Kingdom of Fools

Kingdom of Fools
The unlikely rise of the early church

Nick Page

HODDER

Unless indicated otherwise, Scripture quotations are taken from the
Holy Bible, New International Version (Anglicised edition). Copyright © 1979,
1984, 2011 by Biblica (formerly International Bible Society). Used by
permission. All rights reserved.

First published in Great Britain in 2012 by Hodder & Stoughton
An Hachette UK company

This paperback edition first published in 2013

2

Copyright © Nick Page, 2012

The right of Nick Page to be identified as the Author of the
Work has been asserted by him in accordance with the Copyright,
Designs and Patents Act 1988.

A CIP catalogue record for this title is available from the British Library

ISBN 978 0 340 99626 3
eBook ISBN 978 1 444 70338 2

Printed and bound in the UK by Clays Ltd, St Ives plc

Hodder & Stoughton policy is to use papers that are natural, renewable
and recyclable products and made from wood grown in sustainable forests.
The logging and manufacturing processes are expected to conform to the
environmental regulations of the country of origin.

Hodder & Stoughton Ltd
338 Euston Road
London NW1 3BH

www.hodderfaith.com

CONTENTS

The world of the early church

Alexamenos cebete theon
Graffito from the *domus Gelotiania* in Rome

Introduction: the Kingdom of Fools

On a wall in a schoolroom in Rome, sometime in the late second century a schoolboy scratched a piece of graffiti. It showed a man on a cross. Below to his left is a boy, apparently raising his hand in worship. The crucifixion victim has the head of a donkey. And underneath the schoolboy artist has scrawled in rather dodgy Greek, *Alexamenos cebete theon.* 'Alexamenos worships god.'

It comes from the *domus Gelotiania* in Rome, which was part of the imperial palace of the mad god-emperor Caligula. After his assassination it was used as a boarding school for imperial pageboys. And it was there that a fellow pupil of Alexamenos scrawled his insulting joke. To be fair, Alexamenos probably deserved it. He was weird. Strange. He was a Christian.

It's called onolatry. Donkey worship. Tacitus claimed that the Jews worshipped at a shrine where they had the statue of an ass. This derogatory lie then attached itself to the Christians. 'I hear that they adore the head of an ass,' said the pagan Caecilius of Christians in Carthage, 'that basest of creatures.'[1] Tertullian, writing around the end of the second century, certainly blamed Tacitus for starting the rumour and talked about the widespread 'delusion that our god is an ass's head'. He talked about a vile man who carried around a caricature labelled *Deus Christianorum Onocoetes,* 'The God of the Christians, born of an ass'. It showed a man with the ears of an ass, with one foot and one hoof, carrying a book and wearing a toga.[2]

Those Christians, eh? What are they like?

Good question. This is a book about what the first Christians were like. It's the story of a marginalised, small, frequently oppressed group of people who were determined to live life in a way which was very different from the world around them.

To outsiders these first Christians were dubious characters. They were definitely antisocial and probably criminal. Not to mention stupid. Fools. That was the main thing. Celsus, the first pagan author we know to have written against Christianity, claimed that Christianity deliberately set out to attract 'the foolish, dishonourable and stupid, and only slaves, women and little children'. Celsus claimed that the Christians did not welcome anyone who had been educated, 'or who is wise, or prudent ... but if there are any ignorant, or unintelligent, or uneducated, or foolish persons, let them come with confidence'.[3]

Celsus's criticisms are rooted in his snobbery. He notes how the Christian teachers are wool-workers, leather-workers and fullers (all low-status professions), and illiterate, rustic yokels. These people are quiet before their social superiors, but when they get together with Christians,

> they pour forth wonderful statements, to the effect that they ought not to give heed to their father and to their teachers, but should obey them; that the former are foolish and stupid, and neither know nor can perform anything that is really good, being preoccupied with empty trifles; that they alone know how men ought to live, and that, if the children obey them, they will both be happy themselves, and will make their home happy also.[4]

And the thing is, Celsus was right. Christianity was, from the start, *exactly* for people like that.

Even Paul, writing to the worldly-wise Corinthian church, doesn't deny it:

> God chose what is foolish in the world to shame the wise; God chose what is weak in the world to shame the strong; God chose what is low and despised in the world, things that are not, to reduce to nothing things that are, so that no one might boast in the presence of God. (1 Cor. 1.27–29)

Don't be duped, he continues. It's better to be thought a fool than to think yourself wise in this age. 'For the wisdom of this world is foolishness with God' (1 Cor. 3.18–19).

And the picture in Paul's letters is almost exactly like that in the criticism of Celsus. Paul's letters, and the book of Acts, paint a picture of a movement which grew among leather-workers and tentmakers, fullers and tanners, women, children, slaves.

It didn't stay there, of course. It spread out, gloriously, wonderfully, messily, into all social classes and across all boundaries of ethnicity and religion.

That's the thing about foolishness. It's contagious.

On the margins

This book is all about how this foolish kingdom spread and who spread it. I draw on a wide range of sources, both within the New Testament and from the wider Roman world, to try to understand the world of the early followers of Jesus.

We need to look at it afresh, because the tendency is to project our worldview back into theirs. We imagine the first Christians blithely going to 'church' as we do, singing hymns, listening to a sermon, sitting down with their Bibles and doing a Bible study. But while there are similarities (they did sing and study and learn), all this happened in an entirely different manner and an entirely different context from ours. They lived and worshipped in a society with very different views about the relationship of man to the gods, and in an atmosphere, often, of scrutiny, suspicion and persecution. They didn't have church buildings or national administrative structures. They didn't have centuries of Christian teaching and Christian art, nor libraries of theology. They didn't have Bibles: most of them couldn't read. They didn't have the New Testament. They were living it.

All of this means we are dealing with a church which is constantly learning, discovering, moving. At the beginning, they knew hardly anything about Christianity. The first converts, on that May day in AD 33, knew little of the fullness of what Jesus had done for them, simply because the apostles hadn't worked it out yet.

The amazing thing, the truly astonishing thing, is that this movement succeeded.

Scholars are divided on how many Christians there were in the Empire when Constantine legalised Christianity in AD 313, but assuming that around 10 per cent of the population were Christians, that means that during the previous three centuries, the church grew by around 40 per cent per decade.[5]

That means, if we extrapolate that rate of growth back to the church's earliest days, that there would have been only around 7,500 Christians in the Empire by the year 100.

Easy maths. Perhaps too easy, because, of course, this growth was not uniform. It was lumpy, uneven. Acts suggests remarkable growth in the days of miracles after Pentecost, but after that it slows down. The stories are sometimes of mass conversion, but mostly of households and individuals. But even so, based on this rate of growth, by the middle of the second century, there were still only around 50,000 Christians in an empire of around 60 million people.

This is why they still met in houses and rented rooms. Even had they been allowed to build proper, grown-up churches, they wouldn't have been able to fill them. (The first proper church building we know of doesn't arrive until the middle of the third century, and that was just an extensive remodelling of a house, which mainly involved removing some of the interior walls to create a larger meeting hall.)

The small numbers also explain the relative paucity of archaeological remains relating to Christianity before the late second century. There were only a tiny number of Christians in the Empire, and therefore they only left a tiny amount of archaeology behind.[6]

Small numbers, then. Yet this small group of people nonetheless managed to change the world. This is their story.

Kata Loukan

This book is based mainly on the book of Acts and the letters of Paul. Both Acts and the Gospel we call 'Luke' are anonymous: there is no authorial name attached. The author wasn't trying to hide – he addresses both books to a high-status Roman called Theophilus, who, as patron and recipient, would surely have known who wrote them. But the author is never named in the text.

We do know some things about him, though. He was not an eyewitness to Jesus, but he had met a lot of those who were. He was with Paul for some of his journeys. His native tongue was

Greek, and those who know about such things claim that his is the best Greek style in the New Testament.[7] He did not, on the other hand, know much Aramaic or Hebrew. It is possible that he lived in Philippi. He was generally well disposed towards Roman officials, but also had a regard for artisans and workmen. The feel of the documents supports the idea that it was written by a well-travelled retainer, someone who was in contact with the social elite: well educated, but not high status.

Right from the earliest records of Christianity, that person has been identified as Luke. The earliest extant manuscript of Acts, known as p75, has an inscription at the end: *Euangellion kata Loukan*, 'the good news according to Luke'. This is a papyrus codex which dates from somewhere between AD 175 and 225.[8] The *Muratorian Canon* – a list of the books of the New Testament which may come from around the same time – lists Luke and Acts as the work of 'Luke the physician and companion of Paul'. There are other references as well, including references from the church fathers and a second-century prologue to Luke's Gospel. In fact the early church testimony is unanimous that Luke was the author of this work.

The important factor here is that he is not the obvious choice. He is mentioned just three times by name in the New Testament. He was not an apostle. So if the church was just picking someone to give the work credibility, there are much better candidates: Timothy, for example, or Silas. But the early church believed it to be the work of Luke. And Luke, as I hope to show in this book, fits the bill.

But then there's the issue of the date.

The dating of Acts has been a matter of significant dispute for many years. It is generally claimed that the work was written in the AD 70s, although some who are most determined to discredit it put it into AD 100 or beyond. But there are some significant problems with either of these options. First there are the 'we' passages: the parts of Acts where Luke talks in the first person plural and when the narrator is clearly part of the action. The usual scholarly explanation is that these were part of another source which 'Luke' has inserted into his history. But that doesn't actually make much sense.

Then there is the ending. Acts is a book which ends abruptly. For about half the book it has been building up to a climactic confrontation between Paul and the Roman authorities – and yet it finishes before the climax is reached. There is no trial. The close of the book finds Paul in limbo, under house arrest in Rome. Acts, then, ends not with a bang but a whimper. It's almost as if the author doesn't really know how Paul's story ends.

Finally, there's the curious incident of the temple. In *The Mystery of Silver Blaze*, Sherlock Holmes draws the attention of the detective to 'the curious incident of the dog in the night-time'.

'The dog did nothing in the night-time,' replies the detective.

'That was the curious incident,' answers Sherlock.

In other words, it was the absence of any noise, any barking, which was the clue to the mystery. And there is one great event, one enormous dog-bark of history, which is entirely missing from the New Testament: the fall of the Jewish temple in AD 70.

The fall of the Jerusalem temple was the most significant, climactic event of the first century for both Jews and Christians alike. Yet it isn't explicitly mentioned in the New Testament. Not, that is, as a historical fact. It is predicted, of course, by Jesus. But you might have thought that someone would have cleared the matter up – Luke, for example, writing in Rome for a Roman patron. Would he not have dropped in the line 'and so it came to pass'? But no one mentions it. Not Paul in his letters. Not whoever wrote Acts, with its numerous accounts of persecution by Jewish authorities. Not Mark, who occasionally makes other editorial comments. Not the writer to the Hebrews, whose letter assumes that sacrifice is still going on.

It was this single fact which led one of the most liberal of modern New Testament scholars, John A.T. Robinson, to argue that all the writings of the New Testament pre-dated the fall of the temple.[9] Now, I'm not sure I would put all the writings of the New Testament before AD 70. But the absence of any reference – even of the 'I told you so' type – in the major historical narratives of the New Testament does seem to indicate that they were composed at a time when the final fate of Jerusalem was not known.[10]

It's not just the fall of the temple which is missing from Acts. As already mentioned, we don't see Paul's trial, but nor do we see his death, or the death of Peter, or – most significantly – the perse-cution of the Roman Christians by Nero. These major events are completely missing. They seem rather large omissions.

The reason, I believe, that these elements are missing is the obvious one: because, at the time of writing Acts, *they hadn't happened yet*. Acts closes with an expectation of more to come: you might as well add 'to be continued' at the end.

All of this means that there are strong reasons for considering Luke the author, and that what we have is an account which was written before the fall of the temple and before Paul's death in the mid-AD 60s.

I have to admit, also, that another reason I find myself rooting for an early date is the rather patronising tone of a lot of modern scholarship about the work of the Gospel writers. Here is a typi-cal example:

> We cannot dispense with Acts entirely if we are to have any success in writing a history of the earliest Christians, nor, in practice, should we, for we will find … that in many cases the writer of Acts some-times, perhaps despite himself, has given us credible or worthwhile information.[11]

Heads I win, tails you lose. If Luke gets it wrong, it proves that he's a late and unreliable source. But if he gets it right, it's just a happy accident. As I. Howard Marshall puts it, 'Luke cannot win either way: if the narrative is lacking in concrete details, he is said to have no sources at his disposal, and if he paints a detailed pic-ture of an episode, it is dismissed as legendary embellishment.'[12]

The plain fact is that there are many, many cases where we know Luke *does* get his facts right and where the picture he paints is entirely consistent with other historical, archaeological and lit-erary sources.

This is not to say that there aren't variants and gaps and conun-drums in the text. One of the issues is that there are many differ-ent manuscripts of Acts. Most of these variants are minor, but there is a group of manuscripts, known by the collective term of the Western Text, which contain a number of alternative and expanded readings. (The name comes from the idea that it origi-nated in Alexandria, in Egypt, some way 'west' of Palestine.) In this book I use the initials WT to refer to this source.[13]

A word, too, about other sources. I have drawn information in this book from a range of texts, dating from the first through to the fourth century AD (and occasionally just beyond). There is a list on pages 12-13 of the major sources, their provenance and dating. One has to be careful when extrapolating general conclusions from material which was created at different places and in different times. What was usual for churches in Carthage, North Africa, for example, may not have been customary for churches in Italy or Greece. And a 'church service' in the first century was not the same as one a century or several centuries later. Nevertheless, the basic attitudes and situations do show quite a lot of things in common.

And talking about church services...

You say *ekklesia*, I say synagogue

One of the biggest issues one faces in writing a history of first-century Christianity is working out what terms to use.

Even the most fundamental terms we use about the faith – Scriptures, Christianity, church, apostle, disciple – either had a different meaning, or had not even been invented when our story begins. The disciples had no idea that they were 'Christians'. That nickname was given to them in Antioch, about ten or fifteen years after Jesus' resurrection. And that was only in Antioch; in Jerusalem they were called something different.

In fact, the word 'Christian' only occurs three times in the New Testament (Acts 11.26; 26.28; 1 Pet. 4.16). The word 'Christianity' doesn't appear at all. The earliest instance of that word comes from the *Martyrdom of Polycarp*, written c. AD 150, in which Polycarp offers to teach his captors about the 'doctrine of Christianity'.[14] Before that, what we call Christianity was known simply as the Way (Acts 9.2; 22.4; 24.14, 22).

The book of Acts talks about the first followers of Jesus in a number of ways. There are apostles (*apostolos*), brothers, disciples, the saints, 'those who were being saved'. The commonest term in the early chapters is 'believers'.[15] In Acts 4.23 they are called simply *idios*, which means friends, 'one's own'. The Jews in Judea called them Nazarenes (Acts 24.5), a name which persisted for some time. Tertullian says that the Jews still designated Christians Nazarenes in the early AD 200s. And in the third century, the Babylonian Talmud says that Jews did not fast on the day after the Sabbath 'because of the Notzrim [i.e. Nazarenes]'.[16]

Similarly, there was no such thing as 'the church' (that word comes from a later Greek word, *kyriakos*). The New Testament word which is translated as 'church' is *ekklesia*, and it didn't mean a building – the early church didn't have any church buildings. It was, in fact, a loan word from the cities of the Græco-Roman world, where the *ekklesia* was a gathering of citizens, a meeting in which political and judicial decisions were taken. (It also relates to the Jewish term 'synagogue', which meant 'gathering' and which in the towns of Judea also dealt with local legal and political matters.) The *ekklesia*, then, wasn't 'church' as we know it: it was an alternative assembly, the local government of the kingdom of God, a gathering of the citizens of heaven.

It's the same with their job titles. Their terms for leaders, *episkopos*, *diakonos* and *presbuteros*, are normally translated as 'bishop', 'deacon' and 'elder'. We have created posts for which those are official titles, but the first followers took these terms from the world around them where they simply meant 'overseer', 'servant' and 'elder' respectively. And the 'eucharist' was not the ritual that we know today, but a proper shared meal. The point is that these terms didn't mean then what they mean now.

Why look at the early church?

If so much is different, then, why should we look at the early church? What can we learn from these early Christians? Despite the differences, there are big similarities between their society and ours. We face many of the same issues. And in one crucial way, I think we are living in times very similar to those of the first Christians. In between us and them, there is a great mountain of 'official Christianity'. In AD 313 Constantine, Emperor of Rome, issued the Edict of Milan which legalised Christian worship. Constantine was the first Christian emperor. (Although just how Christian he actually was is debatable. He wasn't baptised until just before his death.) Within a short time, Christianity became the official religion of the Empire. It became respectable and powerful and the social, political and cultural norm.

In Western Europe, at least, that has changed. Writing in 1949, the historian Herbert Butterfield pointed out that, for the first time in 1,500 years, nobody had to go to church any more. Nobody had to be a Christian in order to keep customers or qualify for membership or be socially acceptable:

> This fact makes the present day the most important and the most exhilarating period in the history of Christianity for fifteen hundred years ... We are back for the first time in something like the earliest centuries of Christianity, and those early centuries afford some relevant clues to the kind of attitude to adopt.[17]

So one reason to study the early church is because it can help us address the very real issues facing Christians today. We and they are not so far apart.

There is one major stumbling block, though, for many modern readers, and that is the widespread acceptance of the supernatural in these accounts. The early church believed implicitly in the resurrection of Jesus Christ and also in his ascension. They performed – or were credited with performing – signs and wonders. They were renowned, in fact, for healing and exorcism. Outpourings of supernatural events fill the pages of Acts, as well as featuring in Paul's letters and in the writings of the early church.

This was not something limited to Christians, however. They might have been extreme in some of their beliefs by the standards of the time, but they were far from alone in a belief in the supernatural. Almost everyone, from emperors to peasants, Jew, Greek, Samaritan, men, women and children, believed in demons and spirits, in magic and in gods of various sorts. I'm not going to attempt an apologetic for the supernatural in this book. What I want to do is focus on the social and historical world in which those events were claimed to have taken place.

So why try to learn from the early church? Well, perhaps the best reason comes from one of those early Christians themselves. John Chrysostom, writing about the letter to Philemon, addresses the question of what this little book is still doing in the Bible.

> I wish that it were possible to meet with one who could deliver to us the history of the Apostles, not only all they wrote and spoke of, but of the rest of their conversation, even what they ate, and when they ate, when they walked, and where they sat, what they did every

day, in what parts they were, into what house they entered, and where they lodged – to relate everything with minute exactness, so replete with advantage is all that was done by them … For if only seeing those places where they sat or where they were imprisoned, mere lifeless spots, we often transport our minds thither, and imagine their virtue, and are excited by it, and become more zealous, much more would this be the case, if we heard their words and their other actions.[18]

These are inspirational figures. Their lives, their attitudes, the problems they faced, all have something to say to us today. We can draw inspiration, encouragement and strength from such people.

The world around them considered them idiots. Criminals. Fools.

But looking back, we may just catch a glimpse of some of the wisest people who ever lived.

Major non-biblical sources

Philo of Alexandria (20 BC – AD 50): Jewish Hellenistic philosopher from Alexandria, Egypt. Philo produced a great many works of literature, theology and philosophy, as well as writings that dealt with some of the major historical issues of his day.

Josephus or Flavius Josephus (c. AD 37–100): a Jew who, following the disastrous rebellion by the Jews in AD 67–70, moved to Rome and wrote a history of both the war (77–78) and the Jewish people (93–94).

The Didache, or the 'Training of the Twelve Apostles': an early Christian discipleship manual, probably originating from Antioch in the mid-first century. It offers a unique perspective on the 'rules' for Gentile Christians.

Clement of Rome (first century): probably a Roman Gentile. Possibly he was with Paul at Philippi, although it's not an uncommon name. A church leader in Rome, he wrote a letter to the church at Corinth around AD 90.

Papias (c. AD 60–130): leader of the church at Hierapolis. He knew John the Elder and was a companion of Polycarp. He is notable for having made notes from the testimony of those who had known the apostles.

Polycarp of Smyrna (c. AD 70–157): leader of the church at Smyrna. He is an important link between the apostolic age and the first church fathers. Irenaeus says Polycarp knew John the apostle.

Justin Martyr (c. 100–165): early Christian apologist. Born in Samaria, he became a Christian around 130. He taught in Ephesus where he wrote his *Dispute with Trypho* (c. 135) and then moved to Rome where he wrote his *First and Second Apology* (c. 155). He was beheaded in 165.

Irenaeus (c. 130 – c. 200): overseer of the church in Lyons. His chief work is *Against Heresies*. As a boy he knew Polycarp.

Tertullian, or Quintus Septimius Florens Tertullianus (c. 160 – c. 220): a Christian from Carthage, North Africa and the first major Christian writer in Latin. Became a Christian around AD 197.

Celsus (second century): Greek philosopher and early opponent of Christianity. His work *The True Word* (written around 177) was quoted extensively by Origen and is the earliest known attack on Christianity.

Marcus Minucius Felix (second century): early Christian apologist. Wrote a work called the *Octavius* sometime between AD 150 and 200.

Origen (c. 184 – c. 254): biblical scholar, originally from Alexandria, but moved to Caesarea. He was a brilliant thinker. Among his achievements is the compilation of the Hexapla, a six-column polyglot Bible. In AD 250 he was tortured in prison and he died a few years later.

Eusebius of Caesarea (c. 260 – 340): Christian historian. He became Bishop of Caesarea around AD 315. He wrote many works, but is mainly known for his *Ecclesiastical History* which is our principal source for early church history. It was first published around AD 303, and the final revised edition in AD 323.

Major non-biblical sources

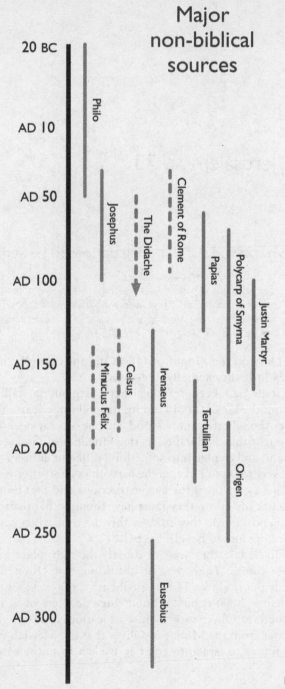

20 BC

AD 10

AD 50

AD 100

AD 150

AD 200

AD 250

AD 300

Philo

Josephus

Clement of Rome

The Didache

Papias

Polycarp of Smyrna

Justin Martyr

Minucius Felix

Celsus

Irenaeus

Tertullian

Origen

Eusebius

1. Jerusalem AD 33

'Why do you stand looking up toward heaven?'

> Then he led them out as far as Bethany, and, lifting up his hands, he blessed them. While he was blessing them, he withdrew from them and was carried up into heaven. And they worshipped him, and returned to Jerusalem with great joy; and they were continually in the temple blessing God. (Luke 24.50–53)

Only on the Mount of Olives did the disciples first grasp just how little they actually understood.

Jesus had been training them, explaining, talking to them about the kingdom of God for around three years. Yet every time they thought they understood what he was saying, every time they thought they had nailed it, this kingdom of God seemed to spin round and change into something different entirely.

According to Luke, in the forty days or so after Jesus' resurrection he gave them further instructions and that morning, on the Mount of Olives, they must have thought that their moment was at hand. 'Lord,' they ask, 'is this the time when you will restore the kingdom to Israel?' (Acts 1.6)

To be fair, they were in exactly the right place to be thinking such things. They were on the Mount of Olives, in the region of Bethany (Luke 24.50), a Sabbath day's walk away from Jerusalem – 2,000 cubits, around three quarters of a mile.[1] But the Mount of Olives was not just a location, it was a symbol, a sign. It was from the Mount of Olives that the Messiah was supposed to return to Israel, to enter Jerusalem from the east and restore

Israel to a position of power. It was all in Scripture, in Zechariah's description of the Day of the Lord:

> On that day his feet shall stand on the Mount of Olives ... and the Mount of Olives shall be split in two from east to west by a very wide valley; so that half of the Mount shall withdraw northwards, and the other half southwards ... Then the LORD my God will come, and all the holy ones with him. (14.4–5)

They had been here before, of course. From the Mount of Olives, Jesus had marched into Jerusalem some fifty days previously. And on the following Friday morning, they had gathered in the early hours to pray in Gethsemane, on the slopes below them. Both times, they must have thought that Jesus was going to establish the kingdom he kept talking about. The Mount of Olives was a place of unfinished business.

So it's no wonder that these 'men of Galilee' think this is their moment. Independence Day. The Romans booted out, the judgement of God delivered on the unbelievers and the faithful (i.e. themselves) rewarded. This, finally, is the moment of power, when Jesus will descend the Mount, storm into Jerusalem and take over.

But instead he goes in exactly the opposite direction. He ascends. Disappears. He tells them that they have a job to do, to preach the good news 'in Jerusalem, in all Judea and Samaria, and to the ends of the earth' (Acts 1.8). And then he disappears, in a cloud.

As an event the ascension is absent from the other Gospels, although in any case, taking things in chronological order, it would have occurred after the ending of both John and Matthew, and Mark's original ending is missing. It's one of those weird events, an explosion of the uncanny, that tend to beat history senseless. Did it actually happen? Purely rationally, of course, it's impossible. And yet it forms a core part of the early tradition of the church. John talks about Jesus returning (John 14 – 17); Paul talks about him descending from heaven (1 Thess. 4.16) and Justin Martyr records it as a tradition which was passed on to him:

> And when they had seen Him ascending into heaven, and had believed, and had received power sent thence by Him upon them, and went to every race of men, they taught these things, and were called apostles.[2]

There are obvious Old Testament parallels, most notably with the departure of Elijah (2 Kgs 2) who promised, we should recall, a double portion of his spirit to his successor Elisha. Any devout Jew would therefore understand this story as more than just a departure: it's a passing on of power, authority and responsibility.

It has been suggested that Jesus' instructions act as a kind of table of contents of the book of Acts: the gospel is taken first to Jerusalem, then Judea, Samaria, infinity and beyond.[3] But one of the interesting things about Acts is that the book simply isn't that neat. Luke puts a shape on things — as all historians do — but the real history has a way of seeping out of such containers. The real history of the early church certainly does not fall into neat sections. It's far more chaotic and exciting than that.

Jesus was gloriously unpredictable, wonderfully messy. He never coloured inside the lines. He never went in the direction that was expected. They expected him to go and take Jerusalem by storm, but to their surprise he left the task to them.

'Show us which one of these two'

With Jesus gone, the 'men of Galilee' rejoin the rest of the followers. Luke describes the group waiting in the Upper Room, the *de facto* headquarters of the new movement. The traditional site of the Upper Room — the setting for both this event and the last supper — is a place in Jerusalem now known as the Cenacle. The present building was built by craftsmen from Cyprus in the mid-1300s, but the presence of a church on this site is attested centuries before that. In Jesus' day the Cenacle was in a rich part of the city. Excavations have revealed graffiti which mentions Jesus, while a visitor in AD 394 recorded that there was a 'little church of God on the spot where the disciples went to the upper room'.[4]

But the church must have dated from much earlier than that, because in the second century the Roman Tenth Legion made their camp directly to the north of the church, around the old palace of Herod the Great. This effectively cut the church off from the rest of the city. Much of Jerusalem was in ruins at the time, following the second Jewish revolt — the Bar Kochba rebellion. To get to the site in those days, Christians would have had to pass through the camp itself, past Roman sentries and suspicious guards. No Christian in his right mind would have chosen to plant a church there in the second century. It would have been too inconvenient. But if they were preserving a traditional site, an incredibly important traditional site, then they would have persevered, despite all the obstacles.[5]

It's very likely, therefore, that the modern building does indeed sit on the site of the little church on Zion, a shrine which itself preserved, despite all the obstacles and difficulties, the place where, in AD 33, everything changed.

It's a large group – Luke says 120 people (Acts 1.15) and we can imagine who was there. Along with the eleven apostles, there were 'certain women', presumably including those mentioned in Luke 8.1–3: Mary Magdalene, Joanna, Susanna. Also the women mentioned in the other Gospels: Mary of Clopas (John 19.25), Jesus' aunt (John 19.25) and possibly Mary the mother of James (Luke 24.10) – a witness to the resurrection. The family of Jesus had other representatives as well, most notably Jesus' brothers (Acts 1.13–14). This is a turnaround. We know from John's Gospel that earlier in his work they did not believe in him. But now they have joined the group. What's changed? Paul's 'official' account in 1 Corinthians 15 tells us that Jesus appeared to his brother Jacob (aka James). But there is more than one brother here. The most likely candidate is Jude. Although some scholars question whether he really wrote the New Testament letter which bears his name, at the very least it shows that he was known to be a follower. If you were inventing a letter and attributing it to someone, you would obviously choose someone who was known to be an apostle of Jesus.

So a good proportion of the people in that room would have been family of one kind or another. There were wives and, presumably, children. Jesus' brothers had wives, and Peter did as well (Matt. 8.14; 1 Cor. 9.5); no doubt others had wives and family there too.[6] Jesus' uncle Clopas may have been present, and possibly Simeon, his son, whom we shall meet later.[7] Along with the 'men of Galilee' there would have been Jerusalem-based disciples as well: the Beloved Disciple, perhaps? Or Joseph of Arimathea? Lazarus of Bethany and his sisters? Joseph Barnabas of Cyprus?

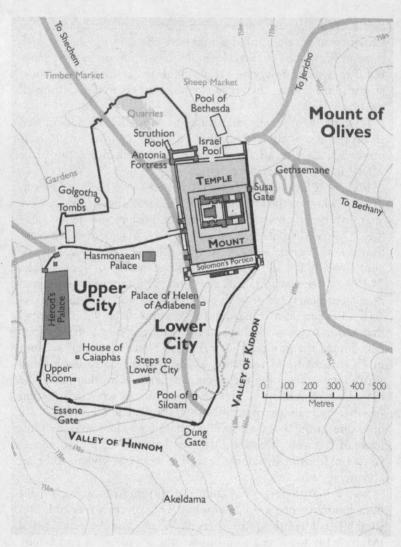

To Shechem

Timber Market

Sheep Market

Quarries

Pool of
Bethesda

Mount of
Olives

To Jericho

Struthion
Pool

Israel
Pool

Antonia
Fortress

Gardens

Golgotha
Tombs

TEMPLE

Susa
Gate

Gethsemane

To Bethany

MOUNT

Hasmonaean
Palace

Solomon's Portico

Upper
City

Palace of Helen
of Adiabene

Herod's Palace

Lower
City

VALLEY OF KIDRON

House of
Caiaphas

Steps to
Lower City

Upper
Room

Essene
Gate

Pool of
Siloam

Dung
Gate

VALLEY OF HINNOM

Akeldama

0   100   200   300   400   500
Metres

Jerusalem in New Testament times

And centre stage in the room there are the apostles: Peter, John, James, Andrew, Philip, Thomas, Bartholomew, Matthew, James son of Alphaeus, Simon the Zealot and Judas son of James. But there's a problem. They're a man down. The 'twelve' are only eleven now.

Judas Iscariot was once a member, of course. But he committed suicide when he realised the full import of what he had done. So the decision is taken to replace him. The two candidates are also in the room: Matthias and Joseph called Barsabbas, aka Justus. Their qualifications are that they have been with the others 'throughout the time that the Lord Jesus went in and out among us' (Acts 1.21). They have history. A track record.

The choice between them is made in what seems to us a rather un-Christian fashion, by the casting of lots. This actually links into traditional Jewish practice. Proverbs records the use of lots as a method of deciding disputes and links it with the will of God (Prov. 16.33; 18.18). Probably what happened is that their names were written on two stones. A designated person would hold one stone in each hand and then someone else would choose a hand. This method is prescribed in the Mishnah to choose which animal to slay and which to release on the day of atonement.[8] (It's significant that the next time such choices have to be made is after the coming of the Holy Spirit, and then lots are replaced by prayer.)[9]

The choice falls on Matthias. He becomes one of the twelve. They are the leaders, the decision-makers. It is, no doubt, one of the most important moments of his life. Sadly, it's also the last we hear of him. This moment of glory is his first and only mention in early church history.

There is a possible later sighting of the runner-up, Joseph Barsabbas. A fragment from the early church writer Papias records that Justus Barsabbas drank a deadly poison and survived. According to Philip of Side, Papias got this story from the daughters of Philip the Evangelist. But nothing more is known of this incident.[10] Of more interest (although drinking snake venom is *pretty* interesting) is the issue of the disappearing apostle. We never hear of Matthias again. And it's not just the new boy who is anonymous: out of the twelve mentioned in this chapter, a full nine disappear from view. In fact, Peter is the only one we hear a lot of: James is only mentioned once more, and John crops up a couple of times.[11]

Why, then, did Peter think it necessary to bring the number back up to twelve? He justifies his action on the basis of a text from Psalm 109. Indeed, the whole of that psalm, with its cries for vengeance against a wicked person, was probably read as a prophecy of Judas and his betrayal. But the apostles' understanding of the kingdom was still rooted in their Jewish understanding of the Messiah. He would restore Israel, and for that you would need twelve men to act as judges. You had to have twelve, because there were twelve tribes of Israel. Later, their understanding clearly changed: when James was beheaded, he was not replaced. But for now, twelve was the magic number.

Luke records this incident faithfully, even though it appears to have had little effect in the wider scheme of things. What it shows is that the apostles were still focusing on Jerusalem, on their own nation. They needed to think bigger. Much bigger.

Tongues of fire

Pentecost was one of the three great pilgrimage festivals of Judaism (the others being Passover and the autumn feast of Tabernacles). It was a harvest festival. Farmers would bring the first sheaf of wheat from their crops as an offering to God. By the first century the festival had grown to be associated with the giving of the law on Mount Sinai, which was assumed to have taken place fifty days after the exodus from Egypt. And there were other traditions and stories as well which attached themselves to the festival. One tells how, originally, God issued the Torah – the law – in all the seventy languages of the world. Philo, writing in the first half of the first century AD, tells how, when the law was given on Sinai, a fire streamed from heaven and, to the utter amazement of the listeners, from the midst came 'a voice, for the flame became the articulate speech in the language familiar to the audience'.[12]

These traditions and ideas seem to feed into Luke's account. The first Christian Pentecost, in Luke's description of it, centres on the giving of a new message, a new power, as a fiery lava flow of words streaming down from heaven, flowing out in the ordinary language of the people around.

If Passover in AD 33 was on 3 April in our modern reckoning, then Pentecost should have begun at sundown on 22 May AD 33 – fifty days later.[13] We can't be exactly sure, though, because the reference in Leviticus says that Pentecost should be celebrated fifty days 'from the day after the Sabbath' (Lev. 23.15–16) and different 'Judaisms' took different views on how this should be reckoned. The Essenes calculated it in a different way from the Sadducees, who calculated it differently from the Pharisees.

And, in fact, it may not be this 'Pentecost' at all. It's always assumed that this event equates to the Jewish feast of Weeks, but the Qumran community celebrated several Pentecosts – and one, in particular, might be linked to this story. The Temple Scroll found among the Dead Sea Scrolls, talks about three Pentecost feasts:

▷ **The feast of New Grain.** Held on the fifteenth day of the third month. This is the biblical Pentecost; the Temple Scroll says, 'It is the feast of Weeks and the feast of Firstfruits.'

▷ **The feast of New Wine.** Held fifty days after the New Grain festival, on the third day of the fifth month.

▷ **The feast of New Oil.** Held fifty days after the New Wine festival, on the twenty-second day of the sixth month.

The second of these festivals is the most interesting, because it may well explain the mocking comments of the onlookers who think that the disciples have been knocking back too much new wine. One of the things which has perplexed scholars for years is why this accusation would surface when the new wine and the new grain were not harvested together. But it makes more sense if they are accusing the disciples of drinking the new wine – wine which they should have been offering as a sacrifice.

So this may not be the main traditional festival of Pentecost, but fifty days later, when the New Wine was celebrated. If that's the case, then we have been celebrating Pentecost at the wrong time for centuries.[14] Perhaps the best we can say is that the event took place sometime between the last week in May and the second week in July, AD 33.

Where were they? Not, apparently, in the Upper Room. The word Luke uses for that in Acts 1.13 is *huperōon*, meaning 'upstairs room'. It's a private place: the same word is used for the room where Dorcas's body is laid and where the small group of Christians in Troas meet (Acts 9.37, 39; 20.8). But the word used here is *oikos*, which means 'house' or 'household'. Now it's conceivable that it's the same building, but there does seem to be a change of scene here. And it's a much more public event than the election of Matthias. The word *oikon* can be used to refer to the temple.[15] It seems to me much more likely that they were either in the temple, or in a building near to it.

The thing about this event is that it draws a large crowd. There is a violent, rushing wind and the participants see something like tongues of fire resting on each of them. And then, without any noticeable scene change, the disciples are surrounded by a huge crowd of people. The temple was really the only public space in Jerusalem where 'thousands' could gather like this – and Peter's statement that it was nine o'clock in the morning (Acts 2.15) implies that the disciples and the people may have gone there for morning sacrifice. As the fire of the Spirit descends on them, the apostles find themselves talking in different languages – languages heard with amazement by the international, cosmopolitan crowd:

> And how is it that we hear, each of us, in our own native language? Parthians, Medes, Elamites, and residents of Mesopotamia, Judea and Cappadocia, Pontus and Asia, Phrygia and Pamphylia, Egypt and the parts of Libya belonging to Cyrene, and visitors from Rome, both Jews and proselytes, Cretans and Arabs – in our own languages we hear them speaking about God's deeds of power. (Acts 2.8–11)

The people speaking here are a mix of resident, immigrant Jews and pilgrims.[16] By this time Jews could be found throughout the Græco-Roman world. Within the borders of the Roman Empire, there were Jewish colonies in all major cities. Jews were particularly numerous in Alexandria and Rome, but they could be found throughout Greece and Asia Minor and North Africa as well. But they had also settled beyond the Empire, far to the east – in Parthia and Medea, in the cities of Susa and Babylon. It was known as the Jewish diaspora, or dispersion.

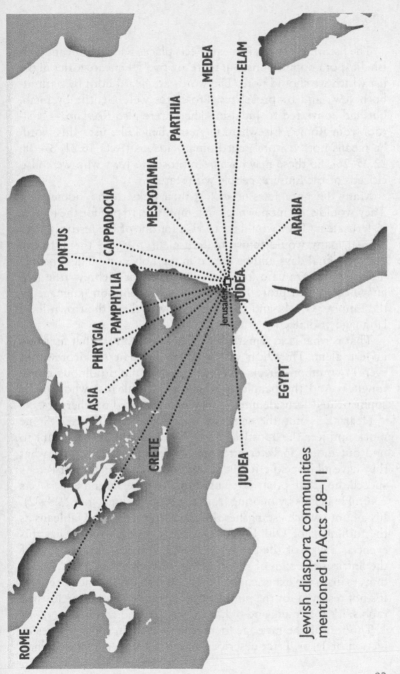

ROME

CRETE

ASIA

PHRYGIA

PAMPHYLIA

PONTUS

CAPPADOCIA

MESPOTAMIA

PARTHIA

MEDEA

ELAM

ARABIA

EGYPT

JUDEA

Jerusalem

JUDEA

Jewish diaspora communities
mentioned in Acts 2.8–11

The list which Luke gives us reflects places with significant Jewish diaspora populations. But there are two other categories in the list which we should note. The words are heard both by natural-born Jews and by proselytes. Proselytes were Gentile by birth, but had converted to Judaism. There were also *Romaioi* – 'visitors from Rome'. Elsewhere in Acts when Luke uses this word, he means not 'visitors', but Roman citizens (Acts 16.21, 37–38; 22.25–26). So these may have been proselyte Jews who were also citizens of the Empire: people with status.

Many diaspora Jews never lost their links to the 'homeland'. They would send money back in temple tax, to pay for the temple in Jerusalem. They would try to visit for one of the festivals. And a great many would return to Jerusalem, to settle there, to live out their final days and be buried in the holy city.[17] These people didn't speak Aramaic (the local language) or Hebrew (the language of the Scriptures). They spoke the common language of the Empire, Greek; and they brought with them their own local language or dialect.

That is what is so remarkable to those present on that morning in Jerusalem. They hear words not in Aramaic or Hebrew, not even in common Greek, but in their own multitudinous native tongues. And the people speaking are 'Galileans' who, to the sophisticated Jerusalemites, are mere uncultured northerners.

Hearing is not the same as understanding, however. Some mock and jeer the apostles and call them drunk; others want to find out more. So Peter attempts to defend and interpret what they have all just experienced. Luke gives us a summary of Peter's speech: he admits that Peter used 'many other arguments' (Acts 2.40). He begins by quoting from the prophet Joel (Joel 2.28–32). It's a quote which establishes the experience of these Galileans as the fulfilment of Old Testament prophecy. It also identifies this event as a sign of the promised age to come: the outpouring of the Spirit is the sign of the kingdom of heaven on earth. And it universalises the experience. This gift is not just for the select few. It's not reserved for the pure Jews, the temple elite or the learned rabbis: it's for young and old, men, women and children.

The rest of the message focuses on one main topic: the resurrection of Jesus. Peter describes him as a wonder-worker, a man of miracles, who was killed by the Romans – 'by the hands of those outside the law' as Peter terms them (Acts 2.23). But this was all part of the divine plan and Jesus was 'freed from death' (Acts 2.24). It is this resurrection which proves Jesus to be the Messiah (Acts 2.31). The message is summed up in the concluding sentence: 'Therefore let the entire house of Israel know with certainty that God has made him both Lord and Messiah, this Jesus whom you crucified' (Acts 2.36).

When people ask how they should respond to this message, Peter tells them to 'repent and be baptized every one of you in the name of Jesus Christ so that your sins may be forgiven; and you will receive the gift of the Holy Spirit. For the promise is for you, for your children, and for all who are far away, everyone whom the Lord our God calls to him.' The other part of his message which Luke records – almost as an afterthought – is the exhortation to 'save yourselves from this corrupt generation'.

The power of the Spirit is evident in the confidence of the message. Peter talks of Jesus of Nazareth – no attempt to hide the very un-messianic origins of their claimed Messiah. No attempt to deny the manner of his death by crucifixion. And no attempt to placate the authorities. If Peter is, as I have suggested, in the temple courts for this speech, then this message is extremely pointed. Statements about corrupt generations are bad enough, but the 'you' in Peter's speech would have been aimed not at Jews *en masse*, but at the people who were running the place where they were standing. He is talking about the temple elite who orchestrated the death of Jesus. He clearly states that Jesus was killed by those outside the law: Gentiles. *Romans*.

So from the start, this message has darker and more political undertones. This is a movement which is not going to kowtow to the establishment. This movement of the Spirit is for everyone, no matter what their class or status: men, women, children, *Romaioi*, whoever. And the Spirit is going to empower them, fill them, inspire them to lives which run entirely counter to the political, social and economic culture of the day.

No wonder, then, that when the establishment get to hear about it, they are immensely concerned.

'Brothers, what should we do?'

Luke records that 3,000 people became followers that day. It's a huge number – although the city was crammed with hundreds of thousands of pilgrims, so it's not unfeasible. The real question is, what were they signing up for? What was their understanding of this new movement? And what were they being asked to do?

Acts 2.38–39 provides information about what was required of the new converts:

> Peter said to them, 'Repent, and be baptized every one of you in the name of Jesus Christ so that your sins may be forgiven; and you will receive the gift of the Holy Spirit. For the promise is for you, for your children, and for all who are far away, everyone whom the Lord our God calls to him.' (Acts 2.38–39)

That's it. That's all they had.

Christian teaching tends to assume that right from the start there was a fully formed theology and understanding of what Christianity was and meant. We assume that the first Christians emerged with all the main credal statements in place, armed with annotated copies of the Old Testament and inhabiting a church structure which was not so different from ours. One frequently hears of the need to 'get back to the early church' – the desire for teaching today to be authentic to early church teaching.

But what did this lot – the earliest of early churches – have for teaching? Huge amounts of Christian theology on subjects like salvation, Christ, leadership, grace, for example, come from the letters of Paul – but we're at least fifteen years away from them. At this point there is no Christian movement. There aren't even any 'Christians'; the name won't be coined for at least another decade. There are no official teachers. There is only Peter, standing up and trying to make sense of it.

This is important because it reflects how the 'church' in Acts is an organisation in a continual state of learning in response to events, both good and bad. Here, for example, they receive the Holy Spirit, experience a miracle of communication and then have to deal with an enormous number of new followers – all on the same day! That's some learning curve.

Not all the people who heard Peter's message on the day of Pentecost were pilgrims. But some of them were. They went back to their countries after Pentecost was over, back into the synagogues in their towns and cities. They knew very little Christian doctrine as such, but they took with them a message of salvation which had never been heard in the world before. Not in any language.

As for those who were residents of Jerusalem, the information is scanty, but after baptism they joined the existing group of believers and 'devoted themselves to the apostles' teaching and fellowship, to the breaking of bread and the prayers' (Acts 2.42).

As the days went by, this developed into a community of believers – the first Spirit-filled Christian community. Presumably there was some attrition. There must have been others who dropped out. But significantly there were others added to their number as well. 'Day by day the Lord added to their number those who were being saved,' writes Luke (Acts 2.47).

The other thing that they carried on doing was going to the temple. The new movement didn't realise that it was a separate movement: it thought it was the next stage in the old movement. The early church was Jewish. The practices, imagery and Scriptures of Judaism were the only language it had in which to express its new ideas. Although it was later to be adopted by people of all cultures and religious backgrounds, Judaism was its birth mother.

We tend to forget all this. For example, Christians are fond of citing Paul's advice to Timothy that all Scripture is God-breathed. What they forget, though, is that Paul isn't talking about the 'Bible' we know. He cannot be talking about the New Testament, which at that stage hasn't been compiled. He's talking about the Jewish Scriptures, which were also the Scriptures of the early church.

The first Christians studied the Hebrew Scriptures; they went to synagogue; and they attended the Jewish temple. In Acts we see Peter and the others going to the temple for morning prayer at nine o'clock and afternoon prayer at three o'clock. These were the two main times of prayer. Sacrifice took place in the temple throughout the day, but the regular daily sacrifices took place at nine and three and at those times crowds flocked to the temple.[18]

This made them good times to beg for alms. Plenty of footfall. And in Acts 4, Peter and John return to the temple to find a beggar waiting for them. A lame man. He is sitting by the 'Beautiful Gate'. It's not known exactly where this is – the name doesn't appear in contemporary Jewish literature – but it was most probably the Sushan Gate which led into the temple forecourts from the Kidron Valley on the east. The beggar asks Peter and John for money, but instead Peter says, 'In the name of Jesus Christ of Nazareth, stand up and walk' (Acts 3.6). And the beggar is healed.

The beggar's reaction is wonderfully portrayed: he jumps and leaps about. For forty years he has been unable to walk, now he is making up for lost time. But this is more than joy at being able to walk. Now he can do more than walk, he can work. He can earn money. In an age when there was no disability benefit, no welfare state, no real office jobs as such, the capacity of disabled people to earn money was extremely limited. Begging was really the only option. So he is restored at the same time to health and to the workforce.

And for the first time in a life of sitting outside it, he can actually enter the temple. Levitical laws were clear on those who were not to be allowed into the temple to present a sacrifice:

> The LORD spoke to Moses, saying: Speak to Aaron and say: No one of your offspring throughout their generations who has a blemish may approach to offer the food of his God. For no one who has a blemish shall draw near, one who is blind or lame, or one who has a mutilated face or a limb too long, or one who has a broken foot or a broken hand, or a hunchback, or a dwarf, or a man with a blemish in his eyes or an itching disease or scabs or crushed testicles. (Lev. 21.16–20)

That's a pretty comprehensive list (and we'll be coming back to the crushed testicles later). But it means that the lame man had never been able to participate fully in the worshipping life of the community. His physical restoration is, therefore, a kind of resurrection. It brings him back to fullness of life. It restores his health, his economic ability and his ability to worship. No wonder he leaps. No wonder he is wildly, ecstatically happy. He has been sitting at the gate for forty years: for the first time in his life, he gets to go in.

Peter uses the occasion to make another speech, and this time the authorities arrive in force: 'the priests, the captain of the temple, and the Sadducees came to them,' it reads (Acts 4.1). The verb used doesn't need to mean 'arrived', it can have a more violent meaning, in the sense of 'to set upon'.[19] It is confrontational. The authorities are present already; now they wade in.

These are heavy hitters, literally and metaphorically. The captain of the temple was the second-highest-ranking official in the temple. He officiated over the daily whole offering and commanded the temple police. He was, in effect, the chief of internal security for the temple regime. He assisted the high priest in ceremonial duties, standing at his right hand. He was also appointed substitute for the high priest during the ceremonies of the Day of Atonement, just in case the high priest was unable to carry out his duties on that day. Often the captain of the temple would go on to serve as high priest.[20] And, crucially, he would have been related to the high priest. He was family.

Luke is absolutely clear. These people arrest Peter for two reasons: he is teaching the people, and he is proclaiming resurrection. And there were two reasons why these activities were such an affront. First, it was the temple aristocracy, more than anyone, who were responsible for the death of Jesus; and second, they were Sadducees.

The Sadducees were theologically conservative and politically powerful. They are entirely absent from the rural Galilean portions of Matthew and Luke. They were an urban elite who seem to have drawn their adherents from among the rich and well connected. Josephus says that the doctrines of the Sadducees were 'received but by a few, yet by those still of the greatest dignity'.[21]

Their theology was based solely on the Torah – the 'Law', the first five books of the Bible. This meant that they rejected the idea of resurrection: it wasn't to be found in the Torah. So that is one reason why they don't like the claims of these followers of Jesus. Another is the whole idea that Jesus was the Messiah, a concept which came from the works of the prophets, not the law of Moses.

In any case, the Sadducees were in power. Why would they welcome the arrival of someone who was going to take over? The Messiah's arrival meant that the overthrow of the current world order was at hand, and that would mean drastic changes for the temple and those who ran it. This was not something which could be countenanced.

The Sadducees were also linked with the high priesthood. We can't say for certain that the high priests at the time were Sadducean, but it is highly probable that they were. Acts talks about the apostles being hauled before the high priest 'and all who were with him (that is, the sect of the Sadducees)' (Acts 5.17). From Josephus we know that one particular high priest was Sadducean: Ananus ben Ananus, the high priest in AD 62. We shall meet him again. For now it is only necessary to note that the people whom Peter and John are brought before on that next morning include Ananus ben Ananus's father, his brother-in-law, and at least one brother.

Acts records the names of those who are ranged against the apostles: 'Annas the high priest, Caiaphas, John, and Alexander, and all who were of the high-priestly family' (Acts 4.6). Annas, or Ananus as he is called in extrabiblical sources, was the founder of a dynasty of high priests, known as the House of Hanin. He was appointed high priest in AD 6 by Quirinius, the Roman legate of Syria. I say 'appointed', but he paid for the privilege. The high priesthood was first bought and sold in the reign of Antiochus Epiphanes IV (175–164 BC), but in the reign of Antiochus Eupator (164–162 BC), Lysias, the king's guardian and kinsman, advised that the high priesthood should be put up for sale every year (2 Macc. 11.1–5). The Romans saw governing the provinces as a means of making money, and selling positions of power was a valuable income stream. A tradition in the Talmud records that the candidates paid a yearly fee for the position.[22] Perhaps this is what lies behind John's cryptic comment that Caiaphas was high priest 'that year' (John 11.49). He had to renew his licence annually.

The high priests more than recouped their costs: they made money from the post. For a start, they had access to the enormous wealth of the temple treasuries. And they could appoint family and friends to highly lucrative posts. They made money from the sale of goods to pilgrims to the temple. It was this practice – and this family – which Jesus condemned in clearing out the temple traders. The family of Hanin and the 'family' of Jesus had history.

Five of Ananus's sons were to be high priests, as well as his son-in-law and possibly a grandson as well. Some of them are in this list. Caiaphas was Ananus's son-in-law. John is probably Jonathan, a son of Ananus who became high priest in autumn AD

36 until the spring of AD 37. Between AD 6 and the fall of the temple in AD 70, Ananus's family held the position of high priest for 37 years. And another son, the Sadducean Ananus ben Ananus, was high priest in AD 62.

This was a family business, and it reflects why Ananus Sr is present here. The high priest is not like a democratically elected mayor who, after quitting, sinks gently into retirement. This is a bunch of aristocrats buying their way into power and sharing it among the family. Ananus may not officially have been the high priest that year, but he was head of the family. He was, quite literally, the daddy. [23]

The high priests were not appointed because of personal holiness. What did the Romans care about that? They were appointed because they knew how the system worked and because they were ruthlessly efficient at handling power. They backed up this power with violence.[24]

It was this family – the House of Hanin – which Jesus had publicly attacked in the temple, in both word and deed. That was the main charge against him at his trial. Jesus' attack on the temple had been a personal attack on them, not just because he was said to have uttered threats against the temple, but because he publicly attacked their profiteering from the sale of goods to pilgrims. When Jesus turned over the tables of the traders he was doing so because their businesses were being run for profit by the temple elite.[25]

The fascinating thing is that nearly all the attacks against Christians in Jerusalem can be linked to times when a member of the House of Hanin is in charge.

High-priestly attacks on followers of Jesus in Jerusalem		
EVENT	YEAR	HANIN FAMILY INVOLVED
Crucifixion	33	Caiaphas/Annas Sr
Peter and John and the beggar	33	Caiaphas/Annas Sr/Jonathan
Apostles arrested	33/34	Caiaphas
Stoning of Stephen	34	Caiaphas
Beheading of James, brother of John	42/43?	Matthias, son of Annas
Death of James, brother of Jesus	62	Ananus, son of Annas

Italics indicate possible involvement.[26]

I don't know about you, but I'm seeing a pattern here. The House of Hanin had a grudge against the followers of Jesus. He had accused them of being thieves. He had challenged their administration of the temple.

This is why the high priests are so concerned over the fact that the disciples don't just teach and perform miracles, but do so in the name of Jesus (Acts 4.8). They even try to order Peter and John not to speak in the name of Jesus. This is personal. The House of Hanin versus the followers of Jesus.

Of course, it doesn't help that the people rocking the boat like this are uneducated, ignorant Galileans (Acts 4.13–17). The term 'uneducated' doesn't mean that they are illiterate, by the way – rather that they have not been trained in the proper religious methods.[27] They haven't got the right theological training.

The temple aristocracy are caught. They can't deny that the miraculous healing has happened: too many people have seen it. And they can't kill Peter and John because, under Rome, they don't have those legal powers. So all they can do is warn them 'not to speak or teach at all in the name of Jesus' (Acts 4.18). Peter and John give an eloquent answer:

> Whether it is right in God's sight to listen to you rather than to God, you must judge; for we cannot keep from speaking about what we have seen and heard. (Acts 4.19–20)

Or, to put it another way, 'No.'

It's a shocking moment. These uneducated Galileans are standing in front of the high priest and they show no fear.

The powers that be are scared silly.

Resurrection is a political message. The early church preached resurrection. That is what Peter and John are saying to the temple powers: the man you killed came back from the dead. Resurrection is a potent, destabilising message. Resurrection gives hope. In the Roman Empire, death was the ultimate deterrent. It was the fear of death which kept nations subdued and slaves obedient. But if people are going to start coming back from the dead, what happens, then, to power? What happens when the ultimate deterrent just doesn't deter people?

This is the moment when the penny drops for the temple aristocracy. These powerful people are suddenly powerless. They can't do anything, because the people are supporting these peasants. They cannot find a way to punish them (Acts 4.21). All they can do is threaten them and let them go.

'To each as any had need'

In the early days and weeks, a distinctive way of life quickly began to emerge among the believers in Jerusalem.

They met each day in the temple, we are told, but perhaps not in the numbers they had before. After Acts 4, and in the light of the antagonism of the authorities, a mass meeting may have been difficult. They kept to their obligations as Jews, but what Acts tells us is that they also met in people's homes (2.46; 5.42). From the start, the Christians began developing a network of house churches. This was something which was going to be crucial to their growth elsewhere in the Empire. They did not need a centralised location. Whereas in Jerusalem Jewish worship was centralised in the massive edifice of the temple, the Christians had to have a network of smaller meeting rooms. From the very start the kingdom grew behind closed doors.

But it did grow. New recruits were added daily. Crucially, this was an inclusive community, a community which looked after one another. We are told that the believers were of one heart and mind, that no one claimed private, individual ownership, but that all things were held in common:

> There was not a needy person among them, for as many as owned lands or houses sold them and brought the proceeds of what was sold. They laid it at the apostles' feet, and it was distributed to each as any had need. (Acts 4.34–35)

Much has been written about this first community, but we should be wary of seeing it as a permanent template. The first followers were just waiting for the imminent return of Jesus which, as far as they knew, could be mere days or weeks away.

The fundamental framework within which the early church operated was eschatologically oriented. The word 'eschatology' has to do with the end times, with the idea that there would be a point when God would step in to bring the present age to a close. Many, if not most, Jews of Jesus' time and afterwards were eschatological in their thinking: expecting the end times. Certainly the early church was. John the Baptist had announced the coming of this new age. The whole idea of the Messiah was linked in with this. Although different Judaisms believed subtly different things about the Messiah, he was generally agreed to be the figure who would usher in this new age (Luke 3.7–17).

But Jesus *didn't* usher in a new kingdom – not in any material, political or military sense. After his resurrection and ascension these new believers had the Spirit, they performed miracles and signs and wonders. But they also still had Roman soldiers and violence and oppression and taxes and all the other stuff that belonged to the old age. The age to come was supposed to be a time without sickness, without death, a time of perfect peace, yet still there were executions and illness and frequent turmoil. So the early church was faced with a quandary: how could the new age be said to have begun when so much of the old age was still stubbornly hanging around?

The answer they came up with was that the new age was beginning. The new kingdom had broken through, but much more was still to come. The blessings and the benefits of the future age could be experienced right now, but their full glory would only be felt in the fullness of time. The kingdom of God was both here and still arriving.

Thus the early church lived in a space between the beginning of the end and the consummation of that end. They proclaimed the Lord's death until he comes (1 Cor. 11.26). They believed that they had been forgiven but not yet fully perfected (Phil. 3.7–14). They had been justified, but there was still to be a future judgement (2 Cor. 5.10). They lived in the kingdom now, but they also prayed with Jesus, 'your kingdom come'.

Everything the first Christians said and did has to be seen in the light of this tension. They were liminal people, living on the threshold between times. They were people of the eschaton, of the end; but the end had only just begun.

This was certainly one impetus behind the sharing of possessions. They were preparing for a radical new future. But even then they didn't give up everything. They sold possessions, but kept their homes. But they did share meals together, and meet to learn and pray.

It was not as though they didn't have models. The Qumran community must have been known to some of them, and that practised a form of communal life in which members had to turn over all their property and possessions.[28] The Essenes (who may or may not have been the Qumran community) also shared everything in common and, significantly, passed their wages to a common treasurer.[29]

But the main model for their behaviour was their founder. He, after all, had told people to sell all they had and give the money to the poor (Luke 18.18–23). And this is what happened. Property was sold as needed and the proceeds given to the community (Acts 2.45; 4.35). And it is in that light that we are, almost in passing, introduced to one of the most significant people in New Testament history:

> There was a Levite, a native of Cyprus, Joseph, to whom the apostles gave the name Barnabas (which means 'son of encouragement'). He sold a field that belonged to him, then brought the money, and laid it at the apostles' feet. (Acts 4.36–37)

A few facts are recorded about Barnabas at this juncture: he was a Levite, he was a Cypriot – he was a Greek-speaking Jew. And he owned – and sold – a field. Indeed, he was so enthusiastic, so supportive, so keen, that the apostles nicknamed him 'son of encouragement'.

The Jews first settled in Cyprus sometime after 330 BC.[30] Barnabas was either born there, or his family had come from there to Jerusalem. Luke later terms him an apostle (Acts 14.14) which would indicate that he had seen the resurrected Jesus. So he must have been a disciple earlier – one of the seventy-two, perhaps, or at least one of the 500 or so who saw Jesus after his resurrection.

He is introduced here, however, simply as a man of generosity and openness of heart. But while Barnabas is giving money, others are holding it back. Luke contrasts the story of Barnabas with the grisly and difficult story of the death of Ananias and Sapphira. Their 'crime' is to sin against the Holy Spirit by keeping back the proceeds of a business transaction. The problem is their evil hearts, dominated by Satan and revealed by Peter's word of knowledge.

This is a judgement miracle – one of two in Acts, the other being the blinding of the magician Elymas (Acts 13.11). Ananias and Sapphira sell some property, but 'keep back' some of the proceeds. When their deception is revealed they are, independently, struck dead.

The verb translated as 'kept back' is often associated with financial fraud.[31] The message is that the followers of Jesus are accountable to God and to the community. Peter throughout emphasises this. It's not as if they *had* to do this. No one held a gun (or a spear) to their head. Unlike Qumran, where selling your property and giving the money to the bursar was a requirement for every incoming member, giving within the Christian community was voluntary.[32] But once they had decided to give, they were accountable.

It's presented throughout as an abnormal, almost inexplicable event, shocking both to the reader and to the community. There is almost an atmosphere of terror permeating through the story. Fear seizes everyone who hears about it (5.5, 11).

The hurriedness with which Ananias is buried reflects this. On the basis of Old Testament texts such as Leviticus 10.1–5 and Joshua 7, it has been suggested that the speed of the burial was to do with the fact that this man had been 'struck down by heaven'. In first-century Judea all burials were speedy by our standards, but some were especially hurried: the suicides, apostates, rebels and condemned criminals. These people had put themselves outside society and were buried without ritual or mourning.[33]

This might explain why even his wife is not informed of Ananias's death. In their culture and understanding, this is not so much a burial; this is quarantine.

Perhaps historically, the most important facet of the story is that it shows that not everything in the garden was rosy. Whatever we think of the event and its outcome, the fact that Luke includes it shows his willingness to record incidents that did not reflect well on the early church: here, the selfishness of some of its members.

Luke gravitates towards big statements, such as the idea that the entire group were of one heart and soul (4.32). But he also shows us the cracks, the fissures, the events which baffle and challenge their emerging theology. This is a learning church. And some of the lessons they have to learn are painful.

'Many signs and wonders'

Signs and wonders. Miracles. Strange deaths, wonderful healings. Illness and demons. Luke talks about people lying in the street so that Peter's shadow might fall on them. (In ancient times, someone's shadow was seen as an extension of their being.) Two groups in particular came from the towns around Jerusalem: the sick and those possessed by unclean spirits.

When it comes to healing, the classic Christian text is the letter of Jacob, or James, the brother of Jesus. In this he writes very simply:

> Are any among you sick? They should call for the elders of the church and have them pray over them, anointing them with oil in the name of the Lord. The prayer of faith will save the sick, and the Lord will raise them up; and anyone who has committed sins will be forgiven. Therefore confess your sins to one another, and pray for one another, so that you may be healed. The prayer of the righteous is powerful and effective. (Jas 5.14–16)

The clear inference here is that healing is not limited to the apostles. It is the leaders of the church – any church – who can and should do it. There is a wonderful matter-of-factness about healing in the early church, even though to outsiders it caused amazement and wonder.[34] Even in later times it was the miraculous which drew people to the faith. Writing some two decades on from this event, Paul points to the presence of the miraculous as proof of apostleship: 'The signs of a true apostle were performed among you with utmost patience, signs and wonders and mighty works' (2 Cor. 12.12).

The miraculous tales of the early church – indeed, of any church – make uncomfortable reading for many people today. In the rationalist modern world such things do not fit comfortably. But we won't understand the spread of the early church until we understand that they lived in a world where the supernatural was taken for granted and where the miraculous clearly happened. At the same time, they were not credulous fools. They understood, more than most of us in the modern Western world, the realities of life: the harshness of poverty, the difference between life and death was very clear to them, you could see it in the streets every day of the week. In any case, we are not dealing here with a handful of tales, but with many accounts of healing, both within the New Testament and from extrabiblical sources.

Further on still, in the fourth century we read of Hilarion, whose healing ministry was so famous that 'people flocked in to him from Syria and Egypt so that many believed in Christ'.[35]

Individuals might come to faith through discussion and argument, or by reading the Scriptures – but the mass of people couldn't read, so those kind of things weren't going to get you far. Gregory, a pupil of the famous Christian scholar Origen, wrote a learned treatise on God in the style of a Socratic dialogue.[36] But what made him famous was the miracles he worked among the populace of north-central Turkey. He was known as Gregory the Wonder-worker, not Gregory the Rather Good Theologian.

Tertullian described Christians as being 'in touch with the miraculous'.[37] Of course we should make allowances for exaggeration or even invention in some of the claims about the early church, but the fact is that there are simply too many instances of healing to dismiss it. There is too much testimony both from the church itself and from its opponents.

Even the enemies of Christianity agreed regarding these powers. Celsus claimed that 'it is by the names of certain demons, and by the use of incantations, that the Christians appear to be possessed of (miraculous) power'. He claimed it was demonic, but he never argued that the miracles didn't happen.[38]

The Christian commentators certainly all concur. Justin Martyr wrote:

> For numberless demoniacs throughout the whole world, and in your city [Rome], many of our Christian men exorcising them in the name of Jesus Christ ... have healed and do heal, rendering helpless and driving the possessing devils out of these men, though they could not be cured by all the other exorcists, and those who used incantations and drugs.[39]

Tertullian describes how the name of Jesus can 'remove distractions from the minds of men and expel demons, and also take away diseases'. And he goes on to give some specifically documented cases, citing particularly how Severus, father of the Emperor Antonine, was healed from sickness by a Christian called Proculus Torpacion: 'How many "men of rank" (to say nothing of the common people) have been delivered from devils and healed of diseases.'[40] Healing was evidence of power, of the presence of God, of resurrection. Theophilus of Antioch described healing as 'the work of resurrection going on in yourself'.[41]

Irenaeus in Gaul wrote about the miraculous healings witnessed by the early church, the giving of sight to the blind and hearing to the deaf, the cure of the 'weak, or the lame, or the paralytic, or those who are distressed in any other part of the body', or those who have experienced 'external accidents which may occur'. One of his fundamental arguments in identifying heretics was that they were not able to perform the kinds of miracles that were manifested among the orthodox believers. And unlike the pagan temples or the chancers in the market squares, Christians refused to take any fee. 'For as she [the church] has received freely from God, freely also does she minister [to others].'[42]

This is just a fraction of the evidence available. What is clear is that, right from the start of the church, healing was a crucial activity: it was demonstration and gift; it was freedom and resurrection; it was new life, and sign, and wonder.

Of course, such activities could not go unnoticed. Soon renewed persecution breaks out in Jerusalem. The high priest's party – and here Luke explicitly identifies them as the Sadducees (5.17) – arrest the apostles and put them in prison. But, in a rather matter-of-fact – even downbeat – description, an angel releases them and tells them to carry on speaking publicly.

We don't know anything more about this incident, although it appears similar in style to the rescue of Peter later on (Acts 12.6–17). What we do know is that they are re-arrested, 'without violence' – because the authorities are fearful of the crowd. Indeed, the temple police are fearful with specific reason: they are scared that the mob is going to stone them (5.26). This remark from Luke is rather important. Although the authorities themselves did not have the power to execute people in Jerusalem, the mob was a different matter.

Fundamentally, the second arrest occurs because they have broken the terms of their probation:

> We gave you strict orders not to teach in this name, yet here you have filled Jerusalem with your teaching and you are determined to bring this man's blood on us. (Acts 5.28)

Once again, what comes to the fore in these charges is that the authorities are taking it personally. What the high-priestly aristocracy don't like is that the apostles are pinning the blame for Jesus' death on them. The apostles' defence, in the words of one scholar, 'consists of slandering the Sanhedrin regarding complicity in the death of Jesus'.[43] No wonder the authorities are furious. But a voice of calm comes from a prominent Pharisee, Gamaliel. Gamaliel's advice is that they should leave these men alone. 'If this plan or this undertaking is of human origin, it will fail,' he says, 'but if it is of God, you will not be able to overthrow them' (5.38–39).

Gamaliel has clout. It is he who orders the council room to be cleared and the apostles to be taken outside. We know a little about Gamaliel the Elder, as he is known in Jewish sources. He was a prominent leader of the Pharisees from around AD 25 onwards. In a list of famous rabbis in the Mishnah, we read that 'When Rabban Gamaliel the Elder died, the glory of the Torah came to an end, and cleanness and separateness perished.' It's possible that his advice here stems from another rabbinic proverb. A later rabbi called r.Yohanan Hassandelar (Johann the Sandal-Maker) says, 'Any gathering which is for the sake of Heaven is going to endure. And any which is not for the sake of Heaven is not going to endure.'[44]

Gamaliel cites two examples of failed messianic movements to support his argument. The first is Theudas, and the second that of 'Judas the Galilean' who is said to have come 'after him'. This seems confused. Judas the Galilean led a tax revolt in AD 6. The only Theudas we know as a revolutionary is mentioned by Josephus as being active between AD 44 and 46. It's possible that Luke, or Luke's source, has his facts wrong. It's equally possible that Josephus, rather than Luke, is wrong. Just as possible is that they are both right and that there was another minor Messiah-wannabee called Theudas. It's a common enough name.[45]

Whatever the details, Gamaliel's speech rings true for a number of reasons. Gamaliel's later reputation for wisdom and righteousness is such that he must have had significant clout in Jerusalem at this time. And it is undoubtedly true that the Pharisees (for all their bad press in the Gospels) were much more likely to support the Christians than were the Sadducees. Indeed, Gamaliel's opposition to the leaders of the council strengthens the theory that the ruling elite of the time were Sadducean.

But we needn't read Gamaliel's intervention as entirely disinterested. He is scoring some political and religious points here as well. For a start, the apostles were released, according to the stories, by an angel. And the Sadducees didn't believe in angelic agents in the world. It did not fit into their Torah-based faith. So the rescue was both a political *and* a theological embarrassment to the ruling party.[46] The longer the apostles retained the support of the people, the more uncomfortable life was for the Sadducees. And upsetting Sadducees was one of the Pharisees' favourite occupations.

Nor does Gamaliel's intervention mean that the apostles go unpunished. They are not just let off with a caution. Unlike their first arrest, this time they are flogged. Jewish law prescribed a maximum of 39 lashes (see 2 Cor. 11:24) with the victim's skin beaten by a tripled strip of calf's hide. It was administered in cycles of three: two blows to the back and one to the chest.

Signs and wonders and unprecedented growth came at a price.

'The Hellenists complained against the Hebrews'

Luke goes on to record a disagreement between the 'Hellenists' and the 'Hebrews' (Acts 6.1). 'Hellenists' is a term which does not appear anywhere in ancient literature before Luke uses it here. Many elaborate theories have been spun about this group, with theologians and church historians reading feverishly between the lines. They have been identified as Gentile Christians, as proselyte Jews, as a group from Galilee and the surrounding regions, as unorthodox former Jews, as members of the Qumran community, or even as Samaritans. But the oldest explanation is the simplest. In the fifth century, John Chrysostom wrote that Luke 'uses "Hellenists" for those who speak Greek'. These are Jews who cannot speak Aramaic.[47]

When Luke talks about 'Hebrews', he is not talking about ethnicity so much as language. He means Aramaic-speaking Jews. Hebrew was used among scholars and as the language of worship and litany, but it was not a vernacular language: everyone spoke Aramaic. All the place names in the New Testament are the Aramaic versions.[48] (And this is how Paul uses the word. He was a Hebrew of the Hebrews: he could speak Aramaic.)

Many of the Hebrews could speak some Greek, because Greek was the common language of the Græco-Roman world. Greek was the language of trade and commerce. Greek allowed you to communicate with the Romans and the Gentiles in less Jewish places like Sebaste and Caesarea and beyond. But hardly anyone would have gone the other way: Greek-speaking people did not learn barbaric languages like Aramaic. And anyway, why would you need to? Even Philo, the Jewish philosopher living in Alexandria, never took the time to learn Aramaic or Hebrew. He didn't need to.[49]

No doubt there were many reasons which took diaspora Jews back to the holy city. For some it would have been returning to their family home. For others there was the understandable urge to return to the fatherland. And many certainly went there to die, to spend their last days worshipping in the temple, back home at last. But once they arrived, they found themselves a minority population in the predominantly Aramaic-speaking Jerusalem. This division must have been reflected within the Christian community too, the majority of whom would have been Aramaic-speaking Jews. The effect was that the Greek-speaking community became isolated to some extent. They were much like expat English-speaking communities around the world today: they were privileged in some ways, and they could get by in normal life without having to learn the local language, but it always put them at a disadvantage.

They were immigrants who could not speak the language. This is not a doctrinal rift: it's a communication problem.

The problem was especially acute for those at the bottom of the social scale. It was one thing to be a Greek-speaking man in Jerusalem, another thing entirely to be a Greek-speaking woman. And another thing again to be a widow. Widows as a group had a tough time in the first century. They were often marginalised, denied an inheritance and merely given a maintenance allowance from their husband's family. The situation must have been worse for those who did not speak the local language, whose husbands had come to spend the evening of their lives in the City of David and who, once that husband had died, found themselves alone. Without skills, without any extended family *in situ*, single older women would have been poor and vulnerable.

What happens here, then, is that Greek-speaking widows who have decided to follow Jesus are missing out on the daily distribution of food. The rabbinic sources describe two Jewish systems of poor relief: the 'poor bowl' and the 'poor basket'. The poor bowl was a daily distribution of food (bread, beans and fruits, with a cup of wine at Passover). The poor basket was a weekly ration of food and clothing. This was probably the arrangement used by the early church. The argument from the widows is simply that they are missing out on the poor bowl distribution.

So the twelve call the community together. 'It is not right', they say, 'that we should neglect the word of God in order to wait at tables.' They ask the community to select seven Greek-speaking Hellenistic Jews to relieve the disciples of such duties and permit them full-time evangelism (Acts 6:1–7). The phraseology 'wait at tables' is a bit misleading. It conjures up images of a huge set of tables outside, like one of those French fêtes, with the seven rushing around with trays. More likely there were many home-gatherings and shared meals being held around the city, and it was the job of the seven to make sure that the widows were invited. Jeremias pictures a centralised system, when the Jerusalem Christians met for a meal and worship. Along with this meal would be a rationing out of a 'poor basket' for the needy, distributed from the food which the believers had brought with them. So there would have been two provisions: the evening meal and the dole of the next day's food.[50]

We have already looked at the necessarily home-based community of the early church. Crowds might gather in the temple, but since the opposition of the temple aristocracy must have made that hard, if not impossible, home was where the heart of the church had to be. Most Jewish homes, though, even of the relatively wealthy, could not have held more than 50 people – perhaps up to 120 if they had an open courtyard.[51] If the numbers Luke records are accurate, and assuming there wasn't a large rate of attrition, then the early church must have met in many separate locations, a network of houses around the city. This gives another obvious reason why communication could break down. Behind the walls of their houses a small community of Greek-speaking women might go hungry – and no one would ever know.

Those appointed to solve the problem are seven men from the Greek-speaking community. All the men have Greek names (which is not to say they were all diaspora immigrants: two members of the twelve had Greek names, Andrew and Philip, but weren't diaspora Jews). Most of them probably were immigrants, or the children of immigrants, however. And one of them – Nicolaus of Antioch – was a proselyte, a Gentile convert to Judaism. Technically, I suppose, this makes him the first clearly identifiable Gentile Christian, even if it was by way of Judaism.

Their role is both leadership and service. The 'seven' are not just administrators or servers at tables, they are preachers, prophets, evangelists. This is not some split between preachers and administrators, or anything of that sort: both the twelve and the seven have serving roles – both roles use the Greek word *diakonia,* 'service'. The seven serve at tables (Acts 6.2), the twelve 'serve the word' (Acts 6.4). There is no implication that the seven do the menial work and the twelve don't. To do that would be to contradict the picture in Luke's Gospel of a Jesus who is consistently sympathetic and sensitive to the needs of widows.[52]

Nor is this solution imposed on the community. Instead, they have to ratify the concept (Acts 6.5). And it is the community who select the seven candidates to set before the apostles. There is also no reason to think that it was the apostles who laid hands on the candidates: the sentence actually goes, 'and they prayed and laid their hands on them' – it doesn't say who 'they' are (Acts 6.6).[53]

Which community are we talking about, though? These Greek-speaking Christians must have met separately for worship in their own language. Most of the Hellenists would not have been able to understand Aramaic teaching about Jesus. They would have needed their own groups and their own forms – or at least translations – of liturgy and prayers. So it seems likely that it is these people who put forward their preferred candidates.

These Greek-speaking Jewish Christians were to have a massive impact on the future of the church, because they were natural missionaries. They spoke the language of the Mediterranean world. They knew there was a bigger world out there. In Luke's account it is the Hellenistic Jews who spread the word outside Jerusalem and Judea.

What we can see is that, just a few months after the death and resurrection of Jesus, the faith being practised in Jerusalem is already far richer and more diverse. There are different communities, worshipping in different places and speaking different languages. There is explosive, difficult-to-handle growth. There is radical community lifestyle.

This episode, therefore, is about the community actively facing and resolving its issues, taking up Jesus' mantle in facing up to rather than ignoring a low-status, marginalised group within their community. It is an act of practical inclusiveness.

But the Greek-speaking widows were not the only marginalised group who found a home in the early church.

'The Most High does not dwell in houses made by human hands'

Their treatment at the hands of the Sadducees, Gamaliel's intervention and the high profile of the Christians within Jerusalem was having a massive impact in the temple itself. A little line in Luke's history reveals that 'a great many of the priests became obedient to the faith' (6.7).

The temple was a mammoth religious industry. It was the biggest single employer in Jerusalem and the basis for the city's economy. While at the top there were the aristocratic, high-priestly families, lower down there were many rural priests whose job it was to assist at the temple twice a year. Priests were divided into twenty-four divisions, each of which went to the temple twice a year for one week, to help out with the services. (One of these was Zechariah, father of John the Baptist.)

The rural priests were part of the peasantry. They were from a very different social class from those who occupied the more privileged positions. The wealth and power of the temple elite drove a wedge between the upper echelons of the priesthood and these rural priests, the 'grunts' who did the day-to-day work in the temple. These poorer, rural priests often became argumentative, rebellious even.

There were plenty of these radicalised priests around. Later on, during the Jewish revolt, the hatred between the 'temple priests' and the 'popular priests' came out into the open, with the two factions abusing each other and even pelting each other with stones. Josephus records how some of the poorer priests starved to death in the days immediately before the Jewish rebellion, because the high priests had seized the tithes which were their only form of sustenance.[54]

The conversion of priests may be one of the reasons why the persecution suddenly goes up a gear. If the priests are becoming interested, then the alarm bells are going to start ringing ever more insistently higher up. This faith is already spreading like a virus among the disaffected, the lower orders, the marginalised, the immigrant community. Now it has infected the temple. Extreme measures must be taken. The infection must be aggressively treated.

The antiviral activity is kicked off, though, not in the temple, but outside it, in the synagogues of the diaspora Jews. One of the seven, Stephen, starts to make a reputation through performing great signs and wonders. We're back to the demonstrative power of the miraculous. These miracles arouse indignation among some Hellenists in the Synagogue of the Freedmen – a Greek-speaking synagogue for diaspora Jews from North Africa and Asia Minor: Cyrenians, Alexandrians (from Egypt), Cilicians and Asians. As the name implies, the synagogue was composed of – or originated from – a group of freed slaves. As a category of individual, the freedman is one of the hardest for us to imagine, because there is nothing similar in western societies. In Rome, freedmen were viewed by the ruling elite as socially inferior. In a far-flung province like Jerusalem, where many families had experienced Roman oppression first-hand, one imagines that the term held less stigma. Many Jewish slaves were prisoners-of-war, enslaved either during the original Roman occupation of Palestine, or in subsequent actions such as when the Romans crushed the revolts that occurred after the death of Herod the Great. Later, once they gained their freedom, some of them clearly returned to Jerusalem and set up their own community. Freedmen were often entrepreneurs. Having learned and mastered skills while slaves, they were often put into business backed by capital from the masters who had freed them. The master may have recognised the freedman's skills and decided to reward them – or make better use of them. One Roman legal source says that 'A reasonable cause for freeing a slave is if he [i.e. the master] frees him for the sake of having an agent.'[55] Many freedmen did very well for themselves and rose to positions of wealth and influence. They were, in many ways, the most dynamic social strata of Roman society: they had experience of the wider Roman world, they had business skills and they had, in effect, gained promotion.

And they spoke Greek. This was a Hellenistic synagogue. There were other Hellenistic synagogues in Jerusalem (Acts 9.29; 24.12). There are references to a Synagogue of the Alexandrians (from Alexandria in Egypt) and a Greek inscription discovered in Jerusalem in 1914 reads:

Theodotus, son of Vettenus, priest and synagogue chief, son of a synagogue chief, grandson of a synagogue chief, had the synagogue built for the reading of the law and for the teaching of the commandments, as well as the hospice and the accommodations and the water-works as lodging to those who need it from abroad, [the synagogue] whose foundations had been put down by the fathers and the elders and Simonides.

This synagogue was for both pilgrims and residents.[56] Such synagogues probably had links to the Pharisees, or were sympathetic to their teachings, at any rate. It is hard to see why the Sadducean temple elite would encourage any kind of competition to the temple. But synagogues could be found in most cities of the Græco-Roman world. There were Greek-speaking synagogues in Egypt and in Rome.

As opposition to Stephen grows, it is the men of such a synagogue who stir up rumours against him and who eventually drag him before the council. The accusation against Stephen is that he is anti-temple. The witnesses claim that he 'never stops saying things against this holy place and the law; for we have heard him say that this Jesus of Nazareth will destroy this place and will change the customs that Moses handed on to us' (Acts 6.13–14).

This is a serious charge, and one which is bound to have an effect on the ruling elite. Notably the witnesses remind the leaders that the same charge was brought against Jesus. And, although Luke says the witnesses are liars, it is noticeable that Stephen's speech does little to reverse that impression. It doesn't actually read like any kind of defence. For the most part it is a recounting of the Torah either through allusion, or using quotes from the Septuagint, the Greek version of the Old Testament. Stephen points to a repeated cycle of behaviour: God sends leaders and the people reject them. And there are many detailed geographical references: God appears to Abraham in Mesopotamia and Haran; there is a long section on Joseph in Egypt; an angel appears to Moses at Sinai. In every case God has appeared outside Palestine. So things are pretty pointed by the time we get to the temple, built by Solomon, which is summarily dismissed with the statement, 'Yet the Most High does not dwell in houses made by human hands' (Acts 7.48). So this speech is all about God appearing to his people, outside the land of Palestine and away from the temple.[57]

In that sense, the speech is, indeed, anti-temple. So it seems that, although they may have been lying about the specifics, there is some basis to their accusations. That may explain why the Hellenistic Jews are so eager to have Stephen dealt with. In the light of their immigrant status, loyal Hellenists would have felt vulnerable to accusations of disloyalty and unorthodoxy. They would have been keen to prove their zeal.

Stephen never mentions the name of Jesus at all, nor does he refer to the Messiah. This is not an evangelistic defence of Jesus' status; it's a denunciation of the people ranged in front of him.[58] It is only right at the end that Stephen introduces Jesus as the 'Righteous One' and denounces the people filling the court as his betrayers and murderers. At this final point Stephen has a vision of Jesus and it is this which tips his persecutors into action: they rush him out of the room and stone him to death.

Which is a puzzle. The Jewish authorities did not have the *jus gladii*, the Roman right to decide on capital cases. That was why they had to have the Romans execute Jesus. For that reason, some have suggested that this must have been during a time of political unrest, perhaps after Pilate's removal from power in AD 36. But a closer look at the story indicates that this is not so much a legal process as mob rule.

The clue lies in who Stephen is and who his accusers are. He's a Greek-speaking Jew. An immigrant. Easy prey, in effect. That's why the leaders let the mob have their way. This interpretation is backed up by subsequent events. Although Luke describes Stephen's death as triggering an outbreak of persecution 'against the church in Jerusalem' (Acts 8.1), the apostles do not have to leave. 'All except the apostles were scattered throughout the countryside of Judea and Samaria,' Luke writes. He cannot mean literally that *only* the twelve remained in Jerusalem. What is more likely is that many of the recent converts left – and especially the Hellenists. This was an attack not on the Aramaic-speaking native church in Jerusalem, but on their sister church, the Greek-speaking Christians.

This isn't a judicial killing: it's the actions of a mob. This group, listening to hostile rumours and clamouring for punishment, may be led by Hellenistic synagogue leaders, supported by the elders and the scribes, but it is a mob, not an official stoning party. The temple authorities did not bring this case. They seem more like passive spectators. It's a mob who take Stephen before the council, and the same mob who drag him out to kill him.

Not that the authorities do anything to intervene. But they could reasonably argue that it's out of their hands. The tumult and chaos rule out any discussion or even formal sentencing. And anyway, if the Romans were worried about a load of poverty-stricken immigrants, the authorities could always point to the anti-temple sentiments of the speech as potentially subversive.

This, then, is the background to the death of Stephen, to the persecution of Saul and to the concerted attack on Jesus' followers. The high priest – probably still Caiaphas – clearly agreed with what was going on: it entirely suited his agenda.[59] But he was not driving this. It was Hellenistic Jews against Hellenistic Christians. This is why Paul is later able to say that he was trying to destroy the community of God (Gal. 1.23). Such a thing would have been impossible among the Hebrews: there were too many of them, and the Christians were too popular. But if he was referring to expelling or crushing the Greek-speaking Christians, yes, that would have been possible.[60]

Stephen is taken away and stoned. The Mishnah states that in stoning, the victims were led outside the city and then stripped of most of their clothes. They would then be thrown down, head first, from a height at least twice the height of a man. If the victim did not die straight away, one of the witnesses would take a huge stone and drop it on the victim's heart. If that failed, then the general mob would join in the stoning.[61] But that was a judicial stoning. This stoning was more about one man being set upon by a mob.

One last small detail reinforces the unofficial, unjust mob-rule nature of the act. Luke records that 'devout men buried Stephen and made loud lamentation over him' (Acts 8.2). The term used for lamenting could refer to pious Jews upholding Jewish burial laws.[62] Who are these people? They are not Christians, clearly. They are, in fact, orthodox Jews, who recognise that an injustice has been done. There is no mention of the apostles or the Christian community burying Stephen and mourning for him. They are too nervous, perhaps. Driven underground. Driven out.

Stephen was accused and killed by his own people: Greek-speaking immigrants from the Hellenistic synagogues. His crime was to speak out against the temple, towards which his executioners, politically vulnerable as they were, were keen to prove their loyalty. And standing by was another immigrant, another Greek-speaker, a young man from the diaspora community in Cilicia. He was not one of the murderers, he was a facilitator, an enabler. Looking after the coats, while the mob did the heavy work. His name was Saul. And, in Luke's chilling words, he gave this mob execution his stamp of approval.

2. Samaria AD 34

'A Jew from Tarsus in Cilicia'

The death of Stephen was the first, thunderous act of a storm of persecution against the Christian community in Jerusalem. At its centre, at the terrible, chilling eye of the storm, stood a man called Saul.* According to Luke, he led the attacks on the church as the persecutors entered house church after house church, dragging all the Christians they could find into prison. His own account confirms this. Writing fifteen or so years later, he describes how 'I was violently persecuting the church of God and was trying to destroy it' (Gal. 1.13).

In his letters, Paul doesn't give us much detail about his early life. There is a brief mini-biography in Galatians, and a description of his background in Philippians: circumcised on the eighth day, an Israelite from the tribe of Benjamin, an Aramaic-speaking 'Hebrew of the Hebrews', a Pharisee, 'a persecutor of the church; as to righteousness under the law, blameless' (Phil. 3.5–6).

More details are furnished from Acts, where we learn that he came from Tarsus, that he studied in Jerusalem under rabbi Gamaliel and that he was born a Roman citizen (Acts 22.3–5, 25–29). That's really all the direct information we have. But there is some detective work to be done, and there are other stories, other traditions.

---

* 'Paul' was his Greek name. Acts refers to him as 'Saul' up until his first missionary trip with Barnabas. For the sake of clarity I will refer to him as Paul, except for the period before his conversion, when he was a Jerusalem-based Pharisee – Paul of Tarsus, or Saul of Jerusalem, as it were.

First, his age. Acts describes him as a *neanias* – a young man – at the time of Stephen's stoning. This term was usually applied to men between 24 and 40 years of age, so doesn't narrow it down much. Writing to Philemon around AD 62, Paul describes himself as a *presbuteros*. The word can be translated as 'ambassador' (and it was also used of the elders of the local Christian communities), but the common meaning is simply an 'old man', someone who had passed his sixtieth birthday. If the letter was written while Paul was in prison in AD 62, that would make his birthday around 1 BC or AD 1 (note that there was no year 0).[1] This would put him in his early thirties when he started attacking the church: well within the range of *neanias*.

Further clues come from early church tradition. According to a fourth-century source, Paul served the Lord for 35 years and died at the age of 68.[2] A pretty late tradition, but it fits with the idea that he was born somewhere around the start of the first century AD.

This makes Paul a direct contemporary of Jesus. And there was another link between the two, because it's likely that Paul came from the same area where Jesus was raised: Galilee. Jerome, writing around AD 388 in his *Commentary on Philemon*, notes, 'It is said that the parents of Paul the apostle were natives of Gischala, a district of Judea, and that when the whole province was laid waste by the Roman arms and the Jews were scattered throughout the world, they were carried away to Tarsus, a city of Cilicia.'[3] He repeats this information a few years later in a biographical dictionary of 135 famous Christian authors.

Gischala was the ancient name for modern el-Jish in Upper Galilee. Although Jerome is a late source – and the only ancient writer who mentions the tradition – he probably got the tale from an earlier source, Origen's commentary on Philemon (now lost). Origen himself was probably recording an oral tradition. There is absolutely no reason why anyone should invent the idea that Paul came from Gischala. It is not mentioned in the Bible and it rivals Nazareth for obscurity. Paul identified himself as a member of the tribe of Benjamin, but Gischala is outside their ancient tribal territories: if you were inventing a town of origin for Paul, there are many better, more symbolic, more famous candidates.

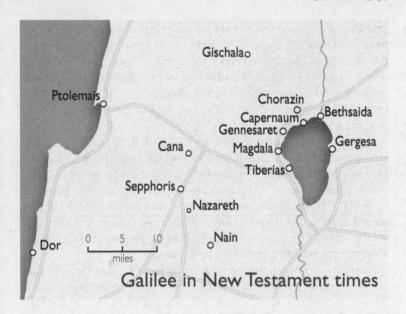

Galilee in New Testament times

But if Paul came from Gischala, it explains how he ended up in Tarsus. Jerome states that Paul's parents were deported to Tarsus by the Romans and sold as slaves. The background to this is the death of Herod the Great in 4 BC, which was followed by disturbances and rebellions throughout Galilee and Judea. In Galilee, the rebels were led by a brigand-chief called Judas, son of Hezekiah, who broke into the armoury at Sepphoris and seized control of the area. The Romans eventually quelled the uprising by razing Sepphoris to the ground and making slaves of the inhabitants.[4] It was not only a form of punishment and retribution, it would also pay for the military action, since the captives would be sold as slaves. When the Emperor Hadrian used the same procedure to pay for suppressing the Bar Kochba revolt in Judea, he sold so many slaves that it created a glut in the market.[5]

Josephus doesn't mention Gischala as being involved in the revolts, but it is not hard to imagine that a Roman army passing through would grab captives as they went; or even that the finance officer of the legion would seek to balance his budget by sending out a raiding party. And it might also explain why, during the

Jewish revolt some sixty years later, the inhabitants of Gischala were 'anxious for peace'. At that time, Josephus describes the inhabitants as mostly farmers 'whose only concern was the prospect of a good harvest' but who had been infiltrated by a powerful gang of bandits who were running the town.[6] The ordinary people might have had in mind what the Romans had once done to them in Gischala.

So we can build up a tentative picture of Paul's origins. Taken into slavery by Roman soldiers in the wake of the revolts after Herod's death, his parents would have been taken north to Antioch on the Orontes – the Roman headquarters in the province of Syria. There they would have been sold to slave dealers, who would have shipped them out of Ptolemais (modern Akko) and up the coast. Offered for sale in perhaps a number of port towns along the coast, they ended up in Tarsus.[7]

Tarsus was a prosperous city in the heart of *Cilicia Pedias* – Cilicia of the Plain, as the Greeks named the region – a rich agricultural country, growing wheat, sesame and rice. Its vineyards produced a muscatel-type wine, and it had a flourishing textile industry. It was also on one of the main trade routes of the ancient world. North of Tarsus lay the Cilician Gates, the narrow pass in the Taurus Mountains through which the overland route led west to Asia and beyond that to Greece and Rome. East were the Syrian Gates in the Amanus Mountains, through which ran the road to Syria and to Antioch. And then there was the River Cnidus, on which the city stood, which led to the north coast of the Mediterranean.

Tarsus was known for a kind of goat's-hair cloth known as *cilicium*, after the province. This was used to make tents, carpets and shoes, so maybe that was where Paul's parents learned their trade.[8] His parents passed on their skills in tentmaking to their son. If his parents were taken to Tarsus in 4 BC, they cannot have remained in slavery for long. Paul describes himself as 'free-born': he was the son of a free citizen or a freedman. So, somehow, his parents managed to escape from slavery and obtain citizenship.

Slaves could gain their freedom in a number of ways. Many were granted freedom – manumitted, to use the technical term – on the deaths of their masters. Sometimes this was a gesture of affection or reward; sometimes the prospect of eventual freedom served as an encouragement to slaves to be obedient and work hard. Others managed to gain enough money to buy their way out. Sometimes slaves were provided with the money to buy their freedom by a synagogue or pagan association. Later the church would help slaves purchase their freedom.[9] It was certainly not unusual for freed slaves to become citizens. Philo describes the Trastavere district of Rome as being the home of many Jews who were 'Roman citizens, having been emancipated; for having been brought as captives into Italy, they were manumitted by those who brought them for slaves.'[10]

There were four main ways in which people would become citizens: they could gain it on retirement from the army; they could be among those granted citizenship if their town was designated a Roman colony; they could gain it as a reward for service or loyalty to the Empire; or they could gain it when they were manumitted.

If Jerome is right about Paul's origins, then probably they were made citizens on their manumission. In AD 4, Augustus passed a series of measures known as the *Lex Aelia Sentia,* which were designed to regulate the manumitting of slaves and clarify some legal aspects of their treatment. According to this, any slave over 30 who was formally manumitted would automatically become a Roman citizen. Formal manumission entailed either an official legal proceeding or freedom being specifically granted in the will of a deceased owner. In the provinces, formal manumission would have to be verified by a local council of twenty magistrates. Although some texts imply that no freed foreign subject could become a citizen, there is evidence that there were Jews who were citizens of Greek cities and Jews were known to be citizens of Tarsus.[11]

Citizenship was a precious commodity in the Roman world. Technically it was illegal to buy or sell citizenship: when the centurion who arrests Paul in Jerusalem says that his citizenship cost him a lot of money, he is talking about an illegal bribe paid to facilitate the process.[12]

We don't know how long Paul remained in Tarsus. In a speech much later he describes how he was 'born in Tarsus in Cilicia, but brought up in this city at the feet of Gamaliel' (Acts 22.3). The implication is that Paul was raised from an early age in Jerusalem, not in Tarsus. This ties in with the fact that he was raised as a Pharisee, and there is no evidence that Pharisees were active outside Palestine at this time.[13] Certainly, later, his sister and nephew were living in the city (Acts 23.16).

However, Paul ties his 'upbringing' in Jerusalem to being a disciple of rabbi Gamaliel and he could not have become a rabbinic disciple before the age of thirteen; probably he was older, if anything. The likelihood is that he was raised until his early teens in Tarsus, before, either with his parents or with other members of his family, making the 500-mile journey to Jerusalem to take up the next stage in his education under rabbi Gamaliel.

Gamaliel's dates are uncertain, as we have seen, but Paul cannot have started as a pupil of Gamaliel earlier than AD 20. It has been argued that he would have been fifteen at this time. But the statement about his being a *presbuteros* in Philemon implies that he may have been older when he joined Gamaliel's circle.

Whatever the case, it was under Gamaliel, that canny and learned rabbi, that Paul from Tarsus became Saul of Jerusalem.

Already fluent in Aramaic and Greek, his rabbinic studies meant Paul had to read Hebrew perfectly as well. He learned to study and memorise the Torah. As a member of the pharisaical wing of Judaism, he was introduced to the decisions, statements and traditions of the great rabbis.

Being a rabbinical student meant more than theoretical study, however. Students lived with their teacher, allowing him to observe their lifestyle. They, in turn, would observe his behaviour and try to copy him. They would also serve the rabbi, performing menial tasks for him. This early training becomes the background to Paul's expectations of his disciples and his followers. Paul is constantly exhorting his followers to learn from his example. It's not because he was arrogant: it's because that's how he learned in the first place.

Jewish rabbinical students were also expected to show a mastery of detail and a knack for developing intricate, even surprising, lines of argument.[14] Paul always excelled at that – perhaps too much. Paul, one suspects, could have started an argument in an empty room. But for rabbinical students, debate and argument were the crucible of learning. Sitting around eating with his rabbi

and fellow disciples, walking together as they talked (later tradition asserted that Gamaliel was renowned for teaching on the
move), there were always discussions and argument.[15]

Perhaps it got a bit overbearing at times. The words of
Gamaliel's son Simeon have a certain poignancy: 'All my days I
have grown up among the sages and I have found nothing better
for a person than silence. The expounding of the Law is not the
chief thing, but the doing of it, and he that multiplies words occasions sin.'[16]

Paul became, according to his own words, a star pupil, advanc-
ing in the law far beyond his contemporaries. What impelled him?
We know Paul always pursued things passionately. His letters are
testimony to that. But what is key is that once again we are dealing with an immigrant. He was not Jerusalem born and bred. He
may have been a rabbi's apprentice, but he was also a Tarsus-born
Roman citizen. Just as later, because of his latecoming to the
faith, he felt keenly any challenges about his position as an apostle, perhaps here he felt keenly the vulnerability of his position as
an immigrant.

Paul's training in Jerusalem, at whatever age he began it, fired
up a passion for the Jewish faith that burned with a fierce flame.
His studies in the Scriptures showed him fierce heroes who had
fought for God. There was Phinehas who killed for God (Num.
25.13). There were the judges. More recently, the Maccabees – the
name means 'hammer' – who struck against the threat to the Jewish faith and drove out the Hellenistic kings.

He came to Jerusalem as Paul from Tarsus. But by the time
he emerged from the shadow of Gamaliel and strode forward to
challenge the followers of this Jesus, that immigrant background
was behind him. He had become Saul of Jerusalem, Saul Macca-
beus: the hammer of the Nazarenes.

'The city of Samaria'

The persecution orchestrated by Saul forced the Hellenistic
Christians in Jerusalem to flee for their lives. They headed out
into Judea and Samaria, and beyond. In a later reference, Luke
tells us that those who had to flee the persecution went as far as
Phoenicia, Cyprus and Antioch. In other words, many went back

'home'; back to their diaspora communities. But not all. One significant – if underrated – figure stayed closer to Jerusalem and started breaking through the boundaries. His name was Philip.

Given his importance, it is astonishing that Philip has received hardly any study from theologians – and yet this is the case. He's almost cast aside, treated as an incidental character; and yet, if the account in Acts is correct, he was the first major missionary of the early church. The Philip who is mentioned in this section is not the apostle, but one of the seven deacons. Luke makes it clear that it was Philip the deacon who spoke to the Ethiopian eunuch and travelled the coastal towns, eventually settling in Caesarea (Acts 21.8–9).[17]

First, though, on escaping Jerusalem, he headed north. He went to Samaria.

The hatred between Jew and Samaritan ran long and deep. It was established 500 years earlier, when the Jews returned from exile in Babylon to find the Samaritans established in the region, and the intervening centuries had done nothing to calm the situation. During the Maccabean era, John Hyrcanus burned the Samaritan temple on Mount Gerizim to the ground because it was an abomination to the Jews. There was only one true temple and it was in Jerusalem, not on Mount Gerizim. He also destroyed the town of Shechem; as Philip made his way into Samaria he would have seen the ruins near the town of Sychar. The hatred simmered on into the first century, occasionally boiling over into sectarian outrages and attacks. To Jerusalem Jews, Samaritans were permanently unclean, impure heretics who spread lies and engaged in underhand tricks. And nothing would ever change that.

At the time Philip travelled there, Samaria was under direct control of the Roman prefect Pontius Pilate. It had not always been that way. It had previously been part of the kingdom of Herod the Great who, in a typically shrewd diplomatic move, invested heavily in the infrastructure of its capital city, also called Samaria. He built a temple dedicated to Augustus and settled the city with 6,000 of his veteran soldiers and sundry neighbouring peoples.[18] He rebuilt it and he renamed it. He called it Sebaste, the Greek version of the name Augustus. From that time people used Sebaste to refer to the city, and Samaria for the region. (Even today the modern Arab village on the site is called Sebastiyeh. Buildings can be burned. Names are hard to kill off.)

It was to this city – the city of Augustus – that Philip went, some time around AD 34. There has, admittedly, been some debate. Luke's Greek could be read as 'a city of Samaria' or 'the city of Samaria'. But the earliest manuscripts of Acts have '*the* city of Samaria': and that can only mean the capital of the region, the Græco-Roman city of Sebaste.[19]

In the first century AD, the city was surrounded by a strong wall, a sign of strength and significance. It had a stadium and in the centre was the magnificent temple which Herod the Great had had built in honour of Augustus, a temple renowned for its size and beauty. Nor was Augustus the only pagan deity in town. There was also a temple to the cult of Kore just to the north of the Augustan temple. Archaeologists have also found statues of Apollo, Dionysus and Hercules.

Sebaste, then, was very different from staunchly monotheistic Jerusalem, with its prohibition of graven images and its temple dedicated to the one true God. It was only 36 miles from Jerusalem, but in every possible way it was foreign territory.

But if this really was *the* city of Samaria, if it really was pagan Sebaste, then it rather explodes the cosy, neat framework attributed to Acts: the gradual expansion of Christianity from Jew to Samaritan (near-Jew) to proselyte Ethiopian (Jewish convert) and only then, finally, to Gentile. Sebaste was full of Gentiles – full of people who believed in Dionysus and Apollo and Kore.

Those Gentiles must have been among those who listened to Philip talk about Jesus, who watched as people were healed and unclean spirits, shrieking and wailing, were exorcised and the paralysed and lame were cured. There must have been Gentile converts who shared in the 'great joy in that city' of which we are told in Acts 8.6–8.

There's also another pointer to the nature of the people who became Christians in Samaria: they believed in magic. Among those who witnessed the miracles surrounding Philip with amazement was a man who traded in that sort of thing, one who no doubt thought of himself as a fellow professional: Simon the magician.

> Now a certain man named Simon had previously practised magic in the city and amazed the people of Samaria, saying that he was someone great. (Acts 8.9)

The ancient world took magic for granted. Every city, every town in the Græco-Roman Empire had its share of magicians and sorcerers, selling quack remedies or charms to ward off evil spirits. Christians were implacably opposed to magic in all forms. In the *Didache*, Christians were instructed not to be augurers, enchanters, astrologers or magicians, since such things 'breed idolatry'. They were instructed not to even desire to see such people.[20]

One of Luke's recurring themes is the supremacy of the power of Christ over the realm of magic. In Cyprus Paul and Barnabas encounter a magician called Bar-Jesus (Acts 13.6). In Philippi Paul and Silas are met by a slave girl with a 'python spirit'. Her liberation results in an outcry by the girl's owners who were making money from her divination. In Ephesus Christian converts burn their books of magic – precious volumes worth a huge amount of money (Acts 19.19).

These examples show the lure of magic, its widespread appeal and the way in which it was economically and spiritually embedded in the culture. There was money to be made. Simon was evidence of magic's lure and its popularity. According to Justin Martyr, who was a local boy himself, Simon was born in the city of Gitta. Simon had built a considerable following in the city, so much so that people thought him some kind of quasi-divine 'Great Power of God'. Philip's encounter with Simon, however, was not as spectacular as the later incidents in Acts. The meeting between the two is dealt with in just a few words: 'Even Simon himself believed' (Acts 8.13). He was baptised and stayed with Philip.

Philip's message is overcoming the other powers in the city. And when news of what is happening in Sebaste reaches the Jerusalem Christians, they decide to send their top brass to check it out.

'The chains of wickedness'

It is Peter and John who are sent to Samaria to give official approval to the work. This is the first case of converts being made outside Jerusalem, outside the sphere of influence of the Jerusalem church, so naturally they are concerned. And soon it becomes clear that there are things that Philip cannot do – or, at least, has not done.

In a passage which has since engendered huge debate, they realise that the people have not quite received the full power of God. New believers have been baptised in the name of the Lord Jesus, but have not received the Holy Spirit. So Peter and John lay hands on the converts and pray for them to receive the Holy Spirit (Acts 8.14–17). It raises many questions. Why does it require a special visit for this to happen? Is Philip not up to the job? Has he not even told them about the Holy Spirit? Has Philip, in fact, rushed it rather?

No, the problem is not Philip. Nor is it that you need an apostle to baptise or to confirm a baptism – the eunuch who is baptised just a little later goes back to Ethiopia and no apostle runs after him; and when Paul is baptised in Damascus there is no need for special apostolic confirmation.

The primary reason why Luke draws attention to this seems to be as a manifest proof that something has changed. These major outpourings of the Holy Spirit occur when someone unusual or unexpected has been added to the kingdom and ratification might be needed in order for the occurrence to be fully accepted. A special dispensing of the Spirit appears when the gospel is received by a new 'group': the Samaritans here; Gentiles in Acts 10.44–48; the disciples of John the Baptist in Acts 19.6–7.[21]

The pouring out of the Spirit is proof that what has happened really is OK. The experience witnessed by Peter and John is, therefore, a stamp of divine approval on these new citizens of the kingdom. They have passed their citizenship test.

The norm in the New Testament is that the Spirit comes with faith (Acts 2.38; 1 Cor. 12.3, 13). These experiences, then, of the two things being separate, are outside the norm. They are special occurrences – but in a positive, not a negative way. Such an outpouring, for example, is absent elsewhere – from the baptism of the 3,000 in Jerusalem (Acts 2.41), the Ethiopian eunuch (Acts 8.36–39), Lydia and her household (Acts 16.15), the jailer in Philippi (Acts 16.29–34), Crispus and others in Corinth (Acts 18.8). Clearly the Holy Spirit was at work in the churches and the letters of Paul show that there were different gifts of the Holy

Spirit being put into action. But the ecstatic eruption of the Holy Spirit at baptism was not a universal norm. The important thing for Luke is that it demonstrates a total experience of the gospel: those who become believers get absolutely the same 'benefits' as anyone else, whatever their background. And it means that no one in the future will be able to argue ethnicity as a barrier.

This is not to say that Philip necessarily got everything right. Perhaps there *was* something missing in his message. This was, after all, the first time anyone had tried to evangelise outside Jerusalem. At the risk of repeating the blindingly obvious, one of the things that we forget about Acts is that it represents a learning curve. Nobody at this stage had had any training in how to 'do' evangelism. There was limited understanding of what this new movement was all about. So there is no reason to think that Philip had things cracked, any more than anyone else did. Peter himself still had a way to go in learning about the parameters of this new belief system.

For the converts themselves, there would have been entirely different levels of response and perception. This is underlined when Simon re-enters the story. Simon looks at the power of the Holy Spirit and immediately desires it – and he does what any magician of his day would have done: he asks if he can purchase an upgrade.

Peter reacts strongly. He spurns Simon's silver and gold and warns him to repent immediately, 'For I see that you are in the gall of bitterness and the chains of wickedness' (Acts 8.20–23). It seems like an extreme reaction, but then this comes after the incident with Ananias and Sapphira, so Peter knows how serious people's obsession with money can be. And it's a warning, not a curse. Simon is, after all, offered a way out: repent and ask forgiveness.

But does he? Simon asks Peter to pray for him, but Luke never says anything about forgiveness. He leaves the conclusion of the story hanging. Perhaps Simon was just too far into that world where magic brings money and power. If later church tradition has any basis in truth, he definitely didn't repent. As Simon Magus, he became a major figure in the literature of the early church. He was a kind of all-purpose villain. Justin Martyr wrote that he founded a sect called the Simonians and eventually ended up in Rome in the company of a former prostitute called Helena. A fellow Samaritan, Menander, followed Simon as head of the Simonians, teaching at Antioch near the close of the first century. Irenaeus, writing around AD 180, called him the source of all heresies.[22] Irenaeus charges that Simon's conversion was feigned and that after the biblical events he set out to learn more impressive magic tricks in order to contend with the apostles. Hippolytus, writing around AD 230, portrays him as a false messiah.[23]

Simon Magus became a convenient peg on which to hang all manner of heresies and gnostic practices, but it is in the pages of Christian fiction that he really becomes the moustache-twirling villain. A largely fictitious work called *The Acts of Peter* which dates from AD 150–200 tells of an all-out miracle contest in Rome: Simon Magus versus Simon Peter. The climax comes when Simon Magus flies above the city of Rome, but is caused to fall by the prayer of Peter.

Winnowing out the truth from these elaborate tales is almost impossible. Acts certainly doesn't go in for any elaboration. In Luke's version he's just a magician on the make.

Perhaps the ongoing story of the city of Sebaste itself mirrors Simon's story. It went on to become a major Christian centre for the early church. During the Byzantine period there was a bishopric there; the bishops of Sebaste were present at the councils of Nicea, Constantinople and Chalcedon and at the Synod of Jerusalem. But paganism ran deep in the city and when Julian II – Julian the Apostate (AD 361–363) – tried to roll back the advance of Christianity, he found a ready following amongst the citizens of Sebaste. They desecrated the tombs and relics of the saints.[24] Jerome talks about strange, appalling religious rites in front of the tombs.

In later times Simon's name was given, on the basis of the story in Acts, to the sin of simony – the act of purchasing ecclesiastical position and power. This is rather unfair. He was after the Holy Spirit, not a bishop's palace and a nice hat. In light of his background, his request is perfectly understandable. (And how many Christians today pay out good money to go on courses on signs and wonders, or fly to exotic American churches in order to 'catch the fire'?)

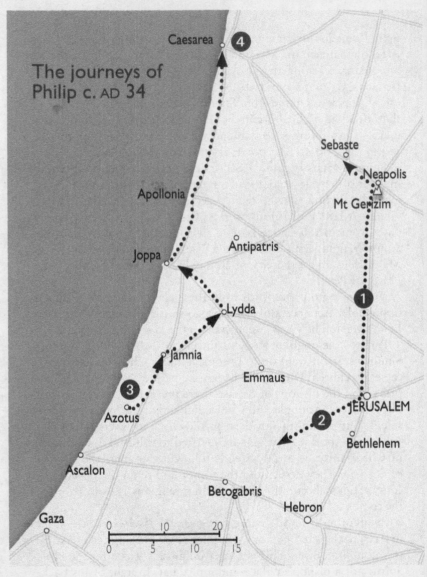

The journeys of
Philip c. AD 34

Caesarea ④

Sebaste

Neapolis

Mt Gerizim

Apollonia

Antipatris

Joppa

①

Lydda

Jamnia

③

Emmaus

Azotus

JERUSALEM

②

Bethlehem

Ascalon

Betogabris

Hebron

Gaza

| 0 | | 10 | | 20 |
| 0 | 5 | | 10 | 15 |

1. Philip goes to Sebaste (Acts 8.6)
2. Philip meets the Ethiopian eunuch in the wilderness on the way to Gaza (Acts 8.26)
3. From Azotus, he travels north along the cities of the coastal plain (Acts 8.40)
4. He eventually settles in Caesarea (Acts 21.9)

But the real import of this story is that Christianity is not magic. It is something far greater than that. It also shows the kind of issues about people's understanding which this new faith has to overcome. In a pagan world, in a city full of gods and goddesses, of magi and miracle-workers, membership of this very different kingdom comes at a price. But it cannot be bought.

God is not for sale.

'From Jerusalem to Gaza'

The failure to fully win Simon – like the Ananias and Sapphira story – is another instance of Luke including unfavourable details. It shows, among other things, that converts didn't always stick and certainly didn't always fully understand what they were getting into – which is hardly surprising given that the apostles themselves were having to work things out as they went along.

There is a roller-coaster feel to the few tales we have about Philip, in which he is whisked from one boundary-breaking experience to another. In the next story in the cycle, he appears on the other side of Jerusalem – to the south.

It's not possible to say when this was. Clearly Luke here is in possession of a number of stories about Philip which are not readily linked together. From Samaria, one would have thought the obvious direction to go would be north, not south – away from the trouble in Jerusalem. So it may be that this event took place at a later date, but has been placed here just to come under the section marked 'Philip'.

Or it may be that, although he is not mentioned as doing so, he returned with Peter and John as they travelled back south towards Jerusalem – proclaiming the message in the villages on the way. But while they go on into Jerusalem, Philip is told by an angel to keep going: 'an angel of the Lord said to Philip, "Get up and go towards the south to the road that goes down from Jerusalem to Gaza." (This is a wilderness road.) So he got up and went' (Acts 8.26–27).

What route he took, we don't know. The normal route from Jerusalem to Gaza would take the traveller south through Hebron and then across to the coast. Eusebius recorded a tradition that the meeting between Philip and the eunuch took place at Beth

Zur, which was some four miles north of Hebron. But mention of 'the desert road' might indicate that Philip branched off and went towards Socoh and into the Elah Valley. There are springs there, where the waters descend from the Judean hill country. It would have made a convenient place for a baptism and the eunuch – and Philip – could then continue west towards Betogabris and the coast.[25]

Wherever it was, he meets a remarkable individual: 'an Ethiopian eunuch, a court official of the Candace, queen of the Ethiopians, in charge of her entire treasury' (Acts 8.27).

Ethiopia, or Nubia, borders Egypt on the south. In the Old Testament it was also known as Cush. That makes the eunuch a black African and it's not insignificant, given Christianity's characterisation as a Western religion, that one of the first non-Jerusalem converts is a black African.

In the first century, Ethiopians symbolised the exotic, the unknown. Ancient literature portrays them in an idealised way, as a mysterious people. Herodotus called them 'the tallest and best-looking people in the world'.[26] Diodorus Siculus wrote that 'it is generally held that the sacrifices practiced among the Ethiopians are those which are most pleasing to heaven'.[27] And they came from the very edge of the earth. Strabo the geographer put Ethiopia on the 'extreme limits' of the Roman Empire. Jesus had said to his followers that they would take his gospel to the ends of the earth (Matt. 28.19): in Græco-Roman terms, that meant Ethiopia.

As well as being an exotic foreigner, the eunuch is a man of high status and high net worth. He's the treasurer to the Candace – which is the Ethiopian term for queen. He is able to ride and read, indicating if we didn't know already that he's educated and wealthy. He has the means to travel in relative comfort and also to afford such a long journey – it would be four months' travel from Ethiopia to Jerusalem.

Why, though, is he making the journey? The most likely explanation is that he is what is known as a 'God-fearer'. The term was an umbrella one, which encompassed everyone from those who supported the synagogue through financial donations (often for local political gain), through those who were interested in Jewish theology, to those who observed some Jewish customs, such as the Sabbath, as well as any who were on their way to becoming a full-blown Jewish convert. We meet such God-fearers at many points in Luke's account. Sometimes they are Paul's opponents, as in the 'devout' women of Pisidian Antioch (Acts 13.50), or those with whom Paul argues in the market place in Athens (Acts 17.17).

The key thing is that such God-fearers had never taken the final step of becoming a proselyte Jew. They had never undergone full conversion. What stopped them? Well, circumcision for one thing: it was seen as part of the bizarre, superstitious behaviour of the Jews and was extremely distasteful to the Græco-Roman mind.[28]

There is evidence that God-fearers could take part to a limited extent in the worship at the temple. They could not go into the inner courts, of course. That was barred to Gentiles. And there were other restrictions. Josephus records that at Passover there were 'many foreigners ... present in great numbers for worship', but that they were not allowed to partake of the Passover feast.[29] Many other Gentile God-fearers, resident in Jerusalem, may have participated to a limited extent in the synagogue worship at some of the Greek-speaking Hellenistic synagogues as well.

God-fearers were looked down on by orthodox Jews. They were pagans, albeit well-meaning ones. This might not have mattered so much in the diaspora world where God-fearers could attend synagogue and spend time with their Jewish friends, but in Jerusalem a God-fearer would have had his secondary status made only too clear to him. He could stand and admire the beauty of the temple, but he could not take part in the festivals. He could pay for sacrifices, but could never actually see the rite taking place. He could go as far as the *soreg*, the low wall which marked the boundary of the Court of Gentiles, but could never enter the inner sanctuary. You can look, but you can't touch.

And for this God-fearer in particular it was even worse. Even had this man wanted to convert, he would never have been able to, because he was a eunuch.

The Greek word *eunochos* could mean a castrated man, or a public official, but more usually it meant both. Court attendants in ancient times were often physical eunuchs (that is to say, they had been castrated). Those associated with queens or other female members of the royal family would be particularly likely to be physical eunuchs – for obvious reasons. Castration was also commonly a mark of slavery or, in some cases, religious devotion.[30]

The Torah was clear: 'No one whose testicles are crushed or whose penis is cut off shall be admitted to the assembly of the LORD' (Deut. 23.1). Such a man was viewed as being in a permanent state of impurity and was thus excluded from full involvement in worship. Eunuchs were particularly suspect. Jewish opinions are reflected in the words of Josephus, who argued for total separation from such people:

> Let those that have made themselves eunuchs be had in detestation; and do you avoid any conversation with them who have deprived themselves of their manhood ... let such be driven away, as if they had killed their children, since they beforehand have lost what should procure them; for evident it is, that while their soul is become effeminate, they have withal transfused that effeminacy to their body also.[31]

Philo, similarly, saw eunuchs as being utterly barred from access to God: 'For [the law] expels those whose generative organs are fractured or mutilated'.[32]

For Jews, then, eunuchs were permanently exiled from the worshipping community. Indeed, throughout the first-century world eunuchs were often viewed with suspicion and distaste. Emperors such as Domitian, Nerva and Hadrian banned the practice of castration within the Empire. Some ancient references portray eunuchs as a kind of third, indeterminate gender.[33] The ancient world was certainly misogynistic. Women were second-class citizens. Anyone, therefore, who had his manhood taken away from him, or who gave it up, was, whatever his social status and wealth, repulsive and unnatural. He had 'opted out of being male'.[34]

Many cults and temples had eunuchs associated with them, most notably, in the Roman world, fertility cults centred around goddesses like Cybele, Isis or Astarte.[35] Many of these pagan eunuchs dressed and acted as women and engaged in sexual activities as such. Tertullian mocked the eunuch priests of this cult as 'a third sex ... made up as it is of male and female in one'.[36]

So this is a man who, for all his power and wealth, will always be marginalised, consistently viewed with disdain. For all his piety he will always be an outsider, never fully a part of God's covenant people.

Well, perhaps not 'never'. In the book he is reading, the book of the prophet Isaiah, there is a glimmer of hope:

Do not let the foreigner joined to the Lord say,
　'The Lord will surely separate me from his people';
and do not let the eunuch say,
　'I am just a dry tree.'
For thus says the Lord:
To the eunuchs who keep my sabbaths,
　who choose the things that please me
　and hold fast my covenant,
I will give, in my house and within my walls,
　a monument and a name
　better than sons and daughters;
I will give them an everlasting name
　that shall not be cut off. (Isa. 56.3–5)

Although it is not this passage he is reading, as Philip speaks to him he must surely recall it. It is, after all, an end-time message, a messianic message: an everlasting name for the foreigner and the eunuch. As Philip speaks about the Messiah Jesus, it must seem to the eunuch as though that time has come. We can even sense the excitement in his voice when he spies some water: 'Look, here is water! What is to prevent me from being baptised?' (Acts 8.36)

So what we have here is a story of perhaps the ultimate outsider, brought into the all-welcoming kingdom of God. And this incident seems to become typical of Philip's developing story, because he is suddenly whisked away and 'finds himself' at Azotus, the old Philistine city of Ashdod, about 20 miles north of Gaza. From there he makes his way up the coast along the cities of the coastal road, proclaiming the good news in all the towns on the way (Acts 8.40). These towns – Azotus, Jamnia, Joppa and Caesarea – were towns with both Jew and Gentile populations.

We can make a guess at the success of Philip's activities in these towns from the fact that when Peter goes over the same territory he finds communities already established, Christian groups which must go back to Philip and others like him. Philip's work helps open up evangelistic activity along the entire coast.

Philip finally settles in Caesarea, home to a substantial colony of Greek-speaking Gentiles. And it is there that Luke meets him, in AD 58 (Acts 21.8).

By that time Philip was one of the grand old men of the church, and perhaps it was then that Luke heard these stories from him – stories of Philip's exploits in Sebaste and Philistia, of whirlwind trips to desert roads and strange, wonderful meetings with eunuchs and magicians.

'Violently persecuting the church of God'

After this interlude on Philip, Luke's account plunges us back into the firestorm following the death of Stephen.

Saul set to his task with zeal and fury. He talks about 'devastation', and this indicates more than the odd arrest. His words in the letter to Galatians indicate that he carried out these activities over a period of time (Gal. 1.13–14).[37] Much later in his life he hinted at one element of his approach: when hunting the Christians, his approach was 'to force them to blaspheme' (Acts 26.11). Were there deaths? Possibly, although Paul doesn't say as much and only Stephen's is recorded in Acts. But it is easy to imagine many of the techniques used – techniques which are still used against Christians, and others, today. Meetings broken up, leaders incarcerated, houses ransacked.

It's unlikely that the Romans would have permitted mob killings on any scale. The odd spate of mob violence was never going to cause them any worry, but systematic 'authorised' outrages against a particular group would more than likely have seen Pilate step in.

Just how 'authorised' was such activity? The virus had spread to Damascus, so Luke reports that Saul went to the high priest for letters of authorisation to hunt down the heresy further afield. It has been pointed out by critics of Luke that this story is implausible. Technically, neither the Sanhedrin nor the high priest had any authority over the synagogues in Damascus. A reference in Maccabees shows that the Romans had, in the past, granted the Jewish high priest power to pursue and extradite fugitives (1 Macc. 15.16–21),[38] but it seems unlikely that they would have extended this power to diaspora Jews in different countries.

One can, however, have different kinds of authority. For devout Jews in the Damascus synagogues, the name of the high priest would have carried a lot of clout, even if legally there was no force behind his words. Power can be expressed in a number of ways. Scholars who are far removed from the realities of religious persecution place too much faith in the notion of legality.

And it was Saul himself, as we are told, who went to the high priest and sought out authority. He was not a recruit: he was a volunteer. Paul from Tarsus, ultra keen to prove that he really was Saul of Jerusalem. So the letters which he took with him wouldn't be some sort of command to the Damascene synagogues to hand over the Jews, but rather letters of commendation: 'Saul has done good work in rooting out the Christians in Jerusalem; if you want to do the same in Damascus, he's your man.'

Saul asks for letters so that he can capture 'any who belonged to the Way' (Acts 9.2). It's the first use of this term in Acts, but it crops up elsewhere too. In Ephesus Jewish opponents speak evil of the Way and a disturbance breaks out (Acts 19.9, 23). Apollos has been 'instructed in the Way of the Lord', but only knows the baptism of John, so Priscilla and Aquila 'explain the Way of God to him more accurately' (Acts 18.25–26). In speeches before Roman governors, Paul talks about 'the Way, which they call a sect' (Acts 22.4; 24.14, 22). This was probably the earliest term for Christianity. But where did it come from?

The Qumran community provides one clue. The Dead Sea Scrolls use the same term to describe that community: their writings contain references to 'those who have chosen the Way', or those who have turned away from it.[39] They based this partly on Isaiah 40.3, 'Prepare the way of the LORD, make straight in the desert a highway', which they took as an injunction to 'separate from the habitation of unjust men and go into the wilderness'.[40]

Significantly, the early church also viewed this text as a crucial prophecy. It is one of the few elements which feature in all four Gospels – where it is associated, of course, with John the Baptist (Matt. 3.3; Mark 1.3; Luke 3.4; John 1.23). This linkage might lie behind Apollos's use of the term 'the Way'. He knew about the Baptist and added to that accurate, but incomplete, knowledge about Jesus: so this terminology goes right back to Jesus' first public work and to his association with John the Baptist.[41]

But Jesus also used and developed the term: he referred to himself as 'the way, and the truth, and the life' (John 14.5–6). And he talked about two paths: the narrow and the broad pathways.

The *Didache* makes this term the starting point of its teaching. It opens with a description of the two ways:

> There are two ways, one of life and one of death, and there is a great difference between the two ways. The way of life is this. First of all, thou shalt love the God that made thee; secondly, Thy neighbour as thyself. And all things whatsoever thou wouldst not have befall thyself, neither do thou unto another. (Did. 1.1–2)

'The Way' is a term with its roots deep in the origins of the Christian faith. Before they were called Christians, before there was such a thing as Christianity, before there were churches and vestments and ritual and liturgy, there was simply 'the Way'.

Bringing us back to the action, as to the other kind of 'way', we can make a strong guess at the route Saul took to Damascus. He would have gone the most common route: along what was known as 'the great north road'. Today the route runs northwards from – unsurprisingly – Jerusalem's Damascus Gate. The road took him through a landscape which reverberated with Old Testament stories: Gibeah, home of his Saul's namesake, the first king of Israel; Michmash, where Jonathan slew the Philistines; Shiloh, where the child Samuel grew to become the greatest judge of all.[42] But it was not until close to Damascus – within walking distance of the city – that the catastrophe occurred.

The story is well known. Proverbial. Even today people talk of a 'road to Damascus' experience. Even within Acts, the story appears three times – once related by Luke and the other times during speeches attributed to Paul himself. He is heading to Damascus when he sees an intense light and hears a voice: 'Saul, Saul, why do you persecute me?' When he asks who the voice belongs to, he gets the reply, 'I am Jesus, whom you are persecuting.' The people with him see nothing. They hear some kind of sound, but only to Saul is it intelligible (Acts 9.4–7).[43] Later, Paul says that the voice spoke to him in the Hebrew tongue – Aramaic – and that the others fell to the ground as well (Acts 26.14).

This was the turning point of Paul's life. It was not some subtle change in philosophies. It was a U-turn, a complete reversal. Conversion. Indeed, when he later wrote about his vision of Jesus – a vision which he believes conferred apostolic status on him – he used vivid, visceral terms. As usual with our English Bible translations, it's given a genteel spin: 'Last of all, as to someone untimely born, he appeared also to me. For I am the least of the apostles, unfit to be called an apostle, because I persecuted the church of God' (1 Cor. 15.8–9).

The phrase translated as 'someone untimely born' is *to ektromati*, 'the miscarried'. In secular Greek it generally means miscarriage, abortion or unnatural premature birth, but its derivation from the word *trōō* 'to wound, injure, damage', carries connotations of something wrong, something monstrous and even deformed. This is the only time it's found in the New Testament. Dunn translates this as 'last of all as to the abortion'. He was miscarried into the faith, aborted, torn out of the womb of pharisaical Judaism. Perhaps, relating it to his persecution of the followers, it carries images of a mother miscarrying because of violence done to her. For Paul this was a traumatic, violent birth.[44]

Perhaps it's not surprising that Paul was drawn to apply an image of childbirth. The effect is to plunge him back into a helpless, baby-like state. He is encased in a womb-like darkness and led into the city, where he sits alone in a room and waits for rebirth.

Damascus was an old city. It was old by the time of Abraham, ancient before Athens and Rome were even thought of. Many kings and emperors had fought to own this city, from the Egyptians under Thutmose III to Alexander the Great. Many Jews also lived in the city. Saul was led into the city, probably through the triple gate at the end of the main street. This was *vicus rectus*, the 'street called straight', and it survives today as the *Tareek es Sultan* which runs east-west in the eastern part of the old city. In those days it was a mile long, divided into three sections adorned with many columns.[45]

Saul was taken to the house of a man called Judas (Acts 9.11) and for three days he sat in the dark neither eating nor drinking. Just praying. Waiting for a man to come and see him. A man to help him see.

Straight Street as it was in the early nineteenth century

That man was Ananias — surely one of the bravest Christians of all times. This disciple, one of what could have been only a small number of Christians in Damascus, knew about Saul's reputation, knew that he had been persecuting the followers in Jerusalem, knew even, according to Luke, that he had come to Damascus with letters of extradition in his possession. Since Ananias had only heard about rather than experienced the persecution in Jerusalem, the implication is that he was not a refugee from Jerusalem, but a long-term resident of Damascus. He must have become a Christian, then, either during Pentecost or in the wake of those events. Despite all this, he went and prayed with Saul. He even addressed Saul as 'brother' (Acts 9.17). Immediately Saul's sight is restored and he is baptised.

Ananias is also the first person other than Saul to be told of Saul's destiny: to take the good news to the Gentiles. God tells Ananias that Saul has been chosen to 'bring my name before Gentiles and kings and before the people of Israel'. And then there is a curious postscript: 'I myself will show him how much he must suffer for the sake of my name' (Acts 9.15). Saul's mission is not one of glory and glamour, but of perseverance, rejection and suffering. How much suffering, God only knows.

After a few days of both instruction and recuperation, Saul heads for the synagogues to argue and debate with the Jews. The persecutor is ready to become one of the persecuted. The way to Damascus is the start of a long, difficult and rocky road.

3. Syria AD 35–37

'Into Arabia'

After the incident in Damascus, Paul stayed away from Jerusalem. Hardly surprising. One can imagine how the Hellenistic Jews might have treated this turncoat. And no doubt Paul was carrying a barrowload of guilt about his actions in Jerusalem, not to mention the nervousness he must have felt over how the apostles might have received him.

Nevertheless, it is not insignificant that Paul's 'career' as a Christian apologist and missionary begins with avoiding the central authority. He does not return to get any kind of mandate, or even to receive absolution or forgiveness. His calling as an apostle is built from the first on divine authorisation – and a hefty dose of self-confidence. Paul is his own man from the start (although he would say, of course, that he was Christ's man).

As to the timing of Paul's vision, I think it highly likely that the first nine or so chapters of Acts are all set in a fairly tight timescale.[1] Paul's encounter with Jesus must, surely, have taken place not too long after the resurrection, otherwise it would be hard for him to claim it as an apostolic vision of the same quality as that of the other apostles. There is an ancient tradition which claims that the resurrection appearances took place over some eighteen months after the crucifixion. Since this tradition appears both in orthodox writings and in gnostic works, it was probably an ancient and fairly widely accepted tradition.[2] So, since Paul claims that his is the final resurrection appearance, that would give us a date of around September/October AD 34.[3]

Luke's data for this period does seem uncertain. He uses a catch-all phrase – 'after some time had passed' – to describe the period of time between Paul's conversion and his eventual return to Jerusalem. It must be quite a time, though, because by then Paul has gained disciples of his own (Acts 9.23, 25a). Indeed, according to his own words in Galatians, he stayed away three years. And he went to Arabia (Gal. 1.17–18).

The name refers to Syrian Arabia and, especially, Nabatea. We don't know for sure what he was doing there, but we can surmise that he was most likely developing the missionary techniques which he was to use for the rest of his life. He found work, he went to the synagogues to argue and debate, and he spent time processing exactly what it was that had happened to him. Paul spent three years in Arabia. According to our calculations above, that probably means from AD 34 to 36. (When Paul later says that it was three years before his first visit to Jerusalem, he is probably following ancient custom and measuring time inclusively, like Jesus' three days in the tomb.)

When he returned to Damascus in AD 36, though, it wasn't long before he had to escape. There are two accounts of the event. In Acts, the Jews are plotting against Paul and watching the gates to kill him, so he has to be let down through an opening in the wall hidden in a basket. Paul's own account is found in 2 Corinthians:

> In Damascus, the governor under King Aretas set a guard on the city of Damascus in order to seize me, but I was let down in a basket through a window in the wall, and escaped from his hands. (2 Cor. 11.32–33)

This is a passage which has exercised many scholars and historians. Paul clearly says that the governor was working for Aretas IV, king of Nabatea. But there is no reference in the works of other historians to the Nabateans controlling Damascus. And even if Aretas was in charge, why would he want to kill Paul?

Aretas certainly wanted Damascus. The kingdom of Nabatea covered what is now southern Jordan and included the famous city of Petra. Aretas had ambitions to expand, but there was really only one direction he could go: north. Heading west from Nabatea brought you to Egypt and the Romans would never let any incursion happen there. South and east was the great Arabian desert. But north led to Trachonitis, the Golan Heights and Damascus. Plenty of Nabatean traders had already migrated in that direction, moving along the King's Highway, the trade route which ran north towards Asia Minor. Damascus was at the junction between this highway and routes north and west. If the Nabateans could get Damascus, it would give them control of all the trade to the Arabian peninsula. (Not forgetting that one of the king's ancestors, Aretas III, had once ruled the city. The Nabateans and Damascus had history.)

We can rule out any idea of Aretas being given control of the city by the Romans. A strategically important, wealthy city like Damascus would only have been gifted to one of Rome's special friends. Aretas was not one of those. That, in fact, was his main problem. It was the emperor's special friends in the region – the dynasty of Herod the Great – who were constantly thwarting Aretas's plans. In 20 BC, for example, Zenodorus, ruler of a small principality near Damascus, sold half his kingdom to the Nabateans, including Trachonitis and the Golan Heights. But the Emperor Augustus, who happened to be in the region, simply revoked this move and handed the region to Herod the Great. Clearly this setback festered with the Nabatean kings. In 12 BC, while Herod was in Rome, they encouraged the Arabs living in Trachonitis to rebel against him, an action which was encouraged by Aretas's minister who was living in the area.[4] So one reason Aretas wanted Damascus was for trade and power. The other reason was revenge.

When Herod the Great died, his kingdom was divided between three of his sons: Herod Philip took the north-eastern part, including Iturea and Trachonitis, Archelaeus took Judea and Samaria, and Antipas was handed Galilee and the Perea. In a shrewd diplomatic move, though, Aretas married his daughter to Antipas. The problem was that Antipas then went to Rome and fell in love with Herodias, his half-brother's wife, and brought her back to Galilee with him. Aretas's daughter, sensing that she was about to be ousted, fled across the border back to Daddy.

Daddy was livid. He threatened Antipas with war. It is in precisely this period that John the Baptist appeared, stirring up the people in the Perea and criticising the marriage of Antipas and Herodias as illicit and immoral. Aretas was in a warlike mood, but there was little he could do. Antipas, fearing that John would spark unrest and weaken his forces, had him arrested and executed, sometime around the end of AD 30. Not only did Antipas have the support of the Romans, his brother Philip the Tetrarch was a strong, efficient ruler who would no doubt have come to his brother's aid. So Aretas merely comforted his daughter and settled down to wait.

Three years later the situation changed. The Roman governor Flaccus died, and his replacement Vitellius did not arrive in Syria until AD 35, resulting in three years of absentee government.[5] Then Philip the Tetrarch died in AD 34. His territory – much to Antipas's irritation – was annexed by Tiberius to the Roman province of Syria, bringing it under direct Roman rule. Clearly this would have been interpreted by Aretas as a sign that Antipas was no longer trusted by Rome.

When Vitellius eventually arrived, he was faced with a region in turmoil. There were conflicts and uprisings in Parthia, Armenia, Cappadocia (the Taurus Mountains north and north-east of Tarsus) and Trachonitis. He was firefighting on a number of fronts.

Aretas took his opportunity. He marched against Antipas and inflicted a crushing defeat on the tetrarch's army at Gamala, in the north of Galilee.[6] The dating of the battle is not certain, but it probably took place in October of AD 36. The defeat gave Aretas control over Trachonitis. More, it gave him influence in the region. It gave him power. And, after all, Gamala was only 50 miles from Damascus.[7]

The Galilean populace interpreted the defeat as divine punishment for the execution of John the Baptist. Herod, in a panic, wrote desperately to Tiberius for help and the emperor instructed Vitellius to march south and to take Aretas 'dead or alive'. Vitellius arrived at Ptolemais in response to Tiberius's order just before Passover in AD 37, after a march that would have taken between one and two months. But for some reason the battle never took place. The chronology is very confused here, but it seems that before Vitellius could take action against Aretas, news arrived of the death of the Emperor Tiberius. All military actions were placed on hold and instead of marching on Aretas, Vitellius and Antipas went to Jerusalem, where the governor received a rapturous welcome. (At the temple he removed the high priesthood from Jonathan and gave it to Theophilos, Jonathan's brother, and another of the sons of Ananus. *Plus ça change.*)

Tiberius was succeeded by Gaius Caligula. Fairly soon, the status quo reasserted itself. By AD 37, Trachonitis was back under Roman control: it was given to Herod Agrippa by Caligula. Aretas probably hadn't expected to hold on to the area for long, but maybe he thought he could exchange it for more territory in the Decapolis. The outline shows that, sometime in the summer or autumn of October AD 36, he was in a position to gain control over Damascus. This lines up perfectly with the account in Galatians of the three-year gap between Paul's conversion and his first return visit to Jerusalem. It might only have been for a short time, but it gives us a window during which Paul had to escape. Through a window.

But *why* did Paul have to flee? Why should Aretas be at all interested in an obscure, wandering tentmaker like Paul? There could be a number of answers. Paul, we know, had been active in Arabia – that is, in Nabatean-controlled territory. Perhaps his missionary practices there had caused problems. Or, another possibility, at this point not much would have been generally known about Christianity, but it would certainly have been known that it originated with a Galilean. Given that Aretas was at war with Antipas – tetrarch of Galilee – any well-known person linked with a Galilean movement could have been suspicious. The subtleties of ethnicity and theology would not have mattered much to Aretas or his representatives. Christianity was a movement whose leaders were Galileans, and Galileans were the enemy.

There were certainly plenty of Nabateans in Damascus to do Aretas's bidding, whether or not he had absolute control of the city. The city even had a Nabatean quarter, in the north-east, between the Roman East Gate and the position of the later St Thomas Gate. Intriguingly, the Ananias Chapel – the traditional site of the home of the faithful disciple – sits right in the centre of this quarter. The tradition for this site goes back to early

Byzantine times. And the official referred to by Paul – the ethn-arch – may have been the head of the Nabatean trade colony in Damascus, a kind of consul, so Aretas need not have been in over-all control for this account to ring true.[8]

There is still the conflict that in Luke it was the Jews who were hunting Paul, whereas Paul says it was the Nabatean governor (Acts 9.23; 2 Cor. 11.32–33). I'm not sure there is a way of rec-onciling this one, except to admit that it is entirely possible that *both* the Jews and the Nabateans wanted Paul dead. He was that kind of guy. Maybe it was the Jewish community who tipped the Nabateans off about Paul's whereabouts. Paul was a known trou-blemaker, linked with some kind of amorphous Galilean move-ment and living in the middle of a Nabatean colony in the city of Damascus: he must have seemed a clear threat.

Whatever the real picture, there is no doubt that Paul had to get away quickly. He hurriedly left Damascus and headed towards Jerusalem, for his first meeting with the apostles. This was the first time he had been in the city since his days as a Christian-hunter. No wonder he – and the disciples – were nervous.

It is at this point that Barnabas steps back into the story. He it is who vouches for Paul (Acts 9.26–27). Perhaps he has contacts with the Christians in Damascus and elsewhere. Presumably he has heard of Paul's work in Arabia. But the truth is that we don't know why Barnabas gets involved.

Nevertheless, he acts as Paul's sponsor. Typically for Paul, immediately after the meeting with the apostles, he gets into trou-ble. He goes back to his old haunts: the Hellenistic synagogues where he was once the golden boy. 'He spoke and argued with the Hellenists,' says Luke, 'but they were attempting to kill him' (Acts 9.29).

I'm spotting a theme here. The apostles wondered, no doubt, if this was going to be the normal state of things with this man (which of course it was), and they sent him home to Tarsus (Acts 9.30), some 300 miles away. He left the region quickly. This is what lies behind his statement in Galatians that he was not known by sight to the Christians of Judea. He didn't hang around to be introduced to any of the other Christian communities in the region. He scarpered – he went home.

There follows what Luke describes as a period of peace. To what extent this is because Paul has left the district, he doesn't say.

'Here and there among all the believers'

In Judea, things had changed. The old enemies had gone. Pilate, after overstepping the mark with a too-brutal suppression of a Samaritan demonstration, had been sent back to Rome. Caiaphas had been replaced by various brothers-in-law. Paul had been quietly reassigned to Tarsus. It was a time of consolidation.

The next section of Luke's history has Peter going to Lydda, Joppa and Caesarea. The most likely explanation for the course of his journeys is that he is following up on the work done by Philip.[9]

Lydda (the Old Testament city of Lod) was an important regional centre. It was a predominantly Jewish town, although with a mixed population. Lydda was about 25 miles north-west of Jerusalem – a day's journey if you really pushed it. Here among the community of believers Peter heals a man called Aeneas who has been bedridden for eight years. This healing has a massive impact among the Christians of Lydda and the area known as Sharon.

The second incident takes place at Joppa (modern Jaffa) which lay on the coast some 12 miles from Lydda. Here we have a woman known by both an Aramaic name, Tabitha, and the Greek equivalent, Dorcas. This is an important woman. Significantly, she is described as 'a disciple', the only point in the New Testament where the word 'disciple' appears in its feminine form (Greek *mathetria*). Everywhere else the term is resolutely masculine.

It is undoubtedly the case that Jesus had women who acted as disciples. People like Mary Magdalene, Martha and Mary of Bethany say and do things which parallel the actions of the male disciples. But culturally speaking it would have been impossible for women to be disciples in the strictest traditional sense. Elsewhere in Jewish culture, women did not receive the kind of teaching that men did. Yet Jesus accorded women a high status. If he did not go as far as calling them disciples, nevertheless they clearly claimed that role. He taught them the same things as the men, and they travelled around with him in exactly the same way.

In the early church this status was continued and there is clear evidence of the high status given to women in the church: a status which stands in stark contrast to the rest of society. In fact, for the critics of the church this was one of the key criticisms: the church gave a role to women – stupid, credulous, foolish women. In the Græco-Roman world, women had no legal status, they could not vote and they were excluded from advanced education. But they were almost scandalously active in the early church. An illuminating passage comes from Tertullian, writing around AD 207, describing why Christian widows should avoid marrying pagan men. He describes how a pagan husband would deliberately arrange to meet his wife at the baths, rather than have her attend a church meeting, or 'if there are fasts to be observed, the husband that same day holds a convivial banquet; if a charitable expedition has to be made, never is family business more urgent'. He gives a graphic description of what the church got up to:

> For who would suffer his wife, for the sake of visiting the brethren, to go round from street to street to other men's, and indeed to all the poorer, cottages? Who will willingly bear her being taken from his side by nocturnal convocations, if need so be? Who, finally, will without anxiety endure her absence all the night long at the paschal solemnities? Who will, without some suspicion of his own, dismiss her to attend that Lord's Supper which they defame? Who will suffer her to creep into prison to kiss a martyr's bonds? nay, truly, to meet any one of the brethren to exchange the kiss? to offer water for the saints' feet?[10]

Both men and women were expected to visit the poor and provide for them from their own food. They were to visit those in prison – criminals who were about to be executed. They were to associate with all kinds of low-life. And they did a lot of this at night. Women were expected to be active participants, apprentices in the Way: the Didache was addressed not to men or women but to both, to *tekton mou*, 'my children'.[11] Needless to say, this is hardly socially acceptable behaviour.

The Tabitha episode demonstrates the important role which women played in the early church. She is described as someone 'devoted to good works and acts of charity' (Acts 9.36). When she dies, Peter is called to her house where he finds widows 'weeping and showing tunics and other clothing that Dorcas had made while she was with them' (Acts 9.39). The Greek phrase indicates that Dorcas had herself made these clothes. She had been living out the Christian faith, clothing those who had no clothes, taking care of the widows. The grammar of the sentence may indicate that what they show to Peter are the very clothes they are wearing. Maybe these were all the clothes they owned. We don't know if Tabitha was the leader of the church, but she was clearly a deeply significant figure in it and influential in the local area.

The port of Jaffa (NT Joppa) c.1910

The story has clear parallels with the raising of Jairus's daughter by Jesus (Mark 5.21–24; 35–43). In fact, the command given by Peter, 'Tabitha, get up', in Aramaic is *Tabitha cumi*, almost identical to Jesus' command to the little girl, *Talitha cumi* (Mark 5.41). Although some have speculated that it is one event spun out into a different story, the events are so different that it's hard to credit that idea. Peter is consciously following Jesus' example, of course, but this is in a different place, with a different person, at a different time.

'God shows no partiality'

Peter stays in the area, but he stays with a tanner called Simon. This is intriguing because tanning – the preparation of leather – was an unclean profession. It was considered ritually unclean partly because tanners would work with the carcasses of dead animals, but mainly because of the sheer smelly filthiness of the procedure.[12] The dirty, bloody hides of the animals would arrive at the tannery, where they would be soaked in water to clean and soften them. After that, any remaining flesh was scraped off and the hair removed by immersing the skin in a vat of urine, or kneading it in a vat of dog's dung mixed with water. The kneading was probably done by the tanner with his feet.[13]

Other Jewish sources describe it as 'a despised trade'.[14] According to the Mishnah, a tanner ranked alongside those who were afflicted with boils or even the person who collected dogs' turds for the tanner to use. The Mishnah states that being a tanner could be considered grounds for divorce. Even though she might have known what his job was before getting married, the new bride was still allowed to change her mind:

> R. Meir said: Although the husband made it a condition with her [to marry him despite his defects] she may say, 'I thought that I could endure it, but now I cannot endure it.'

The Mishnah also tells the story of a woman in Sidon who was married to a tanner and when he died, she refused to follow Levirate law and marry his brother: 'Thy brother I could endure, but thee I cannot endure.'[15] Given what we know of leather tanning, it's not hard to see why she refused to marry into the trade a second time.

Clearly Peter was already not overly concerned with Jewish purity laws. Christianity was drawing in people from outcast professions, not just to the fringes but right to the heart of the action. Peter stayed some days with Simon, in his house by the sea (Acts 9.43; 10.6). The position of the house reflects the fact that tanneries were put at the very edge of the cities or in the poorest locations. The Mishnah directs that tanneries should be to the east of the cities, since the prevailing wind in Palestine was in the opposite direction. Presumably the sea breezes had a similar effect in Joppa. Or maybe the smell of the tannery was negated by the stench of fish.

Anyway, Peter the ex-fisherman is not put off by the smell. And while he is staying with his namesake, one lunchtime he has a vision. The story starts further up the coast, in Caesarea, where a Gentile centurion called Cornelius has a dream. Cornelius's ancestors were slaves. Thousands of slaves had their freedom granted to them by P. Cornelius Sulla in 82 BC, taking the name Cornelius for their own.[16] But he was a free citizen: all Roman legionaries had to be freeborn citizens. He is part of the Italian Cohort, a body of troops originally – as the name implies – recruited in Italy. But while the officers might still have come from Italy, the recruits were probably auxiliaries, recruited from Samaritans and Syrian Greeks. Cohorts had about 600 soldiers and ten cohorts made up a legion of about 6,000 men, which was the main division in the Roman army. An inscription found in Austria records that the Italian Cohort was certainly in Palestine in AD 69, and may well have been there for some years previously. Between AD 41 and 44, though, Caesarea was part of the territory granted to King Herod Agrippa I. He would have had his own, rather than Roman, troops, so this episode has to come from before that time. Although it's always possible that Cornelius is retired.[17]

Cornelius is a God-fearer. The phrase occurs several times in the story (Acts 10.2, 22, 35). He's not a proselyte, a Jewish convert; he has not been circumcised, as Acts 11.3 makes clear. He's a pious man, though: he prays at 3 o'clock, one of the Jewish hours of prayer. And it is then that he receives his 'orders'. He is to send his men to fetch a man called Peter who is in Joppa, in the house of Simon the Tanner, by the sea.

The next day, in Joppa, Peter is praying on the roof at noon, following, perhaps, the orthodox Jewish practice of praying three times a day.[18] It's possible that there was an awning on the roof, to offer some shade. This, combined with Peter's prayerful state and the fact that he is hungry, contributes to a vision he sees, of animals in a sheet, lowered from the sky. The sheet contains all kinds of animals, clean and unclean, and Peter is told to kill them and prepare a meal. When he objects that he has never eaten unclean meat, he is told that this distinction is no longer in force.

As he comes out of the dream there is a knock at the door. Some men have come from Cornelius. It is, by this time, too late to make the return journey to Caesarea, so they stay overnight and then set out early the next morning. Peter does not go alone. He goes with six companions from Joppa. He obviously senses that something significant is happening: he's taking witnesses. According to Acts, it takes them the whole of the next day and part of the one after that to reach Caesarea. When they arrive,

Peter's trip to Caesarea

DAY ONE
⊳ 3 pm. Cornelius has vision

▲ Men travel to Joppa

DAY TWO
⊳ Noon. Peter has vision. Men arrive from Joppa

▲ Men stay with Peter

DAY THREE

Peter and the group return to Caesarea

DAY FOUR
⊳ 3 pm. Peter arrives in Caesarea. Cornelius welcomes Peter to his house.

Peter finds that Cornelius has arranged for his whole family, and others too, to come and hear Peter speak.

Peter makes it clear that he has interpreted his dream as meaning that no man is clean or unclean. As he tells them the story of Jesus, the Spirit descends and they start 'speaking in tongues and extolling God' (Acts 10.46). Peter immediately baptises them and then stays for several days.

Clearly this is a startling, miraculous event. And the 'circumcised believers' who have come with Peter from Joppa are astounded. It is to them that Peter addresses the question, 'Can anyone withhold the water for baptizing these people who have received the Holy Spirit just as we have?' (Acts 10.47). It's a key story for Luke: not only does he tell it at length, he tells it twice (as well as summarising it at the later meeting in Jerusalem in Acts 15.7–9).

Obviously the most important section is the affirmation that Gentiles can receive the Holy Spirit without the need for circumcision or obedience to the usual Jewish laws. But, as we've seen, Cornelius is not the first Gentile to be converted, nor even the first high-status one. So why does Luke concentrate on this? Perhaps because Cornelius is the first high-status Italian convert – the first freeborn Roman national. And this is happening in Caesarea, home of the regional roman government. It's one thing for Ethiopians to become Christians on a road through the desert, another thing entirely when the converts are high-standing Romans at the heart of the Roman administration in Judea.

In antiquity, having dinner with someone meant far more than just the act of eating. To eat with someone was to demonstrate approval of them; sharing a meal was the boundary line between who was in and who was out. This is why Jesus' activities were so shocking to his contemporaries. He kept on eating with people who were ritually impure. And it is why Jesus made the shared meal an absolutely core part of his message: from the first, Christians broke bread together. It showed that they were all OK. It was a sign of unity. Which was fine when all of them were Jews. But what happens with Gentiles?

For a start, Jewish observance of food laws required that Jews not share a table with Gentiles. Foods forbidden by the Torah, such as pork and shellfish, were perfectly acceptable to Gentiles. The early church came to believe that the Torah regulations on this issue had been superseded by Jesus. Mark even inserts an uncharacteristic editorial comment into his Gospel to explain that this was what Jesus had said (Mark 7.19). Paul declared that he had become persuaded that nothing is unclean in itself (Rom. 14.14). Clearly, at some point in the AD 30s or 40s, Jewish Christians came to see that they – or at least their Gentile brethren – could eat any food at all. This was in part an eschatological reality: it was commonly believed that the arrival of the Messiah would make all animals clean.[19]

But Peter doesn't immediately interpret this as a command about diet, nor does he rush down from the roof and order a pork pie. Because this story – and Peter's vision – is about more than just what was on the menu. This is actually about *who* you eat with, not *what* you eat. Certainly that's how Peter interprets it when he arrives at Cornelius's house:

> He said to them, 'You yourselves know that it is unlawful for a Jew to associate with or to visit a Gentile; but God has shown me that I should not call anyone profane or unclean.' (Acts 10.28)

The fact is that, even if the food itself was kosher, there was the problem of moral contamination. Gentiles were morally impure and impurity could be caught, like a disease. If a Gentile touched the same food, or drank from the same vessels, the Jews sharing them would become unclean. The Gentiles themselves were the source of the contamination.

Obviously, this made intermarriage between Jew and Gentile impossible, but even normal social interaction was risky. It wasn't just the food, one of the biggest barriers was idolatry. Idolatry was an abomination to Jews, but the Gentiles were surrounded by idols. You could not walk down the street, nor enter someone's house, without being infected by idolatry. There were idols everywhere. Houses had shrines for household gods. There were paintings of gods on the wall, invocations to the gods as graffiti along the street. Meat was sacrificed to idols and then sold in the market places for consumption at home. It was commonplace – certainly at banquets – for wine being drunk at a meal to be dedicated to a pagan god, like proposing a toast. This made attending any Gentile meal hazardous in the extreme for a devout Jew.[20]

A story called *Joseph and Asenath*, a piece of Jewish romantic-religious fiction from the time, shows this clearly:

> Joseph entered the house of Pentephres and sat upon the throne. And they washed his feet and set a table before him by itself because Joseph never ate with the Egyptians, for this was an abomination to him.

Later he refuses even to kiss the Gentile Asenath in case she has been eating or drinking unclean food:

> It is not fitting for a man who worships God, who will bless with his mouth the living God and eat blessed bread of life and drink a blessed cup of immortality … to kiss a strange woman who will bless with her mouth dead and dumb idols and eat from their table bread of strangulation and drink from their libation a cup of insidiousness.[21]

The 'cup of insidiousness' was joined by other dangers as well: a lot of sophisticated Romans had paintings on their walls which were graphic, to say the least – even pornographic. In Pompeii, for example, archaeologists have found graphic sexual images prominently displayed in private homes, and in inns and taverns.[22]

Practically speaking, this meant that for a Jew to eat in a Gentile home and be certain not to contract impurity, he would have had to bring with him his own food to be served to him by Jewish servants. And he would probably have had to keep his eyes closed most of the time![23] Orthodox Jews did not eat with Gentiles, or even enter their houses, for the simple reason that doing so would make them ritually impure. The rules of the community at Qumran stated that there should be no contact at all with Gentiles on the Sabbath.[24]

This, then, is the problem: it was mandatory for Christians to share the meal together, but it was impossible for a Jew to eat with a Gentile. That is why the outpouring of the Spirit in Cornelius's house is so important. It's an absolute proof that what has happened is OK. And it's also why, when Peter returns to Jerusalem, his opponents say nothing about the baptism. It's not an issue. The issue for which Peter is hauled over the coals is the fact that he has entered a Gentile house and shared a meal with them.

The people who call Peter to account are termed 'those of the circumcision', which refers not to a specific 'circumcision party', but just to the Jewish Christians in general. Their belief is that Gentile Christians should be like proselytes: they should observe the law and be circumcised. And they call Peter before them to explain himself. The whole thing has the air of a hearing – even a tribunal. We see now why Peter took people with him: he needs them to act as witnesses. Peter is forced into giving a step-by-step explanation of the entire sequence of events. In the end he wins the argument – or, at least, his critics are silenced, if not entirely satisfied. For all their theological objections, they cannot deny that the Holy Spirit was poured out on these people; there are witnesses.

It seems to end triumphantly, but one of the really surprising things about this episode is the simple fact that Peter has to justify his actions. Their tone is not at all deferential. Bock claims that their accusation has a certain force behind it: 'You went in and ate with Gentiles, so what about it! Explain yourself.' Verse 2 says that they criticised him.[25]

Clearly Peter, though influential, is no longer the main man in Jerusalem. The leadership has passed elsewhere. There's no suggestion of a coup or a power struggle, but it does show that, after the heady early days of the movement, the Christians in Jerusalem have identified that Peter, the inspirational, talismanic, brave, foolhardy fisherman-apostle, is not actually the best man to lead them.

The truth is that, apart from those very first days, Peter was never really the leader of a church, as far as we know. Tradition calls him the Bishop of Rome, but he was not responsible for the founding of the Roman church and the only evidence we have of him going there at all comes from much, much later. Even in this series of stories about him, he is following in the footsteps of Philip.

That doesn't mean that he wasn't hugely influential, but his influence was of a different kind. He was not an intellectual like Paul, but he had history; he had a track record. He had been there, done that, bought the loin cloth. Sometimes he put his feet on the water and walked; sometimes he just stuck them in his mouth. Such a person can be an inspirational leader on a battlefield, but he's never going to be a good general. For that you need a cool head and a clear strategy.

'Put your sword back into its place'

There is one final question to consider before moving on from the story of Cornelius and, again, it's one that is rarely addressed. Cornelius was a centurion, a military commander, and all the evidence shows that the early church wanted nothing to do with the military.

In the New Testament we know of soldiers who were baptised by John the Baptist, we know of centurions sympathetic to Jesus, and we have Cornelius himself. For these people, living in the imminent expectation of Jesus' return, it may have been possible to stay in post. But in the life of the early church, it was soon accepted that it was impossible for Christians to be soldiers.

Part of the problem was the lifestyle of a Roman soldier. Soldiers made up for their low pay by extortion and robbery, the very things which John the Baptist tells them they can no longer do (Luke 3.14). And it would have been hard for soldiers to stay clear of idolatry. They served the emperor, and the cult of emperor worship was encouraged among the military, along with various other forms of worship such as that of Mithras. But that wasn't the real problem. You could be an honest soldier, and Tertullian indicates that private soldiers could avoid being called on to actually perform a sacrifice.[26]

No, the big problem was the obvious one. Soldiers killed people. Christians didn't. Jesus was a pacifist: he rejected violence and told his followers to love their enemies. A brief selection of quotes from the early church fathers reflects just how adamant they were that Christians should follow Jesus' example:

> We who were filled with war and mutual slaughter and every wickedness have each of us in all the world changed our weapons of war – swords into ploughs and spears into agricultural implements.
>
> (Justin Martyr, c. AD 160)[27]

> If the loud trumpet summons soldiers to war, shall not Christ with a strain of peace to the ends of the earth gather up his soldiers of peace? A bloodless army he has assembled by blood and by the word to give to them the Kingdom of Heaven. The trumpet of Christ is his gospel. He has sounded, we have heard. Let us then put on the armour of peace.
>
> (Clement of Alexandria, c. AD 200)[28]

> God in prohibiting killing discountenances not only brigandage, which is contrary to human laws, but also that which men regard as legal. Participation in warfare therefore will not be legitimate to a just man whose military service is justice itself.
>
> (Lactantius, c. AD 304–305)

Perhaps Tertullian put it most simply: 'But how will a Christian man war, nay, how will he serve even in peace, without a sword, which the Lord has taken away? ... Christ, in disarming Peter, unbelted every soldier.'[29]

The third-century document called the *Apostolic Tradition* (written c. AD 215) was composed in part to remind Roman church leaders of 'traditional' practices of the preceding centuries. It ranks soldiers with astrologers, charioteers, gladiators, prostitutes and magicians as people who should be excluded from the community.[30] Cyprian remarked that homicide is considered a crime when committed by individuals, a virtue when carried on publicly. Cyprian was martyred in AD 258. Close to his grave was the tomb of the youth Maximillianus, executed for his conscientious objection.[31] Of these martyrs, the most famous was Martin of Tours, who refused to take up arms and declared that 'it is not lawful for me to fight'.[32]

It is not until around AD 175 that we get any reference to Christian soldiers: the so-called Thundering Legion, serving under Marcus Aurelius, apparently contained Christians (their prayers supposedly resulted in a thunderous rainstorm which defeated their opponents – hence the name), but this seems to have been a localised exception.[33] Twenty years later, Tertullian refers to Christians in 'the palace, the senate, the forum and the army', but since he is so vehement elsewhere about Christians not killing and since he condemns the idea of Christians enlisting, he is presumably talking of soldiers who had become converts.[34] In such cases, the approach seems to have been that it was possible for Christians to serve in the army on garrison duty or in an administrative role, but it was not permissible for them to take a life.[35] The *Canons of Hippolytus* ordered that 'a soldier of the civil authority must be taught not to kill men and to refuse to do so if he is commanded'.[36]

Even their enemies accepted that Christians hated violence. Athenagoras mocked the Christians who could not 'endure to see a man being put to death even justly'. The Roman Empire was a culture in which death was everywhere. Gladiators fought to the death; condemned men and women were thrown to the wild beasts. Death was entertainment. The fights were a way of siphoning off the natural tendency to violence in a safe way. Turn it against the professionals, or the victims. But Athenagoras states that Christians turned away from all forms of killing, including gladiator fights, abortion and infanticide.[37]

Around AD 250, Celsus felt able to level the following accusation at Christians:

> If all men were to do the same as you, there would be nothing to prevent the king from being left in utter solitude and desertion and the forces of the empire would fall into the hands of the wildest and most lawless barbarians.[38]

To which Origen replied tersely, 'We do not fight under the emperor, although he require it.'[39] Serving in the army would be doing Rome's dirty work. Rome was a bloodthirsty, power-mad regime – Christians knew that as well as anyone. Rome's claims for itself as an empire of peace and justice were scornfully rejected. 'Rome grew great,' Tertullian said, 'not by religion, but by wars which always injure religion.' Lactantius dismissed ideas of Roman 'just war'. He viewed it as simply Rome's way of justifying their subjugation of the world.[40]

For similar reasons, Christians also refused to serve as magistrates. 'We have no pressing inducement to take part in your public meetings,' wrote Tertullian, 'nor is there anything more entirely foreign to us than affairs of state.'[41] The *Apostolic Tradition* says:

> Concerning the Magistrate and the Soldier they are not to kill anyone, even if they receive the order: they are not to wear wreaths … One who has authority of the sword, or a ruler of a city, or who wears the purple, either let him cease or be cast out.[42]

Magistrates were the method by which Rome enforced its power, and they did that by sentencing people to death.[43] Their symbol was the fasces – the bundle of rods which magistrates carried (and from which we get the word 'fascism'). These were not just a symbolic bunch of sticks, they were the rods with which people were beaten. Paul wrote that he had been beaten with rods three times. In Philippi he and Silas were stripped and beaten with rods on the orders of magistrates (Acts 16.22; 2 Cor. 11.25).

The early church, then, was unanimously anti-militaristic. It refused to participate in killing, whether by war or through execution. It refused, even, to be a part of the power structure of the Empire. To work for Rome was to collude with the enemy.

Gradually attitudes began to shift, although the changes were not widespread. The real change in Christian attitude to warfare came, of course, with Constantine, who by incorporating Christianity into the Empire made it impossible for the official church to stand apart from the military. Even so, there remained deep disquiet about the idea of Christians being involved in military action. Writing in AD 313, in the immediate aftermath of the Constantinian settlement, Eusebius first suggested what was over time to become the solution: a kind of two-track approach to Christian behaviour where the laity might take part in just wars (as well as work in otherwise unacceptable trades) while the clergy should embrace pacifism, poverty, aloofness from the world and complete dedication to God. It was a compromise. The fact is that, before Constantine, before the church got a seat on the board, as it were, not a single theologian justified any Christian participation in warfare.[44]

In the Western world since, we have made such accommodation for warfare that we often no longer question it. It's left to those on the 'fringe' – the Mennonites, the Quakers, the Anabaptists – to argue the case for Christian pacifism. Christians have become embedded in the army. As a supposedly Christian nation we have justified some very unjust wars. The leaders of the early church would be horrified at the easy accommodation which the church seems to have made with military and civic violence over the centuries.

So, while we don't know what Cornelius did next, we can guess that he unbuckled his sword. For the early church the situation was simple. You did not kill people. End of story.

A memorial to Marcus Caelius, centurion of the 18th Legion, killed at the Battle of Teutoburger Wald in AD 9. He is depicted wearing his military uniform, and flanked by his slaves. The inscription says he was 53½ years old when he died

4. Antioch AD 38–47

'Those who were scattered'

> Now those who were scattered because of the persecution that took place over Stephen travelled as far as Phoenicia, Cyprus, and Antioch, and they spoke the word to no one except Jews. But among them were some men of Cyprus and Cyrene who, on coming to Antioch, spoke to the Hellenists also, proclaiming the Lord Jesus. The hand of the Lord was with them, and a great number became believers and turned to the Lord. (Acts 11.19–21)

After the sets of stories about Philip, Paul and Peter which we have already looked at, Luke takes us back to AD 34, and the expulsion of the Greek-speaking Christians.

Many of these returned to their homelands along the coast to the Phoenician ports of Tyre and Sidon, or across the Mediterranean to Cyprus. Or they went south and then west to Cyrene, in modern Libya. Some went north, to Antioch, one of the most important cities of the Empire.

Many Jews had relocated to Antioch not long after the city was founded. For the Jewish community, Antioch was an ideal location: it was not too far from Jerusalem, it had flourishing trade and industry and, on the whole, Jews were treated relatively well.[1] They were given privileges and rights, including the right to meet together in groups and share common meals.[2] There were many proselytes in the city as well.[3]

It was very different from Jerusalem, of course. Bigger. More cosmopolitan. Jerusalem, for all its cultural and religious significance to the Jews, was a small city by Roman standards. Antioch, on the other hand, was, according to Josephus, 'third among the cities of the Roman world' after Rome and Alexandria.[4] It was the administrative and military base for Roman control of Syria. It was a major trade and commercial centre and a renowned centre of learning, home to famous schools of philosophy, medicine and rhetoric.[5] Its coins proclaimed it to be 'Antioch, metropolis, sacred, and inviolable, and autonomous, and sovereign, and capital of the East'.[6] Now that's what I call a mission statement.

The first diaspora Jews to arrive in Antioch after AD 34 limited their evangelism to the Jewish community. Nicolaus, one of the seven Greek Jews called to serve as deacons in Jerusalem, was a 'proselyte from Antioch' (Acts 6.5), so he may have returned there with information about the Way. It was only with the arrival of Christians from Cyrene in North Africa, and others from Cyprus, that the message started seeping out to the Greeks. Although most translations talk about 'Hellenists' (Acts 11.20), Luke is not talking about Greek-speaking synagogues. The WT reads *Hellenas*, 'Greeks', rather than *Hellenistas*. Given the story about Peter and Cornelius, this makes a lot more sense.[7]

As to who exactly took the faith to the Gentiles, a couple of candidates are mentioned later on in Acts. Among the leaders of the church in Antioch, by the time Paul is with them, is a man called Lucius of Cyrene, and also Simeon who was called Niger (Acts 13.1). Niger means 'black'. Simeon the Black. So these may well have been a couple of the North Africans who founded the Gentile churches.

Antioch was a place where the Way was almost bound to seep out beyond the boundaries of Judaism. It was a diverse, cosmopolitan city, where many nationalities rubbed shoulders: Greeks, Syrians, Jews, Arabs, Phoenicians, Persians, Egyptians, Indians and Romans. It had a reputation as a place tolerant of different faiths and practices. Not all of these were approved of by the Romans. Just six miles west of the city was Daphne, a city known for the worship of Astarte, Artemis and Apollo. The temple prostituion associated with Astarte, in particular, saddled Antioch with a reputation for loose morals.[8] In Juvenal's *Satires*, the character of Umbricius complains about the dregs of the Orontes – the river running through Antioch – being emptied into Rome.[9]

Clearly there were many in Rome who were distrustful of these 'oriental' customs.

Antioch was a crowded city, too. By the end of the first century the total population was around 150,000, all packed into a city only two miles long and a mile wide. The housing density was probably greater than modern Calcutta. (And in Rome – the megacity of the Empire – the population density was even greater.)[10] All ancient cities were densely crowded, of course. But whereas a place like Jerusalem was hugely crowded with Jews, Antioch was a place where many different races and nationalities crammed together in a tiny space. Restricting such a life-changing belief as Christianity to one ethnic group would be an impossible task.

Antioch is the first major Græco-Roman city where the Way had a real impact. Although Christianity had already been taken to cities like Caesarea and Joppa, Antioch was on a different scale. The establishment of the church among the Gentiles in Antioch was to mark the real beginning of the spread of Christianity: in the major cities of the Roman Empire – Antioch, Corinth, Ephesus, Rome – Christianity found a natural home.

But for centuries, historians have grappled with this paradox. How, exactly, did a faith based on the life and teachings of a rural peasant become such a force amidst the harsh urban cityscapes of the Roman Empire? Acts puts it down to 'the hand of the Lord'. But even those who see God's providence in this growth can still recognise that there were other factors as well. Just what was it that made Christianity 'fit' these places?

For the answer to that – some of the answers at least – we have to look at what those cities were really like. Although some 95 per cent of the Empire's population lived in rural areas, the Roman Empire was unmistakably an urban empire.[11] By our standards these cities were small, crowded and incredibly, unutterably filthy. Very few people lived in proper houses. Most lived in tenements, or over their workshops, or in whatever makeshift accommodation they could find. To imagine what ancient cities were like we have to forget the white marble and the fountains of the Hollywood films: that stuff was for the rich. Instead we would be better to think of the slums and favelas of the developing world.

The streets were narrow. The main street in Antioch – its High Street – was famous throughout the Empire, yet it was only 30 feet wide. In the heart of Rome, inside the old Republican Walls, only two streets – the *Via Sacra* and *Via Nova* – were wide enough for two carts to pass each other or drive abreast. Even the main thoroughfares leading out of the city were narrow by our standards: roads like the *Via Appia*, the *Via Latina* and the *Via Ostiensis* were between 16 and 21 feet wide.

Step off the main street, and you entered a maze of alleyways and tracks, shaded by balconies projecting from the densely packed tenement buildings known as *insulae*, 'islands'. These were three- or four-storey buildings akin to our modern apartment blocks, only without sanitation, and with an alarming propensity to collapse (a propensity made worse by the fact that many of the cities of the Græco-Roman world were in earthquake regions).

So buildings might fall on you. And other things might fall as well. There were no sewers. In richer houses human excrement was stored in cesspits; in most areas it was simply emptied into the gutter which ran down the middle of the street. Often those on the third or fourth storeys of the *insulae* simply emptied their chamberpots out of the windows rather than make the trip downstairs.

Only the wealthiest homes and major public structures were built of stone: most buildings were of wood covered with a layer of thin plaster. In such conditions fire was a major risk. Tacitus blamed the rapid spread of the great fire of Rome in AD 64 on the narrow, winding streets with houses packed so close together.[12]

Water was channelled into the cities via the aqueducts, but most of it went into the homes of the rich and important; for others there was the public fountain. Water was dirty, of course, so throughout the Græco-Roman Empire it was common to add wine to the water as a form of disinfectant. Hence Paul's advice to Timothy: 'No longer drink only water, but take a little wine for the sake of your stomach and your frequent ailments' (1 Tim. 5.23).

These were chaotic places. Crime and disorder abounded. At night people went home and barricaded themselves in their houses. There was no street lighting. If the rich went out, they were accompanied by a retinue of slaves bearing torches. In Rome there were nightwatchmen, the *sebaciarii*, who were supposed to offer protection, but in practice they weren't effective. Juvenal remarked that no sane person went out at night without making their will first. He rated the Rome of his day as more dangerous than the forest of Gallinaria.[13] He was overplaying it, as usual, but there was no doubt about it: these places were urban jungles, mazes where people could easily get lost, like the 'heroes' of Petronius's story who left the dinner table slightly the worse for wear and spent the whole night wandering the unnamed, unnumbered, unlit streets, not reaching home until hours later, just before dawn.[14]

The cities of the Roman Empire were places where people got lost in any number of ways. Rural communities had big problems – debt, famine, drought, taxes. But they also had family structures. People had a place. In the cities these structures were stretched, torn apart. The rich families, of course, had their social networks and established households they maintained. But lower down it was different. In a place like Antioch it was easy to fall through the cracks. For beggars and the sick, the urban environment was harsh indeed.

Among the teeming population of the city, it's easy to see how knowledge of Christianity spread. In such places ideas could spread as fast as disease or fire. Neighbour would talk to neighbour. Stories could jump from one tenement block to another. A miraculous healing, a neighbour freed from a 'demon' – these things would have been the talk of the street, the neighbourhood. And, to begin with at least, Christians made no attempt to hide themselves. Their first meeting places were in the tenements and the workshops of the ordinary people.

But mere proximity – opportunity, if you like – isn't enough to explain why Christianity prospered. For that we have to recognise two simple facts: first, Christians had a distinctive way of life; and second, this way of life actually made life in the cities better.

In the syncretistic, all-gods-welcome atmosphere of Antioch they would have stood out like a sore thumb. It was not just their refusal to worship any of the pagan gods – although that certainly marked them out as weird, as it did the Jews. It was their whole way of life. They had a mission to the poor and the outcast and the sick and the hungry which the other faiths in this melting pot of nationalities and religions simply did not or could not offer.

Christianity promised life after death for its believers, but it offered life before death as well. Christians fed the poor with a daily meal. They clothed widows. They visited those in prison. They healed the sick and cast out demons. They were a counterculture right in the mix of the urban mass. Their sacrificially generous lifestyle had been shaped around their founder's demands that you should 'love your neighbour as yourself' and that it was 'better to give than receive'. Christians created 'a miniature welfare state in an empire which for the most part lacked social services'.[15]

Some of these activities – healings, for instance – come in the miracles, signs and wonders category. But most of what marked the Christians out was just about their living alongside people and helping them. It may not have been signs and wonders, but it was still a wondrous sign. Christians lived lives of baffling self-sacrifice. And nowhere more so than when plague hit town.

Plague was one of the greatest fears. It could decimate entire regions. It has been estimated that during the great plague of the second century, known as the Plague of Galen, between a quarter and a third of the Empire's population died. The mortality rate was so high that Marcus Aurelius spoke of long caravans of carts and wagons being needed to haul the dead from the cities. Cities and villages in Italy and the provinces were abandoned and even fell into ruin.[16] A century later, during another catastrophic Empire-wide plague, in Rome alone 5,000 people a day were dying. Dionysius, Bishop of Alexandria, wrote that 'out of the blue came this disease, a thing ... more frightful than any disaster whatsoever'.[17]

It was in just such panic-stricken, bewildering times that Christianity offered comfort and hope. The Christians stayed on in the cities. The pagans, on the other hand – those who had means, at least – legged it out of town as fast as they could. Even the famous physician Galen left town pronto, retiring to his country estate in Asia Minor until the danger had passed.[18] We have a first-hand account of this through the eyes of Dionysius of Alexandria. This is not some kind of PR spin: Dionysius is writing about the plague in Alexandria to people who had actually been there and who would have known if he had been making it up. Dionysus describes it thus:

Certainly very many of our brethren, while, in their exceeding love and brotherly-kindness, they did not spare themselves, but kept by each other, and visited the sick without thought of their own peril, and ministered to them assiduously, and treated them for their healing in Christ.

Dionysius records how Christians gave the dead a decent burial, 'laying them out decently, they clung to them, and embraced them, and prepared them duly with washing and with attire', and that many of those who 'cured others of their sicknesses, and restored them to strength, died themselves, having transferred to their own bodies the death that lay upon these'. All this contrasts with the pagans, whose behaviour 'was the very reverse':

For they thrust aside any who began to be sick, and kept aloof even from their dearest friends, and cast the sufferers out upon the public roads half dead, and left them unburied, and treated them with utter contempt when they died, steadily avoiding any kind of communication and intercourse with death.[19]

Tertullian claimed, 'It is our care of the helpless, our practice of loving kindness that brands us in the eyes of many of our opponents. "Only look," they say, "look how they love one another."'[20]

We have every evidence that this is not some kind of spin. Christian charity was so well known that a century later, an emperor known as Julian the Apostate complained to the high priest of Galatia that the pagans were not matching the Christian standards. 'The impious Galileans support not only their poor but ours as well,' he complained. 'Everyone can see that our poor lack aid from us.'[21]

And it *did* make a difference. The ancient world did not understand the disease, but just being there, providing food and water for the sick, keeping people clean, must have helped some to survive. Christians offered food and clothing. Health care during the plague. They offered rescue. Resurrection, if you like.

Plague victims were not the only ones who were rescued by Christians. One way in which the Græco-Roman world was very different from ours is that men greatly outnumbered women. It has been estimated that there were 131 men to every 100 females in Rome, and 140 men per 100 females in Italy, Asia and North

Africa. This disparity was due to one simple reason: many girls were killed at birth.

Infanticide was rife. It was common for parents to leave unwanted females or deformed male babies to die on rubbish heaps or to drown in the rivers. Even in large households it was rare for more than one daughter to be reared. One study revealed that out of 600 families at Delphi, only six had raised more than one daughter.[22] The attitude is best summed up in a letter written in 1 BC by a man called Hilarion to his pregnant wife Alis:

> Know that I am still in Alexandria ... I ask and beg of you to take good care of our baby son, and as soon as I receive payment I shall send it up to you. If you are delivered of a child [before I come home] if it is a boy keep it, if a girl, discard it.[23]

Works on gynaecology included sections like Soranus's *How to Recognize the Newborn that is Worth Rearing*. It's hard to overstate the mundane nature in those times of what to us is absolutely horrific. 'The poor do not bring up children,' said Plutarch.[24] But this wasn't just an economic decision: it was a social and cultural choice. As Poseidippos stated, 'Even a rich man always exposes a daughter.'

Tertullian, in rebutting the malicious rumour that the Christians sacrificed babies and drank their blood, turned the accusation into a stinging attack on the child-murder of the pagan world:

> Although you are forbidden by the laws to slay new-born infants, it so happens that no laws are evaded with more impunity or greater safety, with the deliberate knowledge of the public ... you do not kill your infants in the way of a sacred rite, nor (as a service) to God. But then you make away with them in a more cruel manner, because you expose them to the cold and hunger, and to wild beasts, or else you get rid of them by the slower death of drowning.[25]

Christian communities were different. The *Didache* contains an injunction against abortion and infanticide. In fact, Christians would go round rescuing whatever children they could. There was a Christian in Alexandria in the third century whose name literally means 'from the dung heap'. That is where he was found. For him, the salvation of Jesus had a very real and tangible meaning. And it meant that in the church there was an unusually high proportion of women.

Which brings us to the third point about why the early church succeeded in the ancient, urban environment: it included everyone.

Christians offered both food and family. They talked of themselves as a social unit, as a family, as brother and sister. Where the Roman world praised and rewarded the powerful and the wealthy and the well born, the Christians provided a place for the weak and the poor and lowest of the low. The Roman world worshipped the emperor; the Christians followed a peasant who came from the middle of nowhere.

We've seen Celsus characterise the church as a place of 'the silly, and the mean, and the stupid, with women and children'. In Carthage, the pagan Caecilius described Christians as being drawn from the 'lowest dregs' and containing the least skilled labourers alongside credulous women. Even their own leaders agreed that, socially speaking, the church was not the top of the pile. Talking about the Corinthian church, Paul says that 'not many of you were wise by human standards, not many were powerful, not many were of noble birth' (1 Cor. 1.26).

So Christians welcomed those at the bottom of the heap. More than welcomed: empowered. In one of the most radical statements in all antiquity, Paul declares that there is no difference between the different types of people within the church:

> There is no longer Jew or Greek, there is no longer slave or free, there is no longer male and female; for all of you are one in Christ Jesus. (Gal. 3.28)

The common term used among the early church when talking about one another was 'brother' and 'sister'. Those entering the Christian community, whether through contact with a neighbour, through being healed, or through rescue from a dung heap, became part of the family.

One of the main reasons why Christianity grew is that it made life in the cities more bearable. Cities, by their nature, are – to use Mark Mazower's phrase – 'places of both eviction and sanctuary'.[26] They are places where the rich and poweful are greatly outnumbered by the lonely, the discarded and the lost. Christianity, with its emphasis on the poor and the marginalised, on healing and communal feasting and accepting one another, offered a radical alternative to the dog-eat-dog world of the Græco-Roman city. Its founder had declared that he had come to save what was lost, and that is exactly what his followers did: they went out on the streets of the cities of their world and rescued people. The lame in the streets, the beggars at the gates, the babies on the dung heap, the prostitutes in the brothels, the slaves in the markets, all the dispossessed, the desperate and the dying, all those who could only fantasise about acquiring Roman citizenship, suddenly found themselves citizens of the kingdom of God. To Celsius it was foolish, senseless, mad. But to those who were lost and then were found, suddenly life made perfect sense – even in the city.

The people of Antioch were known for their scurrilous wit and invention of nicknames.[27] They turned their mockery onto these weird, foolish people by naming them the *Christiani*. The term comes from two sources. Obviously it's to do with the Greek word 'Christ', meaning 'anointed one': it's a translation of the Hebrew 'Messiah'. Jesus Christ was 'Jesus the anointed'. But the barbed-tongued wits of Antioch were also including another reference, for the word is also a pun on the name *Chrestos*, which means 'good' or 'useful' and which was a common slave's name.[28]

Luke's account that it was in Antioch that the followers of Jesus were first called Christians is corroborated by the ancient literary sources linked with that city. In writings from the first century other than the Gospel, the terms 'Christian' or 'Christianity' occur only nine times. Eight of these are in the letters of Ignatius of Antioch, and the other is in the *Didache*, which was probably composed in the city.[29]

It fitted perfectly. From the start, the *Christiani* used the imagery of slavery to define themselves. They took this imagery from Jesus himself, who had willingly taken on the role of a Gentile slave in washing the disciples' feet and who had then died the slaves' death when he was crucified.

Paul, writing to the church at Philippi, quotes an early church poem or hymn:

> Let the same mind be in you that was in Christ Jesus,
>   who, though he was in the form of God,
>   did not regard equality with God
>   as something to be exploited,

> but emptied himself,
>   taking the form of a slave,
>   being born in human likeness.
> And being found in human form,
>   he humbled himself
>   and became obedient to the point of death –
>   even death on a cross.   (Phil. 2.5–8)

Jesus' followers, in Antioch, followed him to the point that the mocking Gentiles around them gave them a nickname which took the Greek word for 'Messiah' and punningly combined it with that of a slave. They were the *Christiani,* good little slaves, followers of Christ.

'Set apart for me Barnabas and Saul'

The development of the work among the Gentiles in Antioch attracted the notice of the leaders back in Jerusalem and they sent someone to check it out. They sent Barnabas.

Barnabas was the ideal person. It was Cypriot Christians who were planting these churches and Barnabas was a native of Cyprus (Acts 4.36). So, send one of their own. Someone they would trust. But Barnabas seems to have done more than just tick a few boxes and report back: he seems to have taken active control. He approves what's going on, but he clearly feels that more leadership is needed. So he does something quite remarkable: he goes to Tarsus 'to look for Saul'.

The big question is, 'Why?' Why does Barnabas think of Paul at this time?

First, though, timing. It has probably been eight or nine years since Paul was 'encouraged' to leave Jerusalem. We don't know when it was that Barnabas went to Antioch, but we can get the rough period by working backwards. We know that Paul and Barnabas went to Jerusalem in response to a famine and, as we shall see, there are good reasons to date that famine to around AD 46/47.

The famine is predicted in Antioch *after* Paul has arrived in the city. So the latest for the prediction has to be around AD 45 (otherwise it's not much of a prediction). In which case, Paul arrived before AD 45.

There is another possible clue as to timing in the presence in Antioch of a man called Manaen, whom Luke describes as 'a member of the court of Herod the Tetrarch'. This refers to Herod Antipas, former tetrarch of Galilee and the Perea. Manaen is described as a *syntrophos*, a word which indicates that he was a close friend of Antipas and had been brought up with him from childhood. (It's possible that he was one of the sources of the material relating to Antipas in Luke's Gospel.) But what was he doing there? His arrival in Antioch may be linked to the downfall of his childhood friend.

The death of Tiberius brought a new member of the Herodian dynasty to power, the grandson of the old tyrant, nephew to Herod Antipas. His name was Herod Agrippa. Agrippa had been educated in Rome, where he became a close friend of Gaius Caligula. While hosting a banquet for Caligula, he rashly expressed the hope that Tiberius would die so that Caligula could become emperor. His remark was relayed back to Tiberius, who promptly put Agrippa under house arrest.

When Tiberius died on 16 March AD 37, Caligula became emperor. Agrippa was not only freed from jail, he was granted the former territories of his late Uncle Philip together with the title of king. (Although Agrippa visited Palestine in AD 38–39, he did not spend long in his new territory, preferring to return to be with his friend the emperor in Rome.)

This appointment was a slap in the face to Antipas, who had hoped to inherit his brother's territory and had always longed for the title 'king'. So, at the instigation of his wife, Antipas and Herodias travelled to Rome in AD 39 to plead his case. It went horribly wrong. He was outmanoeuvred by his nephew, who persuaded Caligula that Antipas was storing up arms and secretly plotting with the Parthians. Caligula banished Antipas and his scheming wife to Lugdunum Convenarum (modern Saint Betrand-de-Cominges in the south of France). Herod Antipas, the executioner of John the Baptist, the 'old fox', the interrogator of Jesus, ended his days in disappointment and disgrace in the south of France, thousands of miles from his home. And he never got to be called 'king'.

If Antipas was banished in the summer of AD 39, news would have reached Galilee that autumn. His friends and supporters would have had to either transfer their allegiance to the new ruler – Herod Agrippa – or pack up and move on. Perhaps Manaen – *syntrophos* of Antipas – thought that now was the time to move to Antioch. He had either become a Christian already, or became one in that city.

So we're now talking about somewhere between AD 40 and 45. But before Paul comes to Antioch, there is one more date that we need to note. Sometime around this point, Paul had a vision. He only talks about it much later – writing to that troublesome church in Corinth:

> I know a person in Christ who fourteen years ago was caught up to the third heaven – whether in the body or out of the body I do not know; God knows. And I know that such a person – whether in the body or out of the body I do not know; God knows – was caught up into Paradise and heard things that are not to be told, that no mortal is permitted to repeat ... Therefore, to keep me from being too elated, a thorn was given to me in the flesh, a messenger of Satan to torment me, to keep me from being too elated. (2 Cor. 12.2–7)

In some ways this sounds very unlike Paul. He was always an opponent of those who professed hidden mysteries and secret knowledge, but this sounds like exactly that. Except that he wasn't building any theology on it and he doesn't talk about it anywhere else. He wrote to the Corinthians in AD 55, so this vision took place either in AD 41 or 42, depending on whether Paul was counting inclusively or not.

So what was it? It certainly wasn't the Damascus road experience, that was quite different and much earlier (and in any case, he repeated what the Lord said to him there several times). He also had a revelation in the temple during his first visit to Jerusalem in AD 36 (Acts 22:17–21), but again he talks about that and anyway, in that one, the Lord came to Paul, not the other way round. His vision of the man from Macedonia (Acts 16.9) comes from around AD 50, and he also had some kind of vision in Corinth in AD 51/52 (Acts 18.9–10).

None of those fit. It's a mystery, in every sense of the word. But where was he in AD 41? We can't be sure. It's possible that he was already in Antioch, but it's likely that he arrived there a bit later. Perhaps, though, this vision was part of what brought Paul back out of Tarsus and down to Antioch. Whatever the case, it's a formative experience, and one which indicates that the years Paul spent in Cilicia were not fallow ones: there was stuff going on.

That brings us back to the question, 'Why does Barnabas go to fetch Paul?' According to Acts, Paul has been in Tarsus since AD 36, when Barnabas acted as Paul's guarantor at the first meeting in Jerusalem. Now, apparently, Barnabas goes to Antioch and suddenly Paul pops back into his mind. Obviously he's the right man for the job. A Roman citizen, raised as an ultra-orthodox Jew in a Gentile city, he's perfect for relating to the Antioch Gentiles. But even so, it's simply not credible that Barnabas should wave goodbye to Paul in Jerusalem, never see him since that farewell, and then suddenly think of him nearly a decade later.

No. The fact that Barnabas travels to find Paul and enlist him to help implies two things: he knows where he's living and he knows what he has been up to. Barnabas must have kept in contact with Paul. This would not have been that difficult. The Roman Empire had made communication relatively easy and travel relatively safe. It would have been quite possible for Barnabas to meet up with Paul in the intervening years: Barnabas's ancestral home was in Cyprus, only a short boat journey away from Tarsus.

The only logical reason for Barnabas to go and fetch Paul is that he knows he has been engaged in the same form of work. Barnabas would not travel to Tarsus on a hunch that Paul might be good at this sort of thing. Paul must already have been at work, talking to people, arguing, explaining, refining his own theories; above all, engaging with the people of that region, Jews as well as Gentiles. Tarsus was a rich, cosmopolitan city in a wealthy region. It made a perfect missionary base. He might already have made some forays north into Cappadocia. Writing to the Galatians, Paul indicates that reports of his activities had, indeed, drifted back south:

> Then I went into the regions of Syria and Cilicia, and I was still unknown by sight to the churches of Judea that are in Christ; they only heard it said, 'The one who formerly was persecuting us is now proclaiming the faith he once tried to destroy.' And they glorified God because of me.' (Gal. 1.21–24)

Antioch, Tarsus and environs

So they had heard what he was up to, even down in Judea. However, knowing what he had been doing was one thing. Finding him may have been trickier. Luke's phrase 'and when he [Barnabas] had found him [Paul]' hints that perhaps locating Paul wasn't that easy. The WT runs, 'When [Barnabas] found him he exhorted him to come to Antioch,'[30] Perhaps he needed persuading because his own work was going so well; perhaps that success was why Barnabas was so keen to recruit him. Whatever the case, he must have been engaged in mission work among the Gentiles, and it must have been working. As Hengel puts it, 'An unsuccessful missionary would not have been much help to Barnabas in building up the church in Antioch.'[31]

There's a final clue later in Acts, after the apostolic meeting in Acts 15. Ostensibly this was triggered by events in the church in Antioch, and possibly Galatia, but the letter that is sent out from Jerusalem to resolve the issue is sent to 'the believers of Gentile origin in Antioch and Syria and Cilicia' (Acts 15.23, 41). And when Paul sets off on the missionary journey the year after the apostolic meeting, he goes 'through Syria and Cilicia, strengthening the churches' (Acts 15.41). But nowhere in Acts have we seen anyone planting churches elsewhere in Syria and Cilicia. The logical conclusion is that Paul was visiting churches that he had previously planted.[32]

This means that, by the time the Antioch church came to prominence, there were already churches with Gentile Christians in Cilicia and Syria. Paul had spent the years between AD 36 and 45 planting churches and evangelising the region around his home town of Tarsus. That might explain the account of his trials and hardships in 2 Corinthians 11.24–26. The number of shipwrecks, beatings and general Paul-associated disasters in that account doesn't match those few given in the account in Acts, but if he was active in Syria and Cilicia, then suddenly that makes sense. In particular the 'synagogue punishments' mentioned – 'Five times I have received from the Jews the forty lashes minus one' (2 Cor. 11.24) – may well have been meted out during these first years of missionary activity. There was a powerful Jewish presence in Tarsus and its environs.[33]

All of which makes a mockery of the standard description of Paul's first, second and third missionary journeys. Such neatly packaged trips do not reflect the reality. If you had chanced upon Paul on the streets of Athens or Pisidian Antioch or on the wharf at Troas and asked which of his three missionary journeys he was on, he would have looked at you with complete bafflement. He was always on a journey. For Paul, the journey was the destination.

'The church at Antioch'

According to Luke, Barnabas and Paul worked together in Antioch for an entire year. The WT reads, 'When they came, for a whole year a considerable crowd was stirred up...' Yes, that sounds like Paul, all right.[34]

Barnabas probably sent reports back to Jerusalem, and the Jerusalem church sent further emissaries in response. They sent prophets to build up the church. Paul talks about prophets in glowing terms. It's the gift in the church that he most esteems.

> Pursue love and strive for the spiritual gifts, and especially that you may prophesy ... those who prophesy speak to other people for their building up and encouragement and consolation. (1 Cor. 14.1–3)

Paul identifies various types of 'resourcers' of the early church, including apostles, prophets and teachers (1 Cor. 12.28). Many of these would have been itinerant workers, travelling the roads of the Roman Empire. There were apostles, those who had seen the Lord and could tell their eyewitness stories; there were teachers who had knowledge, insight and wisdom to impart; and there were the prophets, who could inspire, encourage and build up. It's likely that the boundaries between these various roles were not distinct. Prophets could be teachers; apostles could be church leaders.

The *Didache* contains instruction about prophets. One of the interesting things is that the prophet had freedom to speak. In the material about the Eucharist in the *Didache*, the instruction is given that after the meal, a prophet is allowed to give thanks 'however they wish'.[35] While others at the meal might have followed more formulaic prayers, prophets are allowed to go 'off piste', as it were.[36] And many of them did – at length. According to the second-century work the *Martyrium Polycarpi*, Polycarp, the famous Christian leader, 'stood up and prayed, being so full of the grace of God that for two hours he could not hold his peace'.[37]

Prophets had important messages to pass on. And one of them – a man called Agabus – predicted a worldwide famine. (Agabus will reappear in a different time and place in our story: he, like others, was a prophet on the move.) The famine referred to by Luke would make a useful chronological anchor for our story, but pinning it down is tricky. There are no references in ancient historians to a worldwide (that is to say, Empire-wide) famine at this time. But there are some hints.

The Empire relied on Egypt. The grain-growing area around the Nile was the breadbasket of Rome. To use a modern phrase, if Egypt sneezed, the rest of the Empire caught a cold. The notes of an Egyptian record office between AD 45 and 47 show that between AD 45 and 46 wheat reached exceptionally high prices.[38] Pliny also records that during the reign of Claudius (AD 41–54) the Nile flooded to exceptional levels.[39] If the flooding coincided with the high prices, then the logical conclusion is that there was a bad harvest in AD 45, followed by the expectation of an even worse one in AD 46.[40]

Josephus also records a famine in Judea which he connects with the procuratorship of Tiberius Julius Alexander (AD 46–48). So probably what we have here is a 'rolling' famine, which spread across the Empire as the shortages began to bite following two failed harvests. It would be those on the edge of the Empire, those in the backwater provinces, who would feel the effects most. The richer parts would have had some cushioning, some protection.

This would explain why money was sent from Antioch to Judea. If there was a worldwide famine there would be little point sending money from one famine area to another. But it's possible that Antioch, as a major trading post, would be less affected by the famine, while Judea to the south was harder hit.

Whatever the case, the church in Antioch made a collection for the saints in Judea. They sent it south with two couriers, Paul and Barnabas. For the second time since he had become a follower of Jesus, Paul was going to Jerusalem.

In the years between his first and second visits as a Christian, things had changed a lot in Jerusalem. As we have seen, Agrippa had been granted control of Galilee and the Perea by Caligula, but he hadn't spent much time in the region, making one quick visit before returning to Rome. At the height of Caligula's insanity, in his last mad months, he conceived the idea that a statue of himself should be erected in the temple in Jerusalem. To the Jews, of course, this was the ultimate sacrilege and, according to Josephus, tens of thousands of them protested, declaring that they would lay down their lives rather than allow such a desecration. Agrippa, to his credit, took the brave step of urging Caligula not to pursue this course of action. At that time it was a life-threatening act to confront the emperor. Meanwhile, the Roman governor of Syria, Petronius, realised that carrying out the order was, literally, an act of madness, and he employed a series of delaying tactics.

Fortunately Caligula was assassinated before the order could be carried out. After the assassination, in January AD 41, Agrippa played a key part in securing the succession of Claudius as emperor. As a reward, the grateful Claudius gave Agrippa the territories of Judea and Samaria to add to Galilee and the other land he had gained from his Uncle Philip. So, by spring AD 41, Agrippa ruled over a territory as large as that of his grandfather, Herod the Great. For the first time in over forty years, there was a king over 'the whole of Judea'.

Even Agrippa couldn't be a king *in absentia,* and his past association with the hated Caligula made it expedient for him to leave Rome. As soon as the seas opened in February AD 41, he headed east. (On the Mediterranean, all ships stayed in port during the winter and the shipping routes opened again around 8 February). It took five to six weeks to sail from Rome to Palestine, so Agrippa must have arrived at Caesarea sometime in the late spring.[41]

When Agrippa returned to Jerusalem in the spring of AD 41, he had some credit with the Jews already, as a result of his resistance to Caligula's mad scheme. And he began to pursue a policy designed to reassure the Jews of his Jewish credentials. He made some immediate changes. Perhaps in need of money, he deposed Theophilos, the son of Ananus, and installed a new high priest, Simon Kantheras of the House of Boethius.[42] He planned a new defensive wall for Jerusalem and he even held a summit meeting of eastern client kings. To the Jews such actions were reminiscent of the heady days of independence. And, in fact, the Romans started to get suspicious...

To devout, zealous Jews the times were propitious: the evil, sacrilegious intentions of Caligula had been thwarted by prayer and by Jewish faithfulness. Now a Jewish king had been restored to the throne. What better time for the Messiah to come?

The Jewish people must have had high hopes for Agrippa. Josephus describes him in glowing terms:

> Now, this king was by nature very beneficent, and liberal in his gifts ... Agrippa's temper was mild, and equally liberal to all men. He was humane to foreigners, and made them sensible of his liberality. He was in like manner rather of a gentle and compassionate temper.[43]

Josephus was a great friend of Agrippa's son, Herod Agrippa II, so maybe he was a little biased. There were questions raised about just how real this Jewish orthodoxy proved. His building projects signify that perhaps the old Romanist Agrippa had not gone away: in Berytus he built a theatre, public baths and an amphitheatre, which he inaugurated by having 1,400 men fight for their lives.[44] And as to his mildness of temper, the church in Jerusalem might have begged to differ.

One of the generous gifts which he bestowed on his loyal Jewish kingdom was a renewed crackdown on Christianity.

'Killed with the sword'

This move may have been motivated by another change of staff. Around this time, Agrippa switched high priest again: Simon Kantheras was deposed and in his place he installed Matthias, son of – you guessed it – Ananus. No doubt a fee was involved, but perhaps as part of this deal Agrippa agreed to further one of the House of Hanin's pet schemes: the annihilation of the followers of Jesus of Nazareth. He launched a wave of persecution against the church and some days before Passover he had James, the brother of John, beheaded.

The event is passed over quickly in Acts: the life of this 'son of thunder' snuffed out in a single brief sentence. When Agrippa saw that this went down well, he had Peter thrown into jail as well. What had happened to James would happen to Peter, as soon as Passover was over. Since Matthias became high priest in AD 42, it is probable the Passover in question is AD 43.[45]

But Peter escapes. In the night he is released by an angel and hurries to the house of Mary, mother of John Mark, where the Christians are praying. Like many houses in the city, it would have had no windows onto the street, just a door in the wall to let guests into a courtyard. Peter knocks at the door and the maid, Rhoda, answers. She is so amazed she forgets to let him in. And while she is telling everyone there's a ghost of Peter at the door, the real live man remains outside, knocking. It's a tremendous story and the notes of humanity and humour reflect, perhaps, the way it was told among the Christian communities that Peter visited. This is a real speaker's anecdote, another classic 'Peter' story.

Despite his miraculous escape, Peter cannot stay in the city, so he slips out of Jerusalem to 'another place' for a while (Acts 12.17). He probably did not return until after the death of Agrippa.

Agrippa had the hapless guards killed, but he did not continue the persecution. Perhaps he thought he had done enough to secure him the support he needed. Maybe he blamed Matthias for the disappearing apostle. At any rate, the next year he had Matthias deposed and replaced him with another priest, returning the privilege to the House of Boethius.

Agrippa soon left Jerusalem for the more congenial surroundings of Caesarea. There he seems to have tired of life as an orthodox Jewish king and embraced the life of a Hellenised ruler. At a meeting with emissaries from Tyre and Sidon he spoke so well that the crowd flattered him, shouting, 'The voice of a god, and not of a mortal!' (Acts 12.22). According to the Christian tradition, he didn't deny this, but accepted the acclaim – an acclaim that Rome would never offer. His blasphemy was punished: he was struck down by the angel of the Lord. Two encounters with angels for Agrippa, then: one releases a man he wants to execute, the other executes the king himself.

The story in Acts is echoed by the account in Josephus. Agrippa had thrown a festival in honour of Caesar, with a music competition, athletic contests, gladiator fighting, wild beasts, horse racing and other lavish and entertaining shows. These festivals had been instituted by Herod the Great and took place every four years on 5 March.[46] According to Josephus, Agrippa appeared at daybreak on the second day of the festival in a garment which so reflected the first rays of the sun that the onlookers declared him to be a god. Shortly after that, however, he looked up and saw a terrible omen: an owl, perched on a rope above his head. He was horror-struck. He had been warned that, should he see such an apparition, he would be dead within five days.[47] Just a few days later, Agrippa was seized with terrible stomach pains and promptly died.

According to Josephus, Agrippa died after 'the completion of the third year of his reign over the whole of Judea'. This would place his death sometime between January and March AD 44.[48] Luke records that he was eaten by worms. It's the usual symbolic fate for the baddies of the first century: Herod the Great, his grandfather, suffered the same fate. Agrippa achieved heights which only his grandfather had achieved and, in the end, his life was cut short in the same way.

'After fourteen years'

If the suggested date for the famine is correct, Paul and Barnabas took the famine relief money to Jerusalem sometime in AD 47 (Acts 11.29–30). The timing and nature of Paul's second visit to Jerusalem after his conversion has caused a lot of debate. Paul's account says:

> After fourteen years I went up again to Jerusalem with Barnabas, taking Titus along with me. I went up in response to a revelation. Then I laid before them (though only in a private meeting with the acknowledged leaders) the gospel that I proclaim among the Gentiles, in order to make sure that I was not running, or had not run, in vain. (Gal. 2.1–2)

This account follows immediately after the account of his first visit, after three years. So the question is, was this fourteen years after his conversion? Or fourteen years after his first visit (and therefore seventeen years after his conversion)? The general consensus is that Paul is dating both visits from his conversion. That, after all, was the key event in his life.

As we have seen, time could be counted inclusively, which means that any fraction of the year could be counted as a year.[49] In Jewish terms, this means that if Paul's conversion was in AD 34, he returned to Jerusalem sometime around AD 47 – plus or minus a year or so.

Paul and Barnabas took the gift to the elders (Acts 11.30). The Greek word is *presbuteroi* and it is the first mention of this strata of Christian leadership. So far we have had apostles and deacons, but nothing else. Luke uses the term several times in conjunction with the church:

▷ Paul's journey in Galatia ends with the appointment of 'elders' in each church (Acts 14.23).
▷ The elders in Jerusalem are present at the Jerusalem conference (Acts 15.2, 4, 6, 22, 23) and referred to in 16.4.
▷ By AD 57, there are elders in Ephesus (Acts 20.17).
▷ Timothy is given instructions on their appointment (1 Tim. 5.17, 19).

The term itself was one used of Jewish local leadership – usually of men who were of some standing in the community. They were present at Jewish councils and hearings, particularly in Jerusalem. With this and other terms, the nascent church appropriated Jewish and secular terminology for their new organisation.

Paul says that the trip was taken because of a revelation (Gal. 2.2). Again this has been used to drive a wedge between the Galatians account and Acts, which says that Paul and Barnabas went up to Jerusalem to deliver the famine relief fund. Paul could have been talking about the revelation of Agabus, who prophesied the famine in the first place. But in any case, it's simplistic to assume that a man can only have *one* motive for doing anything. Paul could have had several reasons to return to Jerusalem. The fund was one thing; another was his conviction – his revelation – that he had been called to preach the gospel to the Gentiles.

He raised this, according to his own words, in a private meeting. Many scholars work on the assumption that the meeting being described here is the so-called Jerusalem Council of Acts 15 and that, once again, poor old Luke has got his facts wrong, because Paul himself says nothing about a famine visit.[50] But clearly they are different meetings. The Acts 15 meeting is a major, public forum – or at least one open to a much wider circle of Christians in Jerusalem.[51] The meeting described by Paul in Galatians, though, is a small meeting. Paul states quite categorically that he saw only the core leaders at this meeting – Jacob (James) and Cephas and John – and that he 'delivered' to them the gospel he was preaching to the Gentiles.

The verb translated 'deliver' (*anatithemi*) means to report facts or information to someone.[52] It's usually assumed that what Paul was seeking was permission. But in the letter which he wrote to the Galatians, he says that even if an angel or Paul himself says something different, they were wrong. There is no impression that Paul thought he needed the permission of the central organisation. What he needed to know was that this approach was not going to lead to him 'running in vain' – that he was not, as it were, going to find himself disqualified from the race. He needed to know that the rug was not going to be pulled from under him later on. (And the fact that it was explains his bafflement and fury.)

Since the whole point of the letter of Galatians is to oppose those who say that Gentile Christians must be circumcised, it seems really odd that Paul doesn't once mention the decision taken by the Jerusalem leadership at that meeting, a decision which would have blown his opponents' arguments out of the water.

This is why, in his letter to the Galatians, Paul swears it is true: this meeting was private, there were no other witnesses.

It also explains why, in Antioch later, there could be such mis-understanding between Peter and Paul. A small, informal, private meeting can lead to misunderstandings and misinterpretation far more easily than a big meeting which issues A Very Important Letter.

The implication then – at least for those who take Acts seriously as a historical record – is that Galatians dates from before the 'big' meeting. It's a meeting that Paul had while he was in Jerusalem delivering the famine relief funds from Antioch.[53]

Paul says that the 'acknowledged leaders' gave the right hand of fellowship to Barnabas and himself: clearly they were the leaders of this mission. But Paul adds that he took Titus as well. Titus was a Gentile, a Greek from Antioch, which was why they took him. He was proof of what had been happening in Antioch. This is living proof of exactly what they're talking about: 'Here's one I prepared earlier.'[54] If so, it must have been a difficult role for Titus. But everything we know about Titus indicates that he was tough. Paul uses him as a troubleshooter. It's Titus whom Paul sends into the bear-pit at Corinth twice: first after he has sent the church there a particularly stinging, strong letter (2 Cor. 1.23 – 2.13) and later to make a collection of money (2 Cor. 8.5–6, 16–24). Later, Titus is sent by Paul to Crete to help establish the church there.

Titus appears several times in the letters of Paul, but not at all in Acts. It's difficult to know why he isn't mentioned. Maybe it's to do with the type of work in which Titus specialised, troubleshooting in problem situations, which Luke may not have deemed significant enough to include in his account. Or maybe it was due to Titus himself: he was a man for the hot spot, but not for the limelight.

In Jerusalem, the leaders were sufficiently persuaded by Paul that they did not insist on Titus being circumcised. On the face of it, it looks like a victory for Paul, but there are hints that, whatever the leaders said, others were not so sanguine. In Galatians, Paul suddenly inserts a strange reference to false brothers being smuggled into the group, spies in the camp. The phrase comes with such force that it entirely fractures the flow. It's as if Paul has suddenly remembered something. He may be referring to a group of Christians in Jerusalem who agitated for Titus to be circumcised.[55] And these may be the same people who visited Antioch later – 'men from James' – coming on the pretence of friendship, but imposing dietary regulations on the church.[56]

Or perhaps the vehemence of the denunciation has something to do with someone a lot closer to home, someone who, by the time of writing Galatians, Paul felt had betrayed him. Because Paul, after gaining the agreement of the leaders in Jerusalem, returned to Antioch and prepared to take his gospel even further into the Gentile world, with the backing of the church in Jerusalem for the first time. He returned with Barnabas, of course, and no doubt Titus. And he took with him a young man called John Mark.

Together, they returned to Antioch. There, 'at the urging of the Holy Spirit', and encouraged, no doubt, by the meeting in Jerusalem, Manaen, Lucius of Cyrene, Simeon Niger and other leaders of the Antioch church laid hands on the apostles and 'sent them off', 16 miles by boat down the Orontes to Seleucia, and then 60 miles off across the Mediterranean to Cyprus, Barnabas's home.

It was the early church equivalent of lighting the blue touchpaper and standing well back.

5. Galatia AD 48–49

'Sent out by the Holy Spirit'

Cyprus. The old and the new. The island was the hub of an ancient trade route between west and east: from at least the eighteenth century BC it had been exporting copper from its mines, while from its forests came the pine which took the island's name. Now the Romans had claimed it. The ancient capital of Salamis had been superseded by Paphos – or New Paphos, as the Romans called it. That became the Roman centre of administration on the island, and the seat of the Roman proconsul.[1]

After initially proclaiming their message in the synagogues of Salamis, Barnabas, Paul and John Mark arrived in Paphos, where they were summoned into the presence of the proconsul himself. According to Acts, his name was Sergius Paulus. Records of proconsuls in Cyprus are patchy, but there have been inscriptions found which testify to the existence of at least one proconsul by that name. An inscription on a boundary stone found in Rome lists the name 'L[ucius] Sergius Paullus' among a group of men who were responsible for checking any flood damage caused by the Tiber when it overflowed. This group was a stepping stone to greater influence. Another on the list of five names, Paullus Fabius Persicus, went on to be proconsul of Asia. It was a kind of Roman quango.[2] There is also evidence that the family of L. Sergius Paullus had strong links with Pisidian Antioch.[3]

Now Sergius Paulus had an advisor, a Jewish magician called Bar-Jesus or Elymas (Elymas is not a translation of Bar-Jesus;

it may be a translation of the Hebrew *holem*, which means an interpreter of dreams).[4] We might be surprised at the linking of a Jew with magic, but Jews had a reputation among the Romans for being involved in spells, incantations and prophecy. Jewish sorcerers from Cyprus seem to have been particularly popular. When the Roman governor Felix wanted to lure Drusilla from her husband Azizus, he sent to her a man called 'Simon, one of his friends; a Jew he was, and by birth a Cypriot, and one who pretended to be a magician'.[5] Juvenal talks of a 'palsied Jewess' who was 'an interpreter of the laws of Jerusalem, a high priestess of the tree, a trusty go-between of highest heaven ... for a Jew will tell you dreams of any kind you please for the smallest of coins'.[6] Later, Paul would encounter the seven sons of Sceva, who tried to exorcise demons and thought that Jesus' name was an incantation.

Elymas tries to interrupt the missionaries, no doubt because he fears losing influence. But in a powerful encounter, Paul speaks out and the magician is blinded 'for a while'. Sergius Paulus is struck by the miracle and 'believes' – although it's unlikely that he makes a full commitment to Christianity.

In the account in Acts it is halfway through the encounter with the magician – a kind of reversal of Paul's own Damascus experience – that Saul has a name change. He becomes Paul. It has been suggested that his triumph in front of Sergius Paulus inspires this change. Others suggest that it is the word 'Paul', which means 'little', hence indicating his humility. The simplest explanation, though, is that Paul was always Saul's Greek name. From now on the Greek world will be his mission field, so he takes the name by which he is known there. Nonetheless, it hints at the change that is in the air. It is Barnabas and Saul who disembark on the island, but Paul and his companions who leave. And from now on – in the book of Acts, anyway – Paul of Tarsus becomes the centrepiece and Barnabas from Cyprus slowly fades into the background.

From Cyprus they sailed to Perga in Pamphylia, and it was there that 'John [Mark], however, left them and returned to Jerusalem' (Acts 13.13). He caught a boat from Perga, which would take him along the coast and back to Syria. What happened? Luke tells us little, but the event was to cause a major row between Paul and

Barnabas later on (Acts 15.38). Was it homesickness? Nerves? An argument? Or something more?

Mark had probably never been this far from home. As he entered the city of Perga, with its hundreds of pagan statues, perhaps it was simply too much for a boy brought up in Jerusalem. Perhaps it was a step too far, too far from home. But he had been through Cyprus. And he had been to Antioch. Surely it can't have been that different?

Maybe Mark had serious doubts about what Paul was doing. He had thought it was just about visiting some synagogues on Cyprus, but here they were, heading off into deepest pagan territory, spreading the word far and wide. So he decided not to go on.

When Mark returned to Jerusalem, what then? He would have been pressed for reports about what Paul and Barnabas were doing and where they intended to go. Luke, after all, does say that this led to a serious breach between Barnabas and Paul. It's difficult to believe that a return prompted only by homesickness or illness would cause such problems. But if John Mark went back and reported what he had seen in Cyprus and Pamphylia, that Paul was welcoming Gentiles without making any legal requirements on them – reports that, even if well intentioned in themselves, led directly to the Jerusalem Council – then that would make Paul's later rejection of him much more comprehensible.[7]

This might explain Paul's outburst in Galatians, about the spies who 'slipped in to spy on the freedom we have in Christ Jesus' (Gal. 2.4). Spies work undercover. Spies wear a secret face. Spies appear friendly, but then turn their back on you. Was this John Mark?

Later, of course, Paul was reconciled to Mark and even asked for Mark to join him in Rome. Maybe the decision of the Jerusalem conference changed things for Mark, who might, as is so often the case with young men – as, indeed, was the case with Paul – have been carried away by his own enthusiasm.

As to why Paul and Barnabas chose this direction, that may well have been something to do with Sergius Paulus, the Procurator of Cyprus. His family – the Sergii Pauli – owned significant estates in central Anatolia.[8] There were several monuments built by the family in Pisidian Antioch, including one probably erected

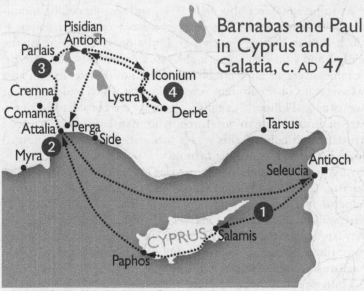

Barnabas and Paul in Cyprus and Galatia, c. AD 47

1. Barnabas, Paul and John Mark sail to Cyprus
2. At Perga, John Mark leaves and returns to Jerusalem
3. Barnabas and Paul go to Pisidian Antioch
4. They travel to Iconium, Lystra and Derbe, establishing Christian communities

by the proconsul's son, also called L. Sergius Paulus.[9] So this was perhaps less a 'Holy Spirit'-inspired itinerary and more a case of the proconsul of Cyprus pointing them to a place where dropping his name might do them a bit of good.

Or not…

'The Saviour of all people'

Barnabas and Paul continued north, along ancient roads winding through daunting mountain passes, before emerging onto the central plateau of Asia Minor. The most likely route was the Augustus Road or *via Sebaste*, a paved Roman highway which linked the colonies established by Augustus: Comama, Cremna, Parlais, Antioch, Iconium and Lystra. Follow the main road: that was Paul's usual habit. Although the *via Sebaste* was less direct than the older route, it was paved to take wheeled vehicles. There would have been more inns and accommodation that way.[10]

At some 3,600 feet above sea level, and surrounded by mountains, Pisidian Antioch was an elevated city in several senses. It was a Roman colony, the civil and administrative centre of the region, and home to some high-status individuals and groups. Colonies were usually established by military veterans (in this case veterans of the Roman Seventh Legion which had fought for Augustus at Philippi). Legally colonies were considered to be a part of Rome. Roman government, Roman laws, Roman social structure and culture: this was a little patch of Rome, dumped down in the middle of Asia Minor.[11]

Augustus. The emperor's name was everywhere. In city names: Sebaste; Caesarea Philippi; Caesarea Maritima. Temples to the emperor in every city. And here, in Pisidia, Paul and Barnabas were walking his road: the *via Sebaste* – the Augustus Road. As they approached Pisidian Antioch, they could see, from miles away, the temple, high in the mountains. A temple to the divine Augustus. A man who was a god.

The temple was the centrepiece of Pisidian Antioch. A broad, colonnaded street – the *Tiberia Platea* – led to a central square where the temple stood. There was a huge terraced platform, surrounded by a two-storey semicircular colonnade set into the hillside. One entered the temple through a triple-arched gateway, reached by twelve steps, which was still being constructed when Paul entered the city. Beyond the gateway and near the temple, there was a long inscription called the *Res Gestae*. Before his death in AD 14, Augustus composed a 2,500-word autobiography in Latin, describing his triumphs and achievements. It was called *Res Gestae Divi Augusti*, 'The Acts of the Divine Augustus'. This text was replicated at various places in the Empire, including Pisidian Antioch.[12]

Augustus began life as Octavian, but after defeating Antony and Cleopatra at the battle of Actium, he returned to Rome in triumph, renamed himself Augustus Caesar and proclaimed himself Rome's first emperor. He had saved the Empire from civil war. He had brought peace and stability. He was, as numerous inscriptions attested, 'the saviour of Rome'.

He became a god. Throughout the Empire, the Romans encouraged a religious cult which viewed their emperors as gods. The words used about Augustus testify to his divine mission and

Above, the remains
of the Temple
of Augustus in
Pisidian Antioch.
The platform on
which the temple
building stood was
set in a huge semi-
circle cut into the
mountainside

Left: the *Tiberia
Platea* in Pisidian
Antioch

status: he was the son of god, saviour of the world, bringer of peace, lord of all, the divine Augustus. Stories were created which claimed that he wasn't, in fact, mortal, that he was the offspring of his mother and the god Apollo. This story began to circulate almost immediately after his victory at Actium in 31 BC.[13]

An inscription from Halicarnassus (now Bodrum in south-west Turkey) describes Augustus as 'Saviour of the common race of men, whose providence has not only fulfilled but actually exceeded the prayers of all'.[14]

The Romans didn't despise Christianity because they claimed a man could be a god – they didn't have a problem with that. Their problem was that the man the Christians worshipped was a despised criminal: a Galilean peasant who died on a cross. The Romans deified men, but only the aristocracy. Their emperors. This changes our perception of the language used in the New Testament. When Christians call Jesus 'Prince of Peace', 'Saviour' or 'Son of God', they are using the terms that the Romans used of their emperor. They are placing themselves in direct opposition to this cultural religion, this imperial propaganda. Every time a first-century Christian said 'Jesus is Lord', they were implying 'and Caesar isn't'. Every time Jesus is described as 'Son of God', it is a denial of Augustus's right to use the term. To follow Jesus of Nazareth, therefore, was to walk the opposite way from the culture around them. To walk the way of Jesus was to go in the opposite direction to the *via Sebaste*.

It was not that the Christians followed a different faith which caused the Roman authorities to clamp down on them. The Romans were intrinsically religious, but they did not defend this religion with legislation. Sacrilege was punishable by law, but the crime referred to actions such as temple robbing, not issues of belief.[15] Nor was novelty the problem. Christianity was a new faith, but there were loads of new faiths. Every time Rome conquered a new region they welcomed some new gods on board.

No, the problem was that they were anti-Roman. Time and again, both in Acts and in accounts of Christians by pagans, it is their anti-Roman attitudes and behaviour which get them into trouble. In Philippi, Paul and Silas are accused of advocating customs 'that are not lawful for us as Romans to adopt or observe' (Acts 16.21).

In Thessalonica they are accused of 'acting contrary to the decrees of the emperor, saying that there is another king named Jesus' (Acts 17.7). In Corinth, Paul is accused of encouraging people to worship God 'in ways that are contrary to the law' (Acts 18.13). This was the crime of the Christians: they were anti-Roman.

They refused to recognise the pantheon of Roman gods. The Græco-Roman world was polytheistic, and then some. Hesiod claimed there were over 30,000 different gods. They differed from city to city and region to region, a rich and heady brew of Greek, Roman, Egyptian, Syrian, any-other-culture-you-can-think-of gods. There were the big players, of course: the Zeuses, Artemises and Apollos, that kind of thing. Most cities had shrines for between 15 and 20 major gods – but behind these lay a vast cornucopia of minor deities, each with their own shrines and devotees.

The Christians wanted nothing to do with all these gods. Along with the Jews, they proclaimed one God. This is why Christians could be described by Romans as 'atheists'. They didn't worship the pagan gods.

Emperor worship soon became a useful test for those trying to root out Christians. Around AD 110, Pliny the Younger, governor of Bithynia-Pontus, devised a three-part test to determine whether someone was guilty of being a Christian. First, they had to repeat after him a simple invocation to the gods. Second, they had to make a sacrifice of frankincense and wine to the gods. Third, they had to curse the name of Christ. Refuse any of those steps, and they were obviously guilty.[16]

The test became widely used. Forty years later, in Smyrna, the aged Bishop Polycarp was offered the chance to save himself. All he had to do was perform the sacrifice to the emperor and his life would be saved. He refused. On 22 February AD 156, he was burned at the stake.[17] As he was dragged into the arena the crowd shouted out their accusation: 'This is the teacher of Asia, the father of the Christians, and the overthrower of our gods, he who has been teaching many not to sacrifice or worship the gods.'

This was the real and biting accusation against the Christians. They refused to worship the gods. They refused to bow down at the altar of Augustus. They followed a different emperor and were citizens of a different kingdom.

'Called to be an apostle'

The Jewish population of Pisidian Antioch had been established there for three centuries. Paul and Barnabas go to the synagogue where, as esteemed visitors from Judea and Syria, they are asked to say a few words. This, with Paul, is the equivalent of ushering a bull into a china shop and inviting it to take a look around, but at first his message is well received. He is even invited to return the next week and Luke – with perhaps a touch of exaggeration – says that the whole city turned out. But 'the Jews' – presumably the Jewish leaders of the synagogue – have now taken offence at this message and start to argue. Paul and Barnabas announce that they will turn to the Gentiles instead. According to Luke, 'many [Gentiles] destined for eternal life became believers' (Acts 13.48).

It's too much for the establishment. Their Jewish opponents stir up the 'devout women of high standing' and the 'leading men of the city'. The devout women are probably well-connected, high-status God-fearers, and they use their influence to get Paul and Barnabas evicted. But the apostles have done enough to establish Christianity in the city, and the new disciples there are filled with both joy and the Holy Spirit.

From Pisidian Antioch, Paul and Barnabas continued along the *via Sebaste*, to the city of Iconium, some 90 miles south-east. Another place named after an emperor: Claudius granted this city the right to call itself Claudiconium. There they remained for a long time, according to Luke, but eventually they were forced to move on again, as there was a plot to stone them, whipped up by the 'Gentiles and Jews, with their rulers' (Acts 14.5) which really makes it sound like most of the city was against them.

There is one more significant detail here: Iconium is the only point in Luke's narrative when Luke gives Paul the title 'apostle', *apostolos* (14.4, 14). It's a curious fact that, despite Luke's obvious admiration for Paul, he seems reluctant to give him this title. It may be that Luke deliberately avoided using the term because, with a historian's precision, he didn't believe it was technically correct. This parsimony with the word on Luke's part does open up a question that was frequently asked about Paul: 'Brilliant evangelist, wonderful writer, brain the size of the Acropolis and all that, but was he really, properly, an apostle?'

In Paul's letters, and in works like the *Didache* as well, the word clearly indicates a wider group than just the twelve. It's worth remembering that, in the beginning at least, the word was a Greek one which just meant 'messenger' or 'emissary'. The apostles were people with a message.[18] When Peter and the others came to choose a successor to Judas, the criterion was that the apostle should have seen the risen Jesus. He should bear 'witness with us to his resurrection' (Acts 1.22). Witnessing the resurrected Jesus was what made Jesus' brother Jacob an apostle (Gal. 1.19), despite the fact that he did not follow Jesus while he was alive. Those who had seen the risen Jesus – those listed, for example, by Paul in 1 Corinthians 15, qualified as apostles. We know that two of Paul's relatives were among this number. Silas was an apostle as well (1 Thess. 2:6–7).

It is harder to fit Paul into this definition. He never saw Jesus in the flesh – he would certainly have said so if he had done. And when Jesus' followers were witnessing his resurrection appearances, Paul was studying with Gamaliel. Yet Paul repeatedly insists that he, too, is an apostle (e.g. 1 Cor. 1.1; 9.1–2; 15.9–10; 2 Cor. 1.1; Gal. 1.1). He describes himself as an emissary with a divine mandate (Gal. 1.1), and he insists on the validity of his vision of the risen Jesus on the road to Damascus (1 Cor. 15.8–10). Virtually every letter he writes begins with a declaration of his apostolic status.[19]

Apostles had a pre-eminent position in the early church. They were Jesus' ambassadors, his representatives. The *Didache* instructs that 'every apostle, when he comes to you, should be received as the Lord'.[20] Their eyewitness accounts were the foundation of the faith. Paul writes that the church was built on 'the foundation of the apostles and prophets, with Christ Jesus himself as the cornerstone' (Eph. 2.20). What he means here is the authentic, validated teaching, stories and traditions carried around the church by those who had been with Jesus.

Paul's insistence on his own status as an apostle, therefore, is a claim to have his teaching recognised as authentic and authoritative. The reason he has to insist so strongly is that his opponents disagreed. In their eyes he wasn't a real apostle. Paul's use of the word *ektrōma*, 'one who was miscarried into the faith', could well have been a term of abuse thrown at him by his opponents. He wasn't a 'true-born' follower. He never saw Jesus like they did. He was a 'mudblood'.

Paul strongly rejected such accusations. In his letters he talks bitterly about false apostles who oppose him, about so-called 'super-apostles' (2 Cor. 11.5; 12.11) who, in his mind, can't hold a candle to his achievements. The accusation needles him, provokes him into 'speaking as a fool' and defending himself by giving a long list of his sufferings and achievements.

That is another key factor, for Paul. An apostle should be able to do things. He or she should have demonstrable power. Signs and wonders were a signifier of true apostleship, a proof of status. Paul mentions 'the signs of a true apostle' (2 Cor. 12.12) – 'signs and wonders and mighty works'. An apostle was validated by other things as well – like healing people.

'The gods have come down to us'

Arriving in Lystra, Paul and Barnabas encounter a lame man. They pray for him, he is healed and the people go mad for them, because the gods are walking the earth.

By now Paul and Barnabas are in the region known as Lycaonia. It is in their native language – Lycaonian – that the crowd proclaim that Zeus and Hermes have come down to earth in human form, which is presumably why Paul and Barnabas don't realise what's happening until the local priest brings oxen to make a sacrifice to them.

Barnabas they call Zeus, Paul they identify with Hermes, Zeus's son and the spokesman for the gods. Clearly Paul was doing most of the talking.[21] Maybe the crowd had in mind the myth about Jupiter (i.e. Zeus) and Mercury (Hermes) visiting the earth and being rejected by home after home, until they are taken in by a poor peasant couple. The couple are rewarded with a never-ending supply of wine, not to mention being saved while the rest of the region is decimated by the angry gods. That story, after all, was set in Phrygia, the region next to Lycaonia.[22]

Zeus was the most worshipped god in Galatia. There were temples to the father of the gods everywhere.[23] And in this region, the local 'type' of Zeus – the one represented in statues – was known as *Zeus Ampelites*, and he is depicted as an elderly man with a beard, with his companion – Hermes – shown as a young assistant.[24] It's quite possible that the appearance of the two apostles reinforced the identification. Barnabas might well have been older than Paul.

In fact, a story written much later and set in the same city of Lystra probably does give us a picture of what Paul looked like. The story is called *The Acts of Paul and Thecla* and it's a curious story about a young woman who becomes devoted to Paul and undergoes many trials before she is miraculously delivered from death at the hands (or the teeth) of wild beasts. It's not an authentic record, in fact we know that it was written by an unnamed church leader in Asia (who lost his post because of it), but it may preserve within it a real story about a woman who was converted during one of Paul's visits.[25] And it probably does contain a picture of the apostle himself. In the book Onesiphorus stands on 'the king's highway that leads to Lystra' and waits for Paul:

> And he saw Paul coming, a man small in size, bald-headed, bandy-legged, well-built, with eyebrows meeting, rather long-nosed, full of grace. For sometimes he seemed like a man, and sometimes he had the countenance of an angel.[26]

While *The Acts of Paul and Thecla* is a work of fiction, this description is so unflattering that many scholars think it reflects an early, authentic description of Paul. Certainly it accords well with the earliest image of Paul, from a medallion in Rome, which shows a bald man, bearded and hook-nosed.

When the oxen arrive for the sacrifice, Paul and Barnabas issue frantic denials. Even then the locals can hardly restrain themselves from offering sacrifices.

We don't know how long they were in Lystra, but we do know their visit ended in violence. Their Jewish opponents from Iconium had followed them and stirred up the crowd against them. Paul was stoned so badly that the crowd believed he was dead. We can assume that he was unconscious or semi-conscious. Luke describes the disciples 'surrounding' Paul (Acts 14.20). Were they praying for him or shielding him? Luke's statement that he got up and went into the city implies that he needed immediate rest and attention. The next day he set out for Derbe.

When Paul writes to the Galatians later, he talks about how he came to them in a bad physical state. In a curious reference, he says, 'You know that it was because of a physical infirmity that I first announced the gospel to you; though my condition put you to the test, you did not scorn or despise me, but welcomed me as an angel of God, as Christ Jesus' (Gal. 4.13–14). What was this physical problem? Paul later says that the Galatians would have torn out their eyes and given them to him. The clear implication is that he had a problem with his sight. It may be that this was a consequence of his experience on the Damascus road; whatever the case, it could only have been made worse by the brutal treatment he endured in Lystra. Perhaps this was his 'thorn in the flesh'. Battered and bruised, he and his companions must have made their way to Derbe slowly. Going there meant leaving the main road and heading down a rough track. But perhaps that was the plan. The Jewish opponents had dogged his tracks along the *via Sebaste*. Perhaps he was giving them the slip now.

Mercifully, Derbe was quiet. Luke tells us nothing more about this visit other than that Barnabas and Paul made many disciples there (14.21). Nothing remains of Derbe now, but the site has been identified following the discovery of two inscriptions. The site is at the mound of Kerti Hüyük, 65 miles south-east of Konya (ancient Iconium).[27]

After spending some time there, Paul and Barnabas returned through the places they had been to previously, appointing leaders in the churches. It would have been easier for them to continue south from Derbe, and so on to Tarsus, but they obviously considered that the job had not been completed. They appointed local leaders, spent time strengthening the churches and gave them a simple instruction: 'It is through many persecutions that we must enter the kingdom of God' (Acts 14.22).

In a region dominated by the kingdom of Augustus, the kingdom of fools had made an entry. But it was never going to be easy.

'Some men from Jacob'

After a brief stop to spread the word in Perga, Paul and Barnabas went to Attalia and then, on a boat, back to Antioch. They must have felt satisfied, if not euphoric. Despite opposition, the gospel had been preached and Christian communities planted. Back home they would be able to relax for a bit.

Perhaps they did. But at some point – and this is around AD 48 – the issue which Paul had discussed in Jerusalem, the issue of Gentiles and the gospel, flared up again. And this time Paul, Peter and Barnabas were all involved.

We don't know how it started. Luke talks about 'individuals … from Judea' (Acts 15.1). Paul is more specific: he talks about Jacob's men (Gal. 2.12).

Luke passes over the dispute rather quickly en route to the Jerusalem conference. He talks about 'no small dissension and debate', but he doesn't give anything like the impression of the full-scale row between the leaders of the church that comes from the letter Paul wrote to Galatia. From that we can piece together something of what happened.

Paul and Barnabas return to Antioch. They either find Peter there (Paul calls him Cephas) or he arrives later. At first they all – Jew and Gentile – eat together. But then some men arrive from Jacob in Jerusalem. Paul describes these as the 'circumcision faction' (Gal. 2.12). They are hardliners, people who have never stopped believing that Christians should be circumcised, and they have obviously been building their power base. They now feel in a position to go to Antioch and force a change in behaviour. They arrive with what the church in Antioch believes to be the full authority of the Jerusalem church. And such is the impact that Peter and even Barnabas stop eating together with the Gentiles (Gal. 2.12–13).

For Paul, worse is to come. He receives news from the new Christian communities in Galatia that Jewish Christians – presumably from the same faction – have been there and informed them that they will have to be circumcised and adopt the full practices of the Jewish law. The Galatians appear to have adopted the Jewish calendar. They may not have submitted to circumcision yet, but they have begun to observe 'special days, and months, and seasons, and years' (Gal. 4.10). The implication is that they are observing Sabbaths and annual Jewish festivals.[28] Despite the assurance Paul received in Jerusalem that he would not run in vain, it looks like he has been disqualified.

Perhaps they told the Galatians other things as well. Paul writes, rather cryptically, 'You have heard, no doubt, of my earlier life in Judaism...' (Gal. 1.13). Is this an indication that he had not told the Galatians about his past? Or merely that he was addressing those who had come to faith in the time since he had left? Or that his opponents had reminded the Galatians just what Paul had been like once?

Some scholars, again arguing about Acts versus Paul's letters, try to separate things out and argue that Galatia means northern Galatia, where the Gauls settled sometime in the third century BC. But the Roman province of Galatia included Lystra, Derbe and Iconium, the places Paul had visited just a few months before. And there is no record – not even a vague tradition or apocryphal record – of a northern missionary journey of Paul.[29] Galatians as a letter makes perfect sense if we suppose it written to the communities of southern Galatia, the places that Paul and Barnabas had just visited.

The letter is passionate, polemical and fantastically outspoken. This is grievous bodily theology. Paul refers to the leaders in Jerusalem as the 'so-called' pillars of the church. He expresses the wish that those people who were recommending circumcision would cut the whole lot off. In most Bible translations it comes over as pretty extreme – and they've toned it down. It's extreme because, for Paul, this was a vital issue and one which he thought he had won. He had been converting Gentiles for a long time now – perhaps dating back to his time in Arabia. Was all that work for nothing? Paul argues vehemently that if the Galatians adopt this, then all his work will have been pointless. They will have put themselves back into slavery: 'For freedom Christ has set us free. Stand firm, therefore, and do not submit again to a yoke of slavery' (Gal. 5.1).

Galatians is nothing if not a roller-coaster ride. It has moments of anger and outrage and classic Pauline overstatement: if an angel from heaven came down and told them a different gospel, Paul would still be right; he talks scathingly of leaders 'who contributed nothing to me' (Gal. 1.8; 2.6). But amidst this bruising polemic, he scales great heights of truth and depths of beauty. In one of the most radical statements ever written, Paul writes that there is no longer Jew or Greek, slave or free, male or female, for everyone is one in Christ (Gal. 3.28). He writes lyrically of the fruits of the Spirit. And he pens the first expression of his great credo: 'Yet we know', he writes, 'that a person is justified not by the works of the law but through faith in Jesus Christ' (Gal. 2.15). This anger that courses through him, this fury, this passion, brings out both the outrageous and the outrageously beautiful.

The Gentiles don't need the law: they have been justified by faith. That becomes Paul's classic, world-changing statement on the nature of belief. That's how he solves the problem of whether Gentiles should obey the Jewish laws.

Why did Paul come to this conclusion? Why didn't he expect Gentiles to follow Jewish customs? After all, it was not as if other Gentiles didn't do it. Proselyte believers became fully Jewish.

Part of the reason was ethnicity. These were *Jewish* laws. Paul has Timothy circumcised because Timothy is Jewish; he refuses to circumcise Titus because Titus is Greek. Paul believed there was something unique about the Jewish people, and he never tries to play that down. It does not make them superior – no difference between Jew and Greek, he wrote – but it does make them different. There is stuff which they have to do and throughout his life, Paul, as a Jew, did that stuff.

As much as anything else, it must have been a pragmatic decision. Paul understood the Hellenistic world in a way that the hardliners did not. He knew that the lives the Gentiles led made it highly difficult, if not impossible, for them to conform fully to Jewish law. These were people, after all, who lived and worked in the Græco-Roman culture. They were slaves in houses which were adorned with pictures of the gods. They worked in the markets where meat sacrificed to idols was sold. He wanted people to accept the salvation found in Christ. And, to put it bluntly, he wanted the cost to them of saying 'yes' to Jesus to be as low as possible. What Paul wanted to do was to remove as many hurdles as possible.

Which is not to say that there was no cost. On the contrary, as we have already seen, following Christ meant swimming against the tide and living lives which were very different. But in Paul's eyes, it did not mean adding to that already demanding discipleship the ritual observance which, he felt, only really applied to Jews.

The argument about circumcision, however, was not the key issue. The conflict between Paul on the one side, and Peter and Barnabas on the other, is not about circumcision, nor is it about the right of Gentiles to be followers of Jesus. The issue is the Jewish Christians' refusal to eat with their Gentile brothers and sisters.

As we have seen, although Jews refused to eat with Gentiles, this was a boundary which Peter had already crossed in his encounter with Cornelius in Caesarea. Now, he seems to have been persuaded to recant. In Caesarea, Peter was convinced that Gentiles could be full and proper followers of Jesus, but in Antioch he does not eat with them.

Such is the pressure on the Jewish believers in Antioch that even Barnabas is caught up in it. Despite his trip through Galatia – a trip in which he simply must have eaten and stayed with Gentiles – he now reverts to the practices of Barnabas of Jerusalem.

For orthodox Jews, the only way of ensuring a 100 per cent Jewish table fellowship was for everyone at the table to be Jews. In discussing this issue, and in Paul's arguments in his letters, his opponents are often referred to as 'Judaisers'. The word gives the impression that they were trying to turn Christianity Jewish, but they were actually trying to keep it Jewish. As they saw it, they were trying to preserve its Jewish origin. One can understand their argument: Jewish identity within the Christian community would disappear if all their characteristic practices were abandoned.[30] There were other factors at play as well. In Jerusalem there was a rising tide of Jewish nationalism which was putting Jerusalem-based Christians under enormous pressure. They continually had to prove themselves obedient to the law.[31] If news that Antioch Christians were no longer observing the law leaked back to Jerusalem, then the Jewish Christians in Jerusalem would be placed under even more pressure. But if they could show that they were, in fact, making Jewish proselytes, albeit to a new strand of Judaism, it might lessen the accusations – and the persecution – against the church in Jerusalem.[32]

Paul recognises this, although he doesn't sound exactly understanding about it. In the final section of Galatians (which, as he says, he writes himself in his own large letters) he claims:

> It is those who want to make a good showing in the flesh that
> try to compel you to be circumcised – only that they may not be
> persecuted for the cross of Christ. Even the circumcised do not
> themselves obey the law, but they want you to be circumcised so
> that they may boast about your flesh. (Gal. 6.12–13)

To Paul, if people weren't persecuting you, you weren't doing it right. But this wasn't about a negative, about embracing hardship and toil. The argument in Antioch and in the small, just-started churches in Galatia was about the positive expression of the kingdom of God. What was at stake here, in Paul's eyes, was that they absolutely *had* to eat together.

'We all partake of the one bread'

To Paul, the Christian practice of the shared meal was absolutely fundamental. He saw the thanksgiving meal – the Eucharist – as a sign, a practical demonstration of what the kingdom of God was like. It fed the poor. It reminded everyone of the story. And it was eaten together.

The name comes from the Greek verb *eucharistia,* which means 'thanksgiving' or 'thankfulness'. In the *Didache* – which originated from this period, and probably from Antioch to boot – the instructions about the community meal form the second-longest section. Taken literally, the opening of this section in the *Didache* runs, 'Now concerning the *Eucharist, eucharistise* in this way.' We might phrase it, 'Now concerning the Thanksgiving, give thanks in this way.'[33] It was certainly not done in the way we do it today. Forget people queuing up to kneel before a bloke in a frock gives them a sip of very bad wine and a fragment of bread, or handing round tiny cups to drink in unison at a command from the front. These thanksgivings were not what Crossan calls 'our present morsel-and-sip ritual', but real, proper meals.[34] At some point within the meal, perhaps, the eating of the bread and the drinking of the wine was given heightened significance. But it was supposed to be about feeding people. In the *Didache* there is a long prayer of thanks which is only supposed to be offered 'after you have all had enough to eat'.[35] The *Didache* states that it happened on the Lord's day,[36] but it doesn't state that it only happened then. Perhaps, at least in wealthier communities, there were more frequent celebrations.[37]

The early Christian community traced this meal back to Jesus. Jesus was always eating and drinking; he depicted the kingdom of heaven as a banquet with an open invitation. The predominant metaphor for the kingdom was a feast. Eating with people was one of Jesus' signature activities. It was also a specific command. Writing to the Corinthians, in a letter which was primarily focused on their failure to 'eucharistise' properly, Paul recalls the specific command that Jesus gave to his followers, to remember him by drinking wine and eating bread, and how Paul had these instructions handed down to him: they were one of the core instructions of the early church.

You learned this stuff straight away. It was important. It was important for a number of reasons. It told the story of Jesus' passion, for one thing. It reminded them all of their identity. Crucially, it was a meal which unified this new type of community. It brought people together. The *Didache* saw the meal as not just unifying a group of individuals in one locality; it also unified the entire church, that network of linked and scattered communities around the Græco-Roman world. In the *Didache*'s eucharistic prayer it has the line:

> Remember your church, Lord, to deliver it from all evil and make it perfect in your love; and from the four winds gather the church that has been sanctified into your kingdom.[38]

This is why we call it 'Communion'. It's all about community. It joins individual believers and communities of believers together and, ultimately, all believers to Christ. No wonder that Paul takes the fracturing of this unity so seriously.[39]

In the later church the debates were – and are – heated over who should preside during the Eucharist and how frequently it should happen. But neither in Paul's writing nor in the *Didache* do we find any discussion of who should preside. This meal was a great leveller of status. This was a meal in which everyone was a brother and sister. This was precisely what made the Romans so suspicious of the Christians' thanksgiving meal. It was not their idea of a meal: banquets in the Græco-Roman world were common, but they were celebrations among equals. There was no mixing of the social classes. To the contrary, Roman banquets were intended to reinforce relationships between the 'right sort of people'. You would eat with those who were socially, racially and culturally accepta-ble.[40] But the Christian meal cut across all these boundaries. Slaves mingled with masters. One cup, one loaf, shared among all.

And it was a meal of peace. It was a visible sign of a group of people committed to living peaceably with one another. This was evident in other characteristic Christian activities associated with the meal. Before you ate together, you were supposed to confess your sins:

> On the Lord's own day gather together and break bread and give thanks, having first confessed your sins so that your sacrifice may be pure.[41]

Then there was the kiss of peace – the holy kiss – which fea-tures in the writings of Peter and Paul, indicating that even very early on it was a feature of the communities' life. This was a star-tling, even scandalous display of unity. By Justin Martyr's time it had become usual to practise the kiss immediately before the Eucharist began. It was a sign that the believers were in harmony with one another. How, after all, can you share the kiss of peace with those with whom you are in conflict, or, indeed, with those whom you consider impure?

The *Didache* urged disciples to ensure that they were at peace with one another before sharing the meal. After seeking forgive-ness from God, the believers were to seek it from one another: 'Anyone who is in dispute with a neighbour must not join you until they are reconciled, or your sacrifice will be defiled.'[42] When churches got bigger, it became a real challenge to ensure that peo-ple could actually visibly make peace with one another. In Anti-och, in the fourth century, Theodore of Mopsuesta suggested that 'everyone gives peace as far as possible to his neighbour'. If the one who had been sinned against was nearby, he suggests that this order of Christ should be put into practice straight away; if he was over the other side of the building, however, then the offender should vow to make peace as soon as possible after the service.[43]

Why is this so important? The Christians were aware that they were modelling something quite unique. Theirs was a community of peace: something that was all too rare in the Roman world. Later on in the life of the church, great efforts were made to ensure that the meal retained this characteristic.

This emphasis on peace could even cut across doctrinal differences. In the mid-second century AD a dispute broke out between the churches of the East and the church in Rome over the date on which the church should celebrate Easter. Naturally many travellers came to Rome from the East and they wanted to do things their way. When Polycarp came to Rome, he and the Roman church leader Anicetus agreed to disagree:

And when the blessed Polycarp stayed at Rome in the time of Anicetus, though they had some trifling disagreements on other matters, they immediately made peace and did not care to quarrel on this subject. Anicetus could not persuade Polycarp not to observe what he had always observed with John the Lord's disciple and the other apostles with whom he consorted; and Polycarp could not persuade Anicetus to observe it, for he said that he ought to hold to the custom of the elders before him. Though such was the situation, they held communion with each other and in the church Anicetus yielded the eucharist to Polycarp, obviously out of respect. So they parted from each other in peace and the whole church was at peace, both those who observed and those who did not.[44]

This, then, is why Paul goes ballistic here. It's not about the rights of Jews and Gentiles to observe their own customs: it's about how observing those customs was actually shattering the ideal of Christian unity. How could Christians claim to be equal if some of them looked down on the others as impure? How could they claim to be united if they couldn't even eat together? And how could they claim to be at peace with one another when they were so visibly torn apart?

Paul was a pragmatist. He knew that the Christian community would be diverse in terms of race, status and gender. But this community *had* to eat together as a sign of peace (Eph. 2.11–22). The only way you could make this work was to be sensitive to the different cultures, not dogmatic. Gentiles did not need to become Jews, nor Jews, Gentiles.

Paul's attitude is made clearer still elsewhere: if the issue did not touch on the core of the gospel, then each person should do what was appropriate for their own conscience. Some would eat only certain foods, others would eat anything. Some set apart certain days as special, others treated all days the same. 'For the kingdom of God is not food and drink but righteousness and peace and joy in the Holy Spirit,' he wrote, '...let us then pursue what makes for peace and for mutual edification' (Rom. 14.17–19).

What is clear here is that peace and mutual understanding are somewhat scarce. The pressure on Peter and Barnabas had split them from the Gentiles, and Paul, diplomat that he wasn't, publicly rebuked them. There was, basically, a blazing row. Paul told Peter he was wrong. To his face. The result was an emergency summit, a crisis meeting to decide the issue.

'Jacob, a slave of God'

Jerusalem was the centre of the Jewish world – both figuratively and literally, in fact, for, geographically, Jerusalem was the centre of the Jewish diaspora. The diaspora stretched as far east as it did west. There were Jewish colonies in Spain and North Africa, but also in Parthia far to the east.[45] The centrality of Jerusalem in the thought of Jews was reflected in the centrality of the Jerusalem church to the early church's life and thinking. It was the mother church. It was the source, the centre, the headwaters.

In Jerusalem, the disciples weren't known as *Christiani*. That was their northern nickname. In Jerusalem, they were probably known as the 'Nazarenes'. Although the term only occurs once in Acts (Acts 24.5), it must be an early term, since it originates from Aramaic, not from Greek or Latin. And it is used by Jews, in Jerusalem, to designate Jewish Christians. It means, simply, 'from Nazareth'.[46] The founder of the sect came from Nazareth and his brother – also from Nazareth – was still in charge. And, when faced with this fundamental issue, it is to this man that they turn: to Jacob, brother of Jesus.

Not James. His name wasn't James, nor could it have been. There is a possibility that his brother Yeshua could have been called Jesus in his lifetime: 'Jesus' is the Greek transliteration of Yeshua. But 'James' as a name wasn't even invented until the eleventh century AD. Everyone who knew him would have called him Yacov, if they spoke Aramaic, or Iakob if they spoke Greek. As to why we call him James, your guess is as good as mine. It's a baffling, illogical, indefensible fact of English Bible translation that the brother of Jesus is always called James, while the grandfather of Jesus – Joseph's dad – is called Jacob (Matt. 1.16). It's the same name! It's not even as if the name Jacob is uncommon nowadays. One of the things that this practice does, though, is to subtly distance Jacob from what was generally agreed to be the most noticeable thing about him: his Jewishness.

So as a blow against this, in this book I'm going to continue to call him Jacob.* 'James' is the name of a Western Christian. Jacob, brother of Jesus, was a Jew through and through. Indeed, his reputation for Jewish piety is not found only in the New Testament but outside the Bible as well. He is one of only a handful of New Testament characters who appear in Josephus.[47]

At the beginning of Acts the church is clearly under the authority of 'the twelve'. But by AD 36, when Paul goes up for his first meeting, he sees only Cephas and Jacob 'the Lord's brother' (Gal. 1.19). And it is Cephas (Peter) whom Paul mainly stays with. At the second visit, around AD 47, Paul sees 'Jacob and Cephas and John' (Gal. 2.9) – and the order of the names is perhaps significant.

By Acts 11, it is simply the Jerusalem church which sends Barnabas to Antioch; specific apostles are not mentioned at all (Acts 11.22). When the famine relief is sent, it is not to the apostles but to the elders (Acts 11.30). Then, when Peter escapes from prison, he leaves a message for 'Jacob and the believers' (Acts 12.17). He does not mention the other apostles – either they are in prison as well, or they have all left the city.[48] The fact that Jacob is not targeted but the apostles are may reflect his status amongst orthodox Jews of the day, or it may signal that this is the point where the leadership of the church finally passes from the twelve to Jacob. The twelve have gone: it's time for Jacob to step in and really take control.[49]

So by the AD 40s, Jacob is in charge of the church, along with the elders. The role and function of the apostles has changed. It becomes a wider term, indicating those representatives, those eyewitnesses, who are out on the road.

Why, though, was Jacob chosen? After all, he wasn't even a believer in Jesus while Jesus was alive (John 7.5). Paul records that Jesus appeared to Jacob after his death (1 Cor. 15.7). This tradi-

---

* Except in quotes from other writers. And I realise that logically I should talk about James, brother of John, the same way. But then it just gets confusing...

tional story also appears in a lost gospel, known as 'The Gospel of the Hebrews'. This was originally written in Greek and aimed at the Jewish-Christian community, and it's the only lost gospel whose actual title is mentioned by contemporary writers. Of the original gospel only fragments remain, quoted in the works of other writers, most notably Jerome, who records an account of Jesus' resurrection appearance to his brother:

> Now the Lord, when he had given the linen cloth to the servant of the priest, went to James and appeared to him (for James had sworn that he would not eat bread from that hour in which he had drunk the Lord's cup until he should see him risen from among them that sleep). And a little further on the Lord says, 'Bring a table and bread.' And immediately it is added, 'He took bread and blessed and broke and gave it to James the Just and said to him, "My brother, eat your bread, for the Son of man is risen from among them that sleep."'[50]

So Jacob had apparently believed the testimony of the other apostles after Jesus' death, which was confirmed by an appearance of the risen Jesus. The story also reflects something else about Jacob: his reputation in the early church for piety and asceticism. He vows to fast until he sees Jesus.

The same reputation is found in Eusebius, who records, right at the start of his church history, that 'James ... whom the men of old surnamed the Just on account of his excellent virtue' was the first leader of the church at Jerusalem. He quotes Clement of Alexandria:

> Peter and James and John after the ascension of the Saviour did not lay claim to glory, as men who had been preferred in honour by Him; but selected James the Just as bishop of Jerusalem.[51]

The term 'bishop' is an anachronism from Eusebius's time, but clearly there was a tradition that Jacob had become the leader of the Jerusalem church at quite an early stage. Over time, reports of his holiness became rather exaggerated. An early church historian called Hegesippus recorded that he was allowed to enter the holy place in the temple and that he prayed so much that 'his knees became hard, like a camel's'.[52] This is clearly nonsense. But Hegesippus also records that he was known as 'Oblias', which in Greek means 'rampart of the people'. Probably this is a version – or corruption – of the Hebrew term 'wall of the people'.

It's not certain where this comes from, but the idea of Jacob as a protector of his community may well go back to the early church. If Peter was the rock, Jacob was the wall.

Along with his reputation for piety and Jewish orthodoxy, there was one other thing which counted highly in the ancient world: he was family. He was the Lord's brother, part of the dynasty. This family connection continued for some time in Judea and Galilee. Jesus' brother Judas (Jude) was a well-known figure in the early church. And when Jacob died, the leadership of the church passed to another relative, Simeon. Eusebius, who gives us this anecdote, wrote that 'He [Simeon] was a cousin – at any rate so it is said – of the Saviour; for indeed Hegesippus relates that Clopas was Joseph's brother.'[53]

Much later, around the end of the first century, there is evidence that two of the grandsons of Jude – Zoker and Jacob [James] – were still farming the family smallholding in Nazareth, but were also leaders of the Palestinian Jewish Christian community. Julianus Africanus reported a tradition that the relatives of Jesus operated as missionaries, starting from Nazareth and Kochaba (a village near Nazareth) and taking the gospel throughout the land. There is a story from the rabbinic literature about a late first-century rabbi encountering a disciple of *Yesû ben Pndr* – 'Jesus, son of Panthera' was their derogatory term for Christians – in a street in Sepphoris. The disciple's name was Jacob of Kephar Sikhnaya and he may have been one of Jesus' relatives. In any case, Kephar Sikhnaya is modern Sakhnin, only four miles from Kochaba.[54]

All of this is backed up by the letter that bears his name. It begins with his name: 'James [Iakob], a servant of God and of the Lord Jesus Christ, to the twelve tribes in the Dispersion...' (Jas 1.1). It is a notably Jewish opening. Scholars are divided over whether Jacob actually wrote the letter, or whether it has been sourced from his teaching. For one thing, the writer has a good grasp of Greek with considerable rhetorical skills. But we needn't assume Jacob was incapable of writing in that way. Or he could perfectly reasonably be working with a trained scribe as an editorial assistant. What's noticeable about the letter is the very low-key opening. He self-identifies as a *doulos*, a 'slave'. Not a leader of the church. Not the brother of Jesus. If you were going to create a letter and attribute it to Jacob, you might want to accentuate his status. Remind us who we're talking about. But if the letter came from Jacob, then that would be played down.

The letter is in the distinctly Jewish tradition of wisdom teaching. 'If any of you is lacking in wisdom,' he writes, 'ask God ... and it will be given you' (Jas 1.5). He draws on many of his brother's words and aphorisms, although he does not quote them exactly. And he presents a teaching with a radical emphasis on the poor and marginalised. In this letter, the rich are the oppressors (Jas 2.6); they store up treasure which rots and rusts (Jas 5.1–5); those who are friends with the world are enemies of God (Jas 4.4); true religion is the care of the widows and orphans in the community (Jas 1.27). This certainly reads as the letter of a man in charge of a poor church, in a city which has seen more than its fair share of oppression.

The letter has often been seen as a counterblast to Paul's assertions about faith, but a close reading of both Paul and the letter of James shows that they have a lot in common. At no point in Paul's letters does he say that you don't have to do stuff. On the contrary, his letters are full of instructions about the right behaviour of Christians. Nowhere in his letter does Jacob say anything about circumcision, dietary laws, Sabbath observance, or any of the other concerns of the more zealous members of his church. It is forgotten that Jacob, in his famous passage on faith and works, is addressing those who are already believers. He may well be seeking to correct a misunderstanding of Paul's gospel – that people were saying it didn't matter what you did. Paul would never have signed up to that. It mattered hugely what you did and how you behaved.

The differences between them have been exaggerated, but they were certainly writing from different perspectives. Paul was out on the periphery, roving around the Græco-Roman world. He was at the edge, looking back to the centre. Jacob was at the centre, looking out.

In any case, by the time Paul arrives in Jerusalem for the big meeting, it's clear that Jacob is the key figure. It's he, and not Peter, who will, in the end, propose the terms of agreement. It's he who stands at the centre of this new movement, seeking to hold the whole thing together. But there were a lot of centrifugal forces trying to split the whole thing apart.

'I have reached the decision'

Although the meeting has been characterised as 'the Apostolic Council', that's too grand a title. It made a major decision, but it has never been listed among the historic councils of the church – that kind of council belongs to a later date and a much more hierarchical organisation. This is a proto-council, at most. A forerunner of the angrier, more convoluted ones which were to follow.[55]

Nevertheless, it's one of the most important events in church history. In Luke's account (Acts 15) it's dominated by three main speeches, but there are other details as well:

▷ Paul and Barnabas and 'some of the others' are appointed by the church in Antioch to go up to Jerusalem.
▷ They pass through Phoenicia and Samaria, and the believers there react with joy to the news of the conversion of the Gentiles.
▷ On arrival they are greeted by the elders and apostles and they report what has been happening through their work.
▷ Some Christians who 'belonged to the sect of the Pharisees' insist that believers have to be circumcised and obey the law of Moses.
▷ The apostles and elders meet together to debate, and following this debate there are speeches from Peter, Barnabas and Paul, and Jacob.

The speeches are interesting. Peter seems to have reconsidered once more. He talks about how he had originally been appointed as the one through whom the Gentiles would hear the good news. 'Now,' he says, 'why are you putting God to the test by placing on the neck of the disciples a yoke that neither our ancestors nor we have been able to bear?'

Barnabas and Paul then give their account of the signs and wonders they have seen among the Gentiles, though their speech is not reported in any detail.

Finally, Jacob stands up and gives what is clearly his ruling to give: 'I have reached the decision,' he says. And the decision is that Gentiles should not be troubled. They are to abstain from 'things polluted by idols and from fornication and from whatever has been strangled and from blood'.

Luke makes it seem very amicable and straightforward, but there are signs that the debate was more finely balanced than that.

First, there are the believers in Phoenicia and Samaria. Their delight in the Gentile work would have been understandable – they too lived in a Gentile environment. But one also feels that perhaps Paul and Barnabas are building support here. Are they getting their allies onside? After all, the church in Judea has had no problem with these people joining the movement in the past. It's fifteen years since Philip first went to Samaria.

Second, there are the 'pharisaical Christians' who get their retaliation in early, as it were, before the meeting has even begun. It's probable that in his entourage Paul has uncircumcised, Gentile believers. The pharisaical Christians demand that all Christians should be circumcised. Right at the start, they are claiming that they cannot have fellowship with these people: they are impure.

It's only after this that the apostles and the elders meet together to discuss the matter. And it's not stated for definite that Paul was invited to that meeting. Certainly from now on Paul and Barnabas are more passive than aggressive: none of their actual words are recorded, unlike those of Jacob and Peter.

Peter has swung back again in the Gentiles' favour, though. Perhaps it was Paul's challenge in Antioch that did it. Perhaps it was the journey back down, which would have taken him via Caesarea and through Samaria, places where he himself had already fought these battles. His speech draws on his personal experience, but it also has a wider focus. And he talks about a 'yoke'. Had this term been used in discussions with Paul? Paul talks about the Christians in Galatians being free from the 'yoke'. Or maybe Peter was using a familiar Jewish image. Later rabbinic scholars talked of 'the yoke of the Torah'.[56] Significantly, Peter also calls the Gentiles 'disciples' (Acts 15.10).

And then we have Jacob. He refers to Peter by his Jewish name, Simeon.[57] He quotes from the Hebrew Scriptures, from the book of Amos (and also a fragment from Isaiah), but the version he uses is the Greek translation, the Septuagint. This is a speech which carefully, diplomatically, straddles the different ethnic groups who are present.

As a leader he must have been a pragmatist. He recognises that Gentiles have already become part of the church. Paul's mission was really just Peter's vision and Philip's Ethiopian convert writ large. You could not put the cork back in the bottle. What could be lived in the holy city of Jerusalem – a city of Torah observance and temple worship – could not possibly be lived out in the emperor-worshipping cities of the Græco-Roman world.

Perhaps more important to Jacob, though, was the belief that this was a pivotal moment, the fulfilment of messianic prophecy. One of the signs of the messianic age was that the Gentiles would be called, without needing to obey the law. This is why he quotes from Amos and Isaiah. Jacob's speech is a statement of messianic promise. The time has come, he says: time for a new building, one that has room for the Gentiles.

The one truly distinctive thing about the Jewish believers in Jerusalem is that they claimed that Jacob's brother – Jesus of Nazareth – was the Messiah. So this is a direct challenge: 'Do you really believe that?' asks Jacob. 'Because if my brother was the Messiah, then according to the prophets, the Gentiles have to come in.'

Even with all that, his conclusion remains something of a compromise. He says that the Gentiles should 'not be troubled', but then he goes on to make stipulations nonetheless. They don't have to be circumcised, but they do have to avoid contact with anything polluted by idols, and keep away from 'fornication and from whatever has been strangled and from blood' (Acts 15.20).

There has been a lot of debate as to what these restrictions mean (and which version of them is the earliest, because some manuscripts of Acts have different versions). They seem to be connected to idolatry, and particularly activities associated with temples. The first refers directly to idols and pollution through their rituals, but sexual immorality also has links with idolatry. The word is *porneia*, which in its basic form means 'prostitution', and often specifically sacred prostitution. Other references in Revelation link the word with Rome and the worship of gods and cults.[58] Pagan temples were associated in the Jewish mind with sexual acts.

Similarly, the apparently odd mention of things which are strangled may have to do with a description of how pagan sacrifices were prepared. And while the restriction on blood reflects the Jewish belief that the blood contains the animal's life force, again there may be a reference to the pagan priest tasting the blood of the sacrifice.[59] In this reading, the pollution of idolatry is a kind of atmosphere that infects those who go near temples. This is not just about the meat from idol worship, but about avoiding the temples altogether. Gregory of Nyssa talks of 'the pollution around the idols, the disgusting smell and smoke of sacrifices, the defiling gore about the altars and the taint of blood from the offerings'.[60] Read in this light, then, what Jacob asks his Gentile brothers and sisters to do is to 'keep away from pagan temples'.

This might seem easy, but would have been quite demanding for the Gentiles. Temples weren't just places of worship, they were places where people met to socialise and do business. They had guilds and associations and other such groups attached to them. So this meant cutting out a large chunk of what was for the Gentiles an important ancient form of social networking.

So was this a victory for Paul? Several scholars have questioned whether Paul really got what he wanted. They point out that Paul's later statements run counter to the decree. In 1 Corinthians, Paul outlines what can only be described as a 'don't ask, don't tell' policy:

> Eat whatever is sold in the meat market without raising any question on the ground of conscience, for 'the earth and its fullness are the Lord's.' If an unbeliever invites you to a meal and you are disposed to go, eat whatever is set before you without raising any question on the ground of conscience. But if someone says to you, 'This has been offered in sacrifice,' then do not eat it, out of consideration for the one who informed you, and for the sake of conscience – I mean the other's conscience, not your own. For why should my liberty be subject to the judgement of someone else's conscience? If I partake with thankfulness, why should I be denounced because of that for which I give thanks? (1 Cor. 10.25–30)

Paul also repeatedly denies that dietary laws are binding on Gentile believers.[61]

Against that, Paul is keenly aware that not everyone feels that way. So in the end he, too, compromises. His argument in 1 Corinthians 8 basically runs, 'Look, you and I know that idols aren't real. But others don't think that way. So don't cause them any grief: just don't eat it.'

The *Didache* adopts similar sentiments, but clarifies the rule about meat sacrificed to idols. Interestingly, it too talks about the 'yoke':

> For if you are able to bear the whole yoke of the Lord, you will be perfect. But if you are not able, then do what you can. Now concerning food, bear what you are able, but in any case keep strictly away from meat sacrificed to idols, for it involves the worship of dead gods.[62]

That last phrase is the key. The decision of the Jerusalem meeting is not primarily about diet. It's about involvement in the world of dead gods.

So Paul took this decree on board, but he sat lightly to it. One of the reasons why he felt able to do so must have been that his opponents ignored it as well. Jewish Christians never let up on Paul: they opposed his work right to the end. He is repeatedly forced to defend his Jewish orthodoxy and expends considerable energy on taking up a collection for the church in Judea, simply to prove the loyalty of the churches in Greece and Asia Minor.

The real truth of the Jerusalem meeting is that it was a score draw. It wasn't a victory for either side. Paul didn't get everything he wanted, but he got enough. It gave him the freedom to go and continue his work in the Gentile world. His opponents, on the other hand, never gave up the idea that he was an enemy of orthodoxy. When Paul returns to Jerusalem eight years later, he still finds enemies spreading rumours about him within the church (Acts 21.20–21).

There is evidence that the animosity against Paul continued in some Jewish Christian circles for a long time. Centuries later, Irenaeus writes about a splinter group called the Ebionites who

> ...use the Gospel according to Matthew only, and repudiate the Apostle Paul, maintaining that he was an apostate from the law. As

to the prophetical writings, they endeavour to expound them in a somewhat singular manner: they practise circumcision, persevere in the observance of those customs which are enjoined by the law, and are so Judaic in their style of life, that they even adore Jerusalem as if it were the house of God.[63]

So the idea that the 'Jerusalem Council' settled the matter proves not really to be true. We shouldn't be surprised. What church council, official or unofficial, ever really settled things one way or another? In the centre ground, minds may be changed, but out on the edges, among the true believers, the fight continues.

So the decision is made. A letter is written: an official communiqué to the believers in Antioch and Syria and Cilicia. But while Paul and Barnabas are delegated to take the letter to Antioch, they are also accompanied by two delegates from the Jerusalem church: 'Judas called Barsabbas' and Silas. Barsabbas and Silas are the representatives of the council, not Paul and Barnabas. It is they who have the authority here.

Of Judas we know nothing more, but Silas – or Silvanus, to give the Latin version of his name – was to become a trusted companion of Paul. Paul calls him an apostle, which means that he was a witness of the resurrection of Jesus. Like Paul, he was a Roman citizen (Acts 16.37–38), and he acted as a secretary for some of Paul's letters.[64]

Luke records that both men exercised more than just a delivery boy role. They were prophets, who spent time in Antioch after the letter had been read out, encouraging and strengthening the believers there, and after that they were 'sent off in peace' by the church at Antioch (Acts 15.33).

Peter's involvement at the Jerusalem meeting is his last appearance in the book of Acts. We don't really know where he goes from here. We know from Paul's letters, though, that Peter went travelling. In AD 54, Paul talks about Peter (here called Cephas) being accompanied by his wife on the road:

Do we not have the right to be accompanied by a believing wife, as do the other apostles and the brothers of the Lord and Cephas? (1 Cor. 9.5)

As we shall see, one of his stops included Corinth. There's also a clue to some of the places he went in the opening of 1 Peter, the letter he wrote from Rome. He writes to Christians in five areas of Asia Minor: Pontus, Cappadocia, Galatia, Asia and Bithynia. A person travelling overland towards Rome from Antioch in Syria would naturally pass through these areas. So the likelihood is that, over the years, Peter made his way west, visiting established churches and planting new congregations, teaching, preaching, building up congregations, sharing stories of his experiences as an elder of the church and a 'witness of the sufferings of Christ' (1 Pet. 5.1).

The rest is lost. Peter leaves the pages of Acts around AD 49, and from there his movements and activities are largely unknown. He peeps out from the mists of history, fleeting, fragmentary. We will meet him once more, walking a road into Rome. But there is a lot more travelling to do before that.

6. Macedonia AD 49–50

'They parted company'

Paul's initial plan, following the kind-of-successful outcome of the Jerusalem meeting, is for him and Barnabas to retrace their steps. He wants to consolidate the gains they made in Galatia and, no doubt, to reinforce the strong message of the letter that he wrote them.

But things have changed. It has been suggested that the split is between the radical Paul and 'the more conservative' Barnabas.[1] But they teach together in Antioch for some time with many others (Acts 15.35). The issue is not Barnabas's conservatism. It's his relative, John Mark. Whatever the original cause of John Mark's 'desertion', Barnabas believes him to be a reformed character, now fully aligned to their purposes and mission. Paul disagrees. Maybe there were other undercurrents as well. Paul may have felt let down by Barnabas's behaviour at Antioch. Despite the resolution of the Jewish council, it must have driven a wedge between them at the time – and perhaps in the longer term too.

So they agree to part. The disagreement becomes 'so sharp' that it severs the partnership (Acts 15.36–40). This is not quite the last we hear of Barnabas, however. We know that he carried on travelling, talking, encouraging. In this instance he and John Mark return to Cyprus – presumably after the sailing season starts again in AD 49, and assuming that the Jerusalem meeting took place around AD 48/49. Luke uses a characteristic link phrase, 'After some days', but that could mean months.

Paul decides to head north by land and to revisit the churches he founded during the previous year. But first he needs to find a new companion. He chooses Silas, who has to be recalled from Jerusalem (15.33). Once Silas arrives, they head off.

According to Acts, Paul and Silas go through Syria and Cilicia, strengthening the churches. As we have seen, we don't actually have any account in Acts of Paul officially proclaiming the word of the Lord in those areas; so Paul was revisiting churches that he – or other unknown Christians – had established before he ever began working with Barnabas. Once again we can see that the account of the growth of the church in Acts is a bit blurred around the edges.

Geographically, these churches lie along the route of Paul's journey back to Galatia. Although Barnabas and Mark sail to Cyprus, Paul and Silas travel overland. Perhaps the time spent recalling Silas from Jerusalem means that the shipping routes have closed for the year. Paul is too seasoned a traveller to risk travelling by sea after October. When he travels at that time of year in the future, it is not of his own volition.

Their journey takes them from Antioch round to Tarsus and then north through the Cilician Gates. Paul's purpose is twofold: he wants to strengthen and encourage the churches that he established on his previous trip, and he is also delivering to them the decision of the Jerusalem council (Acts 16.4).

We don't know when Paul and Silas arrived in Derbe and Lystra: the journey itself would have taken a few weeks, but if they were stopping at churches and Christian communities along the way it may have taken them into the new year before they arrived.

In the meantime the church in Lystra has been growing. There are people here whom Paul has not met, one of whom is a young believer called Timothy. His mother, Eunice, is a follower, but not, apparently, his father, whom Luke merely describes as a Greek (Acts 16.1). In a later letter from Paul, we discover that his grandmother, Lois, was also a believer.

Timothy is a rising star. He is well spoken of not only by the believers in Lystra, his home city, but also in Iconium. Paul recognises something in Timothy that could be of use to the wider church and he takes him on as a kind of apprentice. But before that, as a kind of preparation, Paul does something perplexing, even hypocritical: he has Timothy circumcised. It seems completely at odds with all that we've just been over. Why would he do such a thing?

Acts explains it thus: 'because of the Jews who were in those places, for they all knew that his father was a Greek' (16.3). Timothy came from a mixed marriage: his father was Greek, his mother Jewish. According to the Mishnah, the son of a Jewish mother was considered to be Jewish.[2] Although the Mishnah dates from the third century, Paul's actions imply that the same understanding of Jewish lineage held sway in his time. And the Mishnah records the rabbinic traditions of the Pharisees, exactly the kind of traditions in which Paul had been schooled in Jerusalem. The fact that Timothy was not circumcised clearly indicates that his father had opposed such an action.[3] He might have let his wife raise Timothy as a Jew, but he had not allowed him to be a full child of the covenant. The boy had been raised as a God-fearer rather than a full Jew.

Paul is largely indifferent to circumcision (Gal. 5.6; 6.15). Later he denies that it is any use whatsoever (1 Cor. 7.19) – but there is a pragmatic and even strategic motive behind his actions. Timothy is caught between worlds. To orthodox Jews he would have been regarded as an apostate, a renegade. He had not obeyed the commandments of God. So, pragmatically, Paul is regularising Timothy's Jewish status. But Paul clearly has plans for the boy. He can see his abilities and his potential. It will be helpful for Timothy's work if he is 'above suspicion', seen to be acting in a manner consistent with his Jewish heritage. Timothy's circumcision will facilitate his ministry among Jewish Christians. 'To the Jews I became as a Jew, in order to win Jews,' Paul wrote (1 Cor. 9.20). In that sense, what looks hypocritical is actually the natural outcome of Paul's philosophy. Paul is often portrayed as outspoken, dogmatic, unable to compromise. But a close look at his life shows how often he was prepared to put non-critical things aside in order to further the cause of the gospel.

Paul's journey to Corinth c. AD 49-50

1 Following the Jerusalem meeting, Paul returns to Antioch.
2 He splits with Barnabas over the issue of John Mark. They go to Cyprus.
3 Paul is joined by Silas and they travel through Syria and Cilicia.
4 At Lystra, Paul recruits Timothy.
5 Paul is stopped by the spirit from speaking in Asia. At the border of Mysia he is
    prevented from crossing into Bithynia.
6 At Troas Paul has a vision of a man from Macedonia asking for help. They are joined
    by Luke and cross to Neapolis.
7 At Philippi, Lydia is converted. Paul and Silas are imprisoned and released after the
    earthquake. Luke remains in Philippi.
8 After trouble in Thessalonica and Beroea, Paul travels on alone to Athens.
9 Paul goes to Corinth where he finds Priscilla and Aquila. Silas and Timothy arrive
    from Macedonia.

PONTUS

BITHYNIA

PHRYGIA

GALATIA

CAPPADOCIA

Pisidian
Antioch

lphia
Hierapolis

Colossae   PISIDIA

Iconium

Lystra **4**

Derbe

3

Tarsus

Perga

Attalia   PAMPHYLIA

Side

CILICIA

CIA

Myra

Seleucia   Antioch

2

CYPRUS   Salamis

Paphos

SYRIA

1

Sidon

Damascus

Tyre

Caesarea
Philippi

Ptolemais

Caesarea

Samaria

Joppa

Jerusalem   Jericho

JUDEA

ria

More than that, I think there is a real sense in which Paul is making Timothy like himself, consciously moulding Timothy into his own likeness. In letters written later in his life, Paul calls Timothy his child (1 Tim. 1.2, 18; 2 Tim. 1.2; 2.1). He describes him as his son (Phil. 2.20–22). So Paul moulds Timothy in his own image, makes him a Jew to win Jews, preparing him to carry on the family business. Paul is not so much obeying the law, then, as succession-planning.

So Acts 16.1–5 shows Paul revisiting familiar ground. But once he has checked up on his churches and delivered the council's letter, he does not return to Antioch. Instead he pushes on into the interior, further than he has gone before.

The timing of this is not coincidental. One gets the feeling that Paul wants to take the opportunity afforded by the Jerusalem statement. The more Gentile churches there are, the harder it will be for the Judaistic faction to roll back this decision and impose their rules. He is building up a critical mass.

This move is typical of Paul's travels in Acts, though. His visits 'home' – to Jerusalem and Antioch – act as springboards to ever longer, more daring journeys. It's a kind of cycle: Paul goes to Jerusalem, he 'obtains approval' for some kind of trip, and then he's off. The first Jerusalem visit is followed by his trip to Galatia. The second visit – the apostolic meeting – is followed by an even longer journey, which will take him to Greece and Illyricum. His final visit to Jerusalem will be followed by the longest journey of all. Every visit to the mother ship results in him going further than before – and not just geographically.

'A man of Macedonia'

Timothy joins Paul and Silas. Luke says that they travelled through 'the region of Phrygia and Galatia', which some have seen as implying that he went into north Galatia at this point. But the phrase refers to what was known as Phrygian Galatia and describes the southern part of the region as a whole.[4]

The plan is to push on into Asia, the western part of what is now Turkey. This is the obvious direction. They can travel along the main Roman road to Ephesus, the seat of the Roman governor of Asia. It makes perfect strategic sense.

But it doesn't happen. According to Luke, they are 'forbidden by the Holy Spirit to speak the word in Asia' (Acts 16.6). Strange. Paul isn't stopped from going through Asia, but he is held back from speaking in some way. Along with Ephesus, the province of Asia contained cities like Sardis, Philadelphia, Pergamum, Tralles, Laodicea, Hierapolis – cities which would later house significant churches. But for some reason Paul is not able to speak out in any of them.

In fact, this entire section of the journey seems fraught with difficulties and frustrations. Paul diverts north-west, to Mysia, the westernmost region of the province of Asia, intending to go north and enter the province of Bithynia. But again, he is stopped, this time by the 'Spirit of Jesus' (Acts 16.7), the only use of this phrase in Acts.

They are strange phrases. It's possible that Paul simply doesn't feel right about the mission. He has, after all, just left a region where he felt confident and at home and where he had previously tasted success (albeit with the usual side order of persecution and violence). But the language is emphatic: Paul is 'forbidden', 'not allowed'. It's clear that he wants to speak to people there, but his plans are vetoed.

It's hard to imagine that he would not have found some opportunity to talk in those regions. There were several places which, on the face of it, would have been ideally suited to Paul's approach: Nicomedia in Bithynia, for example, which had a large Jewish colony.[5] Of course, he may have had a vision or a prophecy ordering him to keep silent, but again, it's hard to understand why this would happen.

Perhaps what we are talking about here is an event, or series of events, which he interpreted as divine intervention. Or prohibition. Something occurred which stopped Paul preaching the gospel in these regions, something which Paul and his entourage interpreted as the action of the Holy Spirit or Jesus himself.

Illness, maybe. After all, it's difficult to imagine anything else that would stop Paul. Put him in prison, and he preaches to jailers. Beat him up, and he just carries on. Put him on trial, and he uses the opportunity to preach the gospel. But what if he simply *couldn't* speak? What if there was an illness, or attack, something which stopped him physically speaking – then Paul and his companions might see it as a divine act. Paul himself talks of his 'thorn in the flesh' in such spiritual terms. It's a 'messenger from Satan' which Paul begs to be taken away, but which the Lord decides should remain.

In that case, why keep going? Because he does: after these divinely ordained setbacks, Paul arrives at Troas. Why go there? The answer may lie in Paul's reading of the Bible – particularly the book of Isaiah.

As we have seen, one of the background themes of the Jerusalem council – informing Jacob's speech, certainly – was that the inclusion of the Gentiles was part of God's eschatological plan. The advent of the Messiah opened the way for Gentiles to be made acceptable. The early church got this idea from the book of Isaiah, which became one of their key texts. And the book of Isaiah was certainly important for Paul. He cites the book 21 times in his letters and some of the language he uses about himself echoes this most messianic of books.[6]

Writing to the Galatians, Paul talks about how God 'set me apart before I was born and called me through his grace ... so that I might proclaim him among the Gentiles' (Gal. 1.15–16). This prophetic calling echoes words in Isaiah, who talks of a servant 'called before I was born' and formed 'in the womb to be his servant'. The servant will be 'a light to the nations, that my salvation may reach to the end of the earth' (Isa. 49.1, 5, 6).

But one chapter in particular may have informed Paul's strategy. The end of the book speaks about individuals – 'survivors', Isaiah calls them – going out and preaching to the Gentiles (Isa. 66.19). This, according to Westermann, 'is the first unequivocal mention of mission in the sense that we understand it: the sending out of individuals to distant nations to proclaim the glory of God'.[7]

Isaiah lists the nations to which these people will go. Paul used the Septuagint – the Greek translation of the Hebrew Scriptures – where Isaiah 66.19 runs:

And I will leave signs upon them, and from them I will send forth those who are saved to the nations, to Tharsis and Phoud and Loud and Mosoch and Thobel and to Greece and to the islands far away

– those who have not heard my name or seen my glory, and they shall declare my glory among the nations.[8]

In the Hebrew text there is a slightly different list: Tarshish, Put, Lud, Tubal, Javan. Mosoch is missing. Josephus identified Tharsis or Tarshish with Tarsus.[9] Old Testament Put (Phoud) was identified with North Africa, specifically Cyrene. Lud (Loud) might equally be identified with Africa, but in Genesis 10.22 it seems to refer to the Lydians of Asia Minor. Josephus certainly identifies Lud with Lydia.[10] The Meshechians were identified by Josephus as the Cappadocians, while rabbinic sources identified Meshech (Moshoch) with Mysia.[11] Josephus identifies Tubal (Thobel) with the Iberes – but he also uses the same word for people living in the Caucasus.[12] Rabbinic literature followed the latter identification, identifying Tubal with Bithynia. The Hebrew text has Javan for the final destination, which was translated as Greece in the Septuagint. Josephus believed that Javan was the ancestor of all Greeks.[13] But in rabbinic literature, the rabbis seem to have identified Javan with Macedonia.[14]

So it's a bit complicated, but taken altogether, to a Greek-speaking, Septuagint-reading, first-century Jew like Paul, Isaiah 66.19 suggests that the word of the Lord will go out from Jerusalem to Tarsus, Cyrene, Lydia in Asia Minor, Cappadocia or Mysia, the Caucasus or Bithynia and then Greece or Macedonia and then to the end of the world.[15]

And this, broadly, is what Paul has seen happening. By AD 49 the mission has already infiltrated Tarsus and Cyrene and Lydia and Cappadocia. Now Mysia and Bithynia are closed to him, so next on the list has to be either Greece or Macedonia. If Paul does understand his travels as part of this eschatological pattern, it might explain why he goes to Troas. Troas is the gateway to Macedonia and Greece. He is following Isaiah; he is being obedient to God's plan.

And in Troas, Paul has a vision.

'The beloved physician'

Troas – or Alexandria Troas to give it its proper name – was an important transit town. Augustus made it a Roman colony and populated the city with Roman colonists. From Troas it was a simple boat journey across the Aegean Sea to Neapolis and thence to Philippi, where you could hook onto another major Roman road: the Egnatian Way, the main route across Greece.

We know that there was a Christian community in Troas by AD 57. It may have been founded by Paul on a return visit. Writing to the Corinthians around AD 54, Paul talks about arriving in Troas and finding a door opened 'to proclaim the good news of Christ' (2 Cor. 2.12). But at this point, as he first arrives in the city, Paul is uncertain and unsure, prevented from speaking where he wants to, held back from going where he wishes.

The Spirit is guiding Paul's steps, however, and his next, momentous, step comes as a result of a vision. Paul sees a man from Macedonia saying, 'Come over to Macedonia and help us' (Acts 16.9). Since the vision happens at night, it is probably a dream, although its nature is not defined. But it was commonplace in antiquity for people to receive divine guidance in dreams.

How did Paul know it was a Macedonian? Was it perhaps the most famous Macedonian of them all? Alexander the Great was well known from numerous statues and inscriptions.[16] (Mind you, whoever it was, he does say, 'Come over to Macedonia,' which is a bit of a giveaway.)[17] Perhaps, though, the man in the dream was someone closer to home. Immediately after the vision, the first of the 'we' passages starts – when Luke starts to talk in the first person plural. In Acts 16.9, Paul has the vision and in the very next verse, Luke writes, 'When he had seen the vision, we immediately tried to cross to Macedonia...' So clearly Luke has joined Paul at Troas.

It's possible that Luke himself was the 'man from Macedonia' – that he had met the group in Troas and then reappeared in Paul's dream.[18] Why, though, might Luke have been there? Perhaps this is to do with the way Paul was stopped from speaking in Bithynia and Asia. If Paul was ill, then maybe Luke was there in his official capacity, as a physician. Or maybe Luke was the confirmation of the dream. Maybe Paul had his dream, then woke up the next morning to find – a bit like Peter with the emissaries from Cornelius – that there was a man from Macedonia at the door waiting to see him.

Whatever the reason, Luke now joins Paul on his travels. And from this point on, the times when Luke is accompanying Paul are marked by what are known as the 'we' passages. These passages have been the source of much argument and debate among New Testament scholars. It has been suggested that they are fabrications, that the author has simply taken accounts of sea journeys and inserted himself into the action to add historical credibility to the account.[19] The idea of invention creates far more problems than it solves, however. If Luke is inventing things, then why doesn't he make a great deal more of his presence? If he's trying to claim that he was a bosom buddy of Paul, why not insert himself into other sections and stories? Why does he dip out at Philippi? Why does he just suddenly appear here in Troas? If he's just inventing stuff, why not fill in more of the gaps? After all, there are plenty of other spaces where he could have filled in the blanks with a bit of well-crafted historical fiction (the two-year imprisonment in Caesarea, for example). But he doesn't – because he wasn't there.

The best solution is simply to accept the fact that the 'we' (and non-'we') passages indicate that Luke was not an ever-present companion. The simplest explanation is the obvious one: Luke was there. And later, writing Acts, he relies on both first-hand notes and some kind of travel diary or itinerary of his own. That is why those passages are so detailed. That is why they fizz with marvel and excitement and evince a concern to note down the details accurately. It includes, in fact, the single most detailed account of a sea voyage in the whole of ancient literature. So if it's cobbled together from other accounts, it's an amazing job.

But all of this raises a huge number of questions. How did Luke know where Paul was? Where was Luke before this? Was he already a Christian? If so, what was he doing in Troas? How did he come to join Paul? Who was he?

There are only three mentions of Luke in the rest of the New Testament, all from the time of Paul's imprisonment in Rome.

▷ In 2 Timothy 4.11, Paul reports that only Luke is with him and he wants Mark sent to join them.
▷ In Philemon 24, Paul sends greetings from himself and his fellow workers, including John Mark and Luke.
▷ In Colossians 4.14, Paul sends greetings from 'Luke, the beloved physician'. In this passage Paul implies that Luke is not 'of the circumcision', i.e. that he was not a Jew.

So we know from these references that Luke was with Paul in Rome, that he knew John Mark, that he was a physician and (probably) a Gentile. That's all we know. But we can go a bit further than that. As we saw in the discussion of authorship, he was a fluent writer of Greek, which displays some level of education. And he was comfortable with addressing high-status individuals, although he himself was not one of them. He was familiar with the Septuagint – the Greek translation of the Old Testament – which may indicate that he was a God-fearer at the synagogue before converting to Christianity.[20]

Then there is his name: Luke. This is derived from the Latin name Lucius. It suggests that Luke was a freedman who had taken on the Latin name of his master. This would fit with him being a doctor. Doctors were often Greek and also, frequently, slaves or ex-slaves. They were household retainers, in-house physicians, educated slaves who learned some medicine and attended to the health of the household. When he was freed – when, perhaps, his master Lucian or Lucius died – Luke took his name and carried on with his profession. Certainly in addressing Theophilus, Luke uses the same form of address that subordinates use to Roman superiors throughout Acts (e.g. Acts 23.26; 24.2). And he depicts craftsmen and artisans in a positive light.

There is evidence that shows freed slaves becoming very successful as physicians. An inscription in Assisi records the work of Publius Decimus Eros Merula: 'freedman of Publius, clinical doctor, surgeon, oculist, member of the board of six. For his freedom he paid 50,000 sesterces. For his membership on the board of six he contributed to the community 2,000 sesterces.'[21]

At the time he joined Paul, Luke was probably living in Philippi, in Greece. This is because the 'we' passages in Acts start in Troas (just across the sea from Greece), take us to Philippi and then stop there. Then they pick up again some time later when Paul returns to Philippi. So the likelihood is that Luke came across to Troas to meet Paul, travelled back with him to Philippi and stayed there, rejoining Paul when he returned later. Philippi was a Roman colony, populated by many ex-soldiers and freed slaves.

Whether he originally came from there is debatable. First, if he was already a Christian but came from Philippi, there is the tricky question of how he came to be converted, if the gospel had not yet reached that place. The clear inference in Acts is that Paul plants the first church in Philippi.

There is a strong early church tradition that Luke came from Antioch. An ancient prologue to Luke's Gospel, dating from the end of the second century AD, describes Luke as a 'Syrian from Antioch'.[22] If this is the case, then it makes more sense. Luke could have become a convert in Antioch before seeking out Paul in Troas.

This, again, is not improbable. People travelled long distances in Paul's day. Just as Paul plied his trade from city to city, wherever he found himself, there's no reason to assume that Luke didn't do likewise. Inscriptions show that both male and female physicians were active in this area at this time, and some of them were clearly itinerant.[23] So it's perfectly possible that Luke originated from Antioch, but had come to live in Philippi.

Putting all this together – the way that Paul was 'stopped' from preaching in Asia and Bithynia, the overarching eschatological travel itinerary, the vision of the man in Macedonia and the sudden appearance of Luke – a theory emerges. Paul was ill. The illness was such that it stopped him from working in Asia and Bithynia. Instead the group headed on to Troas, which was the next major stop on Paul's travel plan – possibly inspired by his interpretation of Isaiah 66.19. At Troas they arranged to see Luke, whom Paul knew to be in the region, since he had got to know him in Antioch. The meeting had been arranged some time before, because of Luke's links in Macedonia. But Paul's illness brought it forward and meant that Luke hastened to Troas to meet him.

At that meeting, perhaps doubts were expressed about the general advisability or Paul's physical capability to head across to Macedonia. But those doubts were put aside by Paul's nocturnal vision. The people in Macedonia needed help. On a trip which had up until now been disrupted by the Holy Spirit, this was a clear call: all systems go.

'A leading city of the district of Macedonia'

The crossing from Troas to Neapolis was fast: it could be done in two days. Sailing in ancient times was the fastest method for long distances, but it was not without peril. Sailors in those days relied on the stars to chart their course, or in many cases simply navigated by recognising landmarks on the coastline.[24] Paul's itineraries reflect this. After a day's sailing from Troas, they make an overnight stop on Samothrace, a mountainous, highly visible island, which was an obvious stopping point for ships sailing in the northern Aegean.[25] Paul could have tarried on Samothrace, which had a large and lively population, but he didn't stop there for long, nor at the large island of Thassos, both of which might have proved fertile ground for the gospel. His sights were set on Macedonia.[26]

The winds were obviously with them, since they completed their journey the next day. They landed at Neapolis, on the Macedonian coast. As the best harbour east of Thessalonica, Neapolis was an important commercial centre, but the founding of Philippi had reduced its significance. Paul would have disembarked from the boat and walked up the main street, with the three-tiered aqueduct in the background. Again, he could have stopped at Neapolis, but he didn't. He wanted to get to Philippi.

It would have taken Paul and his company about a day's walk to reach Philippi. The route was straightforward: the *via Egnatia*. This was one of the most important roads of the Roman Empire: the main highway ran for 535 Roman miles (493 English miles) right across Macedonia and connected Rome with its eastern provinces.[27] It was begun soon after the Romans conquered Macedonia and ran from Dyrrachium on the west coast of Greece (in modern Albania) to Neapolis on the north-east coast and then on to Byzantium.[28]

Macedonia had been conquered by the Romans in c. 168 BC. The general Aemilius Paullus had declared that 'the Macedonians were to be free people, possessing their cities and fields as before, enjoying their own lands, and electing annual magistrates; and they were to pay the Roman people half the tribute they had been paying to the king'. A good move. The new masters charged less tax than the old. But don't let the lower tax rate fool you: Rome *was* the master. In a canny move, Aemilius Paullus divided Macedonia into four separate districts. At once, the political unity of Macedonia was destroyed. Divide and rule. Keep the regions apart, play them against one another. The ancient military might of Macedonia, home of Philip and of Alexander the Great, was effectively neutered.[29] Roman control was further reinforced in AD 44, when Claudius placed Macedonia and Achaia under direct control of the Senate in Rome.

They also planted colonies in the region. Colonies like Philippi. Or, to give it its full name, *Colonia Iulia Augusta Philippensis*: 'Philippi, colony of Julian Augustus'. It was named after the masters of Macedonia, the Julian family. Not that it started out that way: it was originally founded by Mark Antony, who in 42 BC granted the land there to veterans of the Roman army. When Antony was defeated, Augustus refounded the colony and it was given the new name.

When Paul arrived, sometime around AD 50, he found a mostly Roman population, including many veterans, and later *liberti* – freedmen and women – who traded as merchants and artisans.[30] It followed that its way of life was more Roman than Greek. Augustus also gave the city *ius italicum* – a kind of honorary Italian status. This gave it legal status as part of Italy, even though it was hundreds of miles away. It was the highest honour a provincial city could attain. This was classic Roman policy: one of the ways they established and strengthened their Empire was to found colonies, little lumps of Rome scattered throughout the Empire.

Colonies could be very different from the region surrounding them. In founding colonies, Rome was essentially planting settlers in occupied territory. The process was simple and has been followed by many occupying nations over the centuries: soldiers would arrive, local residents would be thrown off their land, foreign settlers would move in. This even happened in some regions in Italy, with the refugees flooding to the capital city in distress:

> They came to Rome in clouds, young and old, women and children, to the forum and the temples, uttering lamentations, saying that they had done no wrong for which they, Italians, should be driven from their fields and their hearthstones, like people conquered in war.[31]

If that was true of colonies in Italy, how much harder must it have been for the Macedonians. Philippi was built on the principle of dispossession.

The Romans understood that certain parts of the Empire were great and magnificent cultures, Greece being perhaps the highest example. But for all their heritage and history, such cultures were not Rome. The Romans saw themselves as the perfecters of these people. Thus the colonies were centres of Roman influence from which the humanising, civilising influence of Rome – the *humanitas,* as it was termed – could filter out into the surrounding barbarism. In the colonies, ignorant, backward peoples could taste a bit of Rome: hear some Latin, partake in the imperial cult, watch the gladiators or the animals, see Roman institutions in action.[32] Cicero wrote:

> Africans, Spaniards, and Gauls are repugnant wherever they are to be found, because they stand for everything that is gross and barbarous in humanity. People like the Scythians are even less acceptable. The Roman, on the other hand, is infinitely superior in any number of ways, and he never forgets it.[33]

For all their confidence, in some ways Roman rule in Greece had little effect on the civilisation of the region. In fact, to some extent it went the other way. Roman law was supreme, but in practice, local laws and structures held sway. In Greece, Latin never took root, apart from in a very few areas. Immigrant families from Rome soon lost the language – within a couple of generations. Greek remained the common language of the Empire.

Philippi, however, was a place where the Roman way of life had really taken hold. Philippi wore its Roman status with pride. It was run on Roman law and followed Roman customs and principles. Over 80 per cent of the inscriptions found in the city which date from the first century are in Latin, not Greek, double the proportion in Pisidian Antioch, another Roman colony visited by Paul.[34]

Philippi was, probably, Macedonia's most important town commercially. Luke describes it, literally, as the first city of the area. Technically, that was Thessalonica, the capital of Macedonia, where the proconsul was based.[35] Perhaps Luke is just proud of the town where he lived. Or perhaps he was describing the attitude of the Philippians. Philippi was a Roman colony, Thessalonica was not. Roman colonies thought of themselves as superior to the other provincial Greek cities. Philippi had been founded by Augustus and given his name. *Of course* it was the first city.

The debt to Augustus was reflected in religious life. In the forum was a large temple dedicated to the imperial family and a monument dedicated to Olivia, the wife of Augustus, who had been deified by Claudius. The streets leading to the forum were – the *via Egnatia* excepted – crowded and densely populated. Inside the walls of the city, the streets were only between two and three metres wide and villas and *insulae* – Roman apartment blocks – were built right up to the edge of the forum.[36] Forum apart, there wasn't much open space inside Philippi. For that people had to go out of the city.

Paul and his company entered by the eastern gate, where the *via Egnatia* came in from Neapolis, to run straight through the city, leaving from the western gate on the opposite side, known as the 'Krenides Gate'. And it was probably a little distance outside this gate, in the modern village of Krenides where he encountered a group of women praying by a stream. The area is now known by the name of one of these women: Lydia.

'A dealer in purple'

Synagogue means 'gathering'. Paul's habit was always to go to the synagogue first, but in some places that would not mean entering a building. In Philippi the Jews seem to have met out in the open, by the river. The water would have been used for bathing and washing, for the ritual cleansing which the Jews practised. (Perhaps the choice of a river for their washing indicates a sympathy with the Pharisees, who preferred to use running water when they could.)

It's possible that the lack of a synagogue means there were only a small number of Jews in Philippi. Or, in this very Roman colony, perhaps the attitude towards Jews was harsher than elsewhere. Some Roman colony cities banned foreign cults from operating inside the city walls.[37] The women had gathered to recite the *shema*, to pray, to hear readings from the Law and the Prophets, to discuss Scriptures. That week, they had an unusual guest teacher. Paul and Silas sit down and talk to the women, and Lydia becomes a Christian.

Lydia is a significant figure. She is often called the first convert in Europe, but this is an anachronism: the Macedonians had no idea they were in what we now call Europe, and culturally, they had more in common with the Greeks on the other side of the Aegean than with anyone in Gaul or Iberia. Anyway, Lydia isn't from Macedonia. She comes from Thyatira, on the other side of the Troad, in Asia. Like Paul and Luke, she is a travelling worker. At some point, she made the same journey across from Asia into Macedonia. Indeed, Lydia is the name of a district in Asia. (A bit like calling your daughter Chelsea.) This name may indicate that she was once a slave and took the name of the place where she worked upon being given her freedom. There is inscriptional evidence for the name, including a Julia Lydia who lived in Sardis.

Nor is she Jewish, despite the fact that she has met with the others for prayer. Luke describes her as 'a worshipper of God' (Acts 16.14), a *sebomene*, a Gentile term which Luke uses rather than the more Jewish term 'God-fearer'. We are in Gentile territory now.

And, fittingly in this Roman world, Lydia is a dealer in luxury goods. She is described as a *porphuropolis*, a 'dyer or dealer in purple cloth'. Purple was, for centuries, the most valuable cloth in the ancient world. Its cost came from the labour-intensive nature of the purple dye, which was produced from the shells of murex – sea snails. These were found most notably in Phoenicia, around Tyre and Sidon. You could also use the madder plant to produce the dye. Purple was the imperial colour, as the most expensive material. This was a high-status business.

The opportunities for women in the Roman world were heavily proscribed, but Macedonia was somewhat different – and certainly not like Palestine. This was a place where women could have some status and power. Apollodorus, writing in the fourth century BC, says, 'We have courtesans for pleasure, handmaidens for the day-to-day care of the body, wives to bear legitimate children and to be a trusted guardian of things in the house.'[38] But in Macedonia in subsequent centuries, women had attained greater status and more political power, and Roman women built on this foundation. Technically, of course, Roman women moved from being subject to their father to being subject to their husband: 'Never,' wrote Livy, 'while their men survive, is feminine subjection shaken off.'[39] Nevertheless, many Roman women did, if not shake it off, then rattle it a little loose. In the early Roman Empire, women could be powerful. They could use their wealth and social status to act as patrons. There are records of women holding civic office. Even further down the social scale in Roman society, women could find work in a variety of occupations: as midwives, physicians, musicians, grocery sellers, woolworkers and weavers, and in a number of trades. Here's an inscription from a proud son of the Augustan period:

> My dearest mother deserved greater praise than all the others, since in modesty, propriety, chastity, obedience, woolworking, industry and honour she was on an equal level with other good women, nor did she take second place to any woman in virtue, work and wisdom in times of danger.[40]

Lydia is one such woman. No man is mentioned: she has her own household. Most probably she is a widow, although it is possible she is a single woman. And it is in her house that the church starts to meet. 'She and her household were baptized,' says Luke (Acts 16.15). She later acts as Paul's hostess in the city. So here we have a businesswoman, in a luxury industry, becoming a follower. She is a Graeco-Roman patroness, and this will be her church.

She's not the only prominent woman who comes to faith in Philippi. Writing to the Philippian church a bit later, Paul urges two women – Euodia and Syntyche – to make peace. Clearly they are influential figures who have had a disagreement. One must conclude that women were highly influential in the Philippian church.

'Slaves of the Most High God'

In Philippi there was a slave girl with a spirit of divination. The literal Greek is that she had a *pneuma pythonos,* a 'python spirit'. This phrase originated with the famous oracle at Delphi, which lay in the region of Putho. There, according to Greek mythology, a serpent or dragon lay guarding the Delphic oracle before it was slain by Apollo. (The modern snake gets its name from this ancient serpent.)

Later the word came to be a catch-all designation for diviners and spiritualists – and also, by association, it was used of ventriloquists, who were believed to have such a spirit dwelling in their belly.[41] Plutarch, who had once been a priest at Delphi, dismissed these people as ventriloquists:

> Certainly it is foolish and childish in the extreme to imagine that the god himself after the manner of ventriloquists (who used to be called 'Eurycleis', but now 'Pythones') enters into the bodies of his prophets and prompts their utterances, employing their mouths and voices as instruments.[42]

Eurycleis was a famous ventriloquist. So there was considerable scepticism among some people about the claims of mediums, just as there is today. But in this case there is something else going on. The girl follows Paul, driven evidently by the spirit within her, and crying out, 'These men are slaves of the Most High God, who proclaim to you a way of salvation' (Acts 16.17). The phrase has an authentic ring – as a spirit interpreter of the Greek gods, she would be likely to talk of the Most High God, even though to Jews this would be tautological, since God is the only God. In pantheistic Greek culture, the initial understanding of the Christian God would be that he is top among all the others.

Paul endures this for a long time before finally casting the demon out, almost in a fit of temper. Why doesn't he cast it out straight away? It's possible that in such an overtly Roman environment Paul really does want to keep a low profile. Lydia is not converted through any signs and wonders, but through simple teaching. One gets the sense therefore that Paul is treading carefully, that he knows if he causes too much of a stir in the city things could turn nasty.

He's right. Because once the spirit leaves the girl, her Roman owners get seriously narked. She is, after all, a slave. She is a money-making machine for them. When her connection to the source is cut off, she becomes economically useless.

So they drag Paul and Silas before the courts. (Presumably Luke and Timothy are not involved in the exorcism, or else are dismissed as assistants or subordinates.) This action indicates that the girl's owners had some financial clout and social standing: in that culture you didn't haul people before the magistrates unless you had a good chance of winning.

Their real complaint is that their money-making machine has gone. But they couch their accusation in religious and political terms: Paul and his associates are accused of 'disturbing our city', of being Jews and of fomenting anti-Roman activity. In a city as proudly Roman as Philippi, the latter is a telling charge.

In Philippi, archaeologists have uncovered the *bēma*, or judgement seat, the raised podium from which the magistrates would dispense justice. Although the one discovered dates from a century after Paul's time, it's likely that it was built over the top of the previous structures.[43] The prison into which Paul and Silas were thrown was nearby, or maybe even beneath the *bēma*.

Luke uses two terms for those before whom Paul and Silas are accused: *archontas* and *strategois*, the rulers and the magistrates. It's the first time that Paul goes head to head with the civil authorities. There is no indication that the magistrates give serious deliberation to the charge: rather they seem to be influenced by the agitation of the crowd. When the crowd join in with attacking them, the magistrates simply give in to peer pressure. Paul and Silas are stripped and beaten with rods. This was a particularly savage Roman punishment. Those who wielded the rods were the *lictores*.[44] This was ostensibly a 'lighter' punishment – normally designed for lesser charges or to induce confessions. But 'lighter' is a relative term.

Paul has been the victim of mob violence before – even mob violence instigated by those of high status – but the 'authorities' have not been mentioned. In Philippi, for the first time, the authorities are involved.

The early church had a deep distrust of the authorities. Paul wrote that the powers and the authorities of the world had been ordained by God (Rom. 13.1) – but that did not mean that God approved of them. In fact, the early church took this passage to mean that the power of the state was put in place to curb sinners. Origen compared the state to a chain gang composed of criminals, albeit doing a useful work.[45]

Becoming a Christian meant putting aside such power. The early church assumed that disciples could not be a part of the power structures of the Roman world. Soldiers, as we have seen, had to give up their swords. Magistrates had to put down their rods.

The example of Cyprian shows this in action. Cyprian was a third-century Roman aristocrat who lived in Carthage, in North

Africa. He lived a life of luxury, eating fine food, drinking fine wine and wondering why all of this wasn't actually making him happy. Cyprian felt the call of Christ on his life, but he also felt the pull of the world around him. And he wondered where he was going to get the power to make the change he knew he had to make:

> When does he learn thrift who has been used to liberal banquets and sumptuous feasts? And he who has been glittering in gold and purple, and has been celebrated for his costly attire, when does he reduce himself to ordinary and simple clothing? One who has felt the charm of the fasces and of civic honours shrinks from becoming a mere private and inglorious citizen. The man who is attended by crowds of clients, and dignified by the numerous association of an officious train, regards it as a punishment when he is alone.

Cyprian had held the fasces: he had been a magistrate. He had worn purple, purchased from the Carthaginian equivalent of Lydia. And he knew that he had to give all of that up. He knew that he had to be baptised and join a community who were 'learning to live differently'.[46]

Cyprian eventually became a bishop and lived, according to his biographer, simply and humbly, always showing hospitality to the poor. When he was martyred in AD 258, he was stripped before death. He was found to be wearing a cloak and a hood, but no purple.[47] It is rather ironic that the colour which symbolised luxury and wealth to the early church has now become the official colour of the bishopric. Cyprian literally would not be seen dead in purple.

The magistrates' action was, technically, unlawful. Under the Roman legal code, it was forbidden to bind or to beat a Roman citizen without trial.[48] But Paul and Silas are treated not as Roman citizens, but as *peregrinoi*, wandering foreigners. Vagrants. Later in Jerusalem, Paul plays the citizenship card (Acts 22.25), but not here, which is odd. Surely they could have produced evidence of their citizenship, in the form of the papers which many citizens carried?[49] It has been suggested either that there was no time, or that Paul could not be heard above the crowd, but it's hard to believe that he could not have made himself heard if he wanted to.

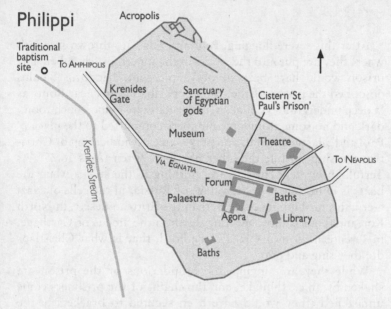

Philippi

Acropolis

Traditional baptism site

To Amphipolis

Krenides Gate

Sanctuary of Egyptian gods

Cistern 'St Paul's Prison'

Museum

Theatre

Krenides Stream

Via Egnatia

To Neapolis

Forum

Palaestra

Baths

Agora

Library

Baths

So why didn't he claim his rights? First, Paul never expected any different. He knew that to be a Christian was to suffer. That had been his message to the new churches in Galatia (Acts 14.22). Paul knew that the message they were preaching was bound to result in persecution and oppression. It was the natural outcome of their challenge to the powers of the world.

He also understood that he was part of the body of Christ. Paul and Silas were part of a community which in Philippi had only just come into being. Not all of these new followers would have been citizens. So perhaps Paul decided not to invoke a privilege which his new disciples did not have themselves. He was one of them. He was on their level. Years later, writing to the church at Philippi, he talks about suffering as part of the normal Christian experience. How could he ever have addressed these people in that way had he chosen to avoid it?

Perhaps he was hoping, too, that if he and Silas took the blame, then the resident Christians would not be treated the same way. Or, perhaps, that the very experience of beating and imprisonment would bring him into contact with the kind of people who would respond to the gospel. Certainly that is what happened, although not in the way that they imagined.

After this severe flogging, Paul and Silas are thrown into jail, where they are put into the stocks in the innermost chamber. The prison would have been deeply unpleasant. Diodorus Siculus described the prison of the colony of Alba Fucens near Rome as 'a deep underground dungeon, no larger than a nine-couch room, dark and noisome from large numbers committed to the place...' Paul and Silas sing hymns and pray – an early indication of Christian worship – while the other prisoners listen (Acts 16.25). As Tertullian wrote, 'The legs feel nothing in the stocks when the heart is in heaven.'[50] In the gulags of Russia, in the cells of Nazi Germany, in shipping containers in the Eritrean desert, in North Korean labour camps, awaiting death in the arenas of Carthage, in seventeenth-century jails in Bedford, that is what Christians do: they sing and pray.

While they are singing, the foundations of the prison are shaken by an earthquake, and the chains of the prisoners come unfastened (they would have been secured to brackets in the walls). The earthquake is an expression of divine power, but we should note that earthquakes were not uncommon in the region.[51] And this one, unlike the one where Peter is rescued, is not accompanied by angels. The jailer's immediate response is to prepare to kill himself. Jailers were responsible for their charges: he would probably have been executed; at the very least he would have been beaten for letting prisoners escape, earthquake or no earthquake.

Paul, however, refuses to leave. The jailer's life is saved – both physically and spiritually, for he brings Paul and Silas out from the jail and into his own house, believes in the Lord, and he and his whole household are baptised.

Clearly, in bringing them out, the jailer shows that he has decided they are innocent. The earthquake is a sign of divine displeasure. This was a usual interpretation of such events: if the earth shook, the gods were displeased. A similar thing happened in Caesarea in AD 305. A Christian was drowned during a bout of persecution, but following his death the city felt an earth tremor and his body was washed ashore. The inhabitants took this as a sign of divine displeasure and the whole town 'confessed the one and only God of the Christians'.[52]

The next morning the magistrates order the release of the prisoners. Clearly they agree with the jailer: the gods are angry. But now Paul reveals that both he and Silas are 'men who are Roman citizens'.

This, then, is another reason why Paul did not claim exemption from the punishment earlier. To put it bluntly, it gave him leverage. Magistrates who had acted this way could lose their posts and face public humiliation. No wonder the magistrates are so scared. They face a double whammy: the gods are displeased with them and, if this gets out, their superiors are going to be angry as well. So Paul is able to make a huge PR coup out of it. He insists that the authorities must 'come and take us out themselves' (Acts 16.37). The magistrates do so. But they also ask that Paul must leave the city. Paul and Silas go to the home of Lydia and 'encourage' the brothers and sisters.

By challenging their economic interests, Paul makes for himself – and for the fresh new church – some significant local enemies. But by forcing the magistrates to apologise, perhaps he hopes that they will think twice in the future about locking up Christians.

Paul always had a soft spot for the Philippian church. He calls them 'my joy and crown' (Phil. 4.1). They had sent him a financial gift, carried to Rome by man called Epaphroditus (Phil. 4.18). Paul reminisces how in the 'early days of the gospel, when I left Macedonia, no church shared with me in the matter of giving and receiving, except you alone' (Phil. 4.15). From the start this church, which met in the house of a businesswoman, supported Paul and helped him. And the first instance of this – the instance which Paul refers to in his letter to them – was in Thessalonica. Which is where Paul heads next.

'Some ruffians in the market-places'

After being 'asked to leave' Philippi, Paul and Silas head west. The 'we' section breaks off here, not resuming until Acts 20 (in c. AD 57) when Paul is once more in Philippi. Luke remains at home. It will be several years – perhaps as many as seven – before he travels with Paul again.

Their journey takes them through Amphipolis and Apollonia. Amphipolis is 30 miles west of Philippi on the Egnatian

Way. Its original name, *Ennea Hodoi*, 'Nine Ways', indicates that it was a well-known hub for travellers.[53] Anyone travelling by land between Philippi and Thessalonica would have had to come through Amphipolis and Apollonia: the only alternative meant an enormous trek around two lakes, Volvi and Cercintis. It was quicker and easier to hug the coast. Perhaps Paul and his co-worker are travelling by mule or horse, since no other locations are mentioned. Both of these staging posts would be reachable in a day's journey on horseback, which would mean that three days after leaving Philippi, Paul and Silas arrive at Thessalonica.

Thessalonica had a long, illustrious past. The capital of the Roman province, to Strabo it was the 'metropolis of Macedonia'. To the poet Antipater it was 'the mother of all Macedonia' (but then he came from there, so he was biased).[54]

It was not a colony, like Philippi, but it certainly benefited from a high level of Roman support. Octavian had made it a free city, which gave it the autonomy to mint its own currency (as well as imperial currency) and to establish its own form of limited self-government. With a well-positioned harbour linking the Bosphorus and the Black Sea and a population of anything between 20,000 and 100,000, it was prosperous and proud.

Paul, Silas and Timothy stay some weeks in Thessalonica: he's there for three Sabbaths (Acts 17.2). As normal, Paul begins with the 'synagogue of the Jews'. Although there is evidence of a synagogue building in Thessalonica, it dates from the late second century.[55] It's the same approach as in Philippi: go to the synagogues. And, just as in Philippi, he has some success, particularly with God-fearing 'devout Greeks' and some of the leading women of the city.[56] But, just as in Philippi, his success brings him opposition.

This time the opposition comes not from the economic powers, nor from disgruntled slave owners, but from the Jewish leaders. Thessalonica clearly had a larger population of Jews than Philippi. Their leaders urge ruffians in the market places to form a mob. Luke describes them as the 'agora men' – probably day labourers hanging around the market place looking for work. Rent a mob – literally.[57]

The city is in an uproar: the mob go to Jason's house – presumably where Paul and Silas are staying – and attack it. Perhaps through chance, perhaps because they are warned, Paul and Silas are not there. In their absence, however, Jason and some others are dragged before the city authorities and accused of playing host to men who are 'turning the world upside down' (Acts 17.6). There are three elements to their accusation: first, they are 'world-upsetters'. Second, they are acting against Caesar's decrees. Third, and most serious, they claim there's another ruler: King Jesus.

Here, in Thessalonica, the Christians are accused of 'acting contrary' to imperial decrees, although it's not clear which specific decrees are being disobeyed. The leaders of a city like Thessalonica would be sensitive to accusations that they knowingly harboured enemies of Roman order. Certainly during the Augustan period, and most probably at this time, the oath of loyalty to the emperor contained the clause that the person swearing would report any sedition.[58] What is clear is that these fools are preaching about a different kingdom. They are seditious, suspicious, traitorous.

The men before whom the Christians are dragged are called by a specific word, *politarchs* (17.6). This designation has been verified by inscriptions found in Thessalonica. Luke's information is specific and accurate. Under Augustus there were five politarchs; by Paul's time there may have been six.[59] The politarchs free Jason and his associates on bail. But clearly the city is not safe for Paul and Silas. Whether they are in hiding in the city, or simply out and about that day, Luke doesn't say. What he does say is that that very night, Paul and Silas have to leave. Timothy, who is with them, is not included in the injunction. As Paul's letter to the Thessalonians indicates, he is free to return to the city. Only Paul and Silas are banned, a fact that Paul takes hard. He describes it as like being orphaned. It is Satan – not the Romans – who is blocking his way (1 Thess. 2.17–18).

'Turning the world upside down'

Subversion. Sedition. High treason.

Such accusations were to dog Christianity throughout its early centuries, for one simple reason: they were true. Christianity *was* anti-imperial. But it went far beyond the claims of their theology, an unusual set of beliefs. The things that the Christians *did* were also seditious and suspicious, and just plain wrong.

Christians certainly refused to worship the Roman emperor, but by extension they refused to venerate the Roman way of life. The imperial cult was the embodiment of Roman values. It was, in fact, the Roman Empire at prayer. So when Christians stood in opposition to it, they were not just in the wrong because of theological differences of opinion, but because of their anti-Roman lifestyle.

Their behaviour was strange. When Pliny started arresting Christians in Bithynia in AD 110, several suspicious things were listed about them. Their habit of meeting before daylight suggested a conspiracy under cover of darkness. Roman history could supply plenty of examples of night-time conspiracies. Minucius Felix reports that Christians were viewed as 'an unlawful and dangerous faction ... which is leagued together by nightly meetings ... a people skulking and shunning the light'.[60]

Nocturnal skulking wasn't the only thing that disturbed Pliny. Christians had a common meal – a clear sign of some kind of close association. And they took oaths and sang songs. Pliny uses the term *carmen* to describe their singing, a word which could also mean an incantation or the casting of a magic spell. And what about the oath – the *sacramentum*? Sure, it could be harmless. It could mean nothing more than the oath of allegiance sworn by a soldier. Or it could be an initiation into a secret society or mystical rite. In the Catlinian conspiracy the conspirators took a solemn oath reinforced by murder and the eating of human flesh.[61]

In fact, the Christians met before dawn because they were commemorating the resurrection – and because many of their members had to go to work later in the day. The oaths were promises to avoid sinful behaviour. But that counted for nothing. The authorities were willing to believe the worst of Christians because they were, genuinely, different. After the passage in Minucius Felix quoted above, the writer goes all *Daily Mail* and accuses Christians of all manner of practices, including killing (and eating) babies, drunken orgies and, strangely, using a dog to turn off the lights so that an orgy could take place:

A dog that has been tied to the chandelier is provoked, by throwing a small piece of offal beyond the length of a line by which he is bound, to rush and spring; and thus the conscious light being overturned and extinguished in the shameless darkness, the connections of abominable lust involve them in the uncertainty of fate.[62]

Christians were a natural target for wild rumour and random punishment. They vehemently denied the wild rumours, but they never denied that there were fundamental differences between their outlook on society and that of the Roman world. That bit was true. They *were* trying to subvert the system. Their accusers were right – although for all the wrong reasons.

This becomes clear once we take a close look at what Paul was teaching in Thessalonica. We can get some idea from the letter that he later wrote to the Thessalonians. He claims that he caused the people of the city to turn from idol worship to the one true God (1 Thess. 1.9); he warned of a day of wrath and judgement (1 Thess. 1.10). He said that Jesus was God's Son (1 Thess. 1.10); he encouraged people to follow the call of God into a new kingdom (1 Thess. 2.12); he urged his spiritual children to live lives of self-control – unlike the Gentiles (1 Thess. 4.5) – and not to exploit each other (1 Thess. 4.6). They were to live independently and quietly. These were all fundamentally un-Roman attitudes.

Clearly Christians were against the emperor. Their eschatological message of a new kingdom was emphatically political. To the Roman Empire, which saw itself as the Empire of all empires, the summit of all achievement, the idea that it would be superseded was foolish at best and subversive at worst.

There are other sticks of dynamite in there too, teaching which looks innocent enough to us but which, viewed in context, shows that Christians were disruptive and dangerous to the social fabric of Roman life. Writing to the Thessalonian church a few months after he left, Paul says that he and Silas 'worked night and day, so that we might not burden any of you while we proclaimed to you the gospel of God' (1 Thess. 2.9). Paul and Silas worked at their trades in Thessalonica which, in Paul's case certainly, and in Silas's possibly, involved being a tentmaker. We shall look at Paul's profession in more detail shortly. But for now we should note that little statement in Thessalonians about independence:

> But we urge you, beloved … to aspire to live quietly, to mind your
> own affairs, and to work with your hands, as we directed you, so that
> you may behave properly towards outsiders and be dependent on
> no one. (1 Thess. 4.10–12)

The Roman world relied on a system known as the patron-client system. It was a system of giving and receiving, of financial and social obligation. It started at the top. The emperor had his favourites, whom he appointed to key positions and who benefited from his patronage. In return he could be sure of their political support. Those who had benefited from the beneficence of the emperor operated the same system to ensure their own support. Provincial governors could help their favoured subjects gain citizenship, offices and high honour from Rome, as well as making sure that any legal decisions fell out in their favour. In turn these honoured citizens, these friends of Rome, had their own clients and benefactors.

These benefactors were expected to demonstrate their social standing by philanthropic works and public service. A typical inscription from Aletrium shows how the system worked. In it Lucius Betilienus Varus records his gifts to the town, which included 'all the street paths in the town, the colonnade along which people walk to the citadel, a playing field, a sundial, a meat market, the stuccoing of the townhall seats, a bathing pool … a reservoir by the gate, an aqueduct about 340 feet long … also the arches and good sound water pipes'. Busy boy. In reward he was twice made censor, his son was exempted from military service and he had a statue erected in his honour.[63]

This system operated right down to the local level. Wealthy patrons had a retinue of clients who relied on them for support. These clients were not beggars. Clients were citizens, freemen. But many didn't have jobs or trades as we know them. Philo says they were those 'knowing nothing of labour'.[64]

There was a code of etiquette which governed this relationship. At the beginning of each day, clients would gather at the house of their patron to be ready to greet him when he appeared and to present their requests. At the second hour, around 7 a.m., they would all parade down to the forum, the patron at the head and all his clients following him. At the forum they might go to the courts, if the patron had business there, or engage in financial matters. After that, at noon, it was off to the baths, which were always at their hottest at that hour, when the wealthy arrived. Following the baths, they might head back to the patron's house for dinner, if invited. At the very least a client was supposed to accompany his patron until the ninth hour, 3 p.m.[65]

The number of clients attending the morning's audience reflected the wealth and status of the patron. The more clients, the more power and influence you had. And since the size of your clientele was a gauge of your social status, it was common for patrons to free slaves so that they could become clients.[66] At the morning's audience, the patron would dole out gifts of money or promise orders of work. The client also received other benefits – legal protection and the occasional meal (albeit sitting at a lower table).

For their part, the clients had obligations to their patron. They might have to do military service for the patron; certainly they would be expected to vote for him. They would do whatever they could to further their patron's interests. Juvenal records the relationship with his usual jaundiced eye:

> A meal is the return which your grand friendship yields you; the great man scores it against you, and though it comes but seldom, he scores it against you all the same ... it is his [the patron's] pleasure to invite his forgotten client, lest the third place on the lowest couch should be unoccupied and he says to you 'Come and dine with me', you are in the seventh heaven![67]

This relationship was the fundamental matrix for social and political affairs. This was how money got made, political influence was gained and positions of power got filled. Of course, at the lower echelons of society, there were people outside this structure: common artisans, ordinary tradesmen and the millions of slaves. But that's the point. No one in their right mind wanted to be down there. Much better to have a powerful patron protecting you, commissioning you, rewarding you. This is why Paul's recommendation to Thessalonian Christians to live independently is so radical. In the context of first-century society, he's actually saying to them, 'Remove yourself from the patron-client relationship as far as you can.'

Christians disdained such obvious displays of patronage. For them service was freely given and without expectation of reward. And the patron-client relationship was one which was deeply threatening to a Christian. What if your duties to your patron – your *obsequium* – came into conflict with your faith? What if it required a trip to the temple? Or the giving and taking of a bribe? The fascinating thing is that the early church took the patron system and transformed it. Turned it upside down. The patrons of the church – Stephanas, Phoebe, Lydia – were clearly the 'leaders', but that leadership, when it was properly exercised, was exercised through service. Jesus had said the leaders should be slaves, so there could be none of that subservience-encouraging, retinue-forming stuff.

Paul also argued that Christians should be benefactors. And he urged all Christians to work, so that they too could undertake good works for those in need. In other words, in Paul's new social reality everyone was supposed to be a benefactor. Everyone was both patron and client.

For Paul, the ability to work independently and with his own hands was vital: it not only allowed him to support himself, it freed him from any obligation to patrons. Paul's innocent-looking statement, then, is in fact a challenge to the way the whole (Roman) world worked. It's a political and economic act. The act of removing oneself from the patron-client relationship, of becoming a low-scale benefactor in your own right, but with no thought of reward, was not only a good thing in itself, it was an act of protest against the entire system. Paul was, indeed, turning the world upside down. Guilty as charged.

We don't know if this kind of teaching had reached the ears of the politarchs, but if so it would have added to their suspicion that these Christians were not the right kind of people. There might have been another cause for their nervousness as well. An edict, indeed, from on high. The year before Paul arrived in Thessalonica, the emperor had expelled the Christians from Rome.

'Claudius had ordered all Jews to leave Rome'

'Claudius had ordered all Jews to leave Rome,' writes Luke (Acts 18.2). Luke's account is backed up by the Roman historian Suetonius and he gives us a glimpse of what caused this edict:

Since the Jews constantly made disturbances at the instigation of Chrestus, [Claudius] expelled them from Rome.[68]

According to Suetonius, the disturbances – the riots – were linked to someone called Chrestus. It has to be admitted that Chrestus was a common name at the time: it was a slave's name which means 'useful' or 'good'. But the implication is that Suetonius's readers should know who he's talking about. The most plausible explanation is that he's using a misspelling of the name of Christ: he's referring to the man who founded the strange little sect of the *Christiani*.[69]

Suetonius does not date the incident, but Orosius, writing, admittedly, a lot later, places it in Claudius's ninth year, AD 49.[70] Although Orosius is writing in the early fifth century, he was working on a research project for Augustine and he claims the date is found in Josephus. No trace of the date can be found in Josephus, but he has no reason to make such a thing up, so it's probably based on a real tradition.[71]

It cannot have been 'all Jews'. Luke must be overstating the case here: there were tens of thousands of Jews in Rome and expelling them all would have been impossible. But expelling some of them, or many of them, or a certain section of them – that would be possible.

It's quite possible that what's being referred to here is not the expulsion of all the Jews, but all the Jewish Christians. That's why Luke uses the term. We can suggest a plausible picture of what happened. Soon after Claudius's reign began, Christianity was established in Rome, planted there by anonymous Christian missionaries who brought the good news into the synagogues. And it became a contentious issue among the Jewish community there. Rome had several synagogues and lots of Jews. Fights broke out between them. Riots. Disturbances. When it came to the ears of Claudius, he banned all the Jewish Christians, all the followers of Chrestus – all the *Christiani*.

News of this might well have reached the leaders in Philippi and Thessalonica. It definitely reached Corinth, because that's where two of these Jews ended up. But the expulsion of the Jews in Rome explains a lot of things. It explains the troubled development of the Roman church. It might explain why the magistrates and the politarchs in Philippi and Thessalonica were so keen that Paul leave the city. And it's one of the reasons why Paul leaves the route of the *via Egnatia* and heads to Beroea.

So, once again, Paul is on the move. He and Silas are smuggled out of Thessalonica by night and head to the city of Beroea.

The 50-mile journey would take them several days. They were travelling on lesser roads now, for Beroea lay some miles off the main road. It was that kind of place. Cicero described it as an *oppidum devium,* a place 'off the high road', out of the way.[72]

Why, then, go there? Precisely because it's out of the way. It's a town of some size, but it's also a place where Paul can lie low for a bit. And maybe Paul has heard of the edict from Rome. If, even at this stage, he has ambitions to get to Rome, there would be no point pressing ahead with that right now. All the Jewish Christians have been kicked out.[73]

If Paul plans to lie low for a while, then he – typically – fails to live up to even his own expectations. Instead he follows the usual MO: he heads for the synagogue meeting. But in Beroea the reception is refreshingly positive. The Beroean Jews welcome the message and scour the Scriptures daily for evidence. This synagogue is clearly a house of study: it has Torah scrolls and other Scriptures which can be consulted and dicussed. And many believe, including 'Greek women and men of high standing' (Acts 17.12). Perhaps one of them is Sopater, son of Pyrrhus, who later accompanies Paul to Jerusalem (Acts 20.4).

It can't last, of course: soon Jews from Thessalonica arrive and, once again, stir up the crowds. But it takes a while to stir them up, and meanwhile Luke writes that 'the believers immediately sent Paul away to the coast' (Acts 17.14), which implies that there must have been a reasonable number of converts by the time this happened. Nonetheless, Paul has to leave again. But by now Timothy has joined Paul and Silas from Thessalonica. They remain to consolidate the work in Beroea. Only Paul seems under threat this time – an indication, perhaps, of the diminishing power of the threat from Thessalonica. So, while Silas and Timothy remain in Beroea, believers from Beroea accompany Paul south, out of Macedonia and on to the cultural heart of the ancient world: Athens.

7. Achaia AD 51–52

'To an unknown god'

Athens was famous. World-renowned. Athens had history. But in a sense that was the problem: history was really all it had. By Paul's day, Athens was a city living on its past reputation. It was still the mythical home of philosophy and learning, but its power had been usurped by Rome, who had strip-mined the Greek culture for what they wanted – the poetry, the theatre, the many gods – and then left Athens to dwell on past glories. The golden age was long gone.

The same was true of many places in Achaia, the province in which Paul now found himself. The two main centres of population were Athens and Corinth. The rest of the cities were small and there was a sense of decline everywhere. Thebes was little more than a village; at Chalcis Dio, Chrysostomos reported cattle grazing inside the city walls while the statues of the gods in the gymnasium were completely obscured by the growing crops.[1] The Roman poet Horace called the capital city *vacuas Athenas*, 'empty Athens'.

Some Romans recognised what had been lost: Pliny lamented that, despite their mastery of the world, Rome had not added much, if anything, to the world's store of scientific or geographical knowledge:

> ... no addition whatever is being made to knowledge by means of original research ... now that every sea has been opened up and every coast affords a hospitable landing, an immense multitude goes on voyages – but their object is profit not knowledge.[2]

No one could accuse Paul of travelling in such a manner. He arrived by boat, docking at the main port of Piraeus (Acts 17.15). Luke depicts him wandering the streets like a modern-day tourist, taking in the atmosphere and seeing the sights. And what he noticed most of all was the huge number of idols in the city. All these temples made by man, in what Paul describes as a forest of idols (see Acts 17.16). This is a place of old myths and new gods. There are the famous monuments: the temple of Hephaistos, the Acropolis and the Parthenon with its statue of Athena; the temple of Ares in the Agora. Not to mention a familiar cult from Galatia, the temple of Zeus Eleutherios (looks a bit like Barnabas). But the new gods are out in force as well. There are four statues in the Acropolis: Augustus, Tiberius, Germanicus and Drusus. The temple of Roma and Augustus dominates the skyline. And all around are dedications to the imperial family, many small altars dedicated to Augustus, a statue of Livia.[3]

Paul subtly changes his approach in Athens. He starts at the synagogue with 'the Jews and the devout persons', but he also goes to the *agora*, the market place, the civic and cultural centre of the city. This was where the philosophers were to be found and arguments were to be had. It was surrounded by long-roofed colonnades known as *stoas*. One of these – the *Stoa Poikile* – gave its name to the group who used to meet there: the Stoics.[4] Their founder was a philosopher called Zeno (340–265 BC). Stoic philosophy praised virtue based on knowledge, self-sufficiency, reason and a devotion to duty.

The other group Paul meets are the Epicureans, who took their name from Epicurius (341–270 BC). Today we think of 'epicures' as people who like fine food. The original meaning was something rather different: Epicurius lived in austerity, withdrew from civic affairs and believed that happiness lay in philosophical discussions.

How happy Paul's discussions are, we don't know. Some of these philosophers dismiss him as a babbler: the Greek word is *spermalogos* and it means 'seed-picker'. He's like a little bird, pecking at fragments of news and ideas. You can imagine him hovering around, taking things in, picking up bits here and there – an obvious newcomer, not worthy of much attention. But there must be something in Paul's twittering that interests them, because he's given a hearing before the Areopagus. The *Areios pagos* – the hill of Ares – was a hill next to the Acropolis. The name can either refer to the place or to the judicial council which met there: just as our word 'parliament' can refer to the group or the building.

Paul's speech to them is fascinating. Like all good speakers, he starts with a topical reference.

> Athenians, I see how extremely religious you are in every way. For as I went through the city and looked carefully at the objects of your worship, I found among them an altar with the inscription, 'To an unknown god.' What therefore you worship as unknown, this I proclaim to you.' (Acts 17.22–23)

There were several altars to unknown gods in Athens; both Pausanias and Philostratus mention them.[5] Paul is doing his best to be a sophisticated Athenian orator and not a provincial religious zealot. He never mentions Jesus by name. He talks about 'the God who made the world and everything in it'. He even quotes from Greek poets: first from the sixth-century BC poet Epimenides and then from Aratus of Soli in Cilicia, a third-century BC Stoic. He does what good missionaries and evangelists have always done: he uses the language, the style and the cultural references familiar to his audience.

And, like all missionaries and evangelists, he has mixed results. The key moment is when Paul mentions the resurrection of the dead. The idea of resurrection was accepted by Jews (albeit in terms of the resurrection at the day of judgement), but it does not feature in any Greek philosophy. Greek attitudes were best summed up by the playwright Aeschylus, who has Apollo say, 'When the dust has soaked up the blood of a man, once he has died there is no resurrection.'[6]

Luke says that Paul makes some believers, two of whom he names: Dionysius the Areopagite – a member of that council – and a woman named Damaris. It's possible that another person becomes a convert in Athens, a man called Stephanas, whom Paul describes as the first convert in Achaia (1 Cor. 16.15), but more of that later.

Athens is an interesting experience for Paul. He is not their kind of person and it is not, really, his kind of place. In Athens,

Athens in the time of Paul

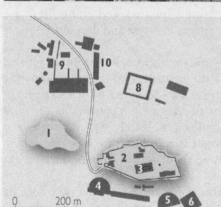

Above: Athens in the early 20th century. A view from the river Ilissus, now completely covered over by the modern city. On the left are the columns of the Temple of Olympian Zeus. In the background, rising above the city, is the Acropolis. The Areopagus was beyond the Acropolis to the west.

0   200 m

1 Areopagus	6 Odeon of Pericles
2 Acropolis	7 Temple of Olympian
3 Parthenon	Zeus
4 Theatre of Herodes	8 Roman forum
Atticus	9 Agora
5 Theatre of Dionysus	10 Stoa of Attalus

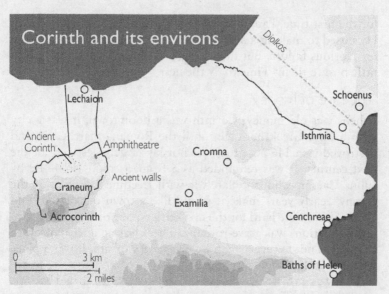

Corinth and its environs

Lechaion

Schoenus

Isthmia

Diolkos

Ancient
Corinth

Amphitheatre

Cromna

Ancient walls

Craneum

Examilia

Acrocorinth

Cenchreae

Baths of Helen

0   3 km

2 miles

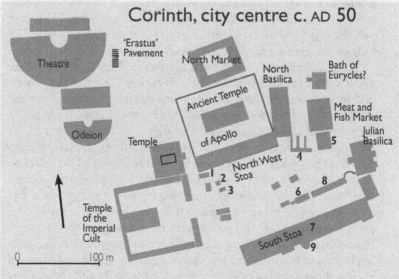

Corinth, city centre c. AD 50

Theatre

'Erastus'
Pavement

North Market

North
Basilica

Bath of
Eurycles?

Ancient Temple

of Apollo

Meat and
Fish Market

5

Julian
Basilica

Odeion

Temple

North West
Stoa

4

1

2

3

6

8

Temple
of the
Imperial
Cult

South Stoa

7

9

0   100 m

1 Temple of Tyche	4 Propylaea	7 'Fountain House'
2 Babbius Monument	5 Fountain of Peirene	8 Central Shops
3 Fountain of Poseidon	6 Bema	9 Bouleuterion (City Council Chamber)

for the first time, Paul is met not with hostility but with apathy. He's used to making a scene. If he can't gain success, he'll settle for glorious failure. But that doesn't work in Athens. He's just a little bird to them. Time to fly the nest.

'The love of money'

Athens was old money; Corinth was a boomtown. It was a city with a long Greek heritage, until the Romans marched in and destroyed it in 146 BC, after which it lay largely deserted for the next century. It was refounded as a Roman colony in 44 BC by Julius Caesar, who populated it with freedmen. Stories of the colony's early years make it sound like a town out of the Wild West. Times were hard for the first settlers: one of the most popular occupations was grave-robbing. There was an ancient proverb that it was not for every man to voyage to Corinth. It was a place where only the tough survived.[7]

That was its history, anyhow. By Paul's day, Corinth had become a jungle of a different sort. Survival was much more about commerce, trade, money-making, enterprise and ambition. This was not the old Corinth of Greek antiquity. It was Neocorinth, the hub of the Mediterranean, the city of self-made men.

The Corinthians would have appreciated the modern estate agent's mantra: location, location, location. The city's commercial success was founded on its position, on an isthmus between the Ionian and the Aegean Seas. This meant that all trade going between Italy and Asia passed through – or near – Corinth, as the shortest route. Strabo described Corinth as 'master of two harbours of which the one leads straight to Asia and the other to Italy'.[8] The two harbours were Lechaeum, on the Italian side, and Cenchreae, on the Asian side. Running between the two ports was a paved road called the *diolkos* which was busy with horses and carts ferrying cargo and passengers from one port to the other. Philostratus describes how a traveller from Smyrna in Asia, 'having landed at Corinth and worshipped the Sun about midday with his usual rites, embarked in the evening for Sicily and Italy'. Corinth's position allowed it to generate huge transit taxes, one of the main sources of its wealth. For travellers, the price was worth paying. That trek across the *diolkos* saved all the time (and the danger) that would otherwise be wasted sailing around the Peleponnese. Corinth, then, was one of the great transport hubs of the first century. All roads might have led to Rome, but most of them went through Corinth.

Above the city towered the craggy rock mass of Acrocorinth, at the top of which was a small temple of Aphrodite. Their choice of goddess to look over the city was meaningful: Corinth was a place known for worshipping the goddess of love. However, some of its reputation has been overstated – probably the result of Athenian propaganda against it. It may well be that Corinth, for all its ways and reputation, wasn't that much worse than any other port city in the Mediterranean of its time.

After all, the real love apparent in Corinth was the love of money. In the heart of the city was a huge *agora*, so big that it was split into two. The Upper Agora was reserved for political and administrative affairs; the Lower Agora was for commerce and trade. Right in the centre of the market place was the chamber where the city council met. There was also the Corinthian *bema* where, as in other cities, the magistrates stood to address the city, receive petitions and issue public proclamations. The *bema* was constructed in marble and was built not long before Paul arrived in the city, sometime between AD 25 and 50.[9]

There were two big basilicas in the Lower Agora: the Julian basilica and the South basilica. They were probably commercial centres filled with a wide variety of goods and traders. All around the market place there were shops; beyond, a few streets away, were the smelly meat and fish markets, the places where Paul was to advise the Corinthians, 'Eat whatever is sold in the meat market without raising any question on the ground of conscience' (1 Cor. 10.25).

Maybe Paul made his way out of the *agora* and towards the theatre: the apartment blocks near there had taverns on the ground floor, offering food to eat and places to stay.[10] If he went in that direction, his steps would have taken him along a pavement with an inscription in letters set into the stone: 'Erastus in return for his aedileship laid [the pavement] at his own expense.'[11] Erastus was the city treasurer, a man of power, influence and wealth. A benefactor. In Corinth, like every city in history, wealth brought you power and influence.

For all that, Corinth was a place where new ideas were welcomed. This vibrant, busy, confident city would inspire Paul and infuriate him in roughly equal measure. It would provoke him to write some of the harshest words he would ever write, and some of the most beautiful words that anyone has ever written. From Corinth he would write perhaps the most influential piece of theological thinking ever.

Paul probably arrived in the city late in AD 50, or even in the spring of AD 51. In some ways it was a good time to reach Corinth. The nearby village of Isthmia was a small place, but every two years it was home to the renowned Isthmian Games, and they were due to be celebrated in April/May AD 51.[12] Lots of people would be coming to Corinth, and they would need tents to stay in, awnings to keep off the heat of the sun. But he needed to find a place from which to work.

He found it with two fellow Jews, two fellow believers. Paul was not the first Christian in the city. When he walked in from Athens, sometime in the winter of AD 50, there were two others there already. Their names were Priscilla and Aquila, and they were in Corinth because they had been kicked out of Rome.

'Prisca and Aquila, who work with me in Christ Jesus'

[In Corinth] he found a Jew named Aquila, a native of Pontus, who had recently come from Italy with his wife Priscilla, because Claudius had ordered all Jews to leave Rome. Paul went to see them, and, because he was of the same trade, he stayed with them, and they worked together – by trade they were tentmakers. (Acts 18.2–3)

Priscilla and Aquila were tentmakers like Paul, which is no doubt why he sought them out in the first place. They were fellow Jews, but most significantly, they were also exiled Christians.

How Paul knew them, we don't know. Perhaps he first encountered them in Corinth. Perhaps he had met them through sharing the same trade. Or perhaps they were related. The WT says that Aquila was 'of the same tribe' as Paul.

They become significant fellow workers of Paul's. He mentions them himself in three of his letters (Rom. 16.3; 1 Cor. 16.19; 2 Tim. 4.19). Paul always calls her Prisca, which is the proper name (Priscilla is a diminutive) and there was a famous Roman family of that name, the *gens Prisca*. Some scholars have suggested that she came from this family, or that she came from another high-status family. This would explain why, in most cases where they are mentioned in the New Testament, her name comes first: in the society of the time, when the wife is named before the husband, she is usually from a family of higher social status.[13] But what this fails to take into account is that she and her husband were tentmakers or leather-workers, and high-status people did not work with their hands.

So why does her name come first in four out of the six mentions? In the patriarchal society of the time, it's unconventional. Perhaps the prominence of her name is not to do with her status in society, but with her status in the church. A close look at those mentions reveals that when it's 'Aquila and Priscilla' (Acts 18.2; 1 Cor. 16.19), the reference is to their house or their occupation. Exactly as you would expect in the culture. But when the subject is their teaching or ministry, it's always 'Priscilla and Aquila' (Acts 18.18, 26; Rom. 16.3; 2 Tim. 4.19).[14] In the New Testament name orders are not accidental. In Acts we read of Barnabas and Saul right up to the point where Paul becomes more dominant, and thereafter it's mainly Paul and Barnabas.[15] Writing in the fourth century, John Chrysostom, hardly what you would call a rampant feminist, noted this. He argues that Paul 'seems to acknowledge a greater godliness for her than for her husband' and says that Paul 'names the woman first, as being I suppose more zealous, and more faithful'.[16] As we shall see from their work in Ephesus, there is a clear indication that Priscilla was the primary teacher of the two.

They had come to Corinth as a result of the expulsion of Jewish Christians from Rome, but they did not originate there – or not both of them, at least – for Aquila is a diaspora Jew from Pontus, a region bordering the Black Sea. Aquila was born in the east, but went west to work in Rome. This was typical. In Rome the businessmen, merchants and craftspeople were composed of freed slaves, lower-class workers and immigrants. Juvenal writes about the immigrant from the east:

> Is doing everything ... surveyor, painter, masseuse, doctor ... he understands everything ... the sailor's wind blows him to Rome together with plums and figs...[17]

They come over here, taking our jobs...

As to where they had come from, Luke just says that Paul went to see them and stayed with them because they were in the same trade. Paul evidently knew they were Christians. We know that they must have been expelled from Rome because they were Jewish Christians. So they were Christians when Paul met them, and nowhere does he claim responsibility for their conversion.

We know that Paul didn't baptise them, either. At Corinth he only baptised Gaius, Crispus and the household of Stephanas (1 Cor. 1.14–16). The fact is that in both Corinth and Ephesus, Priscilla and Aquila are intimately bound up with the planting of the church. In Ephesus, where they go after this, Paul preaches, but it's Priscilla and Aquila who establish the Christian community in their home.

Perhaps they became Christians in Rome; perhaps even earlier. Luke tells us that people from Pontus were present at Pentecost (Acts 2.9). Was Aquila one of those who heard Peter speak that day? The first letter of Peter is addressed to diaspora Jewish believers, including 'the exiles of the Dispersion in Pontus' (1 Pet. 1.1). We don't know when Aquila and his wife became followers. But we do know they were Christians when they left Rome and Christians when they arrived in Corinth. So the clear indication is that these were early, even founder members of the Roman church. If that's so, then it's probable that they were the founder members of the Corinthian church as well.

Corinth was a good place for a tentmaking couple like Priscilla and Aquila to live and to trade until the day came that they would be allowed back into Rome. There was business – the Isthmian Games meant a good demand for tents and awnings – and there were good facilities: throughout the city there were shops set around small squares or markets where artisans could ply their trade.

Typical of these was the North Market, which had shops around all four sides of the square. These were little more than cubicles: 4 metres high, 4 metres deep and with a width varying between 2.8 and 4 metres. Many of them had doors or windows linking with the next-door shop. The only ventilation was the door at the front. In winter workers would have needed a brazier indoors, making the working conditions smoky and uncomfortable. Other shops in Corinth were slightly bigger: 4.5 metres wide by 6 metres long.[18] Shops could also be found on the ground floor of Roman *insulae* or apartment buildings, and in many villas in Roman cities the part of the villa which fronted the street would have shops set into it. Some scholars believe that Priscilla and Aquila were wealthy – sufficiently wealthy to rent a house in Ephesus big enough to accommodate a church (1 Cor. 16.19). But property was expensive. If Priscilla and Aquila had enough money to rent a villa with a shop built in at the front, then why would they need to engage in the hard work of tentmaking? And anyway, such theories are based on the assumption that the church had large numbers. It didn't. It was small, at least at first.

Instead, all the evidence from Paul's own letters is that times were hard. Paul described himself in Corinth as being in need (2 Cor. 11.9). This was hardly a wealthy family or even, perhaps, a profitable enterprise. Their workshop may well not have been in a particularly salubrious area. In Rome, the shoemakers and leather-workers congregated in the notorious district of Subura, where there were also many prostitutes and brothels.[19] The fact is that Priscilla and Aquila were simple artisans. They had enough money to travel, to set themselves up in business. That was no mean achievement. They could rent a shop in Corinth with a room above it. They slept up there, while Paul would have slept in the workshop.

The workshop was where the church began as well. These were not just house churches, they were shop churches. The first *ekklesia* in Corinth must have been that of Priscilla and Aquila. (Maybe it was just those two to start with.) Like Luke in Philippi, there must have been some kind of tiny Christian proto-community of a handful of people, just a flickering spark, waiting for someone like Paul to come along with his usual flame-thrower approach and really get the blaze roaring.

So, they would have met in the workshop. It would not have been clean by our standards, but it would have been orderly, and it would have provided a space where they could close the shutters and share the bread and the wine, read what fragments of

Scripture they had and tell the stories about Jesus. They could do all the things, in fact, that they had once done in Rome.

It was not unusual for artisan-class people to host guests in their place of work. Apuleius describes a meal in the *taberna* of a fuller. The tools of his trade are scattered around the room, the acidic steam from the cloth being bleached tickles the nose. It was not a high-class dining experience.[20]

The early church, whether in Rome, Jerusalem or Corinth, met in domestic settings. There were no church buildings as such: the earliest dedicated church building discovered comes from the Roman border town of Dura-Europas and dates to the late third century. For the bulk of the first three centuries of its life, the Christian church was a house church.

Paul mentions many house churches in his letters. There is the house of Philemon in Colossae, the house of Gaius Titius Justus in Corinth, the household of Stephanas. The church that he writes to in Rome meets at the house of Priscilla and Aquila, just as the church in Ephesus had done. Sometimes these could have been sizeable dwellings, but just as often – maybe more often – they were small spaces, not houses as we think of them.

Ninety-seven per cent of Rome's population lived in *tabernae* (houses with shops on the ground floor) or the larger *insulae*, which were like apartment buildings. *Insulae* were mixed-use buildings. They were built around a central courtyard which offered light and air. On the ground floor, the outer units were shops. Families would live in these shops and they might also have a room behind, for a bit of privacy. Behind them were posher apartments which faced the inner courtyard. The higher you went up in the building, the smaller and humbler the apartments were. These rooms were all bedsits: the entire family lived in one room. And they had no latrines or cooking facilities.

The bigger houses, *domus*-type dwellings, were much rarer. In Rome only 3 per cent of the population could afford those. These had private rooms for the house owner, separate slave quarters and an *atrium* (inner courtyard) with a *triclinium* or dining room attached. There were houses like these in all cities: certainly remains have been found in Rome, Pompeii, Ephesus and Corinth. But even these did not have large amounts of space. In the

Anaploga villa in Corinth, which dates from Paul's time, the *triclinium* measured 5.5 by 7.5 metres, but the floor space would have been diminished by furniture, such as the couches which lined the walls. The *atrium* was directly outside the *triclinium*, but that was a bit smaller at 5 by 6 metres. Once again, the usable space was restricted, this time by the 2-metre-square pool in the middle. Put a congregation of some 40 people in there, and you've got a squeeze.

In Corinth, as we know from Paul's letters, it created problems. If everyone could not be accommodated in one room, the friends of the host would get the best seats in the *triclinium*. Two spaces, inside and out, meant automatic second-class-citizen status for some.

But the first church, the first gathering, must have been in the workshop of Priscilla and Aquila, missionary church-planters in Corinth. They gave Paul a foothold in the city. They gave him somewhere to live and somewhere to worship. They also gave him a job.

'By trade they were tentmakers'

Tentmaker. At least, that's how it's always translated. The word used in Acts 18.3 is *skēnopoioi*. *Skēnopios* does basically mean a tentmaker, but it also has a wider application, of someone who can work in leather and canvas and even linen. Some early church writers such as John Chrysostom and Origen believed that Paul, Priscilla and Aquila were leather-workers by trade. The likelihood, of course, is that like most craftsmen, they could probably turn their hands to work with a range of materials.

Certainly in Rome the tents made for the military were fashioned out of wide strips of leather. There was a guild of tentmakers (*tabernacularii*), part of whose role would be to provide awnings as well. The Roman post of Overseer of Awnings required the post-holder to make sure that, at games and shows in the arena, the seats of the soldiers and court personnel would be shaded from the sun. These awnings were made in the workshops of the imperial *tabernacularii*, the imperial tentmakers.[21]

So Paul's work involved making tents of leather or canvas, and the stitching together of awnings of linen for private houses, for banquets and for corporate celebrations such as the Isthmian Games. And that fits with the idea of Paul as a mobile workman. A tent-stitcher and repairman, a leather-worker, carrying his tools in a bundle: knives, awls, sharpening stone, needles and thread.[22]

In Græco-Roman antiquity the wealthy looked disparagingly upon work.[23] The aim of most workers in the ancient world – even though for most of them it would have been an unattainable dream – was to free themselves from manual labour. This is because manual labour was hard, and most work was manual labour. Conditions would be stiflingly hot in the summer and numbingly cold in the winter. Health and safety meant very different things in the first century! Lucian talks of manual workers being 'altogether demeaned' and Paul did not disagree. He describes himself in Corinth using exactly the same word.[24] The Jewish attitude to manual work was very different: rabbinic sources believed that 'Who doesn't teach his son a craft, makes him a robber.'[25]

It was tough. From his workshop at Ephesus, Paul talks of himself as poorly clothed and 'weary from the work of our own hands' (1 Cor. 4.12). Paul, Priscilla and Aquila spent their daily lives huddled over the workbench, knives and awls in their hands, cutting leather, stitching canvas. They worked like slaves and alongside slaves. Weary from the work of their own hands, they were humble artisans – so humble that some could view them as the 'rubbish of the world' (1 Cor. 4.13).

During Paul's time in Corinth he found out that some of those in Thessalonica were ignoring his example and living in idleness. He responded by pointing to his own example:

> We were not idle when we were with you, and we did not eat anyone's bread without paying for it; but with toil and labour we worked night and day, so that we might not burden any of you. This was not because we do not have that right, but in order to give you an example to imitate. For even when we were with you, we gave you this command: Anyone unwilling to work should not eat. For we hear that some of you are living in idleness, mere busybodies, not doing any work. Now such persons we command and exhort in the Lord Jesus Christ to do their work quietly and to earn their own living. (2 Thess. 3.7–12)

Paul's trade, therefore, was a key part of his make-up. He was Paul the letter-writer, Paul the evangelist, Paul the apostle, of course, but also Paul the tentmaker.[26]

How much he practised his trade is open to question. Certainly in any place where he stayed for more than a few weeks he probably sought out some work, or set up his own workshop. We know that he worked in Thessalonica (1 Thess. 2.9), Corinth (Acts 18.3; 1 Cor. 9.12) and probably Ephesus (Acts 20.33–34). And it's possible that even in Rome, under house arrest, he was able to take on some work.

Later, writing to the Corinthians from Ephesus, Paul defends the right of travelling apostles to be supported by the church. So he was clearly not against this in principle, but in practice it seems that he preferred to support himself where he could. 'The Lord', he says, 'commanded that those who proclaim the gospel should get their living by the gospel,' but in Corinth he deliberately chose not to exercise that right, so that he could make the gospel available 'free of charge' (1 Cor. 9.14, 18). It seems from his letters that Paul accepted financial assistance while he was in Corinth, but he did not accept it from the Corinthians themselves. When he was in Thessalonica he accepted it from those in Philippi (Phil. 4.16). Clearly his principle was not to accept money from those to whom he was taking the gospel. In Corinth, the giving and receiving of money meant entering into a patron-client relationship. Accepting money placed you under an obligation to the donor. Paul rejected this kind of social obligation. The gospel must be free of charge and free from influence.

Paul refused the support of the Corinthian church – a refusal at which some took umbrage. But he recognised that in a city like Corinth, money talked. He did not want to be in anyone's pocket. This refusal tells you a lot about Paul, but also a lot about Corinth.

'To the church of the Thessalonians'

As usual, Paul begins by arguing his case in the synagogue, and that is where Silas and Timothy find him when they eventually arrive from Macedonia. Their arrival brings Paul news from the church at Thessalonica. It's a positive report and Paul writes back full of thanksgiving for this news.

Unlike later letters, the first letter to the Thessalonians contains no quotes from the Hebrew Scriptures. This is probably because the church at Thessalonica is mainly Gentile and they don't know the Hebrew Scriptures. Yet even so their decision to 'turn to God from idols' has become the talk of the people of Macedonia and Achaia. It seems as if he's overstating it a bit, until we realise that the believers in those regions must have been only a handful of people at the time.

The passage shows Paul's expectation of the way in which growth is to occur: it starts with the apostles, with their stories, their testimony, their example. This in turn inspires the church, and then the believers in Thessalonica become an inspiration for the entire region. Paul clearly paints a picture of church growth which is based around imitative behaviour. This was how he learned, at the feet of rabbi Gamaliel: you learn this stuff by doing it.

Paul's letters are not meant as theological essays, a databank of doctrine, to be pored over, dissected and debated. His emphasis is just as much on practice. And this matters, because the Thessalonians are facing real problems. They are imitators in another way: 'For you, brothers and sisters,' Paul writes, 'became imitators of the churches of God in Christ Jesus that are in Judea, for you suffered the same things from your own compatriots as they did from the Jews' (1 Thess. 2.14).

The Thessalonians are grieving. Some of their number have died – perhaps during the same bout of persecution which forced Paul to flee the city, although Paul doesn't make that explicit. But now they are worried: if Jesus is supposed to return in their lifetime, then what will happen to those dead Christians? Will they miss out?

Paul replies that the opposite is true: those who are dead will rise first. They will get their reward. He goes on to describe what he believes will happen when Jesus returns. He will come like a thief in the night, and the dead in Christ will rise to meet him. This passage, which talks of those who are left being caught up in the clouds and meeting the Lord in the air, is what led to the theory of the rapture (1 Thess. 4.13 – 5.11). We should be careful here, however. Paul is speaking in the language of apocalyptic literature, a picture language, mysterious: it should not be interpreted literally.

But again, it reminds us that for the early church time was short. Paul says the same thing to the Christians in NeoCorinth. 'The appointed time has grown short,' he writes (1 Cor. 7.29). It won't be long now...

His first letter must have been sent not long after Timothy and Silas arrived in the city. A little while later he has another letter from Thessalonica. His arguments may have worked a little too well. Some members of the Christian community in Thessalonica believe that the Day of the Lord has already arrived. Paul is uncertain where they have got these ideas from: perhaps it's the first-century equivalent of those who, today, endlessly claim that we are living in the end times.

He counters this by writing of certain things which he believes must happen before the Day of the Lord arrives. It seems to involve a rebellion against God. The 'rebellion' will be a collapse of civil order (Paul may be thinking of the mob rule and anarchy he witnessed in Macedonia) and it will be accompanied by the rise of a figure called the man of lawlessness who will claim divine honours for himself.

The prototype for this figure clearly comes from Daniel 7 – 12, the prophetic section of Daniel, which was the key apocalyptic text for the early church. This was the rootstock from which Paul's ideas grew, and from which the great, exotic foliage of Revelation sprouted in all its florid colours. The passage depicts the blasphemous King Antiochus Epiphanes (175–164 BC) as the 'little horn' with the big mouth (Dan. 7.8), and it portrays another king who will 'exalt himself and consider himself greater than any god, and shall speak horrendous things against the God of gods' (Dan. 11.36). It was from meditating on this kind of imagery that the early church came up with the ideas of the 'lawless one'.

The other important element came from Jesus himself, who warned that after preaching the gospel to all nations, his followers would see the 'abomination of desolation standing where he ought not' (Mark 13:10, 14–27).

But if that's where the ideas originated, who are the candidates for the role? The lawless one 'opposes and exalts himself above every so-called god or object of worship, so that he takes his seat in the temple of God, declaring himself to be God' (2 Thess. 2.4).

That could easily describe Caligula, who in AD 40 commanded that his statue should be erected in the temple at Jerusalem.[27] But anyone who wandered into the forum would have seen plenty of statues of emperors who claimed to be gods. Augustus, Tiberius, Caligula, Claudius: there's no shortage of candidates, no shortage of deified emperors to be identified with the 'man of sin'.[28]

The rebellion, though, is on hold. Something is keeping this in check. What this is, Paul doesn't spell out. It may be that, with the words of Jesus in mind, Paul sees his own mission to the Gentiles as the holding power. Until that's completed, the next stage can't begin. But there's a guardedness about his comments in general which hint at a different solution. Paul has told them all about this when he was with them, but he seems reluctant to name names now. The most obvious solution, therefore, is that he's talking about powers which he sees at work all around him, and he can't say more because the letter might fall into the wrong hands.

The charge against the Christians in Thessalonica was that they were proclaiming an alternative kingdom and a different king. Although the magistrates acted with caution then, Paul isn't at all sure that they will do so again. And the Jewish leaders have been active against the Thessalonian church. So Paul is careful to use an opaque, apocalyptic language.

Early exegetes of this passage believed that the restraining hand was clearly the Roman Empire. It was law and order which was holding the rebellion in check. Tertullian wrote, 'What is this but the Roman state, whose removal when it has been divided among ten kings will bring on Antichrist?'[29] (The reference to the ten kings comes from Rev. 17:12–14). John Chrysostom said:

> Some interpret this of the grace of the Spirit, but others of the Roman Empire, and this is my own preference. Why? Because, if Paul had meant the Spirit, he would have said so plainly and not obscurely ... but because he meant the Roman Empire, he naturally glanced at it, speaking covertly and darkly ... when the Roman Empire is out of the way, then he [Antichrist] will come.[30]

If the man of lawlessness is the emperor, though, how can his own forces hold him back? Well, in some ways this had already happened: Gaius's madness was held in check by his assassination and the accession of the milder, more trustworthy and generally less bonkers Claudius. But how long would that last? What if Claudius was succeeded by another mad-god emperor?

Apocalyptic writing is always tricky. It's Christian conspiracy theory. And 2 Thessalonians is one of Paul's most difficult letters. We see Paul's thoughts through a glass darkly; too darkly, in the end, to be certain of what he means. Perhaps, ultimately, it's safest to go with Augustine, who in the fifth century AD wrote simply, 'I admit that the meaning of this completely escapes me.'[31]

'When Gallio was proconsul of Achaia'

Back to more concrete data. Literally, in fact. For in Corinth, near the market place, just outside the gate on the Lechaeum road, archaeologists have found a broken lintel with the inscription 'Synagogue of the Hebrew'. The date of the inscription is uncertain, but maybe it was here that the Jewish synagogue was sited in the time of Paul.

In the synagogue, Paul is busy 'proclaiming the word, testifying to the Jews that the Messiah was Jesus' (Acts 18.5). It ends, as usual, in a break-up. Paul seems to react fiercely, according to Luke: he shakes the dust from his clothes and declares that their blood is on their own heads. But that's typical Paul. Never knowingly understated. Maybe the breach was not quite as violent as all that, although emotions were clearly running high. In any case, Paul's move to the Gentiles only involves moving to the house next door. He goes to the house of a man called Titius Justus, next door to the synagogue. (This doesn't necessarily mean that Paul moves to live there; what it means is that the growing church in Corinth moves out of the workshop of Priscilla and Aquila and into these larger, undoubtedly posher, premises.)

Titius is a 'worshipper of God', a God-fearer, so obviously Paul's discussions in the synagogue have borne some fruit. It's possible that he should be identified with the Gaius whom Paul mentions in 1 Corinthians 1.14 and who later hosts the whole church (Rom. 16.23). In that case, his full name would have been Gaius Titius Justus. The name indicates a man of Roman extraction.

So Paul doesn't have to move far from the synagogue. And he continues, in fact, to have contact with the people there, because then Crispus, 'the official of the synagogue', becomes a Christian, as do all of his household (Acts 18.8). Crispus is an *archisunagogos,* a 'synagogue leader'. A prominent and visible convert, then, and one which sets tongues wagging in Corinth.

Paul's mission in Corinth goes on for another eighteen months, with some success. We can surmise that the converts were predominantly drawn from the lower social strata of the city. Paul observes that 'not many of you were wise by human standards, not many were powerful, not many were of noble birth'. He goes on to describe the Corinthian church as 'weak' and 'low and despised in the world' (1 Cor. 1.26–28). But 'not many' is not 'none': there were some in the church with wealth, status and power.

It is the power of God which Paul credits with the success. He admits that in appearance he himself is not impressive, and he claims to have none of the clever rhetorical skills which the sophisticated elite of Corinth value:

> I did not come proclaiming the mystery of God to you in lofty words or wisdom ... My speech and my proclamation were not with plausible words of wisdom, but with a demonstration of the Spirit and of power, so that your faith might rest not on human wisdom but on the power of God. (1 Cor. 2.1–5)

No flashy rhetoric, then. No smooth talking. Later on, indeed, Paul's lack of rhetorical flair is used against him by the Corinthians. And it may be one of the reasons why the elite of Corinth do not respond to his message as readily as the lowly and the despised. Græco-Roman orators made a great play of their artistry in public speaking. The tricks of rhetoric and persuasion were studied carefully. Politicians, soldiers, lawyers and public orators used sophisticated rhetorical techniques to make their case more plausible. But for Paul, all that matters is Jesus and the shocking, startling, upside-down message of his crucifixion.

Paul's preaching and teaching, uncultured in style though it is, bears fruit. But it also brings enemies. So much so that Paul fears there will be violent action against him. According to Luke he is reassured by a vision, a promise from the Lord that 'no one will lay a hand on you to harm you, for there are many in this city who are my people' (Acts 18.5–11).

It must have been a comfort to him because, in the summer of AD 51, he was hauled before the proconsul. 'When Gallio was proconsul of Achaia,' Luke writes, 'the Jews made a united attack on Paul and brought him before the tribunal' (Acts 18.12).

Junius Annaeus Gallio was the son of Marcus Annaeus Seneca, a famous orator from Spain. Born in Cordova some time around AD 1, he was the younger brother of the famous philosopher and politician Lucius Annaeus Seneca (4 BC – AD 65), better known to history as plain 'Seneca'. His birth name was Lucius Annaeus Novatus, but he changed it when he was adopted by the famous Roman senator Lucius Junius Gallio and introduced into political life. His reputation was as a cultured, witty man (his brother said, 'No human is so pleasant to any person as Gallio is to everyone', although he was probably biased).[32]

Paul's encounter with Gallio in Corinth is one of the few points in the chronology of Acts which we can date with reasonable precision. The reason for this is the 'Gallio inscription', an inscription in Delphi which equates Gallio's proconsulship to the year that Claudius was 'acclaimed emperor for the 26th time'.[33] The general consensus is that this refers to the the first half of AD 52. The inscription implies that Gallio is no longer in office, which means that Gallio was proconsul of Achaia from the summer of AD 51 to the summer of AD 52.[34]

Paul is probably dragged before Gallio soon after the new proconsul's arrival in Corinth. A new, untried proconsul might be a good target for a strategic complaint. The action takes place at the *bēma*, the judgement seat in the middle of the *agora*, and the accusation, once again, is of anti-Roman practices, of worshipping God 'in ways that are contrary to the law' (Acts 18.13). The problem is, though, that the people bringing the complaint are Jews. Gallio, like his brother, was anti-Semitic. Had these been Greek citizens, maybe he would have been more interested. As it is, he simply dismisses the suit out of hand:

> If it were a matter of crime or serious villainy, I would be justified in accepting the complaint of you Jews; but since it is a matter of questions about words and names and your own law, see to it yourselves; I do not wish to be a judge of these matters. (Acts 18.14–15)

The complaint dismissed, a fight breaks out. The crowd seize a man called Sosthenes – another 'official of the synagogue' – and beat him in front of the tribunal. It's sometimes assumed that they were angry with their leader, but, according to 1 Corinthians 1.1, Sosthenes was a Christian. He could have become a Christian after this treatment, of course, but it seems to me likely that Sosthenes was a target for the anger of the remaining Jewish synagogue leaders. Like Crispus, he was one of their own, one of their leaders to boot, and he, too, had gone to the house next door.

The judgement of Gallio gives Paul a significant breathing space. It secures his position for almost a year and allows him to establish the church in Corinth firmly.

'Farewell to the believers'

Paul remained at Corinth for 'some considerable time', during which time the church expanded and his hard work was rewarded (Acts 18.18). To Titius Justus and Crispus, we can add other names. Chloe and her household. Sosthenes. Fortunatus and Achaicus – two slaves, judging by their names. There was Gaius as well, who may be the same as Titius Justus, but who was one of a handful of people baptised by Paul himself. Gaius may have been more wealthy, since in AD 57 the church was meeting in his house. There was also a man called Stephanas and his household, whom Paul describes as 'the first converts in Achaia' (1 Cor. 16.15–17).

There's a riddle here, because Corinth was not Paul's first stop in Achaia – that was Athens. But if Stephanas was a Corinthian, how do we reconcile that statement with Luke's statement that some people in Athens believed? Perhaps the easiest solution is that Stephanas was in Athens, not Corinth, when Paul met him. Later he moved, or went back, to Corinth.

There was also a woman called Phoebe: a church had been established in Cenchreae under her patronage (Rom. 16.1–2). She had been a benefactor of Paul and of many others. It was a short walk from the centre of Corinth to the eastern Corinthian port of Cenchreae. Paul had no doubt made the 9-kilometre journey lots of times during the eighteen months he was there.

In the summer of AD 52, Gallio left Corinth. Cultured he may have been, but something in Corinth got to him. He left office, according to his brother, because of a fever. His brother said, 'When, in Achaia, he [Gallio] began to feel feverish, he immediately took ship, claiming that it was not a malady of the body but of the place.'[35] In other words, he was both physically and metaphorically sick of Corinth. Political life made Gallio – and it also destroyed him. In AD 59 he had to act as compère for Nero when he notoriously appeared playing the lyre and singing on the stage.[36] He was convicted of being involved in the Pisonian conspiracy – a plot to assassinate the Emperor Nero. Despite the Senate testifying to his innocence, he was forced to commit suicide.

Perhaps it was rumours of the proconsul's departure which decided Paul to move on. Better not risk another appeal from the Jews before an incoming proconsul. Time to head back to Judea. The Way had been established in Macedonia and Achaia. Time to head home. He went first to Cenchreae, accompanied by Priscilla and Aquila.

Before departing, though, Paul had his head shaved because of a vow (Acts 18.18). The implication is that this was some sort of Nazirite vow. Perhaps he had made a thanksgiving vow to God for keeping him safe at Corinth after the turbulent times at Philippi and Thessalonica. Or perhaps it was to do with his vision. But it seems that Paul had not cut his hair while in Corinth, and now he was leaving he was free to have it cut. Usually at the completion of such a vow, the hair would be cut at Jerusalem and then offered as a sacrifice.[37]

'To the Jews I became as a Jew, in order to win Jews,' Paul wrote to the Corinthians. 'To those under the law I became as one under the law (though I myself am not under the law) so that I might win those under the law' (1 Cor. 9.20). So it may be that as part of his ongoing dialogue and dispute with the Jews in Corinth he took a vow and lived it out. He became a Nazir, a Nazirite.

As usual, Luke has been attacked by some for historical or even theological inaccuracy. It has been argued that Paul would not have taken such a vow, because of his strong ideas about grace. But that is putting words into Paul's mouth. Why on earth would Luke invent such a thing? He doesn't explain it. He just knows it happened and puts it in. The uncomfortable fact for those who would seek to put Paul in a box is that he refused such easy categorisation. At the end of the day, he was Jewish, and you can take the boy out of Judaism… We certainly know that Paul voluntarily submitted to other Jewish customs and rites: indeed, he would later do so in Jerusalem. What he always complained about was people being forced into rites and rituals which they did not need to do and which they could not comprehend. A vow taken voluntarily hardly falls into this category.

Head shaven, accompanied by Priscilla and Aquila, their tools and supplies wrapped up and carried with them, Paul boarded a small freighter and sailed out of the harbour, past the enormous statue of Poseidon holding a dolphin and a trident. They left the harbour and headed east. Across the Saronic Gulf to Ephesus, the chief city of the province of Asia. Some two years before, he had been stopped from going there by the Spirit. Now there was no such hindrance.

The visit was a brief one, however. Despite being urged by Jews in the local synagogue to stay and discuss further, Paul wanted to return to Syria. He promised to return, but he made haste to Jerusalem.[38] He left behind him Priscilla and Aquila. No doubt they had business in the city, but perhaps Paul left them there to do some groundwork for a later visit.

Luke gives us no details of the journey, but after Paul arrived in Caesarea the text says that 'he went up and greeted the church, and then went down to Antioch' (Acts 18.22, NIV). The implication – spelled out as definite in many Bible translations – is that he went to Jerusalem. Certainly, had he been heading for Antioch, he would hardly have gone via Caesarea, which was a long way south. But he intended to report back on all he had been doing. He was performing his duty to the leaders in Jerusalem. It was just like getting his hair cut.

Then it was back to Antioch. Two years and 2,700 miles since he had set out with Silas, he was back home.

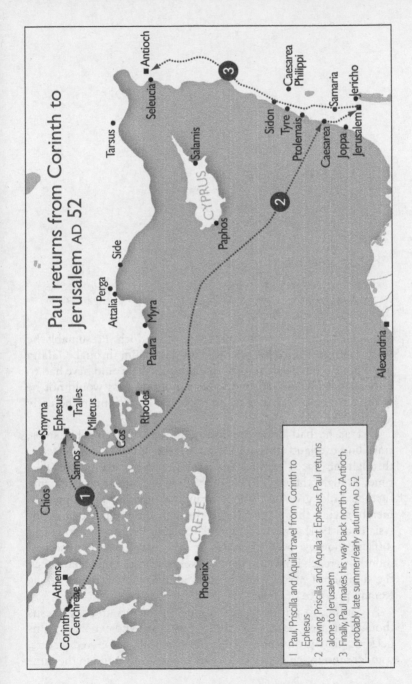

Paul returns from Corinth to Jerusalem AD 52

1 Paul, Priscilla and Aquila travel from Corinth to Ephesus

2 Leaving Priscilla and Aquila at Ephesus, Paul returns alone to Jerusalem

3 Finally, Paul makes his way back north to Antioch, probably late summer/early autumn AD 52

211

8. Ephesus AD 53–57

'Through the inland regions'

> After spending some time there he departed and went from place to place through the region of Galatia and Phrygia, strengthening all the disciples. (Acts 18.23)

We don't know how long Paul spent at Antioch. Presumably he wintered there: since his next journey takes him through Galatia and Phrygia 'strengthening all the disciples' he would have had to go via the Cilician Gates and that mountain pass would not be easily navigable over winter. So probably he set out in the early spring of AD 53.

Just as he had done previously, he was retracing his steps, travelling overland through Lystra, Derbe and then further east, through the places he, Silas and Timothy had visited before. This time, though, there was no Spirit stopping him from exploring further. Luke gives us little information about Paul's itinerary, merely saying that Paul passed 'through the inland regions' of Asia (Acts 19.1). Overland from Antioch to Ephesus is a long and difficult journey: over 700 miles. It must have taken Paul several months to reach Ephesus. So at the very earliest, it must have been the summer of AD 53 when he arrived in Ephesus, capital of the Roman province of Asia.

According to an inscription found in the city itself, Ephesus thought of itself as a 'most illustrious city'. The extensive ruins back up that proud boast. Visitors can walk the paved streets, wander among the upper and lower forums and stand in the huge

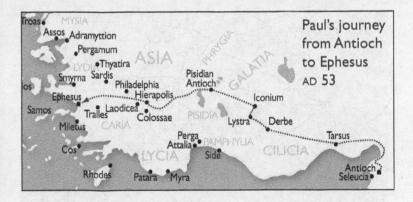

Paul's journey from Antioch to Ephesus AD 53

theatre mentioned in Acts 19.29. They can see the outlines of the lavish houses, sit in the public toilets – and even read a sign saying, 'This way to the brothel.'

Ephesus had grown extensively during the reign of Augustus, benefiting from the increase in commerce under the *pax Romana*. Strabo said that 'because of its advantageous location ... [Ephesus] grows daily, and is the largest emporium in Asia this side of the Taurus'.[1] That word 'emporium' is significant. Like Corinth, Ephesus was a wealthy city. And, again like Corinth, it derived its wealth from its port. The port required a lot of attention and sophisticated civil engineering. The tendency of the river to silt up meant that the port was only kept open through extensive dredging (today it lies 5 miles inland). But Ephesus had the money and the skills to innovate. It had all the latest inventions: *insulae* apartment blocks with running water piped to every level (unknown even in Rome and Ostia). On the ground floor were shops, including the first-century equivalent of cafés, selling warm drinks and snacks.[2]

The city was crammed with impressive building schemes and monuments. Archaeologists have discovered many dating from the time of Paul: the Upper Agora, temples of Dea Roma, Divus Iulius, Isis, Augustus and Apollo, the Stadium, the Fountain House, the Palace of the Proconsul, the Theatre, the Harbour Gate, the Korassian Gate, the Magnesian Gate. The list goes on and on – and those are just the ones we know about.[3]

Left: Artemis of the Ephesians. A statue of the goddess from Ephesus

Right: 'This way to the brothel'. A street sign for visitors to Ephesus

Below: Ephesus today, looking down towards what used to be the harbour

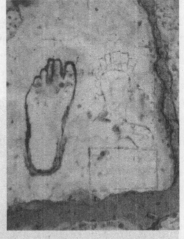

The most important monument, the one for which Ephesus was famous, was the Artemisium, the temple of Artemis, one of the seven wonders of the ancient world. The original temple had burned to the ground in 356 BC, on the night of Alexander the Great's death.[4] It was rebuilt about five years later and this second temple was magnificent. Measuring 130 by 70 metres – four times the size of the Parthenon in Athens – the building was adorned with 128 pillars of the finest Parian marble, each over 18 metres high. This semi-translucent, pure white, flawless marble came from the island of Paros. On its own it was stunning, but in the temple of Artemis it had even been inlaid with gold.[5]

The original Artemis was a daughter of Zeus and sister of Apollo, a virgin hunter-goddess. The Romans knew her as Diana, goddess of forests and groves. Artemis of the Ephesians was a mutation of this original. She was more of a mother-goddess, a fertility symbol, a kind of mash-up between Artemis, the Phrygian mother-goddess Cybele and the Phoenician Astarte. Her statues show her as a multi-breasted woman wearing a crown of city walls.[6] Her priestesses were called 'bees', while the priests – all eunuchs – were 'drones'. As well as these, the temple had a huge staff of attendants and functionaries.[7]

By Paul's day she was famous around the Græco-Roman world. Pausanias writes, 'All cities worship Artemis of the Ephesians and individuals hold her honour above all the gods.' He puts her fame down to 'the antiquity of the sanctuary', the size of the temple and the 'eminent' status of Ephesus.[8] Wherever you were in the Græco-Roman world, you would have found adherents of Artemis of the Ephesians: she was the Manchester United of ancient gods. The magnificence of her temple and the cult surrounding it drew visitors and pilgrims from far and wide. So Ephesus was, in some ways, like Jerusalem. It was a pilgrimage city. Religion was one among the many things on sale in the great emporium of Ephesus.

Its position made it the perfect strategic base for Paul. To the east were the Christian communities he had founded in Galatia and Cilicia. To the west, Macedonia and Achaia. There were sea routes to the Aegean, the Bosphorus, Egypt, and east to Palestine and Syria. Two great highways left the city, heading east. One was the *koine hodos*, the Common Highway which wound up the

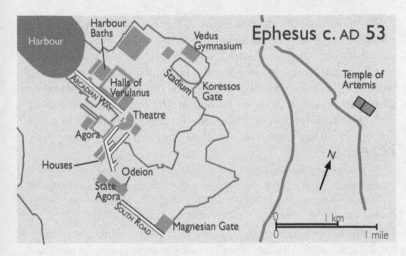

Meander Valley to Tralles and beyond. Or you could go north to Sardis and then pick up the ancient Persian Royal Road which ran all the way to Susa, via Galatia. This is why the Romans chose the place as their administrative capital in Asia. Using these excellent transport connections, the Romans set up a college of *tabellarii* – messengers or couriers – in the city.[9] Ephesus was a hub of ancient communication (this must have been a key reason why Paul originally wanted to go there in AD 50). This is why Luke is able to say that as a result of Paul's work in Ephesus, 'all the residents of Asia, both Jews and Greeks, heard the word of the Lord' (Acts 19.10): what happened in Ephesus would radiate out rapidly throughout the region.

There's one more thing, too: Ephesus had a Christian community. Priscilla and Aquila had stayed after leaving Corinth with Paul. And sometime around AD 53, an Alexandrian Jew arrived in Ephesus. His name was Apollos.

'A Jew named Apollos'

Apollos probably arrived after the sailing season opened in the spring of AD 53. An Alexandrian Jew, he arrived, perhaps, on one of the first grain ships of the year from Egypt. The Empire relied on Egypt's grain, taken around the Mediterranean by enormous ships – the tankers of the day.

We know little about the origins of Christianity in Alexandria, which is surprising considering the role the city was to play in the course of Christian history. Alexandria was the home of the first Christian training college – the famous Catechetical School. From Alexandria come the great codices, the first complete bound Christian Bibles. It grew to be one of the four great centres of early Christianity. But in the New Testament we only hear of one Alexandrian Christian: Apollos. And even he is only *partly* a Christian:

> [Apollos] was an eloquent man, well-versed in the scriptures. He had been instructed in the Way of the Lord; and he spoke with burning enthusiasm and taught accurately the things concerning Jesus, though he knew only the baptism of John. (Acts 18.24–25)

There is no question in Luke's eyes – just as there was none for Priscilla and Aquila – that Apollos was anything other than a *bona fide* believer. This was no false teacher, no charlatan or freeloader. This was a man with enthusiasm and skill who taught accurately about Jesus. But there is that curious, difficult detail: Apollos, Luke says, 'knew only the baptism of John'.

It seems a contradiction in terms: how could a man teach accurately about Jesus, but only know the baptism of John? And why did Priscilla and Aquila have to take him to one side and explain the way of God to him more accurately?

There are two main possibilities. The WT says that he was 'instructed in his own country in the word of the Lord'. It's not impossible that he learned about Christianity in Alexandria (although the phrase 'word of the Lord' may simply refer to his Jewish upbringing). It may be that some of those who dispersed because of the persecution after Stephen's death went back to Egypt and, as we saw with Philip, they were not fully acquainted with the baptism of the Holy Spirit. But it seems hard to believe that in twenty years no one had brought a wider perspective.

For another possible answer, we have to go back a bit further, to the early days of Jesus' public work in AD 29–30. From the end of AD 29 to John the Baptist's arrest in early AD 31, Jesus was working alongside John. According to John's Gospel, Jesus was baptising in the Jordan, while John was at Aenon near Salim (John 3.22–24). Many people were baptised at this time by Jesus and his disciples while they were still working alongside John. Say one or two people from Alexandria had been on a pilgrimage to Jerusalem in the autumn of AD 30. There they discovered a new teacher, Jesus, offering John's baptism of repentance. They were baptised and became, at that point, followers of Jesus. Since that time they had picked up other information about Jesus, odds and ends, but they had never been presented with the big picture.[10] There were disciples of Jesus who had known him only when he was working alongside John.

It was from people like this that Apollos learned about Jesus. We know that there were still followers of John the Baptist around; Paul met twelve of them when he arrived in Ephesus. These disciples were ignorant of the Holy Spirit and had only encountered 'John's baptism'. Paul prayed for them and the Spirit descended: they spoke in tongues and prophesied (Acts 19.1–7). It's quite possible that around the Mediterranean there were others who had only ever seen a part of the picture.

Whatever the case, Apollos's information was incomplete. So Priscilla and Aquila took him under their wing. Again, the order of the names is important. John Chrysostom believed that it was Priscilla who did the teaching. 'She took Apollos … and she instructed him in the way of the Lord and made him a teacher.'[11] Now fully equipped, Apollos became an important and effective evangelist and when his travels took him across to Corinth, the believers in Ephesus supplied him with letters of recommendation. Apollos proved to be a big success in Corinth (Acts 18.27–28). Later, Paul may be referring to these letters when he writes to the Corinthians, 'Surely we do not need, as some do, letters of recommendation to you or from you, do we?' (2 Cor. 3.1–2)

Later on in Corinth the Apollos faction characterised themselves as inspired Spirit-filled believers – in contrast to Paul's converts (1 Cor. 1 – 4). Ironic, considering that when he came to Ephesus, Apollos didn't even know that the Holy Spirit existed.

'Extraordinary miracles'

In Ephesus, Paul naturally joined forces again with Priscilla and Aquila. A church had grown up in the city, perhaps sparked off with Paul's brief visit, but mainly, one imagines, from the work of Priscilla and Aquila in the intervening months. It certainly met in their house. We also know the name of one possible Ephesian church member: writing to Rome, Paul sends greetings to Epaenetus, 'who was the first convert in Asia for Christ' (Rom. 16.5). Paul does not claim responsibility for this conversion. Epaenetus had moved to Rome by the time Romans was written in AD 57, and Priscilla and Aquila had also returned to Rome. It seems probable that all three of them moved there together and that Epaenetus was the first convert in the fledgling Ephesian Christian community.

From Priscilla and Aquila, Paul must have heard the story of Apollos and, indeed, it must have been soon after this that Apollos returned from Corinth. Perhaps Paul sent for him – certainly he would have wanted to meet him. We should note, in light of what's going to happen, that Paul never once criticises him. Nor does he seek to order him around. He acknowledges that they each have a unique gifting:

> What then is Apollos? What is Paul? Servants through whom you came to believe, as the Lord assigned to each. I planted, Apollos watered, but God gave the growth. (1 Cor. 3.5–6)

Various other claims have been made for Apollos over the centuries, most notably Luther's suggestion that he was the author of Hebrews. In the end, however, all we know of Apollos is that he was an eloquent, capable speaker, a committed evangelist and a supportive colleague of Paul who refused to become involved in any of the factionalism which later struck the Corinthian church.

Apollos was not the only travelling Christian evangelist to visit Corinth in the years after Paul left. Peter and Barnabas probably visited there as well. Paul later refers to them in his correspondence to the Corinthians (1 Cor. 1.12; 3.22; 9.5). Corinth, given its strategic position geographically, must have received a steady stream of famous and not-so-famous apostles and teachers.

In Ephesus Paul applied his trusted procedure: into the synagogue, preach for a bit, get thrown out of the synagogue and move elsewhere. Although this time, Luke records that he lasted for three months before he was evicted. Maybe he was mellowing (Acts 19.8–10).

In Corinth he had moved to the house of Titius Justus. In Ephesus, Luke records that he hired a local venue, the lecture hall of Tyrannus. The name Tyrannus means 'tyrant': perhaps it was a nickname for the teacher who had taught there. According to the WT, he hired the hall from 11 a.m. to 4 p.m. Since public life in cities like Ephesus finished at midday and everyone who could afford to headed for the baths, or home for a siesta, it would have been cheaper at this time. (It has been suggested that more people would have been awake in Ephesus at 1 a.m. than at 1 p.m!)[12] If this is correct, it means that Paul would work from dawn till 11 a.m., then go to the lecture hall to discuss and debate. The man had stamina. So did his listeners.

There are two time markers for Paul's stay in Ephesus. The first is Acts 19.8–10, which says that Paul spoke in the synagogue for three months and then continued to lecture in the hall of Tyrannus for two years. The second is in Acts 20.31, where Paul, speaking to the Ephesian elders, says that 'for three years I did not cease night or day to warn everyone with tears'. Bearing in mind Paul's typical use of inclusive time, this doesn't mean that he was in Ephesus for three full calendar years. Paul was probably in Ephesus from the summer of AD 53 to AD 55.[13]

Paul's stay brought the good news to a lot of people. 'All the residents of Asia, both Jews and Greeks, heard the word of the Lord,' says Luke (Acts 19.10). It must have been at this time that Christianity spread out from Ephesus to the surrounding region, up the Lycus Valley to cities like Laodicea, Colossae, Hierapolis. Paul did not found those churches (Colossae was probably founded by Epaphras), but he knew of them.

Meanwhile in Ephesus the miraculous was happening. As a religious centre, the city had a reputation for magic and miracle, especially healing. Artemis the goddess was specifically associated with acts of healing. Strabo records that her name derived from the fact that she made people *artemeas,* that is, 'safe and sound'.[14] She was believed to listen to the prayers of her followers, to help those in need. This was a city where miracles were requested. But in Ephesus, tales of the miraculous soon attached themselves to Paul. According to Acts – and in a verse that has long been a severe embarrassment to staunch Protestants – even 'relics', cloths and aprons which he had touched, brought healing and exorcism.

In a city where magic held so much sway, it was unsurprising that this power started to attract the attention of the other mystics and magicians. The first to take notice were some itinerant Jewish exorcists known as the seven sons of Sceva. Luke calls Sceva a Jewish high priest, but his name does not appear among any of the high priests from the time. Possibly he means that they were part of a high-priestly dynasty, but more probably this man was not a Jerusalem-based high priest at all, but a renegade Jewish leader of a localised cult. There were other temples of Judaism in the ancient world. There was one, for example, at Elephantine in Egypt. These seven sons tried to exorcise a man by invoking the name of Jesus. They were soundly thrashed by the demon. Jesus' name is not some magic spell or incantation to be bought in the market place.

The event had a marked effect on the local adherents, who burned their very valuable books of magic ritual. People were turning away from paganism and towards Christianity. And in a city which was famous for its pagan roots, that was going to cause problems.

Talking of problems...

'It has been reported to me by Chloe's people'

Libraries of books have been written on the letters of Paul to the Corinthians and his relationship with the Corinthian church, but pinning down the sequence of events is tricky. References to what happened are scattered through Paul's letters to the church – at least one of which is lost.

Luke doesn't mention the problem, but that's hardly surprising. He's not out to wash dirty linen in public. And anyway, what happened in Corinth, in the grand scheme of things, was not really that important. No one died. The civil authorities were not involved (except in a roundabout way). It was an internal matter.

But clearly what happened in Corinth occupied a lot of Paul's time and energy between AD 53 and 54. And it resulted in two (or maybe three) of Paul's most influential and important letters.

So, what did happen?

In the New Testament there are two letters from Paul known as 1 and 2 Corinthians. But we know from internal evidence that he wrote at least four, which I'm going to call, with stunning originality, Letters A, B, C and D.

▷ *Letter A*. Referred to in 1 Corinthians 5.9–11. The first letter about dealing with sexual immorality in the church. This is missing.

▷ *Letter B*. This is what we call 1 Corinthians. A much longer letter addressing numerous problems.

▷ *Letter C*. Referred to in 2 Corinthians 7.8–9. This is a 'harsh' letter, written in terms that even Paul came to think might have been too strong.

▷ *Letter D*. A reconciliation letter: what we call 2 Corinthians.

So, two letters are missing. Or are they?

It has to be said that 2 Corinthians is a strange letter. Written after Paul has left Ephesus, it starts off full of joy and light and relief that the problem has been solved. Paul suggests that the person who caused the problem should be welcomed back and forgiven (2 Cor. 2.5–11). At the beginning of the book, Paul addresses the fact that he has not come and visited the Corinthians as he thought he would. He says that he didn't want to have another painful visit, after he had been forced to write them a harsh and painful letter (2 Cor. 1.15 – 2.4). But that is the only real note of contention in the opening chapters. The tone of the first nine chapters of this book is one of relief and forgiveness.

But then, at chapter 10, everything changes. The tone alters entirely. Paul is suddenly on the defensive: justifying his conduct as an apostle, talking of 'punishing disobedience' (2 Cor. 10.6), recounting his history, talking sarcastically of 'super-apostles', answering claims that he has been deceitful (2 Cor. 12.16) and saying that he is ready to come to the Corinthians a third time (2 Cor. 12.14). When he comes, he fears that he will find all kinds of problems – 'quarrelling, jealousy, anger, selfishness, slander, gossip, conceit, and disorder' – and that he will have to mourn over 'many who previously sinned and have not repented of the impurity, sexual immorality, and licentiousness that they have practised' (2 Cor. 12.20–21). He warns that he will not be lenient (2 Cor. 13.2).

What happened? One minute it's all sweetness and light, all joy and forgiveness, the next minute it's biting sarcasm, withering put-downs and Paul waving the big stick. As one writer has commented, 'the text ... seems to show some very rough seams'.[15] That's an understatement. If this was one of Paul's tents, you would send it back.

Clearly something is wrong. Those who argue for the unity of 2 Corinthians suggest that Paul has sweetened the pill: having been positive to build them up, he now lays into them. But that's hardly convincing. The gist of the first nine chapters is that the situation has been largely resolved. If it hasn't, if there's still back-biting, dissension and sexual immorality, then Paul is not sweetening the pill, he's just lying.

Another suggestion is that there's a gap between Paul finishing chapter 9 and then starting chapter 10, and in that gap things went wrong again. So Paul, instead of starting the whole letter again, changes tack and starts writing sternly. But that doesn't make sense. If things had relapsed since he started writing, if the whole situation had suddenly reversed, then why would he send the first part of the letter at all?[16]

Then there's the question of the visit. In 2 Corinthians 12 – 13, Paul threatens to visit for the third time. But in 2 Corinthians 1, he's apologising for not visiting.

The obvious solution is that 2 Corinthians 10 – 13 is actually from Letter C – the harsh letter. If one reads the text in a different order, it seems to work:

▷ There's a problem and Paul responds (1 Cor.).

▷ The problem gets worse and Paul responds more harshly (2 Cor. 10 – 13).

▷ The problem is resolved and Paul is joyful (2 Cor. 1 – 9)

So trying to piece together what happened is complicated by some textual problems. Another problem is dating it. But here, perhaps, the sailing season comes into play. It was only a short hop across from Ephesus to Corinth: the journey took four to seven days heading east (with the prevailing wind) and seven to ten days going west. So making a visit and sending letters would have been simple. No one, however, would try it when the sea routes were closed in the winter. So most news would be received and most travel carried out between March and September. It's possible, therefore, that there were long gaps between Paul sending a letter and then receiving the response.

Given all this, we can work out a rough plan of the course of events, and even give it a suggested timetable. Much of it is supposition, of course, but here's my precis of what happened.

When Paul arrived in Ephesus, Apollos had gone to Corinth. The trip went well. In fact, in a way things went rather *too* well. Apollos, schooled in the rhetoric and oratory of sophisticated Alexandria, was a more impressive figure than Paul. Some of those in the Corinthian church were comparing Paul to Apollos and not liking what they saw: 'His letters are weighty and strong,' they said, 'but his bodily presence is weak, and his speech contemptible' (2 Cor. 10.10). Around this time there had been other visitors to Corinth as well: famous visitors like Cephas and Barnabas. They, too, seemed more substantial as teachers than the bald tentmaker with the bandy legs.

The make-up of the church was changing. Some Christians in Corinth now were taken from among the 'wise' and the 'powerful'. Erastus, the city treasurer, had become a Christian. He was a high official in local government and it was very likely the same Erastus who sponsored the building of the pavement.[17] He had money, power and influence. Erastus is not implicated in the scandal, but he may represent a new type of Christian convert in Corinth: someone who had wealth and connections and who brought into the community cultural expectations and attitudes from the city around them. They were used to the best things in life: the finest food, the best houses and the best in Greek rhetoric. The humble origins of the Corinthian church and the humble people in it were, perhaps, something of an embarrassment to them.

In Ephesus, Paul hears rumours. Whispers. Reports of sexual immorality among the Corinthian church. If Apollos returned before the close of sailing in AD 53, then perhaps he passed a letter of greeting from the Corinthians to Paul. And perhaps he reported on what he had seen and heard.

So Paul sends them a first letter: Letter A, which is now lost (1 Cor. 5.9). He advises them not to allow any immoral person in

among them. He doesn't expect the Corinthians to avoid all contact with the sexually immoral – in a city like Corinth that would
have been impossible. But they should not share the thanksgiving
meal with them; and they should be excluded from the brethren
(1 Cor. 5.9–11). He sends Timothy with this letter, hoping that his
young protégé will be able to nip any problems in the bud (1 Cor.
4.17–18). Then the seas close and everything goes quiet; during
this period Paul moves into Tyrannus's lecture hall.

Things in Corinth deteriorate. Some in the community think
that Paul means they shouldn't associate with any sinners (Paul
corrects this in 1 Cor. 5.9–13). Perhaps this misunderstanding further erodes confidence in Paul among the community. Timothy
gets a hostile reception.

When communication reopens in spring AD 54, the Corinthian church sends a letter to Paul asking for clarification on some
issues. But it is what the letter does *not* say that concerns Paul.
Paul gets an update on the situation from Timothy and also from
'Chloe's people' (1 Cor. 1.11–12), which means either a Christian
household or probably a mini-church that meets in Chloe's house.
The 'people' may be Stephanas, Fortunatus and Achaicus, who
we know visit Paul in Ephesus (1 Cor. 16.16–18). Paul also gets
information from Sosthenes, who also comes across to Ephesus
and who is 'co-author' of Paul's reply (1 Cor. 1.1).

The news is not good. There is a tsunami of issues to deal with.
Not only has a case of sexual immorality not been dealt with,
there are loads of other things: lawsuits between believers; selfishness at the thanksgiving meal; factions within the church.

So Paul sends Timothy back with Letter B. Or, as we call it, 1
Corinthians.

'I belong to Paul'

It is written just before Passover, probably in AD 54. When he
writes to the Corinthians he uses Passover imagery and refers
to the fact that they are to celebrate the Passover festival (1 Cor.
5.6–8). There are indications in the letter that things are tough in
Ephesus. Paul talks of being in want, being hungry and thirsty,
even being beaten. It may be that he's talking about his career as
a whole, but there are other hints. In one remark, right at the end

of the letter, he talks about how he 'fought with wild animals at Ephesus' (1 Cor. 15.32).

Has he really faced wild beasts? Unlikely. While facing wild animals in the arena was a common sentence in Rome, it was much rarer out in the provinces. Anyway, Paul was a citizen, and it was illegal for a citizen to be given such a punishment. But this little reference inspired several legends about Paul: Hippolytus, in his commentary on Daniel, refers to an apparently widespread belief that Paul was condemned to the beasts but that the lion which 'was set upon him lay down at his feet and licked him'.

Nice story, but this is clearly a metaphor. The image is of the *venatores* or *bestiarii*, professional gladiators who were trained to fight against animals as part of a spectacular show. Excavations in the theatre in Corinth revealed paintings of life-sized figures engaged in fighting with beasts, so they would have recognised the image. Paul isn't a victim here: he's a trained *bestiarius* who has fought a battle. In his letter to Rome, Ignatius writes, 'All the way from Syria to Rome I am fighting wild beasts, on land and sea, by day and night, chained as I am to ten leopards, that is, a detachment of soldiers, who prove themselves the more malevolent for kindnesses shown them.'[18] Unlike Ignatius, Paul's beasts in Ephesus were probably not soldiers: he says there is a great opportunity in Ephesus and enough security to allow him to stay there until after Pentecost (1 Cor. 16.8). Possibly he is talking about the local Jews in the synagogue.

But it is a struggle, a fight. Which is why he reacts so strongly to the news from Corinth. It's bad enough your opponents attacking like wild animals, never mind those who are supposed to be on your side...

Paul starts by addressing factionalism. There are people who claim adherence to Apollos, or to Cephas, or to Paul (1 Cor. 1.10–14). In the ancient world it was common to declare yourself someone's 'man' in political contests. There were no political parties as such: political factions were named after the individuals whose interests they served. There was the 'faction of Marius' or the 'party of Pompey'. It was the patron-client relationship writ large: political parties consisted of groups of clients pledged to their patrons.[19] In Pompeii thousands of political slogans have been found on the walls of the buildings to do with the election of magistrates. They were painted by the candidate's friends and neighbours, or by groups such as the dyers, the fullers, the gold-smiths, the garlic-dealers and the poultry-sellers (a bit like get-ting the union vote). They consist of simply the candidate's name and his office, the sponsoring individual or group, and a verb of adherence or support. They were done by professional signwrit-ers, probably working late into the night.[20]

This faction business is not about theology, it's simply a reflec-tion of the political world of the Græco-Roman city. It's church politics. It's about power and influence and wealth. Paul's response is to discredit completely the so-called 'wisdom' of the world and the pompous pride of the high-status Corinthian elite who have taken control. God has chosen the foolish, the lowly, the weak, the 'low and despised' to shame the wise (1 Cor. 1.26–29). The people against whom they are discriminating truly reflect the wisdom and power of God. This passage must have seriously annoyed some of the people in the Corinthian church – which is, presumably, exactly why Paul wrote it.

He goes on to stick the theological boot in further. The Cor-inthians are still drinking milk, not solid food (1 Cor. 2.14 – 3.4). Paul is telling them to 'grow up'. And their attempts to interro-gate Paul (1 Cor. 4.3) are met with a wondrous piece of satire: he describes how lowly the life of the apostle is:

> We are fools for the sake of Christ, but you are wise in Christ. We are weak, but you are strong. You are held in honour, but we in disrepute. To the present hour we are hungry and thirsty, we are poorly clothed and beaten and homeless, and we grow weary from the work of our own hands. When reviled, we bless; when persecuted, we endure; when slandered, we speak kindly. We have become like the rubbish of the world, the dregs of all things, to this very day. (1 Cor. 4.10–13)

Paul's conditions were surely tough in Ephesus. But he's delib-erately overstating things here, in order to shame the wealthy Corinthian church leaders.

Then Paul deals again with the sexual immorality in the church: 'a man is living with his father's wife' (1 Cor. 5.1) – which means his step-mother rather than his birth-mother. Even the pagans, says Paul, wouldn't stoop that low. He's not exaggerating. Incest was a criminal act under Roman law. If the young man was sleeping with his step-mother, and his father was still alive, then both parties would be punished by permanent exile under the Roman civil code.[21] But the Corinthians have not even exiled the man from the church. Possibly he was of high social standing, and the patron-client relationship meant that they felt compelled to go on eating with him. Paul will have no truck with such things.

There are lawsuits within the church, too. Paul's exasperation is clear:

> Can it be that there is no one among you wise enough to decide between one believer and another, but a believer goes to court against a believer – and before unbelievers at that? (1 Cor. 6.5–6)

The Christian communities are supposed to be outposts of peace in a world of conflict. How can they claim that if the members of the church are suing one another?

The fundamental issue in the Corinthian church is simple: it's too much like Corinth as a whole. They criticise Paul for his appearance, his lack of sophisticated rhetorical skills. And he's nothing more than a tentmaker, a manual labourer. The factions in their church behave like the political factions in their city, and some of them are mimicking pagan priests as well.

'Something on his head'

In the imposing Julian Basilica in Corinth there was a statue. The figure stood, looking slightly to the right, his hands outstretched, as is common in statues of Romans making a sacrifice. It was a statue of Augustus and he was making a sacrifice, and his toga had been brought up so that his head was covered.[22]

This statue is not unique to Corinth: statues like this have been discovered throughout the Empire. The image also appeared on coins.[23] The image reflects Augustus's religious beliefs. In 13 BC, Augustus became *pontifex maximus* – chief priest of Rome. He wanted to restore traditional religious values to the Empire. As chief priest he made sacrifices, and he did so with his head covered. The same is true of his successors. In the same basilica archaeologists found a head of Nero, with his toga pulled up over his head.

Augustus as Pontifex Maximus

Covering your head, then, was what the emperor and pagan priests did during sacrifices. It's not that everyone covered their heads: only those taking a leading part in the rituals. Those people would have been drawn from the local elite.

When Paul writes, then, that Christian men must pray or prophesy with their heads uncovered, at least part of what he's saying is that the church is not to ape the culture of the society around. It's only a part – he also grounds the argument in a wider first-century understanding of the nature of men and women – but it does indicate that there was a cultural aspect to covering your head.

When it comes to the women, though, Paul does want them to wear their hair covered. 'Any woman who prays or prophesies with her head unveiled disgraces her head,' he says (1 Cor. 11.5). There have been many arguments about this, but one theory holds that Paul is probably not talking about 'women' here so much as 'wives'. The word *gunē* can mean either an adult woman or a wife specifically.[24] Paul uses the same word in 1 Corinthians 7.39, where it certainly does mean the latter: 'A wife [*gunē*] is bound as long as her husband lives.' It makes more sense here, because Paul is not talking about the full veil, but the kind seen on coin portraits of people like Livia, the wife of Augustus. It was a half-head covering, and it was associated with marriage; a bit like wearing a wedding ring today. Many Roman men had mistresses or courtesans as a matter of course, and these women would not wear the marriage veil.

This is why Paul says that if a woman (a *wife*) will not veil herself she should shave her hair off. Head-shaving was the female punishment for adultery.[25] It's Pauline hyperbole, of course, but he's saying that if a married woman takes her head-covering off in order to prophesy or pray, she is dishonouring her husband and it's as bad as committing adultery.

Clearly, though, in some circles in Corinth it was OK for women to be unveiled. All but one of the portrait statues of women from ancient Corinth show women with their heads uncovered.[26] These were respectable women, so bareheadedness in itself was not disapproved of or scandalous. But women in later antiquity are much more frequently shown wearing head-coverings such as Livia's veil. This may be why Paul then seems to backtrack slightly and ask the Corinthian church to judge on the issue for themselves (1 Cor. 11.13). Tertullian, rather reluctantly, acknowledges this reading: he says that until close to his time the matter of women wearing veils was left to free choice, like the question of whether to marry.[27] Certainly, veiling seems to have been common practice in the east, which is why Paul says, 'We have no such custom, nor do the churches of God' (1 Cor. 11:16). In Paul's day, in many parts of the east, complete veiling of women was common and considered respectable. Dio Chrysostom praises the modesty of the women in Tarsus and notes that when they go out no one sees any part of their faces.[28] He is writing around AD 100, but he says that the custom has been common since the days of Augustus. Complete veils were common in Arabia and Syria.[29] Jewish women covered their heads. The rabbinic evidence (collected some time later than Paul) shows that women were expected to keep their heads covered, sometimes even in the home.

So Paul's instructions have to be interpreted against the background of contemporary culture. When we look at the statues and consider the everyday life in Corinth, the principles of head-covering and the issues around hair become much more about the distinctive Christian lifestyle and the importance of unity. Don't do that which others find offensive. And if Augustus's head is covered, then Christians should uncover theirs.

We get into similarly murky cultural waters when we consider Paul's instructions on the role of women in worship. Paul paints a picture of a 'proper' orderly church worship meeting, where 'each one has a hymn, a lesson, a revelation, a tongue, or an interpretation'. He goes on to talk about the gift of speaking in tongues and the need for interpretation to be given:

> Let two or three prophets speak, and let the others weigh what is said. If a revelation is made to someone else sitting nearby, let the

first person be silent. For you can all prophesy one by one, so that all may learn and all be encouraged. And the spirits of prophets are subject to the prophets, for God is a God not of disorder but of peace. (I Cor. 14.29–33)

Then he inserts a strange piece about how women should be silent in churches and not permitted to speak, and how this is the case 'in all the churches of the saints'. The strange thing about this is that it quite clearly goes against so much of what we know about church worship in the first century. First, women were in positions of patronage and leadership. Chloe, from whose people this report first came, is a woman who holds some kind of position of authority. Was she a householder? A wealthy widow? The phrase seems to imply that there was a church which met in her house. We know that Phoebe was a deaconness in Cenchreae. Was she silent all the time?

Paul has also just contradicted himself. In 1 Corinthians 11.5 he has said women *can* prophesy, provided they have their head covered. And we know of other female prophets. Philip had four daughters who were noted for prophetic gifts. Both Priscilla and Aquila were teachers and, as we have seen, even a gnarled old misogynist like John Chrysostom admits that Priscilla was probably the prominent teacher. There are churches where women have leadership roles (Rom. 16.1–4; Phil. 4.2–3).

Faced with all this, we have to believe either that this passage doesn't mean quite what it says, or that none of these prominent women actually exercised their ministry in a church service – or that, if they did, they did it entirely in mime.

Once again the issue may be to do with how you translate *gunē* or *gunaikes*: whether you go for 'women' or 'wives', as it were. Since the issue is one of subordination, the latter would make more sense. In which case, when Paul talks about not talking in church but seeking instruction at home, what he's talking about is wives not asking questions or challenging what their husbands are saying. Or it may be linked to the issue of speaking in tongues; they may have been challenging the interpretation given. In the culture of the time, this would bring public dishonour on the husband.[30]

It's about ensuring a display of unity – and that's the real theme of this letter.

'One goes hungry and another becomes drunk'

The whiff of social superiority is everywhere in 1 Corinthians. The elite Gentiles cover their heads when sacrificing, so the Corinthian men follow suit in their services. The elite Gentiles look down on manual labourers, so Corinthian Christians start to look down on Paul. The elite praise Greek wisdom and Roman rhetoric, so the Corinthian Christians look down on the unimpressive, plain-spoken apostle.

And the elite eat the best food...

Few things make Paul as angry in this letter as the behaviour of the Corinthians at the thanksgiving meal:

> When you come together, it is not really to eat the Lord's supper. For when the time comes to eat, each of you goes ahead with your own supper, and one goes hungry and another becomes drunk. What! Do you not have homes to eat and drink in? Or do you show contempt for the church of God and humiliate those who have nothing? (1 Cor. 11.20–22)

It's easy to see why Paul is so angry. This meal is something he has staked his reputation on in the past. He has stood against the pillars of the church. He has risked friendships. The thanksgiving meal is *the* sign of unity among the early church. But the Corinthians have turned it into a pagan banquet.

Roman banquets, like most of Roman society, were run along lines of strict social hierarchy. Eating meals together was common; having guests of inferior social status – as long as they were freedmen – was also common, but sharing the same table and the same food with slaves and women? Incomprehensible.

Where guests of different social status were at the same meal – at a patron-client meal, for instance – the wealthy and the powerful would get the gourmet fare, while the lowlier guests got the 'set menu'. It was generosity, but at the same time it was ritualised social humiliation. The poet Martial complains, 'While the throng of invited guests looks on, you, Caecilianus, devour the mushrooms.' Dining with a man called Ponticus, he complains that they don't 'eat the same fare'.[31]

To Pliny the Younger, such a display was a sign of ungentlemanly breeding. He describes how some elegant dishes were served to the hosts and a few chosen guests, while the rest had the cheap stuff. And there were three grades of wine as well. Pliny's solution was to serve everyone the same, but to eat cheaply so as not to have to spend too much.[32]

This is exactly what Paul describes as happening in Corinth. The rich are eating the better food and then leaving. The church is meeting on the first day of the week by now (1 Cor. 16.2), which, of course, is an ordinary working day. (Sunday didn't become a day off until the fourth century.) The rich patrons and their clients arrive first, because they don't have jobs to do. They get the best food and drink, while the rest go away hungry. To Paul, this shows complete and utter contempt for the 'church of God' (1 Cor. 11.22). This is not a problem of doctrine. It's not that one side believes in transubstantiation and the other doesn't. The problem is 'not that the Corinthians are profaning a holy rite, but that they are fragmenting a holy society'.[33]

Paul reminds them of the story he was taught and which he passed on to them. The order 'learned' by Paul may indicate that the early church thanksgiving meal had three stages. It began with the invocation and breaking of the bread:

The Lord Jesus on the night when he was betrayed took a loaf of bread, and when he had given thanks, he broke it and said, 'This is my body that is for you. Do this in remembrance of me.'

It then moved into a supper and concluded with the invocation and sharing of the wine:

In the same way he took the cup also, after supper... (1 Cor. 11.23–25)

The point is that everyone does it together. It's about unity. It's about equality in action. Equality was a core concept of early Christianity and one which put them on a very different plane from the society around them. Paul argues in his letters that there is no difference between Jew and Gentile, slave and free, Greek and Barbarian.

The idea, clearly, came from their founder, who continually argued that all were equal, who said that the least in the kingdom of God was greater than John the Baptist, and who used the image of a little child as a model for roles within the kingdom.

The idea was also informed by the strong belief that they were living in the end times. Equality was eschatological: the love that stretched among Christians across social and racial strata was a sign of the end times.

In other Jewish writing, equality would come on the Day of the Lord. The *Sibylline Oracles*, a collection of Jewish and Christian oracles, describes a transformed world:

> The earth will belong abundantly to all, undivided by walls or fences. It will then bear more abundant fruits spontaneously. Lives will be in common and wealth will have no division. For there will be no poor man there, no rich, and no tyrant, no slave. Further, no one will be either great or small any more. No kings, no leaders. All will be on a par together.[34]

The life of the church, then, would have been read by some as a sign of a transformed world. The kingdom had already arrived and here was the proof. This idea of a new age, ushered in by the arrival of Jesus the Messiah, was an important underpinning to the shared meals of the Christians. These were practical examples of Christian love, of course, but the idea of a feast to which the poor and the outcasts were invited was a core component of messianic expectations. Here's a passage from Isaiah:

> On this mountain the LORD of hosts will make for all peoples
>   a feast of rich food, a feast of well-matured wines,
>   of rich food filled with marrow, of well-matured wines strained
>   clear. (Isa. 25.6)

This would be an age of peace. Micah describes how the nations:

> . . . shall beat their swords into ploughshares,
> and their spears into pruning-hooks;
> nation shall not lift up sword against nation,
> neither shall they learn war any more;
> but they shall all sit under their own vines and under their own fig trees,
> and no one shall make them afraid;
> for the mouth of the LORD of hosts has spoken. (Mic. 4.3–4)

And one more eschatological sign: the inclusion of the Gentiles. Zechariah, a prophet whose works were mined for messianic references, describes how all the peoples of the world will come to worship the Lord:

> Thus says the LORD of hosts: Peoples shall yet come, the inhabitants

of many cities ... Many peoples and strong nations shall come to seek the LORD of hosts in Jerusalem, and to entreat the favour of the LORD. Thus says the LORD of hosts: In those days ten men from nations of every language shall take hold of a Jew, grasping his garment and saying, 'Let us go with you, for we have heard that God is with you.' (Zech. 8.20–23)

This stuff was more than just a nice idea. It was more than a growth strategy for the successful church. It was confirmation of the messianic status of Jesus. The Messiah was expected to usher in an age of feasting, equality, peace and unity. If that was blown apart by squabbling within the church, then what did that say about Jesus as Messiah?

Paul views equality in the church as so fundamental that he even proposes a compromise: he says that if the Corinthians really must keep the best stuff to themselves, then they should have some food before they come to the meal (1 Cor. 11.34). I can't imagine Paul feeling that this is a good solution, but it shows the power and influence of the factions he's up against.

The letter ends with some housekeeping matters. He urges the Corinthians to collect some money for the saints in Jerusalem. He states his intention to come to them after passing through Macedonia. And he closes with greetings.

Paul suggests that he might send Timothy with the letter: 'If Timothy comes,' he writes, 'see he has nothing to fear among you' (1 Cor. 16.10). It may be that Timothy stepped once again into the lion's den. Or it may be that Paul sent the letter with Titus (2 Cor. 12.18) and an unnamed 'brother' – someone whom the Corinthians would respect. One of their own – Erastus, perhaps. Stephanas, maybe. The heavy mob. People to whom the Corinthians would listen.

Not Apollos, at any rate. Paul asked Apollos to visit Corinth, but Apollos refused to go. Clearly Apollos had no wish to be drawn into these arguments. Or perhaps he, too, had suffered from the rumours and accusations rife among the Corinthian church.

All this – and a great deal more – is crammed into Letter B, 1 Corinthians. It's tough. Hard-hitting. But along with the corrections and the rebukes and the clarifications, amidst the detailed arguments about unity and division and sexual criminality, it also contains some stunning writing, some of the most sublimely beautiful words ever committed to paper (or papyrus). There's Paul's famous passage on love; his image of the body as being made up of many parts; his powerful description of the resurrection of Christ.

Despite all that he was going through, despite the wrongheadedness of the Corinthian elite and the hardships of his working life, there is such beauty in this writing that at times it takes your breath away. Amidst the rebukes and the counter-arguments and the clarifications, there are moments when the Holy Spirit sets light to Paul's words and he just soars. Ironically, the rhetorically challenged tentmaker who was the object of the Corinthians' scorn has proved to be one of the greatest writers who has ever lived.

Beautiful it may be, but it still didn't work. So Paul had to go there himself. It proved to be a painful experience.

'Another painful visit'

In 2 Corinthians, Paul says that when he visits again it will be his third time (2 Cor. 12.14). The first time was when he established the church in AD 51–52. The third visit will eventually take place in AD 57. So when was the second one? Perhaps in the summer of AD 54, after he sent the first two letters.

As we have seen, the journey across to Corinth took days rather than weeks. It would not be hard for Paul to cross to Corinth, nor need he have stayed long. Acts doesn't mention the visit, but maybe that's because it was so brief. Or maybe because it was a complete disaster.

Paul describes it later as a 'painful visit' (2 Cor. 2.1). In Corinth he came up against a group of people he witheringly terms 'super-apostles' (2 Cor. 11.5; 12.11). He was accused of freeloading, of hypocrisy. His speech and demeanour were criticised.

You would think that Paul would give as good as he got, but he actually talks about being humble face to face, but bold when away (2 Cor. 10.1). So maybe he tried a gentle approach which simply didn't work. Maybe he was, for once in his life, outgunned. Whatever the truth of it, he had to retreat to Ephesus. There he regathered his thoughts and wrote another letter. And this time he let them have it with both barrels.

We don't know when Paul wrote this letter – Letter C in our plan. It can't have been earlier than the summer of AD 54. We have to allow for Letter B to get there, and then for news to return that it has had no impact, and then for Paul to make the painful visit and return. That would take a few months.

We don't have an authoritative text for this letter. But if, as I've argued above, some of it is preserved as 2 Corinthians 10 – 13, we can get an idea of what the main issue was: it was all about Paul. Who he was. His personality, his history, his very credibility as an apostle. The letter includes a lengthy CV, an apologia for his life. He had gone to Corinth and been put down. 'The Corinthians thought me unimpressive in the flesh, did they? Well, here's a taste of what I've been through...'

So, in sentence after piledriving sentence, Paul batters the Corinthians and their super-apostles with his apostolic credentials. He lists his sufferings for the Lord; he talks about his visionary experiences; he reminds them that he was the founder of the Corinthian church (2 Cor. 10.14); tellingly, he points to the indicators of a true apostle: not social status and fine rhetoric, but 'signs and wonders and mighty works' (2 Cor. 12.12).

And he deals with one of the more toxic accusations which have been whispered about him behind people's hands: accusations about work and money.

These super-apostles, apparently, did not work at anything as demeaning as a manual trade. In his first letter Paul defended the right of an apostle to receive support, but then said he didn't exercise that right. He said, in fact, that he would rather die than be supported (1 Cor. 9.15). At first glance, it's difficult to see what the problem was, but in this letter it becomes clear. It wasn't that Paul turned down money to support him: it was that he turned down *their* money. While working to support himself in Corinth, Paul received gifts from elsewhere:

> And when I was with you and was in need, I did not burden anyone, for my needs were supplied by the friends who came from Macedonia. (2 Cor. 11.9)

AD 53

▷ Apollos comes to
Corinth

Paul and Corinth:
a suggested timeline

▷ Paul arrives in Ephesus
▷ Reports of problems in Corinth. Paul sends **LETTER A**
(missing). (1 Cor. 5.9–11)
▷ He sends Timothy to them. (1 Cor. 4.17)

SEA CLOSED

AD 54

▷ Chloe's people (1 Cor. 1.11), Stephanas, Fortunatus and
Achaicus visit Paul in Corinth (1 Cor. 16.17-18). There are still
problems. The Corinthians send a letter (1 Cor. 7.1; 8.1).
▷ Sends **LETTER B** (1 Corinthians) Titus goes to Corinth, either
with this letter or later (2 Cor. 12.17–18). Problems persist.

▷ Paul makes a visit: the 'painful visit' (2 Cor. 2.1). He returns to
Ephesus.
▷ Sends **LETTER C**: the harsh letter (poss 2 Cor. 10 –13) (2 Cor.
7.8-9). Sent via Titus.

Paul in Ephesus

SEA CLOSED

AD 55

▷ Silversmiths' riot in Ephesus (Acts 19.23–41). Paul flees to
Troas where a door is opened for the gospel (2 Cor. 2.12).
▷ Paul crosses to Macedonia. (2 Cor. 2.13). He finds Titus who
reports the repentence of the Corinthian church.
▷ Sends **LETTER D** (2 Corinthians: poss. chaps 1-9). He sends it
via Titus and others (2 Cor. 8.16–18, 22).
▷ Titus returns to Corinth. Then goes on to Crete (Tit. 1.5)

▷ Paul travels through Greece to Illyricum (Rom. 15.18–19).

He was probably supported by money from Philippi. Now this was being held against him. It's easy to imagine the Corinthians' criticism: *their* money wasn't good enough. The church (or key members of it) were offended that Paul wouldn't accept their support and upset at his stubborn refusal to leave the workshop and enter a proper, Corinthian-style patron-client relationship. In the heavily politicised atmosphere of Corinth, Paul refused to be beholden to anyone. Clearly the super-apostles had no such scruples, and they encouraged the view that Paul's refusal of the Corinthian money meant that he didn't love them.[35]

Paul's principles, though, were unalterable. He knew that to take their money would compromise his ability to share the truth freely and (where necessary) forcibly. And he knew that the minute you started down the road of apostles-for-hire, you entered some very murky and difficult waters.

'There will be false teachers among you'

Very truly, I tell you, whoever receives one whom I send receives me; and whoever receives me receives him who sent me. (John 13.20)

This is what Jesus said and the early Christian communities trusted in that. Ancient culture was an oral culture: for the most part news and teaching was spoken, heard, learned and remembered. It was written down, of course, but it was mostly handed on verbally, in a world where very few people could read. So the good news about Jesus was taken out through the Roman Empire by a steady stream of travelling apostles, teachers and prophets, telling their stories, passing on what they had learned and serving the church.

The first Christian communities supported these travelling apostles and provided for their needs. But such a system is open to abuse – and some people decided that there really was such a thing as a free lunch. We can see this in action, in an account from outside the church.

Lucian of Samosata was an Assyrian-born speaker and satirist who wrote in Greek in the mid-to-late second century. His works contain one of the earliest pagan accounts of Christians. It comes in his mocking story of a cynic philosopher called Peregrinus, a man Lucius depicts as a charlatan and conman. In his tale,

Peregrinus goes on the run after murdering his father. He ends up in Palestine where he decides to become a Christian and tricks a group of Christians into making him their leader:

> It was then that he learned the wondrous lore of the Christians, by associating with their priests and scribes in Palestine. And – how else could it be? – in a trice he made them all look like children, for he was prophet, cult-leader, head of the synagogue, and everything, all by himself. He interpreted and explained some of their books and even composed many, and they revered him as a god, made use of him as a lawgiver, and set him down as a protector, next after that other, to be sure, whom they still worship, the man who was crucified in Palestine because he introduced this new cult into the world.

He was thrown into prison, much to the consternation of the church, who continued to support him:

> From the very break of day aged widows and orphan children could be seen waiting near the prison, while their officials even slept inside with him after bribing the guards. Then elaborate meals were brought in, and sacred books of theirs were read aloud, and excellent Peregrinus ... was called by them 'the new Socrates'.

Lucian portrays this behaviour as normal for Christians:

> Indeed, people came even from the cities in Asia, sent by the Christians at their common expense, to succour and defend and encourage the hero. They show incredible speed whenever any such public action is taken; for in no time they lavish their all. So it was then in the case of Peregrinus; much money came to him from them by reason of his imprisonment, and he procured not a little revenue from it. The poor wretches have convinced themselves, first and foremost, that they are going to be immortal and live for all time, in consequence of which they despise death and even willingly give themselves into custody; most of them. Furthermore, their first lawgiver persuaded them that they are all brothers of one another after they have transgressed once, for all by denying the Greek gods and by worshipping that crucified sophist himself and living under his laws. Therefore they despise all things indiscriminately and consider them common property, receiving such doctrines traditionally without any definite evidence. So if any charlatan and trickster, able to profit by occasions, comes among them, he quickly acquires sudden wealth by imposing upon simple folk.[36]

We should take this account with a fistful of salt. For one thing, Peregrinus is worshipped as 'a god' – an impossible thing for any Christian leader. Lucian is a satirist, not an historian. Lucian's satire mocks Peregrinus because, in the end, he chose to commit suicide and throw himself into a blazing funeral pyre. That doesn't sound much like the work of a charlatan and con-artist. It seems to me that at the root of Lucian's warped account is the true – and tragic – account of someone who was desperately searching for something, who perhaps underwent a radical conversion – and who was a genuine leader and disciple for a time.

But, leaving that to one side, the work shows us what pagans like Lucian believed of Christians. The faith is inherently Jewish: Lucian uses terms like 'synagogues' and 'priests' and 'scribes'. The community includes widows and orphans. It supports its members in prison. And it's open to exploitation by con-artists and false prophets.

It's interesting to examine what Lucian says about the beliefs of Christians as well:

▷ They worship Jesus, 'the man who was crucified in Palestine because he introduced this new cult into the world'.

▷ They suffer imprisonment for their beliefs.

▷ They have a network of communication so that other Christian leaders come to offer support.

▷ They believe they will live for ever, a belief which makes them 'despise death' and 'willingly give themselves into custody'.

▷ They believe they are all brothers and sisters.

▷ They deny the Greek gods.

▷ They have goods in common and give their wealth away.

This demonstrates clearly some of the most wonderfully scandalous qualities and beliefs of the Christians: they were equal, they were unafraid of death, they despised possessions and they denied the Greek gods. They were, in all respects, not proper Romans.

The picture is startlingly reminiscent of that in Acts and in Paul's letters. And it demonstrates how vulnerable these communities were, not only to persecution and imprisonment, but to exploitation by cheats. If you have 'welcome' written all over you, people do rather tend to treat you like a doormat.

Incidents of false teachers became so acute that the Christian community came up with rules to sort out true apostles from those who were just after a free lunch. The *Didache* explains:

Let every apostle who comes to you be welcomed as if he were the Lord. But he is not to stay for more than one day, unless there is need, in which case he may stay another. But if he stays three days, he is a false prophet. And when the apostle leaves he is to take nothing except bread until he finds his next night's lodging. But if he asks for money, he is a false prophet.[37]

Further advice claimed that if visiting Christians wished to settle among the community and they had a craft, then they were to work for their living, but if they refused to co-operate they were 'trading on Christ'.[38] This fits in precisely with Paul's practice of supporting himself by his own craft. Interestingly, in the *Didache* there is no distinction between apostle and prophet; clearly in some cases the roles were combined. And, as Paul wrote in 2 Corinthians, the true apostle/prophet was shown by their actions as well. 'Not everyone who speaks in the spirit is a prophet, but only if he exhibits the Lord's ways ... if any prophet teaches the truth, yet does not practise what he teaches he is a false prophet.'[39] The *Didache* even gives an example of one of their tricks: ordering meals 'in the spirit' – perhaps by speaking in tongues and then giving their own interpretation. It says that 'any prophet who orders a meal in the spirit shall not partake of it; if he does, he is a false prophet'.[40] (So remember, if anyone, in the middle of worship, suddenly orders a pizza, they are not allowed even one slice.)

There were leaders who did live permanently with the communities and the *Didache*, like Paul, recognises the right of these people to be supported.

But every true prophet who desires to settle among you is worthy of his food. In the same way a true teacher is also worthy, like the workman, of his food ... But if you don't have a prophet, give them to the poor.[41]

The issue of true and false prophets, and their financial relationship with the people they serve and teach, is almost as old as the Christian church. We have seen it throughout history, and we see it today. Around the world, Christian leaders making themselves fat and rich on the back of their prophetic ministries. The medieval popes, Byzantine patriarchs and Anglican archbishops in their palaces. The American TV evangelists and African mega-church pastors in their Bentley Continentals and their sharp suits. Paul, and the *Didache*, would have had them thrown out.

'Great is Artemis of the Ephesians!'

Paul sent Titus with his harsh letter and settled down to wait for the result. He had promised – or threatened – to make his third visit. But then events got in the way. In Ephesus there was a riot. When Paul talks later about 'the affliction we experienced in Asia', his language is filled with the vocabulary of death and despair:

> We were so utterly, unbearably crushed that we despaired of life itself. Indeed, we felt that we had received the sentence of death so that we would rely not on ourselves but on God who raises the dead. (2 Cor. 1.8–9)

By then he is in Macedonia, having left Ephesus in a hurry (2 Cor. 2.13). Acts tells us more of the story and, once again, it has to do with magic. And money.

As we have seen, Ephesus was a centre for religious pilgrimage. It brought in visitors, trade and cash – and then some. Ephesus had innkeepers, grocers, guides, prostitutes – all the sophisticated

amenities of a Græco-Roman tourist hotspot. And, of course, there were souvenir salesmen, in particular the silversmiths. They made their money from selling statues of the goddess, small replicas of her shrine.

The ringleader in this episode is a man called Demetrius, who gives a lot of business to the artisans of the city. Presumably he's a retailer, and like all good retailers before and since, he can spot a trend. And the trend he spots in Ephesus is one of sales heading downwards. People are turning to Christianity, which means turning away from the traditional gods. Every day, in the lecture hall of Tyrannus, Paul is saying, 'Gods made with hands are not gods.' That's bringing his religion into disrepute. Worse, it's hitting his profits.

Demetrius can see that if pushed to its logical conclusion, then even the great temple itself will be threatened. So he whips the artisans up into a frenzy. It's possible that this event took place during the *Artemision*, a week-long spring festival dedicated to the goddess, but it could have happened at any time when the traders felt their profits threatened by this attack on 'their goddess'.

Shouting and chanting 'Great is Artemis of the Ephesians', they process from the guildhall to the theatre, having first grabbed

The theatre at Ephesus. In Paul's day the road would have led to the harbour. Now it is silted up

some Christians called Gaius and Aristarchus. Conveniently, they are foreigners: two Macedonians, described as Paul's travelling companions. (Travelling where? Corinth, perhaps?) Gaius is probably the same Gaius who is listed as one of Paul's travelling companions in Acts 20.4. Acts says the man was from Derbe, but the text could be read as simply referring to Timothy. The WT actually reads *Douberios* (instead of *Derbaios*), which like Thessalonica is also a Macedonian town.[42]

Aristarchus is a Jewish Christian from Thessalonica (Acts 20.4; 27.2; Col. 4.10). Later, in Rome, he may have been in prison with Paul, although the word Paul uses, *sunaichmalōtos*, literally means 'prisoner of war', so Paul may be speaking metaphorically.[43]

It has been suggested that, since Aristarchus appears prominently in some of the 'we' passages, Luke knew him and therefore got a first-hand account of the events. Certainly Luke's account is full of accurate historical details. He uses the phrase 'temple-keeper' correctly with respect to Ephesus (Acts 19.35); he knows about the silver shrines that were produced; he calls the powerful local political figures 'Asiarchs' (Acts 19.31) – a name which crops up in many local inscriptions and which has now been shown to date from the first century AD.[44]

The town is filled with confusion, with rumours and noise spreading like wildfire along the narrow streets and among the closely packed *insulae*. The mob gather in the one place where big meetings are held in the town: the huge theatre, a great arc carved out of the side of Mount Pion with a capacity of close to 25,000 people. Paul, typically, wants to go down and face the protesters, who are now described as a *demos*. Technically that refers to a gathering of citizens in a free city; this is a mob trying to look like a respectable assembly. Paul's fellow Christians do not allow him to go. Their advice is reinforced by the Asiarchs. It's a strange group to associate with Paul: the Asiarchs were the leading men of the province, members of the nobility, with a range of civic responsibilities, including overseeing festivals and promoting the imperial cult.[45] It may be that Luke is trying to suggest to his Roman patron that these people did not see Paul as a threat. More likely Paul had a friendly, interested patron or two of his own among the Asiarchs.

Meanwhile, things are getting out of hand. The Greek towns-people, not caring much for the niceties of this eastern superstition, do not distinguish between Jew and Christian. A Jew called Alexander is pushed forward and attempts a defence, but as soon as the crowd realise that he's a Jew, he's shouted down. For two hours, the crowd chant. It must have been terrifying for those against whom this wall of sound was directed.

Eventually the riot is brought under control by the *grammateus*, the town scribe or record keeper. This sounds to us like a minor official, but it was a highly responsible post. The temple of Artemis served not only as a place of worship, but also as a bank, so he probably kept records associated with that, and with the general running of the city. We should imagine someone more like a company CEO. He calms everyone down, threatens them with the proconsuls and warns them that they might be accused of rioting. The Romans have accorded privileges to Ephesus: if the conduct of the mob is interpreted as being seditious, the Romans might intervene.[46] Nothing, in the eyes of the town clerk, justifies the people acting in such a way. Gradually, the crowd disperse.

Luke's account perhaps underplays the danger of the occasion. It's clear that Paul has to leave the city, and leave quickly. Paul's statement that 'we felt that we had received the sentence of death' gives the clear impression that he feared for his life. It has been claimed that Paul was imprisoned in Ephesus and that this is what he's referring to, but there's no evidence of that. No, the obvious point when Paul felt he was facing death was when the mob were baying for his blood.

He was saved through the help of others. Writing to the Christians in Rome a few years later, Paul refers to Priscilla and Aquila, commending them as two people 'who risked their necks for my life' (Rom. 16.3). Did they hide him in their workshop while the mob were looking for him? Did they smuggle him out of Ephesus as he had once been smuggled out of Damascus? What's clear is that Paul did leave Ephesus at some speed. Probably accompanied by Gaius and Aristarchus, he went down to the harbour and took the first boat he could for Troas.

Not for the first time, Paul was forced to flee.

'I have complete confidence in you'

The boat landed him up the coast at Troas. According to 2 Corinthians, there were opportunities there for the gospel, but Paul
couldn't linger. He boarded another boat and crossed to Macedonia. Possibly he went to Philippi or Thessalonica, since that was
where Aristarchus hailed from.

It was a hard time. Paul says that 'our bodies had no rest, but
we were afflicted in every way – disputes without and fears within'
(2 Cor. 7.5). Hardly surprising. The last time he had been in this
region he had been hounded out, imprisoned, beaten. So: head
down. Keep a low profile.

The one thing that brought him comfort was the arrival of
Titus with good news: the Corinthian church had repented of
their behaviour. Paul's letter to them (Letter D) is full of peace-
making words. They are not to blame themselves; they are not
to lose heart; the ringleader has been punished by the majority;
now he should be forgiven and received back into the community (2 Cor. 2.6–7).

The one tiny bone of contention was the suspicion that Paul
was not keeping to his word. He had promised to visit and had
not done so (2 Cor. 13.1–2). Paul, quite reasonably, points to what
happened in Asia. He reminds them of his plan to come to them
after going through Macedonia. He says that he only stayed away
to spare them another painful visit (2 Cor. 1.8, 15 – 2.4).

One might expect him to rush south to see them. But he didn't.
We know, though, that he sent Titus and two other brothers down
to Corinth to take this fourth letter and to organise a collection
for the churches in Judea. Who these brothers were we don't know,
since Paul is frustratingly coy about naming them. One is 'famous
among all the churches for his proclaiming of the good news' and
has been 'appointed by the churches to travel with us'. The other
has been 'tested and found eager in many matters' and now has
confidence in the Corinthians (2 Cor. 8.18–19, 22). Candidates for
this pair have included Luke, Barnabas, Aristarchus and Apollos,
but we really don't know.[47] Personally, I would plump for Apollos
and Timothy: given their own experiences at Corinth, that may
be why Paul is coy about the names. However, your guess is as
good as mine.

What is significant is that Paul didn't go to Corinth. Despite welcoming their change of heart, he didn't rush to see them. He was too battered and bruised from his Ephesus experience, perhaps. It was to be many months before he eventually returned to the city.

It was now probably late summer AD 55. In one of those phrases which seem to cover a multitude of details, Luke says that Paul

... left for Macedonia. When he had gone through those regions and had given the believers much encouragement, he came to Greece, where he stayed for three months. (Acts 20.1–3)

As Bruce writes of the Greek text, 'the first ten words of this verse possibly cover the lapse of as much as a year'.[48] Paul eventually went to Corinth in AD 57, but he left Ephesus in AD 55, or the spring of AD 56 at the very latest.

So what happens? He seems to disappear. He drops off the radar, goes under cover. He's feeling his age, maybe. Tired. He faced death in Asia, and in Macedonia things aren't much better. It's easy to imagine that, at this point, Paul has simply had enough. Enough of being responsible, enough of being criticised, enough of being threatened. And also, perhaps, there's a bit of stubbornness. He isn't going to be at the beck and call of the Corinth church. So he goes where no one knows him.

He goes to Illyricum.

'As far around as Illyricum'

Writing from Corinth in AD 57, Paul talks about his journeys:

By the power of signs and wonders, by the power of the Spirit of God, so that from Jerusalem and as far around as Illyricum I have fully proclaimed the good news of Christ. (Rom. 15.19)

As far as is recorded in Acts, he never went near Illyricum, which was the region on the western side of Greece. But Paul's own testimony is clear. So when did he go? It must have been after the experience in Ephesus. Acts doesn't mention Illyricum, but it does say that he spent that time in Macedonia, a region which stretched the whole width of Greece, from Philippi and Neapolis in the east to Apollonia and Epidamnus in the west. And just north of Epidamnus – around 5 miles – was the border of Illyricum.

Paul was a pioneer. He loved going to new territories. But for the past few years he had been forced into church maintenance, not church planting. He had been dealing with disputes and division, with doctrinal advice, dishing out pastoral concern. What would be more natural for Paul than to keep going along the *via Egnatia* and head west across Greece? So it was probably in this period that he went to Illyricum. Intriguingly, there is another reference to Paul being on the west coast of the Greek mainland – in a letter to Titus, where Paul writes:

> When I send Artemas to you, or Tychicus, do your best to come to me at Nicopolis, for I have decided to spend the winter there. Make every effort to send Zenas the lawyer and Apollos on their way, and see that they lack nothing. (Titus 3.12–13)

Titus is one of the disputed letters. When attributed to Paul, it's usually placed late in his career and assumes that Paul was released from imprisonment in Rome and later went to Crete. This is because Paul says, 'I left you behind in Crete...' (Titus 1.5). The Crete trip is also a mystery. According to Acts, Paul only went to Crete once, and that on his final trip to Rome. As he was a prisoner at the time, it's unlikely that he got the chance to do much church planting! But does the phrase 'left behind' have to mean that Paul himself went there? From Cenchreae it would have been easy to get a boat to Crete. So it's possible that Paul sent Titus to Crete via Corinth and then 'left' him there, rather than recall him to Macedonia. Nothing in the letter of Titus says that it was necessarily Paul who planted the first churches on the island.

The letter to Titus is often described as 'pseudepigraphical', i.e., written by someone else and attributed to Paul. Scholars point to differences in style with Paul's other letters, to vocabulary which is not used elsewhere, and to content which seems to reflect the church at a later stage.[49] In fact, the evidence shows that the church reacted strongly against such ghostwriting practices. Tertullian talks about a church leader in the second century who forged a third Pauline letter to the Corinthians. He was discovered and lost his position in the church.[50] More recent surveys into pseudepigraphy in the ancient world show that such books were usually intended to deceive. Pseudepigraphy was common among the gnostics, for example, who attributed their own works to people like Thomas and Peter, but without exception these were identified as such by the early church and declared uncanonical. There were debates in the early church about the authenticity of some of the letters which subsequently made their way into the Bible, but no one raised any concerns at that point about those letters attributed to Paul.[51]

In terms of style, we have to remember that there were several people involved with the creation of these letters. Paul worked with a secretary, someone who wrote down what he dictated. These people may have been given leeway to express things in their own style – particularly if they were trusted by Paul. And it's dangerous to assume that the other letters give us enough information about Paul's style. He must have written many more letters than those which we have preserved.

Paul's letter to Titus talks about the appointment of elders and 'bishops' (Titus 1.5, 7) and some have argued that these titles come from later times. The terms that are used here are not religious titles, however, but secular loan-words. The word translated 'bishop', *episkopos*, just means 'guardian' or 'overseer'. It's used many times in classical Greek literature. It crops up in the Dead Sea Scrolls.[52] It also seems to have been used early on: it appears in Peter's speech right at the beginning of Acts (Acts 1.20). Paul uses it in Acts 20.28 when he talks to the leaders of the Ephesian church at Miletus, an event which is set just a year after his trip to Illyricum. Crucially, Paul uses it to describe himself and Timothy at the beginning of Philippians, written from Rome c. AD 62:

> Paul and Timothy, servants of Christ Jesus, To all the saints in Christ Jesus who are in Philippi, with the bishops [*episkopois*] and deacons [*diakonois*]. (Phil. 1.1)

Translating it as 'bishop' is the anachronistic bit. It makes us think of old blokes with big hats and cathedrals, but the early Christian communities were small, closely knit communities who met in houses where everyone knew everyone else. (Even in the second century, when we have a single 'bishop' overseeing several churches in a city, these would likely have numbered a few hundred Christians at most.) They were far from the lordly figures they became in later ages. In fact, their problem was rather one of insignificance. The *Didache* advises communities, 'Appoint for yourselves therefore bishops and deacons worthy of the Lord, men who are meek and not lovers of money, and true and approved,' but it goes on to underline that 'they also perform the service of the prophets and teachers. Therefore despise them not; for they are your honourable men along with the prophets and teachers.'[53]

Even later on, when the role was bigger and carried more kudos, the bishop still had to know his place. Part of the bishop's role was to make sure that the poor and needy had somewhere to sit – especially if they were elderly. And, according to the *Didascalia Apostolorum* (written c. AD 230), if no place was available, then the bishop had to give up his seat:

> Do thou, O Bishop, with all thy heart provide a place for them, even if thou have to sit upon the ground; that thou be not as one who respects the persons of men.[54]

This is indeed the *episkopos* – the guardian – as servant: authority exercised in a Jesus-shaped manner, in service and respect and the simple act of giving up your seat.

Given all this, there's nothing inherently anachronistic about arguing for Paul writing to Titus in AD 55/56, during his 'hidden' years. A mission to Crete could have been launched at any time, using Titus as the spearhead. Particularly from busy ports like Ephesus or Corinth. A sea journey to Crete would have taken only a few days. And the fact that Paul is 'sending' Zenas and Apollos to Crete to take the place of Titus ties in perfectly with the idea that this was a delegated mission. The letter is also the only other mention of Apollos outside Acts and the Corinthian correspondence (Titus 3.13). Apollos was not, as far as we know, with Paul in Rome. The only documented time when they were together is in Ephesus. It makes sense to date the letter from this period in Paul's life.

As part of his trip to the west side of Greece, Paul could easily have wintered in Nicopolis. The route from Illyricum towards Achaia would have taken him right through it. Even if he made the trip by boat, making short hops down the coast, Nicopolis would have been a natural stopping point.[55]

Nicopolis was established to celebrate Octavian's defeat of Mark Antony and Cleopatra at the sea battle of Actium in 28 BC. Its very name means 'City of Victory'. Octavian – who later became Augustus – established the city to secure the westward end of the *via Egnatia*, but also, according to Suetonius, 'to extend the fame of his victory at Actium and perpetuate its memory'.[56] 'You are now entering Victoryville' – and don't you forget it. Augustus turned the tent where he had planned and commanded the battle into a huge monument, adorned with the modest slogan, 'From here I went forth under heavenly protection to complete my divine mission and fulfil Rome's imperial destiny.'[57]

Once again, Paul came face to face with the visible demonstration of Roman authority. And maybe it got him into trouble during this period, for there's another little detail which crops up in Romans, when Paul sends greetings to two important people: 'Greet Andronicus and Junia, my relatives who were in prison with me; they are prominent among the apostles, and they were in Christ before I was' (Rom. 16.7).

Junia is both a woman and an apostle. Well, at least in most Bible versions. Some versions render her as Junias – making her male. This despite the fact that nobody in antiquity has ever been called Junias. Ancient sources supply over 250 examples of the name Junia, but not a single mention of Junias. Nor is it an abbreviation for the male name Junianus: there's no known case of Junia being used to abbreviate Junianus.[58] Others take a different strategy, translating the phrase as 'well known to the apostles' (Rom. 16.7), thus allowing her to stay a woman, but removing her status as an apostle.[59]

It's hard not to see these kinds of things as acts of wilful mistranslation. The early commentators assumed it was a woman, Junia, which is a common name. What we have here is another husband-and-wife team, much like Priscilla and Aquila. Their names might indicate a slave origin.[60] These were probably Hellenised Jews who became Christians before Paul. The word rendered 'relatives' can also mean 'compatriots' or 'fellow countrymen' or 'kinsmen'. Paul could be saying that they were Jewish, or that they were his blood relatives. Either way, they would be Jewish Christians. And the Greek word used about their status, *episemos*, means 'splendid, outstanding, prominent'.[61] The fact is – and it's an uncomfortable fact for some theologies – that this husband-and-wife team are two prominent apostles.

The interesting thing here is that they were in prison with Paul. This must have happened before AD 57 when Romans was written.

But when Paul writes to the Corinthians and lists his sufferings for the gospel, he doesn't mention being imprisoned (2 Cor. 11.25–27). Acts only mentions one incident up to this point: the overnight jailing in Philippi. But Junia and Andronicus are not mentioned in relation to that event; indeed, they don't feature in Acts at all.

If we're looking for a point when Paul could have spent time in jail, and when he could have been accompanied by these two famous apostles, then the time spent in western Macedonia and Illyricum might just fit the bill. There's no proof, and Paul makes no reference to it, but perhaps he spent time during this period with Junia and Andronicus before they went to Rome. And perhaps, in one place, their work did not go down well with the authorities.

Whatever the case, it seems highly likely that Paul followed the *via Egnatia* west at this time, across Macedonia to Dyrrachium or Apollonia. It would surely have been tempting for him to continue, to make the short hop to Brindisi and thence to Rome. Perhaps that was what Junia and Andronicus did.

But Paul didn't press on to Rome. It might have been in his mind, though, because when he arrived in Corinth eventually in the spring of AD 57 he wrote a letter to the church at Rome, a letter full of profound thought, a letter which may well have been the product of a long period of reflection, tramping the roads of Macedonia, Illyricum and Greece.

'To all God's beloved in Rome'

Paul arrived in Corinth around the beginning of AD 57. Luke says that he spent the Passover at Philippi (Acts 20.5–6), but before that three months in 'Greece', which probably means Corinth.

While there, he was hosted by Gaius (Rom. 16.23), but this one is probably not the same Gaius who faced the mob in Ephesus. This Gaius was one of the few people in Corinth whom Paul had personally baptised. His house was host to 'the whole church' in Corinth, which implies some degree of wealth (Rom. 16.23). His Latinate name, and the fact that he sends greetings to people in Rome, might indicate that he was a freed slave who had come from Rome and done well for himself in Corinth.[62]

The letter to Romans is a different kind of letter for Paul, in that he's writing to a church that he has neither visited nor founded.

There had been a Christian community at Rome since sometime in the AD 40s. Priscilla and Aquila were expelled from Rome along with other Christians in AD 49, so we know that a church existed in the capital long before apostles like Paul or Peter visited. (Although Peter is sometimes credited with introducing Christianity to Rome, there's no evidence that he went there before the late AD 50s or early 60s.)

With the death of the Emperor Claudius in AD 54, the Jewish Christians from Rome began to return. Priscilla and Aquila had returned after Paul left Ephesus in AD 55. Perhaps they even travelled west with him, before boarding a boat at Dyrrachium. By the time Paul is writing, they were back in Rome (Rom. 16.3). Probably, as in Ephesus, they hosted a church in their house.

Romans is Paul's most influential letter, a letter which literally changed the world. It has always held a pre-eminent position: in the New Testament it appears first of all Paul's letters. It has been characterised as his *magnum opus*, a summary of Pauline theology. Which is not strictly true. There's nothing in Romans about the resurrection of Christ, the future resurrection of believers, the church understood as the body of Christ, or the Eucharist, all significant planks of Paul's theology.

We can make some guesses as to the kinds of problems which Paul was seeking to address in this church in Rome. There seems to be – shades of Corinth – some disunity in the church, along the classic Jewish and Gentile faultlines. Clearly there were tensions between the Jewish and Gentile believers, the same tensions that had been apparent in Antioch and Corinth, and elsewhere. In a long passage, he appeals to the Christians in Rome not to judge one another and to seek unity (Rom. 14.1 – 15.6). There were also problems about religious observance:

> Some judge one day to be better than another, while others judge all days to be alike. Let all be fully convinced in their own minds. Those who observe the day, observe it in honour of the Lord. Also those who eat, eat in honour of the Lord, since they give thanks to God; while those who abstain, abstain in honour of the Lord and give thanks to God. (Rom. 14.5–6)

Perhaps this means that in Rome not all Jewish Christians had changed their day of thanksgiving to a Sunday. Or it may be about

Jewish and Gentile fast days. In the *Didache* the Christian fast days are defined as Wednesday and Friday; Jews fasted on Monday and Thursday. But Paul is remarkably relaxed about the whole thing: let your conscience be your guide.

Romans is a complicated letter. In the words of Bernard Green, 'Paul can contrive to be a very unclear writer at the best of times but he surpasses himself in the letter to the Romans.' For all its complexity, however, its power is evident. There are images and phrases which strike with the impact of an arrow, and moments of sublime beauty when you sense that Paul's spirit simply takes flight:

> For I am convinced that neither death, nor life, nor angels, nor rulers, nor things present, nor things to come, nor powers, nor height, nor depth, nor anything else in all creation, will be able to separate us from the love of God in Christ Jesus our Lord. (Rom. 8.38–39)

Perhaps, though, there's a paradox behind Romans. For all its power, it was written against a background of weakness and anxiety. Paul wrote it as he prepared to return to Jerusalem, a place where he was to be accused of encouraging Jews to ignore the law. At times in the letter one gets the feeling that Paul is not writing to address a specific problem situation, but is trying to create a workable and convincing theology for himself. Returning to Jerusalem would put him back in front of some of his harshest critics. He had just emerged from three years of hard conflict with the church in the city where he was writing the letter. There had been mistakes and misjudgements; people had misunderstood his teaching. His emphasis on the freedom of Christians had led the Corinthians to go overboard in that direction.[63]

That's why Romans has such dizzying depths. It's Paul's *credo*, his statement for the defence. He sends it to Rome because he wants them to know what he's really about. But it's not just about them and their situation: it's also about Paul himself. Romans is much more than a letter to some Christians at Rome: it's a letter from Paul at Corinth.

And, for all its theological density, Romans is about real life. It's packed with advice about the stuff that Christians are supposed to do, and the people and churches who are charged with doing it. Paul talks about the need for humility and patience, for Christians to bless those who hate them and not to seek revenge. He addresses the need for Christians to be subject to the authorities and, in words which must have struck many before and since as deeply ironic, he says that 'rulers are not a terror to good conduct, but to bad' (Rom. 13.3). The arguments are still used today as justification for the removal of liberties: 'If you're not guilty, you have nothing to fear.' But that can't be Paul's position. This is a man who has been imprisoned, beaten, falsely accused. This is a man who, when he finally gets to meet the recipients of this letter, will be in chains.

Finally Paul reiterates his intention to come to Rome, but not as his final destination. He intends to stop there on his way to Spain.

Romans 16 contains a long and fascinating list of names of Christians in Rome. We shall look at these in due course, but it's clear that there are many people in that community at Rome whom Paul knows well. The church includes friends, co-workers, relatives, even: Priscilla and Aquila, Junia and Andronicus; people whom Paul calls 'beloved': Ampliatus, Urbanus, Stachys. The letter was couriered to Rome by one of the church leaders in Corinth, Phoebe, a deacon at Cenchreae and a benefactor of both Paul and the church in Corinth.[64]

Paul remained at Corinth until the spring of AD 57. Although the problems in the church appear to have been solved, there was danger from other quarters. Thus Paul was forced to leave Corinth in a hurry – as he had done from so many cities – because of a plot against him by the Jews.

We are not sure what this plot was. Paul was certainly a man who moved his enemies to violence, but perhaps while he remained in the city he could be protected against this. After all, he had some influential friends there, like Erastus. But outside the city, out at sea, on a boat, then things might get sticky. It's possible that Paul was planning to board a ship full of Jewish pilgrims going to Jerusalem for the festivals. The idea of Paul on board a ship full of zealous Jews was a recipe for disaster. So he decides, wisely, to go in a different direction, sailing north via Macedonia.

As Paul left Corinth by the road north – the same road by which he had entered some seven years before – he was escaping a threat against his life. Maybe it was an omen.

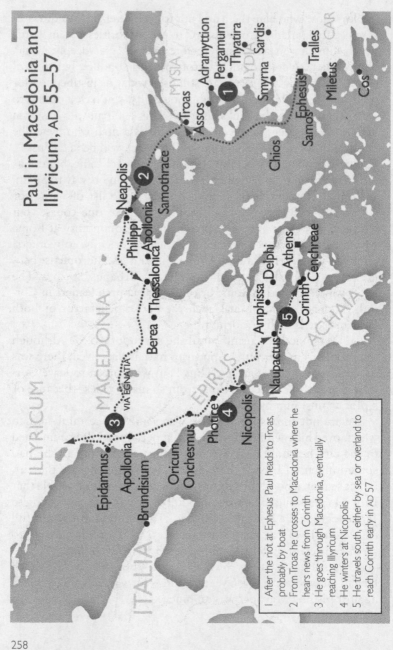

Paul in Macedonia and Illyricum, AD 55–57

ITALIA

ILLYRICUM

Epidamnus
Apollonia
Brundisium
Oricum
Onchesmus
Phoenice

MACEDONIA

VIA EGNATIA

Berea • Thessalonica
Apollonia
Philippi
Neapolis
Samothrace

EPIRUS

Nicopolis

Naupactus

Amphissa
Delphi
Athens
Corinth Cenchreae

ACHAIA

Troas
Assos

MYSIA

Adramyttion
Pergamum
Thyatira
Sardis

LYDIA

Smyrna

Chios

Samos
Ephesus
Tralles
Miletus

CAR

Cos

1. After the riot at Ephesus Paul heads to Troas, probably by boat
2. From Troas he crosses to Macedonia where he hears news from Corinth
3. He goes through Macedonia, eventually reaching Illyricum
4. He winters at Nicopolis
5. He travels south, either by sea or overland to reach Corinth early in AD 57

9. Caesarea AD 57–59

'Holding a discussion'

Paul wanted to get back to Jerusalem to deliver the collection monies he had been gathering for a long time now. He was also taking representatives of the various churches and regions. Luke lists a group of people travelling with him which includes Sopater son of Pyrrhus from Beroea, Aristarchus and Secundus from Thessalonica, Gaius from Derbe or Douberios, Timothy from Lystra and Tychicus and Trophimus from Asia (i.e. Ephesus) (see Acts 20.4).

It sounds more like a diplomatic mission than a pilgrimage. It's clear that Paul believed he still had to prove himself and the validity of his mission. The Jerusalem meeting nearly ten years before had created space for Paul to launch his mission into Asia and Greece, and for the Gentile church to develop and grow – but it hadn't silenced the opposition back in Jerusalem. So Paul was taking back two kinds of proof: a gift of money and the finest examples of Gentile Christianity.

The group seems to have sailed to Philippi. And while the bulk of this party went on to Troas, Paul stayed in Philippi for Passover and the feast of Unleavened Bread (Acts 20.3b–5). In Philippi he was reunited with Luke: the second of the 'we' passages begins here (Acts 20.6). It's six years since Luke made the short journey from Troas to Philippi with Paul.

Luke's presence adds in the kind of specific chronological details which are missing in the rest of Acts. Particularly for the first part of the journey, Luke is very precise. It took them five days to sail to Troas, where they rejoined the rest of the party. According to William Ramsay, Passover in AD 57 fell on Thursday 7 April. It's difficult to be quite so precise when dealing with the ancient world, but we can say with confidence that Paul arrived in Troas in mid-April.[1]

Paul's aim was to get to Jerusalem for Pentecost, which gave him a window of 49 days: Pentecost would have fallen around 29 May.[2] He stayed seven days at Troas.[3] The stay probably ran from the Tuesday to the following Monday morning, which would mean that he left Philippi on the Friday before.

The night before he left, Paul attended a meeting of the local Christian community. It's the only depiction we have of an early church meeting in the New Testament. Paul gives us hints in his letters about what their services contained, but this is the only time we see a local church meeting.

It takes place on the first day of the week – literally 'the first of the sabbath', the same phrase Luke uses to describe the day of the resurrection (Luke 24.1). So we are talking about a Sunday meeting.[4] The implication is that these Christians were meeting on Sunday evening, and because Paul was going to sail the next day he wanted to make the most of his time.

The meeting took place on the third floor of a building. This can only have been a room in one of the *insulae*, the first-century apartment blocks. The poorer people lived on the third and uppermost floors of these apartments, which were often shoddily built. 'We inhabit a city supported to a great extent by slender props,' wrote Juvenal, 'for in this way the bailiff saves the house from falling.'[5]

Clearly the church at Troas was small – it must have been to meet in a third-floor apartment. And there, a young man called Eutychus fell asleep while 'sitting in the window' and fell three floors to his death on the street below. Paul went down and he was miraculously restored to life.

In most versions of the Bible you will find Paul 'speaking to them' or 'addressing them' or 'preaching' (Acts 20.7). Many translations give the impression that Paul's sermon went on and on, until the young man was literally bored to death. But a close look reveals that it wasn't like that at all.

First, his name – which, ironically, means 'lucky' – was a slave's name. And he was a young man, a *neanias*. So here we have a young slave, and one who had been working hard all day (remember: no day off on Sunday). They were in Turkey, in spring. The room was lit by small oil lamps which would have shed more heat than light. So it was hot and dim. It was very late. No wonder he dropped off. Literally.

And more than that, Paul wasn't preaching at all. The Greek word to describe what he was doing is *dialegomai*, which means 'discussion' – from which we get our word 'dialogue'.[6] This was not some sermon, but a long discussion. It could still have been dull, of course. By his own admission, Paul wasn't a great speaker, so perhaps it did get too technical and detailed for a young slave to follow. But it wasn't a sermon, and Paul wasn't preaching.

Paul came from the rabbinic tradition, where teaching was about question and answer, dialogue and debate. Jesus, too, used this format. He never preached a sermon in his life, not in our sense of the word. And that same style was probably adopted by the early church. Even the terms we use for the classic Christian speech – 'sermon' and 'homily' – reflect much more discursive origins. 'Sermon' comes from the Latin word *serma*, which means 'conversation'. 'Homily' comes from the Greek word *homileō*, which means – wait for it – 'conversation'. The first actual sermon that we have comes from the mid-second century.

The early church was a question-and-answer community. Paul's letters often arise in response to questions that he has been asked. They are not transcripts of theology lectures. In Troas we see that in action: a small, compact group sharing dialogue.

And sharing food. The implication is that they shared the thanksgiving meal (20.11). What we have here is much closer to a housegroup meeting or even a church supper than a modern church service.

The apartment was probably owned by a man called Carpas, if we accept 2 Timothy as genuine. Before leaving the next day, Paul left some stuff there: a cloak, some notebooks and scrolls. He intended to return, it seems, probably on his way to Rome.

Wrong.

Paul and companions travel from Corinth to Jerusalem: spring AD 57

1 Paul and companions arrive in Philippi for Passover.
2 They sail to Troas, staying there 7 days.
3 Paul walks across the headland to Assos, joining the others there. They then sail to Mitylene.
4 They stop opposite Chios.
5 Passing Samos on the west, they sail to Miletus, where Paul spends time with the elders from Ephesus.
6 They sail to Cos, then Rhodes, then Patara.
7 They sail across to Tyre.
8 At Tyre they stay for a week, waiting for a ship to take them south.
9 After a brief stop at Ptolemais, they arrive in Caesarea, where they stay with Philip.
10 They make their way to Jerusalem, arriving for Pentecost and lodging in the house of Mnason.

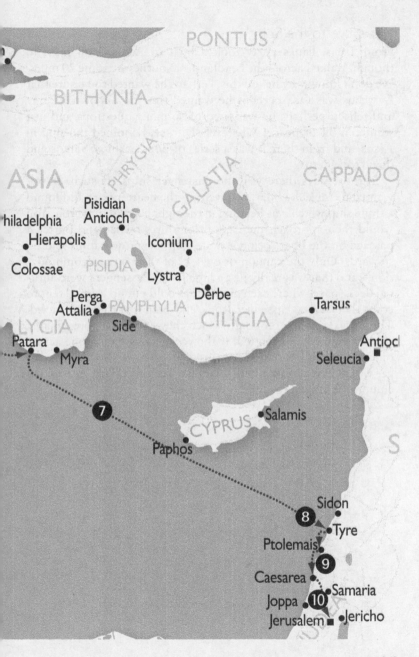

PONTUS

BITHYNIA

ASIA

PHRYGIA

GALATIA

CAPPADO

Pisidian
Antioch

hiladelphia

Iconium

Hierapolis

PISIDIA

Colossae

Lystra

Perga   PAMPHYLIA   Derbe

Attalia

LYCIA   Side   CILICIA   Tarsus

Patara   Antioch

Myra   Seleucia

7

CYPRUS   Salamis

Paphos

S

Sidon

8   Tyre

Ptolemais

9

Caesarea

Samaria

Joppa   **10**

Jerusalem   Jericho

'A captive to the Spirit'

From Troas, Paul's party took a boat to Assos. Paul himself, though, walked across the headland – a journey of some 20 miles. We don't know why he did this. Perhaps he wanted to be sure that Eutychus was OK; perhaps he wanted time on his own to pray and reflect; perhaps he was tired of so many questions and just wanted a bit of peace! Whatever the case, he joined the ship in Assos, and from there it was a series of hops – Chios, Samos and down to Miletus.

In those days there were no passenger ships, as such. If you wanted to travel by boat, you went to the nearest port and found a trade ship which was heading in the right general direction. You would then approach the captain or ship's owner and barter a passage on the boat. Being a trade ship meant no cabins and no stewards. Only the captain or owner got their own accommodation – and that was really just a large box.[7] Passengers were allotted deck space, where each night they could put up a small tent to cover themselves. Passengers took and prepared their own food. There was a galley on board which they could use, presumably after the crew had been fed. If the voyage was a long one across open water, they would need a lot of provisions.[8] So any passenger would have to take along their own sleeping quarters, cooking equipment and all the food they needed.

Two ancient boats from Herculaneum. Left: A trade ship with a figure sitting on the deck (presumably the owner) giving instructions. Right: Detail showing the roof of one of the cabins on deck (circled)

Many voyages, in any case, were a series of short hops from port to port, allowing passengers to leave the ship at night and find accommodation in an inn in the port. This was what happened on the first leg of Paul's voyage back to Syria, and even on his return as a prisoner, where he was allowed off to spend the night with friends in Sidon (Acts 27.3).

Acts tells us that Paul sailed past Ephesus and stopped instead at Miletus. Luke says it was because he wanted to get to Jerusalem, but the stop in Miletus was more time consuming, because he had to summon the leaders from Ephesus to meet him there – a journey of around 30 miles each way. This actually added to the travel time of the journey. The issue, surely, was the risk. In Ephesus Paul still had enemies – there might have been the risk of arrest. Luke says he didn't want to 'spend time in Asia'; if he had stopped in Ephesus, he might have found himself doing time rather than spending it.

So he went to Miletus instead and called across the leaders of the church in Asia. Paul gave them a speech. Whether it's recorded verbatim is uncertain, but it must catch the gist of what was said. It contains a glimpse of Paul's working methods:

I did not shrink from doing anything helpful, proclaiming the message to you and teaching you publicly and from house to house, as I testified to both Jews and Greeks about repentance towards God and faith towards our Lord Jesus. (Acts 20.20–21)

This fits in with what we know of the situation of the early church: small, tight-knit communities; Paul travelling from house to house, where the Christian communities met.

Paul says that 'I am not responsible for the blood of any of you' (Acts 20.26), which probably means that he has discharged his duty to them. They are grown-ups now. One of the interesting things about the speech is that it quotes a saying of Jesus which is found nowhere in the Gospels: 'It is more blessed to give than to receive' (Acts 20.35). We do know that in the early church several gospels of Jesus were circulating as well as collections of the sayings – the *logia* – of the Lord. Luke himself records that others had tried to set down a record of events (Luke 1.1). This presumably comes from one such collection.

Paul's journey to Syria: April-May AD 57

Paul left Philippi after Passover and arrived in Jerusalem for Pentecost. It has been estimated that, in AD 57 Passover would have been on Thursday 7 April and Pentecost on 29 May. At least for the early part of the voyage, Luke's details are very specific, allowing us to make a plausible reconstruction of the voyage.

Place	Miles	Km	Poss. Date	
At Philippi			c. 7–15 April	We sailed from Philippi after the days of Unleavened Bread, and in five days we joined them in Troas, where we stayed for seven days. (Acts 20.6)
To Troas	130	209	c. 15–19 April	
At Troas			c. 19–25 April	
To Assos	35	56	c. 25–29 April	
To Mitylene	31	50		When he met us in Assos we took him to Mitylene. (Acts 20.14)
To Chios	59	95		... on the following day we arrived opposite Chios. The next day we touched at Samos, and the day after that we came to Miletus. (Acts 20.15)
To Samos	59	95		
To Miletus	44	70		
At Miletus			29 Apr – early May	
To Cos	46	74	Early May – mid May	... we came by a straight course to Cos, and the next day to Rhodes, and from there to Patara. (Acts 21.1)
To Rhodes	71	114		
To Patara	71	114		
To Tyre	404	651		We came in sight of Cyprus; and leaving it on our left, we sailed to Syria and landed at Tyre. (Acts 21.3)
At Tyre				
To Ptolemais	27	43	Mid May – late May, arriving in Jerusalem for Pentecost around 29 May	
To Caesarea	34	55		
At Caesarea				
To Jerusalem	65	105		

The speech appears to show that Paul knows he's heading into trouble. He even appears to give a prediction of his death. But appearances can be deceiving. Paul never says that he won't see them again: that's what *they* think, because of his words. They know how dangerous it is for Paul to return to Jerusalem. Nor, in fact, does this passage include a great deal of prophecy – at least not the type of supernatural predictive prophecy we might be thinking of. Paul says that 'the Holy Spirit testifies to me in every city that imprisonment and persecutions are waiting for me' (Acts 20.23). But it would hardly take a great prophet to predict that: it happened in virtually every city he ever visited and was the reason why he couldn't stop in Ephesus on this journey. And as I say, nothing in the speech says anything about Paul's death. If Luke were inventing this speech – or if Acts were written a long time after Paul's death – then why is it nowhere predicted in the text? There are two more prophecies about Paul's future in Acts and neither of them mentions Paul's death (Acts 21.11; 23.11). Throughout, the writer of Acts is unaware of Paul's final fate.

'He would not be persuaded'

The meeting with the elders and overseers from the churches lasted perhaps a day. After that it was back on board a ship and then a further series of daily hops: Miletus to Cos, Cos to Rhodes, Rhodes to Patara. Patara was on the south coast of Lycia, not far from Myra, where Paul had embarked all those years ago with Barnabas. The journey was coming full circle.

At Patara they changed ship, finding a freighter taking cargo to Tyre. They rounded Cyprus, arriving at Tyre, probably after a journey of three days or so.[9] At Tyre they found a group of disciples and they stayed there for a week. We know nothing of this church, but it was presumably founded sometime in the early days of Christianity, when the message spread north, through Samaria and into Syria.

The men, women and children of this Christian community urge Paul not to go on to Jerusalem (Acts 21.4). They speak 'through the Spirit', but Paul ignores it. Which raises some interesting questions. Is Paul disobedient? Probably the prophecy is conditional: 'If you do X, then Y will follow.' Elsewhere, Paul says that prophecy has to be weighed, judged, assessed (1 Cor. 14.29). The Tyrian Christians know what will happen and believe that this is an instruction not to go. Paul knows what will happen and goes anyway.

From Tyre it's a short hop down the coast to Ptolemais, a sea port about 30 miles south of Tyre. Again they find another group of believers there and after a day spent with them, Paul and the companions go on to Caesarea.

At Caesarea it's time for a blast from the past. They meet one of the giants of the church, a grizzled veteran from the frontier days: Philip the evangelist. Some 24 years have gone by since Philip took the gospel first to Samaria and then to Gaza and the towns of the coast. Since then his daughters have grown to become noted prophets in the church.

Paul and Philip have history. It was Paul, of course, who was responsible for Philip ending up in Caesarea. Paul's persecutions, under the name of Saul, forced Philip out of Jerusalem. Then another historical figure arrives: Agabus, the prophet from Antioch who predicted the famine in Judea and elsewhere (Acts 11.28). Again, his prediction led to Paul's visit to Jerusalem with the gift, and the private meeting with the leaders which sent him off to Cyprus and Galatia. Now we have Paul on his way to Judea with another gift. Like the elders in Asia and the house church in Tyre, Agabus believes that Paul will be imprisoned in Jerusalem, an act he demonstrates by symbolically tying Paul up with his belt.

What was it that made everyone think this way? Prophecy, of course: the power of the Holy Spirit. But also other factors, which must have backed up those Spirit-inspired, prophetic warnings. Anyone in the region – certainly any Jews – would have been aware of the rising political temperature.

Even Caesarea was divided. The city was created by Herod the Great as a sophisticated Græco-Roman centre, with amphitheatre, hippodrome, a palace by the sea and a magnificent, artificial harbour, developed at huge cost and utilising the latest in Roman technology. The city had been named in honour of Augustus. The temple of Caesar, a landmark which could be seen a long way out to sea, contained a statue of Augustus and one of Roma, goddess of Rome. Caesarea became the natural place for the Roman prefect of Judea to dwell, very different from the fevered religiosity of hot, dry, dusty Jerusalem.

But by the AD 50s, some of the atmosphere of Jerusalem had spread to Caesarea, like a virus. Jews and Greeks were arguing over ownership of the city. And if it was like that in Caesarea, then how much more so in Jerusalem? Decades of Roman rule, crass, inept and avaricious, combined with a rising Jewish nationalism to make the city a combustible mixture. Paul was heading into the fiery furnace. Everyone knew it.

Paul knows it too. Writing to the Romans before he sets out on his journey, he asks for their prayers 'that I may be rescued from the unbelievers in Judea, and that my ministry to Jerusalem may be acceptable to the saints' (Rom. 15.31). It's not just the Jews in Jerusalem from whom he expects trouble: it's the Jewish Christians as well.

Luke's closing phrase to the stay in Caesarea almost sounds like a sigh: 'Since he would not be persuaded, we remained silent except to say, "The Lord's will be done"' (Acts 21.14).

On his way into Jerusalem Paul stays with a man called Mnason of Cyprus, whom Luke calls 'an early disciple' (Acts 21.16). The most natural reading of the earlier text indicates that his house was in Jerusalem and that it was there that the brothers greeted Paul warmly. Mnason's name may be a Greek version of the Hebrew name Manasseh. He was probably among that early group of Cypriot Christians who, in the aftermath of Paul's persecution, took the gospel to Cyprus and then on to Antioch (Acts 11.19–20). Mnason, then, was probably one of the Hellenised Jewish Christians going right back to the time of the appointment of the seven deacons. Since most of Paul's eight Gentile companions were uncircumcised, they might not have been welcome in many establishments in the city during the festival. But Mnason offered them hospitality and some form of accreditation.[10]

The shadows of the past are coalescing around Paul. He's returning to the city where he first encountered the Christians, back to the place where he hunted them down and imprisoned them. What goes around, comes around. Paul has made it safely across the sea from Corinth to Jerusalem, but in the landlocked Holy City he finds himself in very deep water indeed.

'This man is a Roman citizen'

Mnason may have welcomed Paul and his travelling companions, but the next day, when Paul goes to meet the elders of the Jerusalem church, the reception is somewhat more mixed. The account in Acts (21.18–26) is notable for the coolness of Paul's welcome. Although the leaders 'praise God' for what has been achieved through Paul, they immediately launch into a warning:

> Then they said to [Paul], 'You see, brother, how many thousands of believers there are among the Jews, and they are all zealous for the law. They have been told about you that you teach all the Jews living among the Gentiles to forsake Moses, and that you tell them not to circumcise their children or observe the customs. What then is to be done? They will certainly hear that you have come.' (Acts 21.20–22)

Clearly no one knew in advance that he was coming. And what's more, the thousands of Jewish Christians still believe that Paul is undermining their faith. No gift of money from the Gentile churches is going to solve that. Indeed, despite the fact that it was Jacob who specifically asked the Gentile churches to remember the poor, there must have been some – perhaps many – in the church in Jerusalem who would have seen this 'Gentile' money as tainted.

The picture in Luke's account is quite startling. It shows that there are those in the church who are spreading rumours – either maliciously or ignorantly – about Paul. And the leadership of the church in Jerusalem has been unable, or unwilling, to counter these accusations.

Such is the level of suspicion about Paul that he has to prove his Jewish credentials: the elders decide that he and his Jewish travelling companions should very visibly observe 'the customs'. Paul goes through the act of purification (i.e. ritual bathing) to enter the temple, and then pays the expenses of four men who have to make sacrifices to fulfil their Nazirite vows. The fulfilment of a Nazirite vow required the sacrifice of a year-old unblemished male lamb, as well as an unblemished female lamb as a sacrifice for sin, a ram as a peace offering and a basket of unleavened loaves and unleavened wafers and cereal offerings (Num. 6.14–15). That would not have come cheap. The lambs cost four denarii each, the ram eight denarii. Sixteen day's wages, and they were probably more expensive at festival time.[11]

Paul would hardly have the money to pay for this personally. So where does the money come from? Possibly from one of the travelling companions or, more probably, from the collection money itself. That would be a canny political move from Jacob: Paul's enemies could hardly complain about the money if it had been acceptable enough to be used to pay off a Nazirite vow.

But how would Paul view this? Money collected from people who had been justified by their faith, used to pay for Jewish rites, rituals and sacrifices? And what of that purification undergone by Paul? The purification ritual was designed to purify someone from uncleanness, from contagion through contact with some form of impurity – like, well, Gentiles, for instance. One can imagine Paul having to swallow hard at some of the potential implications that could be taken from this, and bite his tongue. Two or three months earlier, he wrote, 'We who are strong ought to put up with the failings of the weak, and not to please ourselves' (Rom. 15.1). Now he has to live that out.

The gesture might have done something to satisfy his critics among the Jewish Christians, but it's no help against his opponents in orthodox Judaism. They jump on it to accuse him of taking Gentiles into the temple.

Paul is alleged to have taken Gentiles into the inner courts of the temple. His accusers, interestingly, are some Jews from Asia – diaspora Jews from the Ephesus area. This, presumably, is how they know Paul and recognise Trophimus, who is with him and is an Ephesian. 'Fellow-Israelites, help!' they call out. 'This is the man who is teaching everyone everywhere against our people, our law, and this place.' It's fundamentally the same rumour which is circulating against Paul among the Jewish Christians: Paul is anti-Jew, anti-Moses, anti-temple. The Jews accuse Paul of taking the Gentile Trophimus into the inner temple. Gentiles were forbidden to go beyond the Court of the Gentiles: there were signs up in both Greek and Latin warning of the death penalty should they cross the low balustraded wall which separated the courts.[12]

Immediately a riot breaks out. Luke records that the gates are shut – presumably by the temple police who want to secure the area. But it's not the temple police who seize Paul and take him out of the temple: it's the Romans.

Overlooking the temple from the north-west was the Antonia Fortress, the Roman garrison in Jerusalem. It was rare to have a garrison in a major city, but Jerusalem was a special case and the positioning of the garrison, overlooking the temple, indicates its main purpose. When trouble kicked off, it usually kicked off in the temple. So the job of the troops was not to police Jerusalem – that, ironically, was the job of the temple police – but to control the temple itself, especially at the crowded festival times. Josephus wrote that the feasts were 'the usual occasion for sedition to flare up'.[13] There was a stairway from the Antonia which allowed the troops quick access to the Temple Mount.[14] The cohort, under the command of a tribune called Claudius Lysias (Acts 23.26), would only have numbered around 600 men, not nearly enough to defend themselves in the case of a full-scale riot, but they could be used to remove troublemakers quickly from the scene.

Claudius Lysias sends a snatch squad down to drag Paul away. Paul is bound in double chains, which sounds excessive – but not to the tribune, because he thinks that he has captured a ringleader of the group known as the Sicarii.

The Sicarii were a new type of bandit. They worked in broad daylight and committed their atrocities in the heart of the city. And they were particularly dangerous during the festivals when, according to Josephus,

> they would mingle with the crowd, carrying short daggers concealed under their clothing, with which they stabbed their enemies. Then, when [the enemies] fell, the murderers joined in the cries of indignation and through their plausible behaviour, were never discovered.[15]

Given this background, it's easy to see why the tribune acts as he does. According to Luke, he believes that Paul is the Egyptian who led a group of 4,000 *sikarios*, or Sicarii.

'The Egyptian' was a Jew who had come to Jerusalem at the head of many followers. Claiming to be a prophet, he led his followers to the Mount of Olives, from where he planned to attack the city and overpower the Roman garrison. Josephus says in a parallel account that he believed that the walls of the city would fall, Jericho-like. In the end the Egyptian's force was destroyed, not just by the Romans under Felix, but by the people of Jerusalem as well.[16] Although he appears to have had large numbers of followers (Josephus says

30,000; Luke's figure of 4,000 is much more plausible), he clearly didn't have widespread support in Jerusalem. His followers were massacred, but the Egyptian himself escaped.

Now the tribune believes that he has caught his man, in the act of murdering someone during the festival: just as the Sicarii were known to do.

It's only when he gets Paul back to the stairway leading to the barracks that he realises he's mistaken. Instead of an Aramaic-speaking Jew, he has caught a Greek-speaking Jew, from Tarsus in Cilicia. The misidentification is the tribune's first mistake. His second is to let Paul address the people. Paul makes a defence to the crowd – the first of three lengthy 'speeches for the defence' that Luke records in this section of Acts. This one reveals some crucial details of Paul's life: his apprenticeship under Gamaliel is one, but also his vision of Jesus in the temple, in Jerusalem, telling him to take the message to the Gentiles.

At this point the crowd break out in renewed frenzy. A vision of the hated Jesus in the heart of the temple – the very institution which he both vocally and symbolically attacked! Given that Paul has just been accused of bringing a Gentile into the inner courts, reminding them of his calling might not be the most subtle thing to do. Once again, the Roman troops have to intervene. The centurion decides that Paul should be flogged before being interrogated. This kind of scourging – known as *verberatio* – was delivered with the *flagrum*, a whip which tore the flesh and could even shatter bone. It was this kind of beating which, in effect, killed Jesus. The law of Augustus – *Lex Iulia de vi Publica* – explicitly forbade its use on Roman citizens. It was a punishment restricted to slaves and foreigners. Cicero put it like this: 'To bind a Roman citizen is a crime, to flog him an abomination, to slay him almost an act of murder.'[17]

So when Paul says that he's a Roman citizen, the process stops at once. (All he said to the tribune before was that he was a citizen of Tarsus, not a Roman citizen.) The commander is incredulous. His citizenship cost him a lot of money, probably in the form of a bribe given to officials in the imperial secretariat who would then have put his name on a list of candidates to be put before the emperor.[18] But what about this ragged Jew?

Paul is hastily reprieved from the flogging. But he is not freed. He is taken into custody in the Antonia Fortress. The next day, he is to be put before the Jewish council.

'The resurrection of the dead'

It's actually the tribune who orders that the chief priests and the entire council should meet (Acts 22.30). This may be a religious matter, but Rome is calling the shots. So Paul, after spending the night in custody, is brought down from the Antonia to the place where the Sanhedrin are gathered.

There is no chance here for Paul to tell his story. He barely gets out his opening line before the high priest orders him to be struck across the mouth. Paul reacts angrily, but then seems to apologise: 'I did not know you were the high priest,' he says.

This seems surprising. The high priest at the time – Ananias son of Nedebaeus – was not new in post; he had been appointed high priest in AD 47, ten years earlier. At one point he had fallen foul of Quadratus, governor of Syria, and, along with others, had been sent off in chains to Claudius.[19] They were released through the influence of Agrippa II. He used his wealth to bribe individuals and to influence a later Roman procurator, Albinus. He was seen as pro-Roman, and in AD 66, at the beginning of the revolt, his house would be burned to the ground. He managed to flee to the palace of Herod the Great, but he and his brother were captured and executed by the Zealots.[20]

This is not a man renowned for piety. In that context, Paul's reply, and his use of a quote from Exodus, may be disingenuous, suggesting that a real high priest would not act as he does. Paul's next comment is certainly disingenuous. Seeing the Pharisees in attendance, he calmly lobs in a theological hand grenade:

When Paul noticed that some were Sadducees and others were Pharisees, he called out in the council, 'Brothers, I am a Pharisee, a son of Pharisees. I am on trial concerning the hope of the resurrection of the dead.' (Acts 23.6)

If there's one thing Paul knows how to do, it's how to create a disturbance. Paul claims theological kinship with the Pharisees and then reframes the charges: this is not about the temple or about the law of Moses, it's about resurrection. Technically, of course, his claim is true. But the key point is that it's hugely inflammatory. The Pharisees believe in the resurrection of the dead, but the Sadducees do not. The consequence is a theological brawl which turns violent and as a result of which the trial descends into chaos. Given that the Pharisees start to defend Paul, it seems that Luke did consider Ananias a Sadducee.[21] Paul is removed by the tribune for his own safety and taken back into the Antonia.

That night, in a cell in the Roman fortress, Paul has a vision. Jesus appears to him, just as he appeared to him in the temple so many years ago. Just as he appeared in Corinth when he was under threat. Just as he appeared all those years ago outside Damascus. He says to Paul, 'Keep up your courage! For just as you have testified for me in Jerusalem, so you must bear witness also in Rome' (Acts 23.11). Jesus doesn't say anything about a trial. The implication is simply, 'Don't worry, you'll make it to Rome.'

Which is what happens. Although not, perhaps, in the way Paul might have imagined it.

'There would be a plot'

Jerusalem is tense. Febrile. A swirling pool of rumour and complaint. Already there's a sense of fragmentation about the city, a depiction of small groups and sectarian intrigue, the kind which, when revolution does come, destroy it from within through conflict and betrayal.

There's a conspiracy. Luke talks of over 40 Jews who swear to take no food until they have killed Paul. They hatch a plot, telling the 'chief priests and elders' to ask for Paul to be brought down so that they can make a 'thorough examination'. At which point they will assassinate him. It's the first-century equivalent of shooting someone on the steps of the court house.

Their plan is foiled when Paul's nephew gets to hear about the plan. He warns Paul, who passes on the information to the tribune. The tribune writes a letter explaining the situation, then sends Paul to Caesarea, accompanied by 'two hundred soldiers, seventy horsemen, and two hundred spearmen'. One man, who has done 'nothing deserving death or imprisonment' according to the tribune's letter (23.29). Accompanied by 470 troops.

Hmm. Having spent a lot of time defending Luke's historicity, surely this is stretching it a bit?

Let's have a look at the details. First, Paul has family in Jerusalem. His sister lives there, and with her his nephew. Perhaps the nephew, like his uncle in the past, is involved with radical religious politics. He cannot have become a Christian: how would a Christian hear about a plot organised by ultra-nationalist zealots?

Or maybe there's a different explanation. The involvement of the Jewish authorities seems, at first glance, very problematic. Why would they agree to be involved in something which they know will enrage the Romans? But Luke's description talks merely about the chief priests and elders. A small subset of the Sanhedrin. Or maybe it's a larger, more formal group, but they never intend to go along with the plot. So they tip off Paul's family. It offers a way for them to get out of the situation without angering either the zealots or the Romans.

Then there's those fanatics. We should remember that Paul is in Roman custody. This attack would be a strike not just against the heretic Christians, but also against his Roman protectors, who have dared to decide when the Sanhedrin should meet and who should be punished. There's an intensely political angle to this plot.

Which explains the tribune's reaction. This one man could become the spark which sets the whole forest alight. So let's remove him from the situation. Send him to the governor at Caesarea, and let him handle it.

But what about all those soldiers? You don't need 470 soldiers to guard Paul. Perhaps the tribune fears a more general uprising. In the tense political atmosphere, such an ambush and attack could be the start of something incendiary. Why take any risks?

Or he may be simply taking advantage of pre-planned troop movements, sending Paul with a group of troops who would be returning to Caesarea anyway. At festival time the troops in the Antonia would have received reinforcements to deal with the crowds. As a diversionary tactic, it's not bad: a load of Romans returning north to their base. Who would think that hidden away in the middle of them all an insignificant Jewish troublemaker is being spirited out of the city? Certainly the accurate details – the distances, the hours, the terminology – all lend credibility to the account.[22]

Paul's journey back to Judea has been book-ended by death threats. The Jews in Corinth planned to tip him off the boat; the zealots in Jerusalem planned to murder him during the tribunal. So Paul is spirited away once again. Luke's geography is spot on. He goes first to Antipatris, a military station on the Samaria/Judea border where they halt for the night. The next day Paul is taken by horse to Caesarea. He's given a cursory hearing by the governor Felix. And then is put back into jail. Safe. Secure. Under lock and key.

'His excellency the governor Felix'

Five days after the incident, twelve days after Paul arrived in Jerusalem, a delegation arrives at Caesarea. The group includes Ananias, the high priest, some elders and a lawyer called Tertullus. Tertullus begins with a bit of flattery, before launching into his main charge: Paul is a pestilent fellow (the word *loimos* refers to a disease or plague), a notorious Jewish agitator known around the world, 'a ringleader of the sect of the Nazarenes' who has tried to profane the temple. The language is clever. It's similar to that used by Felix's mentor Claudius when talking about Jews in Alexandria whom he accused of 'stirring up a common plague throughout the world'.[23]

The charge is calculated to get a response. Although the Romans wouldn't be concerned with profaning the temple, they would be concerned with someone doing so to incite a riot. Paul denies the charges, but does admit that he belongs to 'the Way, which they call a sect' (Acts 24.14). He then goes on to give an account of what has happened to him and why he was taken.

Interestingly, Felix is familiar with this sect. He's 'rather well informed about the Way' (Acts 24.22) and, far from going along with the prosecuting party, he simply dismisses them and adjourns the case until he can hear from the tribune. In the meantime, Paul is allowed to receive visitors in jail to bring him what he needs, and no doubt he's helped by the Christians in Caesarea.

Felix – or Marcus Antonius Felix, as he was probably known – was a freed slave of the Emperor Claudius, or perhaps Claudius's mother, Antonia. He was a favourite of Claudius, who rewarded him with a command in Palestine. This did not go down well with the aristocratic traditionalists, who muttered darkly about Claudius's habit of giving excessive power to freedmen.[24] Before AD 52 he was probably governor of Samaria and Judea, with Ventidius Cumanus in charge of Galilee. But Cumanus fell from grace after letting a conflict between Samaritans and Jews get out of hand. So Felix took complete control of the province.[25]

Under Felix, though, things got worse, not better. Judean society began to fall apart. Brigands and rebels began to roam the countryside, urging others to join them and threatening death to anyone who sided with the Romans. Felix took some strong action against them. And when more trouble broke out in Caesarea, he tried negotiation, rather than use force straight away. He even referred the matter to Nero.[26] He was criticised by the former high priest, Jonathan – yet another son of Ananus. Indeed, so bad was the relationship between the two that it was even rumoured that the procurator paid a close friend of the high priest to arrange Jonathan's assassination. (And the people who killed Jonathan were the Sicarii.)

Felix and his wife Drusilla, a Jewess, are among Paul's visitors. They listen to him talk. Drusilla was the daughter of Herod Agrippa I. She had been married to Azizus, King of Emesa (in Syria), but Felix seduced her and she bore him a son, named Agrippa, after her father. He died during the eruption of Vesuvius in AD 79. As a Jew, Drusilla was probably a good source of information for Felix about 'the Way'. According to Suetonius, Drusilla was one of three 'queens' whom Felix married. He was also said to have married a granddaughter of Antony and Cleopatra (who, confusingly, may also have been called Drusilla). His third royal wife has not been identified. Whatever else he was, Felix was a big fan of the monarchy. And, apparently, women called Drusilla.[27]

Contemporary judgement on Felix is coloured by snobbery: he was an ex-slave, after all. And there's a rather prurient streak in these accounts: an ex-slave and a princess (or three). Tacitus said that Felix 'with all cruelty and lust wielded the power of a king with the mentality of a slave'.[28] Still, snobbery aside, you can't help but notice that every single historical source is unanimous in its hostility towards Felix. Even Luke is critical. He writes that Felix was hoping to get some money out of Paul for his release.

This may be why Felix and his wife are 'alarmed' by Paul's talk. Paul talks about 'justice, self-control, and the coming judgement' (Acts 24.25). Hardly a seeker-friendly message for a greedy serial adulterer.

By now we have reached the summer of AD 57. How long Felix stayed in office is unclear, but the data in Suetonius and Josephus strongly suggests that Felix was in Caesarea until at least AD 59.[29] During that time, Paul remained in prison.

'Felix left Paul in prison'

We don't know what Paul did for those two years. We know he was living in the *Praetorium* of Herod the Great (Acts 23.35). The palace served as the administrative headquarters for the Roman occupying forces in Palestine. It had a magnificent dining room with a near-Olympic-sized swimming pool right next to it. It also had a Roman military holding facility for troublemakers and criminals.

For the first five days Paul was held in solitary confinement. It was only at the second hearing that Felix allowed him to have visitors (Acts 24.23). Indeed, after this hearing the conditions of his imprisonment were relaxed and he was allowed some measure of liberty.

When assigning guards to a prisoner, the Romans took into account the seriousness of the crime and the status of the individual involved. The emphasis was on guards with experience. Paul was assigned to a centurion. It's doubtful that this man was currently in charge of 100 men: more likely he was part of the administrative staff of the HQ.[30] As to the 'relaxation', a parallel might be found in the imprisonment of Agrippa by Tiberius. Agrippa was also a Jew and a citizen – albeit one of a much higher social status than Paul. When Agrippa was imprisoned, it was really a form of house arrest. Josephus says of Agrippa that after he was transferred from the camp to his own house, 'the watch on his daily activities was relaxed'.

So Paul might have been assigned slightly better quarters in the palace complex and given freedom to communicate with the outside world. Surely he wrote letters. We don't have any that we can securely date to this time (although some have assigned various prison letters to this period), but later, when Festus examines Paul, he says literally that too much *grammata* has driven Paul insane (Acts 26.24). *Grammata* can mean 'learning', but it also means 'writing', especially writing letters. When Paul arrives in Rome, the Jews tell him, 'We have received no letters [*grammata*] from Judea about you' (Acts 28.21).

It's impossible to imagine Paul just sitting quietly in Caesarea. He would doubtless have been beavering away. Discussing, debating, thinking, writing, studying the Scriptures: his body in prison, but his mind flying wherever it would take him.

In AD 59 Felix was recalled from Judea and succeeded by Porcius Festus. Josephus describes Festus as a peaceful, conscientious procurator, who strove to bring some stability to an increasingly fragile province. That's probably why, three days after his arrival in the province, Festus went to Jerusalem. Grasp the nettle straight away.

Sometimes governors marked the end of their period in office by releasing prisoners. Not so Felix. Paul remained in custody. It was a favour to the Jewish temple authorities, who also wanted Paul's removal to Judea. By now there was a new high priest, Ishmael, son of Phabi, who had been appointed by Herod Agrippa II in AD 59.

Agrippa II was the last of the Herodian kings and tetrarchs. He was the son of Herod Agrippa I, the king who had killed James and died a suitably gruesome death for acting like a god (Acts 12.1–11, 20–23). In AD 52, Agrippa II was given the territories of Iturea and Trachonitis, as well as parts of Galilee and the Perea, and granted the title 'king'. He had cultivated good relations with the Romans; it was his sister, Drusilla, who was married to Felix.

Festus was in no hurry to grant concessions. Instead he invited the Jerusalem leaders to come to Caesarea. Festus remained in Jerusalem for about eight to ten days – Luke is characteristically precise where he can be – and then went to take up residence in Caesarea. Thus it was that, two years after his first hearing, Paul was paraded before the new governor and his Jewish accusers.

Festus offered Paul a choice: 'Do you wish to go up to Jerusalem and be tried there before me on these charges?' Paul, mindful of his reception in Jerusalem last time, and also of his vision of going to

Rome, took the only other option which was available to him. As a Roman citizen, he invoked his right to be tried in Rome.

Paul knew his chances of a fair trial in Jerusalem were virtually non-existent. (They weren't that good in Rome, but at least his hearing would not be held in such a religiously violent atmosphere.) There was also that vision he'd had in the Antonia Fortress. Two years before, Jesus had promised Paul that he would 'bear witness in Rome'. Faced with a new governor, then, Paul took his chance to move things on. He would get to Rome any way he could. Anything was better than going back to Jerusalem.

'Several days' after Paul had his initial hearing before Festus, King Agrippa II and his sister Bernice came to Caesarea on an official visit. Agrippa II was on a charm offensive. He had maintained cordial relations with Felix, but that old crook was gone now, so it was time to make a good impression on the new boss. During their stay, Festus brought up the subject of Paul. Agrippa expressed a wish to hear Paul speak. Nearly 30 years earlier, his great-uncle Antipas had listened to both John the Baptist and Jesus. Now he had a chance to listen to one of the key followers of the sect these strange prophets had spawned.

The next day Paul was brought up from the cell and put in front of the 'military tribunes and prominent men' of Caesarea. Festus enquired as to what he should write on the charge sheet about Paul. 'I have nothing definite to write to our sovereign about him,' he complained to Agrippa (Acts 25.26).

Once again, Paul gets the chance to make his testimony speech, this time the longest and most detailed of all his defence speeches in Acts. It is, in a way, the climactic speech of the book: Paul's hearing before both Roman and Jewish powers. It's not, in any way, a judicial speech. It contains no counter-accusations, no rebuttal of any charges. Instead it's an *apologia*, a 'here I stand' moment. Indeed, since most of it revolves around Jewish covenant history, it must be pretty incomprehensible to Festus, who gets frustrated enough to accuse Paul of madness (Acts 26.24).

It's a Jewish speech, this one. It's aimed at Agrippa and Bernice. Despite his experiences, Paul has clearly never given up the hope of evangelising Jews. Paul argues that the king knows all about the messianic ideas and must be aware of these events.

'King Agrippa, do you believe the prophets?' Paul asks. 'I know that you believe' (Acts 26.27).

The speech is careful, calculated. It has elegance and style. It shows signs of preparation. Paul even begins by stretching out his hand, the sign of an orator about to begin.[31] He has clearly been rehearsing for these occasions, getting ready, perhaps with Rome in view.

But he fails. At the end of the encounter, Paul is still in chains, Agrippa is still a Jew. Such is the nature of the exchange, however, that it must have given Paul hope. In the courts of the Romans, before the emperor himself, Paul would be allowed his say.

There were good reports about the emperor. Nero had become emperor in AD 54, following the somewhat suspicious death of Claudius. (Poisoned? Some thought so; on the other hand, he was 63 years old.) Due to his relative youth, he was under the influence of his mother Agrippina and his tutors, the Praetorian prefect Sextus Afranius Burrus and, especially, Gallio's brother, the philosopher Lucius Annaeus Seneca. The first five years of Nero's reign were, by all accounts, something of a golden age. His first political act was the deification of Claudius, who joined Augustus in the pantheon of dead emperors. Nero's official nomenclature ran, 'Nero Claudius Caesar Augustus Germanicus, son of the deified Claudius, grandson of Germanicus Caesar, great-grandson of Tiberius Caesar Augustus, great-great-grandson of the deified Augustus.' Two gods in your lineage. Not bad.[32] After Claudius's funeral, Nero delivered a speech to the Senate in which he promised that excessive court influence would be moderated, that there would be no more grants of citizenship through bribery and that there would be no more politically inspired, malicious prosecutions. Maybe Nero's statement about bribery lies behind the tribune's comment in Acts 22.28.

Nero also pledged to end the practice of exercising imperial jurisdiction behind closed doors. Trials of this kind were usually for treason (*maiestas*), a charge which came to be a kind of catch-all for imperial enemies, but which certainly covered disrespect to the emperor. Perhaps this gave Paul confidence that his trial would be public and significant. Those cases that Nero did try showed good judgement. He never gave judgement immediately, but heard the case carefully, then withdrew to consider written opinions, before giving his decision the next day.[33] However, all this was mainly spin for public consumption. In the end it became clear that Nero really wasn't interested in hearing cases at all.[34]

But Paul, in jail a long, long way away, might not have known that. And he could not have realised that the golden years of Nero were about to dissolve like a dream. Nero became convinced that his mother was plotting to kill him (and he was probably right). So he took action. The stories of her death – and Nero's involvement in it – are wild and fantastical and involve poison, booby-trapped falling ceilings and lead-lined ships, designed to sink and so make her death look like an accident. Whatever the real truth, it does seem that Nero was heavily involved in her death in March AD 59. He came to be haunted by it. He heard voices, the sounds of trumpets on distant hills. Unable to get the image of his mother's simple grave out of his mind, he moved to Naples to try to get some peace.[35]

Paul had appealed to the emperor, however, so to the emperor he must go. It was AD 59, and the emperor was hearing voices in Naples.

Not for the first time, Paul had got his timing completely wrong.

'It was decided we were to sail for Italy'

Paul was taken out of the prison, along with a batch of other prisoners, and put under the guard of Julius, a centurion of the Augustan Cohort. This cohort, the *speira Sebaste* or *speira Augusta*, appears in first-century inscriptions. Largely composed of Syrian auxiliaries, it was stationed in Syria for most of the first century AD.[36] At some time during the reign of Agrippa II, the Augustan Cohort were stationed in Batanea, east of Galilee.

Anyway, Paul and his fellow prisoners were marched down to the harbour and put on a ship from Adramyttium, a town in Mysia, the region where Paul had been hindered by the Holy Spirit nearly ten years before. The town was on the north-west coast of Asia Minor, opposite the island of Lesbos, so the ship had made a long journey to be in Caesarea.[37]

The Roman imperial government did not have special prison ships. They simply commandeered passage on whatever ship was going in the right direction. This one was heading west, so it would do for a start.

Paul was accompanied on the journey by Luke and Aristarchus. Aristarchus was the Macedonian who had initially accompanied Paul to Jerusalem as a representative of the church in Thessalonica (Acts 20.4). He had been arrested as well and was accompanying Paul. In a letter written after Paul has arrived at Rome, Paul describes him as 'my fellow-prisoner' (Col. 4.10). We don't know why Aristarchus was arrested. Perhaps he was caught up in the Jerusalem riot and arrested at the same time.

But Luke is not a prisoner. How did he get on the ship? It's possible that he booked his passage like others, that he made separate arrangements with the ship's captain, and the Roman centurion allowed him to look after Paul.[38] This would have been unusual, however. Although there may have been other passengers on board, we know from another account that prisoners seem not to have been allowed to be accompanied. A letter from Pliny tells of a Roman prisoner called Paetus. When he was brought from Illyricum to Rome, his wife Arria was not allowed to accompany him. But then, he was allowed to take certain slaves with him.[39]

So perhaps that's it. Luke was probably an ex-slave. Did he, for the duration of this voyage, slip back into that role and take on, willingly, the mantle of slavery? As Paul's 'slave', he might have been allowed on board, arranging the meals and serving as Paul's physician.

You have to admit, reading the account, he does seem to have enjoyed it. For all the terrors the journey held, Luke's detail in this sea voyage is utterly convincing and completely enchanting. It is, in fact, the most detailed description of a sea voyage in the whole of ancient literature. There isn't anything else quite like it. The writing is filled with the breathless excitement of someone who just wasn't used to this kind of adventure.[40] You can taste the salt on your lips and feel the spray in your hair.

They probably set off from Caesarea in the late summer of AD 59. Julius treated Paul kindly, according to Luke. The centurion was probably an older man, and also a citizen. He had the power to confine Paul below decks if he wished, although the evidence of the account shows that Paul spent most of his time above deck.[41] Although the members of the Augustan Cohort were drawn from local recruits and were probably, therefore, hostile to Jews, Julius seemed to favour Paul. At Sidon, he allowed Paul to go and stay with friends – accompanied, of course, by a guard.

After that the ship went into the lee of Cyprus (when he had come on the outward journey, they had gone past Cyprus on the other side – perhaps this is why Luke noticed this detail) and then they worked their way along the Cilician and Pamphylian coast to Myra in Lycia. It was hard work, trying to make headway against the prevailing west wind of the late summer.[42] Already it was late in the sailing season and the winds were difficult. According to one manuscript of Acts, the ship took 15 days to travel along the Cyprio-Pamphylian coast. It's an addition to the text, but is probably well informed.[43]

At Myra they had to change ships, for the ship they were on would head on up the coast of Asia Minor to Adramyttium. It was painfully slow going. They would never make it to Rome that year on these little coast-hugging vessels. They needed a ship that could make the straight run, across the open sea. But this late in the sailing season there were few ships crossing the open sea to Italy. What they needed, therefore, was a big, ocean-going ship – one which was carrying a cargo valuable enough to encourage the owner to take risks.

That's what they found at Myra.

'An Alexandrian ship, bound for Italy'

Around AD 150, a ship was blown off course and ended up in Athens. It was travelling late in the season and it was a ship the like of which the Athenians had never seen before in their harbour.[44] It came from Alexandria, in Egypt, and this 'great monster of an Egyptian corn-ship' became an instant tourist attraction. The satirist Lucian of Samosata went to see it, and his description is so wonderful it's worth quoting in full:

> I say, though, what a size that ship was! 180 feet long, the man said, and something over a quarter of that in width; and from deck to keel, the maximum depth, through the hold, 44 feet. And then the

height of the mast, with its huge yard; and what a forestay it takes to hold it! And the lofty stern with its gradual curve, and its gilded beak, balanced at the other end by the long rising sweep of the prow, and the figures of her name-goddess, Isis, on either side. As to the other ornamental details, the paintings and the scarlet topsail, I was more struck by the anchors, and the capstans and windlasses, and the stern cabins. The crew was like a small army. And they were saying she carried as much corn as would feed every soul in Attica for a year. And all depends for its safety on one little old atomy of a man, who controls that great rudder with a mere broomstick of a tiller! He was pointed out to me; Heron was his name, I think; a woolly-pated fellow, half-bald.[45]

It was one of the Alexandrian grain ships, the oil tankers of their day, enormous vessels capable of holding over a thousand

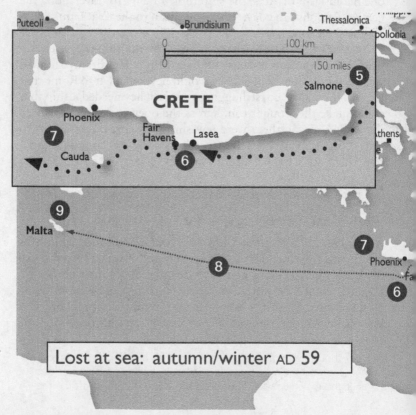

Lost at sea: autumn/winter AD 59

tons of grain, which is three times as much as any other vessel before 1820.[46] Like Paul's vessel, this ship was blown off course during a storm which had driven them as far west as Sidon. It took them 70 days of risky sailing – often at night – to reach Piraeus. The captain put their rescue down to a 'bright star – either Castor or Pollux – which appeared at the masthead, and guided the ship into the open sea'.

The Alexandrian grain tankers were the biggest vessels to sail the seas for nigh on two millennia. The reason they were so big was Rome's insatiable need for grain. Rome relied on its supplies of grain from Alexandria. Such was the importance of securing supplies that Claudius even offered government insurance schemes to encourage ship-owners to transport grain across the

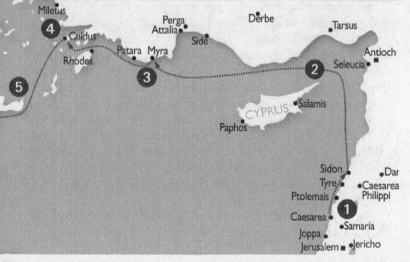

1 Under guard, Paul leaves on a ship bound for Adramyttium.
2 After changing ships at Sidon they sail under the lee of Cyprus.
3 At Myra, they change ship, boarding an Alexandrian grain ship bound for Italy.
4 High winds make it impossible to dock at Cnidus.
5 They struggle along the coast of Crete, under the lee of Salmone.
6 The ship docks at Fair Havens but cannot stay there as it is too late in the season.
7 They try to make Phoenix, but the north-east wind forces them away and south of Cauda; they attempt to reinforce the ships with ropes.
8 The ship spends two weeks adrift at sea in the heart of the storm.
9 They are shipwrecked on Malta.

Mediterranean in winter.[47] This huge demand and limited supply meant that big money was to be made on these voyages. Especially for those who were prepared to take a few risks.

That autumn, there was an Alexandrian grain ship in port at Myra. And the good news for the centurion and his prisoners was that its captain was prepared to risk a straight run for Rome. So the prisoners were transferred and the ship set out. It sailed slowly for a few days, limping along the coast to Cnidus. But it could not dock there, so it headed for Crete, with the aim of putting in at the port of Salmone. The winds, however, were against them, so they had to continue until they came to a place called Fair Havens, near the city of Lasea. Here they had another issue: the ship was too big. The harbour was not large enough to offer the ship protection during winter. Time was now of the essence. 'The fast' had gone (Acts 27.9) – *Yom Kippur*, the Day of Atonement – which was observed in the autumn, in late September. They were now, therefore, into October. No one in their right mind sailed during October.

Paul – who, let's remember, had spent a lot of time at sea – advised them not to set forth. It's not framed as a prophecy or word of knowledge, merely the advice of someone who has spent a lot of time at sea. A seasoned traveller. But they ignored the advice of a mere prisoner and decided to make a run for Phoenix, another port on Crete, which would offer them more protection. When a moderate south wind sprang up, they thought they could make it, so they weighed anchor and set out.

Then the wind changes.

It's a violent north-easter that drives the huge ship away from the island, past a small island called Cauda, where they hoist the ship's boat (used to transport passengers to shore) on board to stop it smashing against the sides of the ship. Luke mentions this detail because he's involved in it: *we* hauled the boat up, he says (Acts 27.16). They also use a technique called 'frapping' – tying cables transversely around the boat to keep the timbers together. The sailors fear the wind is so fierce that it might drive them far south onto the reef of Syrtis. But there's nothing they can do except endure the onslaught.

The storm drives them out to sea. The next day they start throwing the cargo overboard. On the third day they start throwing the ship's tackle over. In the gloom and darkness of the tempest, having abandoned cargo and equipment, they begin to abandon hope.

At this point Paul *does* give a word of knowledge – another of his visions. This time he sees an angel by him who promises him that they will all be saved. He ends his rather stirring speech, however, with the rather downbeat ending, 'but we will have to run aground on some island' (Acts 27.26). It's hardly guaranteed to raise a cheer. Various scholars have questioned the credibility of this speech, but there's nothing inherently unreasonable with the idea of Paul giving an encouragement to the crew at some point. He's not exactly unused to shipwreck and disaster, after all.

Despite this, for two weeks they remain at sea, adrift in the face of the gale. They are driven across the Adriatic and eventually they near land. They are able, at last, to put down anchors from the stern. At one point the sailors try to escape the ship and leave it to its doom. Paul advises Julius, 'Unless these men stay in the ship, you cannot be saved' (Acts 27.31). It's not a prophecy, more a statement of the obvious: if the sailors go, there's no hope of landing the ship. Julius cuts the ropes and lets the ship's boat go free. No one is running away from this. Save some, save all.

Then, in the midst of all this, Paul holds a thanksgiving meal. Well, sort of. It's not really the Eucharist: there's no wine, and all we see is Paul setting an example, by breaking bread and giving thanks, as any Jew did before eating. But there's a certain symbolism here. In the midst of the storm, a thanksgiving meal. Thanksgiving for salvation, for rescue from the perils of the deep. One of the favourite stories of the early church, and an image which appears often in their art, is the story of Jonah. They saw themselves as a rescued community. They would have recognised the symbolism here. It must seem utterly mad, but the sailors, the guards and the rest of the prisoners join in. According to Luke, there are 276 people on board this ship. And right at the end, they throw away the rest of the grain. The hope of profit has gone completely.

Dawn reveals their situation. They are a little way offshore, but there's a bay with a beach where they can hope to run aground. This is their last chance. They cut the ropes holding the anchors and aim to drive the enormous ship straight onto the beach. It doesn't work. There's a reef offshore, some kind of underwater barrier, on which the ship grounds itself. After two weeks of being driven before the wind, the ship is finally falling apart.

The modern identification, known as Saint Paul's Bank, does have a good chance of being correct. In Paul's day the sandbar was much bigger. Dio Chrysostom reports a feature of the area which created 'two seas', i.e. a sandbar.[48] The ship is stuck and the stern is being smashed up by the waves. The soldiers' first thought is to kill the prisoners. As with the jailer at Philippi, they will be held responsible for their prisoners. If they escape, the soldiers' lives may be forfeit. Better kill them than run that risk. The prisoners are saved by Paul's relationship with Julius. He does not want to kill the apostle. So he orders everyone to get to land as best they can: some swimming, some floating on planks.

Thus it is that Paul's prophecy proves correct. Not a hair on their heads is hurt. And this travelogue – the most exciting sea voyage in ancient literature – comes to an end. They have reached dry land. Some 17 days after leaving Crete, they land on the island of Malta.

It's raining and cold. The natives make a fire to warm them. While collecting wood to feed the fire, Paul is bitten by a viper. The natives see this as divine vengeance: clearly the man's a murderer who is being punished by the gods. But Paul simply shakes the reptile off with no ill effects, so they change their minds and decide he's a god. This story about Paul had some afterlife in the church. In the longer ending of Mark (which is not original) it states that Christians would be able to pick up snakes in their hands without any harm (Mark 16.18). This ending was written later than the Gospel to which it is attached – probably late second or early third century AD. Even today there are some snake-handling cults among the fringes of Christendom.

In modern times Malta doesn't have any poisonous snakes, and if it was a viper then they don't fasten themselves onto their victims: they bite and withdraw. It's possible that the creature was *coronella austriaca*, a kind of constrictor which is found on Malta. It's not poisonous, but the ancient world believed all snakes were poisonous. And anyway, it's the natives who believe that Paul has had a miraculous escape. Luke is recording their reactions, not claiming it as a miracle himself.

Indeed, the whole story of the shipwreck would have been interpreted by a first-century audience as a vindication of Paul's innocence. In a world which believed thoroughly in divine retribution, it was assumed that those guilty would suffer misfortune and death and that even innocent people might sometimes be caught up in that. The sea, particularly, was a place where the gods caught up with you. So Paul's survival of both snake bite and shipwreck were clear demonstrations, to pagan and Christian mind alike, that God was with him.

Which is not to say that the miraculous didn't happen on the island. The travellers are given refuge at the house of a man called Publius. Presumably he's the governor, or one of the wealthiest citizens. For three days he gives them hospitality, during which Paul lays hands on his father and cures him of sickness. It gives Paul instant celebrity status, and those who are sick begin to visit him. Luke records that the people of the island show their gratitude by giving them provisions when they come to leave.

'The island was called Malta'

They stayed on Malta for three months, until February AD 60, when the seas reopened. Another Alexandrian ship gave them passage off the island: the *Dioskouroi*. Gemini. The twins. Its figurehead was a carving of Castor and Pollux, the two sons of Zeus, venerated by sailors as guides and protectors. The same who protected the Alexandrian ship that ended up in Piraeus.

From Malta they made the short journey to Syracuse on the east coast of Sicily, where they stayed for three days. Then it was on to Italy, Rhegium first, and then a day later to Puteoli.

Puteoli, on the Gulf of Naples, was the pre-eminent port on the west coast of Italy and the main harbour for ships coming from the islands. Although Claudius had opened up the harbour of Ostia, Portus, to serve Rome, it was not until the late second century that grain fleets were redirected to Ostia. Before then Puteoli remained the main arrival point for travellers from Egypt and further afield. (Josephus landed there in AD 64.) In Puteoli, where

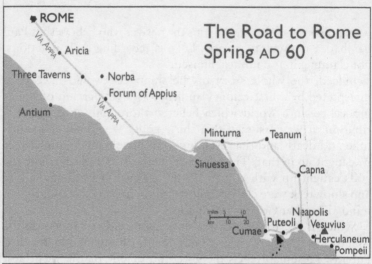

The Road to Rome
Spring AD 60

ROME

Via Appia

Aricia

Three Taverns

Norba

Forum of Appius

Antium

Minturna

Teanum

Via Appia

Sinuessa

Capna

Neapolis

Puteoli

Vesuvius

Cumae

Herculaneum

Pompeii

miles 5 10
km 10 20

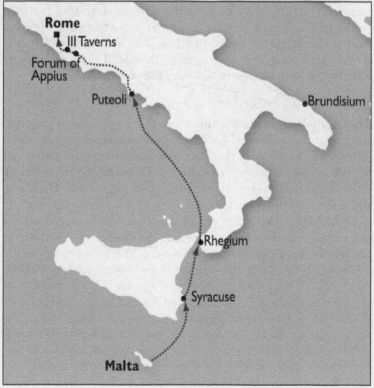

Rome

III Taverns

Forum of
Appius

Puteoli

Brundisium

Rhegium

Syracuse

Malta

they stayed for a week, Paul and his friends discovered, apparently to their surprise, a community of believers.

We don't know the origins of this church. Its members most likely came from the east, from Asia or Syria, blown along with the tradewinds, carried along among the packs of merchant travellers. Puteoli, with its flourishing Greek community and strong contacts with Asia, was a gateway for eastern goods and eastern ideas.[49] We know that other faiths spread up from Puteoli to the capital: there was a temple of Serapis in Puteoli in 105 BC, but it is not until AD 79 that we know of there being a similar temple in Rome.[50] Compared to Serapis, Christianity's progress was rapid.

The route from here was straightforward, if not easy. They would take the *via Compania* to the junction with the *via Appia*, then it was north, 130 miles of walking. Maybe that's why they tarried in Puteoli. Getting their strength up.

The *via Compania* had a reputation as a rough path. In the *Acts of Peter*, that second-century fantasy, Peter arrives at Puteoli and a character called Theon entreats him to refresh himself, because the road from Puteoli to Rome is 'a pavement of flint'. But if the *via Compania* was a pavement of flint, the *via Appia* was as smooth as silk. It was one of the great roads of Roman times, 'the queen of the long roads' according to Statius.[51] News of Paul's arrival ran ahead of him along the road and as they drew nearer to Rome, a delegation from the church came out to welcome him. The believers met Paul and his companions – and his guards – at the Forum of Appius and the Three Taverns.

The Forum of Appius lay about 40 miles south of Rome. It was a market place which Horace described as being stuffed with sailors and surly landlords.[52] The Three Taverns – *tre tabernii* – was about 10 miles further on.

Finally, six months or so after he had left Caesarea, Paul was brought to Rome. He had made it at last. He had longed to visit the city and, in the end, he arrived in chains. He had come for his triumphant encounter with the emperor, when he was to get to preach the gospel to Nero himself.

It didn't work out that way at all.

The Via Appia. Paul walked along this road to enter Rome in AD 60

10. Rome AD 60–70

'And so we came to Rome'

Into Rome. The belly of the beast. When the first Christians write about Rome, it's with horror and disgust. Rome becomes Babylon, the great whore, the beast, terrifying and repellent. But Paul arrives before the beast turns on the church, before it begins to prowl, to roar.

Even so, to a provincial like Paul, Rome must have been a frightening creature to encounter. Rome was huge: 'No city has existed in the whole world that could be compared to Rome in size,' wrote Pliny.[1] The city had grown inexorably, spreading out after Augustus had dismantled the old republican walls. Building was the great Roman passion: bathhouses and sanctuaries, basilicas, shops, theatres, circuses, aqueducts, fountains – they filled the available spaces and surged outwards in search of more land to devour.

The population had surged as well. It may well have been as much as one million people, all crammed into the available accommodation. The rich lived in *domus*, private houses, but these constituted only a tiny fraction of the living accommodation of the city. Most people lived in *insulae*, or rough on the streets. In the fourth century there were 1,797 *domus* compared to 46,602 *insulae*. And, of course, the *insulae* contained a great many inhabitants, whereas the domus contained only one family and their slaves.[2]

In such a place, privacy was reserved for the wealthy or the divine. The imperial family and retinue had their private spaces such as the Palatine Hill. The gods had the Campus Martius, 200 hectares of temples, porticos and tombs of the illustrious dead, where no human habitation was allowed. The rest of the people did the best they could.

For those who were not used to it, Rome must have been an overwhelming assault on the senses. (It must have been pretty overpowering for those who *were* used to it.) Noise. That's what so many accounts of the city seem to emphasise. The noise. Well, the noise and the smell. And the sights. And everything, really.

By day there were crowds everywhere. The *tabernae* crowded with diners and drinkers, the shops spilling their wares out onto the streets. Barbers shaving customers in the middle of the thoroughfares. Beggars, tinkers and hawkers of cheap goods at every corner; the groans and grunts of people exercising in the baths; the varied cries of 'the sausage dealer and the confectioner and the peddlers of cook shops hawking their wares, each with his own particular intonation'[3]; the drone of schoolmasters teaching their children in the open. Soothsayers peddling their charms and fortunes. A funeral procession walking solemnly by, flutes playing, horns blowing, a long cortége of relatives and clients and hangers-on, the body on a hand-barrow, making their way out of the city to the funeral pyre. And the smells – the tang of urine from the tanners, the greasy smell of the cookshop as sausages fried in the pan; the smell of bread being baked; the blood from the animals being slaughtered in the shambles – or in the temples as sacrifices.

By night it wasn't any quieter. That was when the traffic started. By imperial decree, all carts and wagons were banned from Rome during the day, because the streets were too crowded with pedestrians. So they came in at night. The only 'vehicles' which were allowed in during the day were those taking part in religious processions or triumphs. Or the contractors' carts which were allowed in to work on buildings. If you wanted transport during daytime, then, you had to be carried on a litter, or ride a horse, or simply walk. The passage of carts and carriages in the narrow winding streets, and the swearing and abuse of the drivers caught up in the inevitable traffic jams, filled the night. 'It takes great wealth to sleep in the city,' said Juvenal.[4] it was, indeed, an expensive place to live. 'A great price must be paid for a wretched lodging, a great price for a slave's keep, a great price for a modest little dinner.'[5]

So, a great mix of noises and smells and sights. And a great mix of nationalities as well. Rome was cosmopolitan: filled to the brim with immigrant workers and slaves. It was a huge net importer of labour, relying on a constant supply of foreign labourers in order to survive. Not everyone welcomed these Greek-speaking immigrants. On the one hand, Romans were proud of their city, which they called 'a single fatherland of all the nations of the world'. On the other hand, these people who came to Rome from the outposts of the Empire were foreigners. Barbarians. 'The coming of the Greek has brought us a Jack-of-all-trades – grammarian, rhetorician, geometrician, painter, wrestling manager, prophet, rope-walker, physician, magician; he knows everything.'[6] Slaves, foreigners, the few rich and the many, many poor: this was Rome. And the Roman church was a mirror image of the city it called home.

By the time Paul walked through the gates of Rome under escort, Christianity had been in the city for at least 20 years. Priscilla and Aquila were among those expelled in AD 49, so it must have been established before that.

Who brought it? Well, Jews, in the first place, who arrived probably in the decade after Jesus' crucifixion. Travellers from Jerusalem and the east, tradesmen and women, arriving from the east at Puteoli and carrying their tools and their faith along the trade route to Rome.[7]

And that's how the Romans thought of Christians, at first: they were Jews. The Romans didn't much like the Jews. There were tens of thousands of Jews in Rome. They had been there for many years. The earliest reference to them in Rome dates from 139 BC, but the numbers grew dramatically after 65 BC when Pompey the Great returned from capturing Jerusalem, bringing with him many thousands of Jewish slaves. When Herod the Great died, 8,000 Jews assembled in Rome to call for an end to his dynasty.[8] In AD 19, 4,000 of them were conscripted for military service in Sardinia. So it has been estimated that the total number of Jews in Rome was between 40,000 and 50,000 at this time, perhaps 5 per cent of the total population: a sizeable minority.[9]

Julius Caesar had given them special privileges. He granted them freedom of worship and association, the right to raise money to support the temple in Jerusalem, exemption from military service and the right to adjudicate legal cases among Jews without recourse to civil courts. Such was his support that when he was assassinated, crowds of Jews came to mourn at his tomb. These privileges were renewed after his death.

The Jews kept themselves to themselves: they were prickly and exclusive. This only served to exaggerate the myths about them. Tacitus is typical. His account of Jews mixes together reality and near-hysterical myth. He correctly records that they observe the Sabbath, abstain from pork, eat unleavened bread and regard killing an unwanted child as a crime. But he also adds that they worship at a shrine where they have the statue of an ass, which, apparently, commemorates finding water in the wilderness, whence they were led by a herd of wild asses. He says that they look after their own, but hate everyone else. They eat separately and refuse to have sex with foreign women. But 'among themselves, nothing is illicit'.[10]

Not all Jews tried to keep separate. Some tried to assimilate. Others even tried to keep their identity a complete secret. Martial, writing around AD 80, refers to an actor whose jockstrap came off during a performance, revealing him to be Jewish, something he had been trying to hide.[11]

There is no evidence of widespread synagogue attendance. When Philo visited in the first century, there were only four or five synagogues in the city, while evidence from third- and fourth-century Jewish inscriptions shows that there were only twelve synagogues in Rome at that time. Some of these would have dated back to the time of Paul: the synagogue of the Augustiales might have owed its name to Augustus; the synagogue of the Agrippans might refer to Herod Agrippa, or else Vipsanias Agrippa, Augustus's close friend. But synagogue cannot have played a significant role in the life of the Jews in the city: a community of 40,000 people served by five synagogues mitigates against regular attendance.[12] (This relative paucity of synagogues explains how Claudius was able to close them for a time in AD 41. There weren't that many to close.)

Instead the Jewish faith as followed in Rome was essentially a home-based, personal rite: the customary prayers, the Sabbath observance, dietary regulations and the keeping of the command-ments. So Judaism in Rome may well have differed substantially in style from that of the cities of the eastern Mediterranean, with its emphasis on synagogue and its population of mobile, urban Jews who owed their allegiance to Jerusalem. Rome was much further away, in every sense.

And what of the church? It began with Jews, but in AD 49, as we have seen, the Jewish Christians were expelled by Claudius, not returning until after the emperor's death six years later. That means that between AD 49 and 54, the church in Rome must have been almost entirely Gentile, kept alive by Gentile converts made before AD 49, or arriving in the interim.

It's interesting to speculate, therefore, on what happened when the Jewish Christians returned in AD 54. Did they try to reassert control? Was there a culture clash between the Jewish Christians and the Gentile leadership which had grown up in the intervening years? When the Jewish Christians returned, the Gentiles were no longer God-fearers who had joined the Jewish community and found salvation within it: they were the leaders of the church. They were the ones who had kept it alive. They were equals.

'I desire, as I have for many years, to come to you'

Perhaps there are clues to the make-up of the church in the letter which Paul addressed to it in the winter of AD 56–57, particularly from chapter 16, which is a set of greetings to the church. We call the letter Romans, but the title may be misleading. Although Paul writes to 'all God's beloved in Rome, who are called to be saints' (Rom. 1.7), he's not necessarily writing to all the Christians in Rome. It's more likely that he's addressing one specific church, namely the church of his friends Priscilla and Aquila. Paul sends greetings to Priscilla and Aquila and 'the church that meets in their house'. He does talk about members of other households: Aristobulus, Narcissus, Asyncritus and brothers, Philologus and the saints – but he doesn't specifically mention 'the church' that met in these households.[13]

If it were one church, one Christian community, then it would explain a lot of things in the letter. It would explain how they could all greet one another with a kiss. And it would explain

why the theological differences between them were so critical. As
Bernard Green points out:

> The simple fact is that if the Roman church were not one commu-
> nity he would not have addressed them one letter; if they did not
> meet together he would not have suggested they greet one another;
> if they did not eat together there would have been no problem for
> Paul to try to resolve between Christians who observed the Jewish
> law and those who did not.[14]

So that list in Romans 16 may be the members of one church.
Some of these Paul knows well; some he only knows by name.
Some he doesn't know at all – he only knows they are part of
a certain person's household. He lists by name only 28 people.
There's no reason why all those mentioned in the letter couldn't
have been accommodated in one place.

Of course, it could have been intended for, and circulated
among, other Christian communities in the city. But even so, there
may not actually have been that many churches in the city. The
Roman church in the mid-50s might only have been several dozen
strong. Even later, when the Christians were more numerous, the
churches remained small in size. In AD 165, Justin Martyr was
interrogated about the church he attended in Rome:

> Rusticus the prefect said, 'Where do you assemble?' Justin said,
> 'Where each one chooses and can: for do you fancy that we all
> meet in the very same place?' ... Rusticus the prefect said, 'Tell me

where you assemble, or into what place do you collect your followers?' Justin said, 'I live above one Martinus, at the Timiotinian Bath; and
during the whole time (and I am now living in Rome for the second
time) I am unaware of any other meeting than his.'[15]

What Justin depicts is a small congregation which met above
the bath of Myrtinus. He talks about other congregations, but
he doesn't know where they are and doesn't appear to have been
to any of them. Another example comes from under the church
of Santa Prisca in Rome. There, way down below the present
Renaissance building, is the original meeting place: a room in
a building, which was leased by Christians but which was separated from its non-Christian neighbours only by a door. They
met in small, ordinary spaces – above the baths, in a workshop,
in a rented room.

Santa Prisca is one of nine churches in Rome which claim association with Christians from the first two centuries AD. These are
known as *Tituli* churches and are named after such people as San
Pudenza (Pudens) and San Clemente (Clement). The legends surrounding these churches originate from the fifth century – far too
late for us to reliably connect them with the real historical characters. But they do tell us something of the development of Christianity in the city. For a start, they seem to congregate in certain areas:
three on the Aventine and two in Trastavere; two on the Vicus Patri-
cius and Clivus Suburanus; and two at the foot of the Caelius.[16]

The Roman Forum. Looking south-east from the base of the Capitoline hill.

Rome in the time of Peter and Paul

Paul entered the city through the Porta Capena, the gate through which the Via Appia entered Rome.

The inset map below shows the locations of early churches – including the so-called *Tituli* churches – mapped against the Rome of Paul's day. We can see the concentration of churches in the Trastavere and along the Appian way. Christians were probably concentrated in the shaded area.

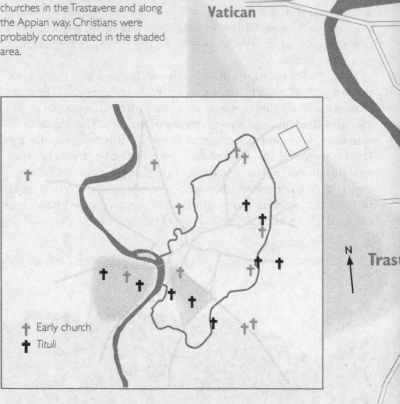

Circus of Nero

Vatican

N

Trast

† Early church
✝ *Tituli*

0
1 km
0
1

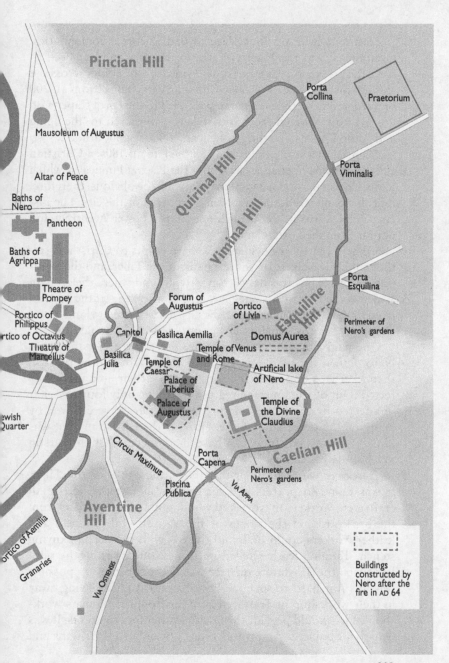

Pincian Hill

Porta
Collina

Praetorium

Mausoleum of Augustus

Porta
Viminalis

Altar of Peace

Quirinal Hill

Viminal Hill

Baths of
Nero

Pantheon

Baths of
Agrippa

Porta
Esquilina

Theatre of
Pompey

Forum of
Augustus

Portico
of Livia

Esquiline Hill

Perimeter of
Nero's gardens

Portico of
Philippus

Capitol

Basilica Aemilia

Domus Aurea

rtico of Octavius

Temple of Venus
and Rome

Theatre of
Marcellus

Basilica
Julia

Temple of
Caesar

Artificial lake
of Nero

Palace of
Tiberius

ewish
Quarter

Palace of
Augustus

Temple of
the Divine
Claudius

Circus Maximus

Caelian Hill

Porta
Capena

Perimeter of
Nero's gardens

Piscina
Publica

VIA APPIA

Aventine
Hill

ortico of Aemilia

Granaries

VIA OSTIENSIS

Buildings
constructed by
Nero after the
fire in AD 64

Trastavere is an obvious place to find Christian communities, given that it was the Jewish quarter of the city and had been so since the first century BC. But other evidence also points across the river, to the Aventine. The early Christian catacombs (from AD 200 onwards) were on the *via Appia*, which led to the Porta Capena on the Aventine. Juvenal records that Jews had moved to 'the aging and damp Capena', settling as beggars in its neighbourhood.

There's other evidence as well. In the late AD 180s, a Christian called Callistus opened a bank near the Piscina Publica in which many Christians deposited money. It would be obvious, therefore, that this bank would be in a 'Christian' area of the city. The Piscina Publica was in the twelfth region, the Lower Aventine, and not far from the Porta Capena.[17]

So the fragmentary evidence we have points to Christians settling in the Trastavere on the left bank of the Tiber, and the Aventine on the opposite side, particularly around where the Appian Way met the Porta Capena. They settled where the traffic arteries from the east met the fringe of the city. These were lowland areas. Damp. Unhealthy. Inhabited by poor people and immigrants.

One final clue: after the great fire ravaged the city in AD 64, Nero pinned the blame on the Christians. Why did he pick on them? Perhaps one of the reasons was that their area was unaffected. Out of the fourteen regions of Rome, only four were left unaffected by the blaze: one of these was Trastavere, saved by being on the other side of the Tiber. If the Christian area was largely untouched, it would have made accusations of arson much more believable.[18]

Trastavere was a harbour quarter on the banks of the Tiber. It was home to porters and merchants, shopkeeprs and small craftsmen, workers in ivory and wood, potters and workers from the brickyards on the slopes of the Vatican Hill. Tanners and leather-workers could be found there – with the accompanying stench. Tanning leather relied on urine, sourced from the public toilets: the Trastavere quarter was piss-poor in every possible way. It's not hard to imagine Priscilla and Aquila slaving away in their workshop in Trastavere, not far from the tanner's workshop which would provide them with leather for their tents. It was densely populated. And it was home not only to Christians and

Jews, but to many other cults and religions from the east: Dea Syria, Hadad, Sol of Palmyra, Cybele. Near where the façade of St Peter's is today, there was a temple of Isis.[19]

The Porta Capena was similarly poor – or at least parts of it were. It was the gateway into Rome from the end of the Appian Way, the entry point into the city proper. It was the ancient Roman equivalent of the railway station. And it was through the Porta Capena that Paul was led, one day in AD 60.[20]

'Greet one another with a holy kiss'

Back to those names. Say it was one *ekklesia*, meeting in the workshop/dwelling of Priscilla and Aquila, somewhere in the Trastavere area. If we went there sometime before dawn on a Sunday morning in AD 57, who would we meet? Here's the list (from Rom. 16):

▷ Prisca and Aquila, who work with me in Christ Jesus, and who risked their necks for my life… also the church in their house.

▷ My beloved Epaenetus, who was the first convert in Asia for Christ.

▷ Mary, who has worked very hard among you.

▷ Andronicus and Junia, my relatives who were in prison with me; they are prominent among the apostles, and they were in Christ before I was.

▷ Ampliatus, my beloved in the Lord.

▷ Urbanus, our co-worker in Christ.

▷ My beloved Stachys.

▷ Apelles, who is approved in Christ.

▷ Those who belong to the family of Aristobulus.

▷ My relative Herodion.

▷ Those in the Lord who belong to the family of Narcissus.

▷ Those workers in the Lord, Tryphaena and Tryphosa.

▷ The beloved Persis, who has worked hard in the Lord.

▷ Rufus, chosen in the Lord; and his mother – a mother to me also.

▷ Asyncritus, Phlegon, Hermes, Patrobas, Hermas, and the brothers and sisters who are with them.

▷ Philologus, Julia, Nereus and his sister, and Olympas and all the saints who are with them.

So we have a total of 26 named individuals, plus two unnamed (a mother and a sister) as well as family members and various other 'saints'.

What we see by analysing these names and descriptions is that they were a very mixed bunch.

They were both Jew and Gentile. There are five definite Jews: Andronicus, Junia, Herodion, Priscilla and Aquila. Probably Mary and Rufus were also Jews, if Rufus was the son of Simon of Cyrene. Most of the rest were probably Gentiles. Some of these may have originally been God-fearers, who found in Christianity a faith that welcomed them fully, instead of keeping them on the fringes of the synagogue. This diversity is reflected in documents associated with the city. For example, both the Gospel of Mark and the letter to the Hebrews are traditionally associated with Rome, yet they seem to appeal to a very different readership. Mark explains all his Hebrew terminology; Hebrews certainly doesn't.[21] Also 1 Clement, written in Rome in the AD 90s, contains quotes from Jewish apocryphal writings and references to Jewish traditions.

Twelve of the 26 people are immigrants or have strong links with the east. We know that Aquila (and Priscilla?) came from Pontus. Epaenetus was converted in Asia; Andronicus and Junia were, presumably, from Palestine or Syria; Urbanus had previously worked with Paul. Rufus and his mother were Cyrenians with links to Judea. Ampliatus, Stachys, Persis and Apelles are all personally known to Paul. At some time they have lived outside Rome, or travelled extensively enough to become known by Paul.

Some of them were relatives of Paul: Herodion, Andronicus and Junia. Paul mentions other relatives of his: he mentions Lucius, Jason and Sosipater, who are in Corinth (Rom. 16.21). There were a number of close relationships, in fact. Husbands and wives (Priscilla and Aquila, Andronicus and Junia, possibly Philologus and Julia); family members (Nereus and his sister, Rufus and his mother, probably Tryphaena and Tryphosa).

It was a socially diverse group. Paul begins his letter to them by identifying himself as 'Paul, a servant [*doulos*/slave] of Jesus Christ' (Rom. 1.1). This was something which had special resonance with those listed in Romans, because 18 of those named in this list bear names associated with slaves. Slaves were often named after mythological beings (Hermes, Nereus, Narcissus) or after the person they had served (Herodian, Patrobas). Some of them may still have been in service. The names Philologus and Julia (Rom. 16.15) were common among members of the imperial household.[22]

At the other end of the scale, we appear to have royalty in the list – or, at least the household of royalty. Paul greets all those in the household of Aristobulus. Although Aristobulus was a fairly common name, it's possible that the one mentioned here was a grandson of Herod the Great and brother of Agrippa I. Josephus records that he died as a 'private person', in other words he was not in high office or involved in public affairs. His brother Agrippa lived in Rome for a long time and was friendly with the Emperor Claudius. It's probable that what Josephus means is that Aristobulus was kept under close surveillance until his death, which may have been in the late AD 40s. (His brother died in AD 44.) Even if he had died earlier, his household would still be known by this name, and any Christians among the household would have been identified by this name as well.

Then there are the women. Four people in this letter are praised for their hard work – Mary, Tryphaena, Tryphosa and Persis – all of them women. Of the 26 individual Christians in Paul's list, 8 are women (31 per cent) and 18 are men (69 per cent). But when we look at those who are singled out as being active in the community, these percentages shift dramatically. They are Priscilla and Aquila, Mary, Andronicus and Junia, Tryphaena and Tryphosa, Persis and Urbanus. (Other possibles for this list are Rufus's mother, Apelles, and Rufus himself.) This indicates a 6/3 split between women and men (or 7/5 if we include the possibles).[23]

Paul uses the word 'to work hard', *kopiaō* in Greek, as a sign of praise. And the interesting thing here is that it's a word he associates with apostolic activity. He uses it to describe himself in Galatians (4.11) and 1 Corinthians (15.10). What we see here are active women, working hard in an apostolic capacity. Take Tryphaena and Tryphosa, for example, 'those hard workers in the Lord'. It was common to give family members similar-sounding names, so it's probable that they were sisters. And their hard work may suggest that they were freedwomen, with some independence. (There's a joke here as well: their names mean 'Dainty' and 'Delicate'.)[24] Also the description of Persis as 'the beloved' rather than 'beloved' (as in Rom. 16.5, 8, 9) may indicate that she was known as beloved by the wider church, not just Paul.

In other words, we have women here getting on with the business of church and being given the freedom to do so. Later generations of the church became more patriarchal and the role of women was suppressed. Yet despite this, women were still active. Even as late as Augustine's time (c. 400) it was still women who were leading the way in evangelism. 'Oh you men,' he wrote, 'who all fear the burden imposed by baptism. You are easily beaten by your women. Chaste and devoted to the faith, it is their presence in great numbers that causes the church to grow.'[25]

There were people there with deep historical roots in the faith. Andronicus and Junia were famed apostles, who were in Christ before Paul. And then there's Rufus. It's generally agreed that the Gospel of Mark was written in Rome. In Mark 15.21 we get the story of Simon of Cyrene, carrying the cross of Jesus:

> They compelled a passer-by, who was coming in from the country, to carry his cross; it was Simon of Cyrene, the father of Alexander and Rufus. (Mark 15.21)

The interesting thing is not only that Mark mentions Rufus and Alexander, but that he makes no attempt to clarify who they are. So we can assume that they were well known to the Christian community. Since the Christians at Rome were probably not numerous at this time, it seems likely that the Rufus mentioned in Romans 16.13 is the son of Simon of Cyrene – and therefore his mother mentioned in the same verse is Simon's wife. These were eyewitnesses, people with their own stories of Jesus.

In addition, although wealthy benefactors were converted, for the most part the church in Rome was a church of low-status individuals. Clement of Rome includes a prayer from the liturgy of the time which shows the kind of people who were citizens of this most unlikely kingdom:

> We beseech Thee, Lord and Master, to be our help and succour. Save those among us who are in tribulation; have mercy on the lowly; lift up the fallen; show Thyself unto the needy; heal the ungodly;

convert the wanderers of Thy people; feed the hungry; release our prisoners; raise up the weak; comfort the fainthearted.[26]

In the heart of the greatest city on earth, in the shadow of its glory and splendour, a different kingdom had been established. It was populated by the poor and the weak, the lowly inhabitants of the Trastavere, the tentmakers, the freed slaves and many more.

Thus, in what on the surface just looks like a list of names, we have a rich source of information about the make-up of this group of Christians in Rome. How far we can extrapolate from this to the wider Christian community is impossible to say, but there's no reason to think that this community was anything out of the ordinary. It was full of slaves and ex-slaves. It had reached into various layers of society. There were women and men, there were those with deep roots in the faith and those who had come to Christ recently. It was to people like this that Paul came in AD 60. But were they pleased to see him?

'He lived there two whole years'

The final chapters of Acts can blind us to a simple fact. All those fine speeches, all that excitement of the shipwreck get in the way of the fact that for the last four years of his career as described in Acts, Paul was in jail.

He arrived, as we have seen, through the Porta Capena and thence to the Praetorian barracks. The only record of the custodial deposition is found in Acts 28.16, which tells us nothing more than that Paul was allowed to live by himself with one guard. The WT adds more useful details:

> The centurion handed over the prisoners to the garrison commander [*stratopedarchos*]. Paul found favour with him to stay outside the headquarters with a soldier to guard him.[27]

The *stratopedarchos* was probably attached to the Praetorian camp, situated on the eastern side of Rome. The camp prefect, the *Praefectus Praetorii*, had the task of overseeing prisoners from outside the city of Rome and from the provinces. It's not likely that the prefect himself would deal with someone like Paul; one of his officers would most likely have seen to it. But Paul would probably have been held in a room near the Praetorian camp, located near the Porta Viminalis to the north-east of the city.[28]

The picture given in Acts is, essentially, a reasonably light form of house arrest. Paul had a guard assigned to him, to whom he was loosely chained by the wrist. He was not a valuable or significant prisoner, just an insignificant provincial. The more dangerous the prisoner, the higher the rank of guard allotted to him. In Rome, Paul was guarded by a simple soldier. So he was neither high status, nor high priority. He spent two years in this situation.

Where, though? Only the wealthy could afford to rent a *domus*. Paul, like virtually all the other million inhabitants of Rome, rented a room in an *insulae*. Given that Jews (with their religious purity standards) were happy to come and visit him, his conditions could not have been too degrading. And we know from other documents that he had space to think and write. The most likely picture is of a man chained up at night, but by day allowed limited access outside his room and the courtyard of the *insula*.[29]

Acts records that he had meetings with the local leaders of the Jews; with, as usual, mixed results. Some believed, others rejected him. But in Rome he was not the big hitter that he had been in Ephesus and Corinth.

When he first meets the Jews, in Rome they tell him:

> We have received no letters from Judea about you, and none of the •
> brothers coming here has reported or spoken anything evil about
> you. But we would like to hear from you what you think, for with
> regard to this sect we know that everywhere it is spoken against.
> (Acts 28.21–22)

In other words, 'Sorry mate, never heard of you.' What they do know is that this sect – the Christians – are spoken against everywhere.

What's curious is that even the local church seem to take no notice of Paul. Luke tells us nothing of his relationship with the local church. Paul meets with Jewish leaders, we are told, but there's no mention in Acts of his meeting Christians in the city itself. OK, so the Christians seem to have been operating largely undercover in any case, but there must be a real question over whether the Christians in Rome actually welcomed Paul's arrival. For the Jewish Christians, it was only six years since they had been allowed back into the city. And for the Gentiles, it would have been one thing to welcome Paul as a visitor, but he was a prisoner – and one with plans to take his case before the emperor. By now everyone in Rome knew what it may have taken Paul longer to grasp: the emperor was a madman. It may be for these reasons that the Christians seem absent from the end of Acts. Paul is willing to pay the ultimate price for his witness, but perhaps some of the others don't want to get caught up in the crossfire.

Nevertheless, Luke ends the book on a positive note – with Paul welcoming all who come to him, 'proclaiming the kingdom of God and teaching about the Lord Jesus Christ with all boldness and without hindrance' (Acts 28.31). No doubt that's what he's doing. No doubt people do come to meet with Paul. And, Paul being Paul, of course he's going to talk about the kingdom.

But behind those positive lines, what's the truth? Paul is stuck in a tenement room in Rome, and he's there for two years. Nobody in the Roman legal system is taking a blind bit of notice of him. In Jerusalem Paul was a somebody. In Rome he's just another provincial Jew, rotting away in a tiny room near the Praetorian barracks.

And that's the end of Acts. The book ends with more of a whimper than a bang. It doesn't really end at all, in fact. Many scholars argue that of course it does, it ends with Paul having preached the word in Rome. Except that, well, he hasn't – not really. Not magnificently, as he had hoped. Theologians might argue that the book ends perfectly acceptably. As a writer, I *know* that it ends abruptly. For the second half of his work, Luke has been leading up to Paul's encounter with the emperor. That's the big narrative arc, which was going to end, inevitably, with *Paul versus Nero*. But that never happens. And, in fact, we never get to hear anything about the final fate of Paul. It's inconceivable that the early church did not know Paul's fate. If Luke – or whoever wrote Luke-Acts – was really writing after AD 70, after the fall of the temple and the death of Paul, why doesn't any of that appear in the book? Why would an author so good, so keen on detail, so strong on narrative events, not record the single event which he has been building up to through the whole of the final section of the book?

The answer is obvious to anyone who hasn't already made up their mind about the dating of the book: he didn't put it in, because he didn't know. Acts ends in the way it does because that's all Luke knew. Paul spent two years under house arrest. And during that time nothing happened. Nothing at all.

So what happened next? For that we have to leave Acts behind. We have to look at fragments, traditions, myths. And the letters, of course. Paul was speaking in Rome, but he was also writing.

'Paul, a prisoner of Christ Jesus'

No chains could keep Paul entirely captive. We know that he was in contact with Christians in the emperor's household. This doesn't mean the house of the emperor, but refers to the imperial civil service.[30] So perhaps he was making inroads among those in the imperial service. We get this information from a letter Paul wrote to the church at Philippi. The letters which Paul wrote at this time include the group known as the 'Prison Letters': Ephesians, Colossians, Philippians and Philemon and at least one letter to Timothy. Although claims have been made for imprisonment in Caesarea, or in Ephesus, most scholars accept that they were written in Rome.

The internal evidence as to the place and dating of the letters is not clear. There is plenty of evidence within the letters that Paul was in prison, but few points where he mentions Rome. Three of the letters appear to have been written at the same time: Colossians, Ephesians and Philemon. They share some links:

▷ Twice he mentions the same mailman or courier: Tychicus (Eph. 6.21–22; Col. 4.7–8).
▷ In Colossians and Philemon he mentions the same group of five companions who send greetings: Epaphras, Mark, Aristarchus, Demas and Luke (Col. 4.10–14; Philem. 23).
▷ Philemon 2 and Colossians 4.17 both send greetings to Archippus, who was apparently a member of the Colossian Christian community. Not only that, they met in the house of Philemon.

So it's most likely that these three letters were sent at the same time, and they were sent to Asia. Ephesus was the principal city of Asia, and any messenger heading for Colossae from the west would have had to pass through the port. At no point in these letters do we get a definite confirmation that Paul is in Rome, but the collection of people seems to suggest that. Luke is present (which is not the case in Ephesus) and Mark has strong links with Rome. Aristarchus was Paul's fellow prisoner from Caesarea. There is also Jesus Justus and Epaphras (also, apparently, a prisoner) and Demas (Col. 4.10–14; Philem. 23).

So the evidence suggests that while in Rome, Paul wrote letters to churches in Asia. Indeed, he sent more than just these three. Along with these letters, Paul also wrote one to the church in Laodicea, which was just some 18 miles from Colossae. There the church met in the house of Nympha – another female church leader. Paul also refers to a church in Hierapolis, again just a few miles from Colossae (Col. 4.13–16).

This set of letters – Ephesians, Colossians and Philemon – are filled with matter-of-fact advice about social relationships and management of the Christian communities. And they are optimistic in tone. Although Paul signs off the letter to Colossae with the phrase, 'Remember my chains' (Col. 4.18), he expects to see them again. He asks Philemon to prepare a guestroom. Paul is in chains, but he is directing things – sending envoys hither and thither, surrounded by his 'team'. He is by no means isolated.

There is an indication, as well, that Paul has not yet had his moment. He asks the Christians to pray for him so that 'when I speak, a message may be given to me to make known with boldness the mystery of the gospel, for which I am an ambassador in chains. Pray that I may declare it boldly, as I must speak' (Eph. 6.19–20). So we can tentatively date these letters not long after Paul's arrival in Rome in AD 60. Things are still on course. At this stage at least, the plan is working.

One of the letters in particular deserves special attention. It's all about the man whom Paul uses as a courier for this set of letters: a man called Onesimus.

'No longer as a slave'

In virtually every sermon, study guide or commentary about Philemon you get presented with the incontrovertible fact that Onesimus, the person who is with Paul in Rome, is a fugitive slave who has stolen money from his master Philemon, come to Rome and been converted by Paul.

So it comes as something of a surprise to find that nowhere does the letter say this. That he was a slave is strongly indicated. He has a slave's name, for one thing: Onesimus means 'useful'. And Paul says that he is returning him as 'more than a slave'.

> Perhaps this is the reason he was separated from you for a while, so that you might have him back for ever, no longer as a slave but as more than a slave, a beloved brother – especially to me but how much more to you, both in the flesh and in the Lord. (Philem. 15–16)

But just because Paul refers to Onesimus as a slave doesn't mean he was one. Paul refers to himself using the same Greek word, *doulos* (1 Cor. 9.19; Rom. 1.1; Gal. 1.10; Phil. 1.1). And references outside the New Testament imply that Onesimus had considerable status in the church. The letter of Ignatius to the church at Ephesus, written in AD 107–108, says:

> I received, therefore, your whole multitude in the name of God, through Onesimus, a man of inexpressible love, and your bishop in the flesh, whom I pray you by Jesus Christ to love, and that you would all seek to be like him. And blessed be He who has granted unto you, being worthy, to obtain such an excellent bishop.[31]

This seems to make more sense. If Onesimus became the overseer of the church at Ephesus, and a significant local leader, then it would explain why this little letter has been preserved. It recorded the first meeting of this man with Paul in Rome. It had significance, this letter, not because of what it contains so much as because of what Onesimus had become.

But the letter of Ignatius makes no mention of Onesimus's background at all. No mention of slaves or running away or anything like that. And a further mention by Tertullian, written around AD 208, groups Onesimus with other famous names, in a passage which recommends that Christians should not attempt to buy their way out of persecution:

> When did Onesimus, or Aquila, or Stephen, give them aid of this kind [i.e. money] when they were persecuted?[32]

Here, far from being a slave, he's assumed to have some kind of wealth. The fourth-century *Apostolic Constitutions,* though, is certain he was a slave. It even uses him as an instruction about allowing slaves to be ordained:

> We do not permit servants to be ordained into the clergy without
> their masters' consent; for this would grieve those that owned them.
> For such a practice would occasion the subversion of families. But if
> at any time a servant appears worthy to be ordained into an high
> office, such as our Onesimus appeared to be, and if his master allows
> of it, and gives him his freedom, and dismisses him from his house,
> let him be ordained.[33]

Mind you, the same work also had Onesimus down as the
bishop of Beroea.[34]

So far, then, we have the tradition that Onesimus was a leader
of the local church, and the idea that he was a slave. But what
about the runaway bit? Well, surprisingly, this does not appear
until the late fourth century, around AD 386–400, in the works of
John Chrysostom: 'There was a certain household slave Onesimus, an abominable runaway.'[35] Other references in Chrysostom's
works make it plain that Onesimus was both runaway and thief:

> Moreover also the blessed Paul not only welcomes Onesimus the
> unprofitable runaway thief, because he was converted, but also asks
> his master to treat him who had repented, on equal terms of hon-
> our with his teacher.[36]

It is from Chrysostom that we get the idea that Onesimus was
a fugitive slave, who had stolen money and who was baptised by
Paul and sent back to his Christian master. But the point is that
the first mention of this theory dates from some 350 years after
the letter was written. Before that there's no mention of the runaway thief theory.[37] Chrysostom had a clear social and political
agenda. He was part of the post-Constantine world, and he was
using this homily to argue that slaves should not be freed. That's
why he sees Onesimus as a runaway thief who gets returned to
slavery by Paul.

But it's not in the text. It's all inferred: from Onesimus's name;
from Paul sending Onesimus back; and from Paul's statement that
if Onesimus has wronged Philemon he (Paul) would repay.

The letter itself says nothing about theft. Nothing about running away. Within the letter there's no evidence that he was on the
run. And if he was a fugitive, then why would he go to Paul – a
man who was accompanied, let's remember, by a soldier? Paul
may have been willing to forgive a fugitive, but the Roman author-

ities were not so forgiving. The punishments for runaway slaves were brutal. Yet Paul makes no mention of them in his appeal to Philemon.[38] Not only that, but he says nothing about any repentance on the part of Onesimus, nor is there any explicit appeal for forgiveness or pity on the part of the master.[39]

Nor does it say anything about Paul converting and baptising Onesimus. That theory is based around Paul's statement about Onesimus 'whose father I have become during my imprisonment' (Philem. 10). Well, that *could* mean that Onesimus was converted. But many people were converted by Paul. Much more likely, surely, is that they developed a close relationship, similar to that which Paul had with Timothy. As we have seen in the letter to the church at Rome, Paul talks about people who are like family to him.

There was, clearly, some kind of dispute between Onesimus and Philemon. And money seems to have been involved. It has been suggested that this is to do with the *amicus domini*, the idea that Paul has been asked to arbitrate in some serious dispute between the two. This was a common Roman practice: the *amicus domini*, the friend of the master, was a mediator between two parties.[40] The problem with this is that Rome was 900 miles from Ephesus. It's a heck of a long way to send someone just to mediate in a dispute.

What if the primary purpose of the visit was not to solve a dispute, but to transport money? And what if some of that money got used in some other way, which might not have been originally envisaged? Because one of the things this letter does show is that news of Paul's imprisonment had reached far and wide, and that he was receiving emissaries from Asia, from the places where he had always had influence. Assumptions just get multiplied. Once you come up with the compelling narrative – that a runaway slave steals money and flees to Rome and gets converted by Paul – it's so much more exciting than the idea that the slave was sent on a journey to take money to Paul, perhaps with the idea that as a side-benefit Paul might also settle the argument between them.

In the end, we don't know what the nature of the dispute was. We don't know why Onesimus was once useless and is now useful. And we don't know what wrong he may have done to Philemon.

There's one other thing which we don't know, but we would really like to: why doesn't Paul condemn slavery?

'Taking the form of a slave'

In AD 61, around the time that Paul was writing to Philemon, a prefect of Rome, Pedanius Secundus, was murdered by one of his own slaves. According to Roman custom, that meant all the slaves in his household should be executed: 400 men, women and children in all. There was an outcry among the people against this injustice and the Senate was besieged. But inside the Senate, a senator called Gaius Cassius argued that it simply had to be done: 'Whom will rank shield when it did not avail the prefect of the city?' he said. 'Whom will a large number of slaves keep safe, when four hundred did not protect Pedanius Secundus?' The issue was made worse by the presence of foreign slaves among them: 'Now that we have in our households foreigners with customs different from our own; with alien religions or none at all, you will not restrain such a motley rabble except by fear.' In the end the execution was carried out. The condemned were led away to their deaths, and Nero had the entire route lined with soldiers to prevent any interference.

Those in power lived in fear that slaves would organise and rise up. Seneca reported that on one occasion a proposal was made by the Senate to distinguish slaves from freemen by their dress. 'It then became apparent how great would be the impending danger if our slaves began to count our number.'[41]

The owners lived in fear of rebellion; the slaves lived in fear of death. To keep them under control, slave owners kept their slaves terrified of the consequences of stepping out of line. Slaves knew that if they rebelled it would mean one thing: crucifixion.

Crucifixion was the slave's death. It was a punishment reserved for slaves and foreign criminals. Its terror was the point: it was the fear of crucifixion which kept the slaves obedient. The slave rebellions of the second century BC culminated in mass crucifixions; the victorious Crassus had 6,000 slaves crucified, lining the main road into Rome. A slave could expect this terrible punishment for all manner of offences.[42]

In examining the early church's attitude to slavery, we have to remember one thing: their founder had died the slave's death. On the night before that, he had acted like a Gentile slave, taking off his outer clothes and washing the disciples' feet. Acceptance of slavery was built into the core of their beliefs about Jesus. About this time in Rome, Mark began writing his Gospel. He related a story in which Jesus told his disciples that 'whoever wishes to become great among you must be your servant, and whoever wishes to be first among you must be slave of all' (Mark 10.43–44). This was taken up by the early church and even sung in their services. Paul quotes one of the hymns of the early church in a letter he wrote from prison in Rome. It begins:

> Let the same mind be in you that was in Christ Jesus,
>> who, though he was in the form of God,
>> did not regard equality with God
>> as something to be exploited,
>> but emptied himself,
>> taking the form of a slave,
>> being born in human likeness...   (Phil. 2.5–7)

One of the reasons why the early church did not say much about rejecting slavery is that they considered themselves all slaves. Some were literally slaves, of course; but amazingly, some actually chose to become slaves. In 1 Clement, there's evidence that some Christians in Rome actually sold themselves into slavery to feed their fellow Christians.

> We know that many among ourselves have delivered themselves to bondage, that they might ransom others. Many have sold themselves to slavery, and receiving the price paid for themselves have fed others.[43]

Even by the terms of the kingdom of fools, this must have seemed madness. Who in their right mind willingly chose slavery? Slaves were commodities. They were even dumped, like scrap cars. To save them the trouble of caring for sick or worn-out slaves, owners would dump them on the island of Aesculapius in the River Tiber in Rome. So many were being abandoned there that Claudius was forced to rule that if any recovered, they would receive their freedom.

So one of the reasons why Paul and the early church did not speak out against slavery is that they actually saw it as part of their calling. Another is that they paid little attention to status.

We have already seen the radical equality which the church offered its members. Paul actually shows a revolutionary disregard for the idea of slavery. There wasn't any difference, actually, between slave and free. That's obvious in this letter to Philemon, where he tells Philemon that Onesimus is something beyond a slave: a brother. To any right-thinking citizen of the Roman Empire, such a statement would be incomprehensible and downright dangerous.

But perhaps the most compelling argument as to why the early church writers didn't call for the mass freeing of slaves is their conviction that they were living in the end times. They believed that the second coming of Jesus was imminent. At that point all injustice would be abolished.

One of the main statements of this comes from Revelation, that subversive, anti-imperialist tract written by a prisoner of the state on the island of Patmos. The writer depicts the fall of a great and wicked city, Babylon, an evil city, a city which has 'glorified herself and lived luxuriously'. But judgement will fall on the city and her trades, her fine luxuries all destroyed:

> The merchants of the earth weep and mourn for her, since no one buys their cargo any more, cargo of gold, silver, jewels and pearls, fine linen, purple, silk and scarlet, all kinds of scented wood, all articles of ivory, all articles of costly wood, bronze, iron, and marble, cinnamon, spice, incense, myrrh, frankincense, wine, olive oil, choice flour and wheat, cattle and sheep, horses and chariots, slaves – and human lives. (Rev. 18.11–13)

That last bit. Slaves. And human lives. One day, the evil city will fall. And with it will fall an economic system which exploits greed, avarice, sin and human misery.

The New Testament writers didn't issue a downright condemnation of slavery because they believed that soon the entire system would be abolished anyway. In any case, they gave to slaves a dignity and status which was incomprehensible to the wider Roman world. They viewed slave and free as equal. They talked about themselves as slaves. And they looked to the imminent future, when an entirely new society would be in place.

The city which Revelation condemned was built on the blood of innocent people. By the time John was scribbling away on Patmos, that violence had been turned against the church itself. 'And in you [Babylon]', he wrote, 'was found the blood of prophets and of saints, and of all who have been slaughtered on earth' (Rev. 18.24).

He wrote 'Babylon', but no one was fooled. What he meant was Rome.

'Sorrow upon sorrow'

Those first letters are lighter, then. Optimistic. But in later letters, the indications are that, like so many of Paul's journeys, he has run into deeper and darker storms.

There's the letter we know as 2 Timothy. There has been much debate about the authorship of this letter: if it was pseudonymous, then the author is one of the greatest historical fiction writers ever, because it abounds in the kind of small detail which would be hard to make up. Clearly Paul is in Rome, but he's more remote than before, more isolated. He writes to Timothy and talks about Onesiphorus, who came to Rome and 'eagerly searched for me and found me' (2 Tim. 1.17).

One of the dominant themes in the letter is shame. Paul tells Timothy not to be ashamed of 'the testimony about our Lord or of me his prisoner' (2 Tim. 1.8). He goes on to say that he's not ashamed of his own suffering (2 Tim. 1.12). The implication is that some people clearly are ashamed. Something has happened now, something which has changed Paul's situation. He claims that 'all who are in Asia have turned away from me, including Phygelus and Hermogenes' (2 Tim. 1.15). At his first defence hearing, 'no one came to my support, but all deserted me' (2 Tim. 4.16). He also says that 'Demas, in love with this present world, has deserted me and gone to Thessalonica' (2 Tim. 4.10). Not only that, but other members of the team are dispersed, elsewhere: Crescens in Galatia, Titus in Dalmatia, Tychicus sent to Ephesus, Erastus in Corinth, Trophimus in Miletus. Only Luke is there. Paul wants Timothy to join him and to bring John Mark, who, he says, will be 'useful in my ministry' (2 Tim. 4.10–11).

We are not sure what event he's describing here. But the idea that Paul has been deserted is clearly linked with his first hearing before the Roman authorities. Not only have his supporters and friends from Asia left him, but 'no one' supported him, including, presumably, the Christians in Rome. Paul may be overstating the case, though: at the end of the letter he sends greetings from Eubulus, Pudens, Linus and Claudia, 'and all the brothers and sisters' (2 Tim. 4.21).

Probably this was a preliminary hearing before the magistrates, held to determine the identity of the accused and the general validity of the charges against him. It was a public hearing, at which supporters and friends would be invited to testify. At such hearings they could even advise on points of law. Yet no one was there. Nobody stood alongside him. This must have made the magistrate suspicious, cautious, likely to pronounce a verdict of *Amplius*, 'more is needed'.[44]

Where is Timothy? Ephesus, perhaps, because Paul sends greetings to the household of Onesiphorus. But he also sends greetings to Priscilla and Aquila, and last time we saw them they were in Rome. Perhaps, once again, they have been forced to relocate. Wherever he is, Timothy is going to pass through Troas on his return and Paul asks him to bring with him some objects: 'When you come, bring the cloak that I left with Carpus at Troas, also the books, and above all the parchments' (2 Tim. 4.13). At the time when Paul was writing, though, Timothy himself may have been in prison. 'I want you to know', writes the unknown author of Hebrews, 'that our brother Timothy has been set free; and if he comes in time, he will be with me when I see you' (Heb. 13.23). We don't know anything more about this episode, but it shows that Timothy was not free from persecution either.

Whatever the case, Paul is clearly believing that things could turn very bad indeed. He's now close on 70 years old. For three decades his body has carried the marks of the death of Jesus (2 Cor. 4.10). Now winter's coming and it feels like everything's running down. This sense of abandonment and doom is also present in the letter he wrote around the same time to the church at Philippi.

By that time, Timothy has joined him (Phil. 1.1), but the letter hints at a deeper turmoil. There's an undercurrent of friction and antagonism in the background.

Paul argues that what has happened to him has been good – it has served to spread the gospel. And 'most' of the brothers and sisters have been empowered to talk more boldly about the gospel (Phil. 1.14). Then he starts talking about conflict, about mixed motives.

> Some proclaim Christ from envy and rivalry, but others from good-will. These proclaim Christ out of love, knowing that I have been put here for the defence of the gospel; the others proclaim Christ out of selfish ambition, not sincerely but intending to increase my suffering in my imprisonment. What does it matter? Just this, that Christ is proclaimed in every way, whether out of false motives or true; and in that I rejoice. (Phil. 1.15–18)

Only Timothy, it seems, remains in his confidence. All the others 'are seeking their own interests, not those of Jesus Christ' (Phil. 2.21).

The whole letter is shot through with a sense of abandonment and betrayal and the language of struggle. It contains some of Paul's most outspoken writing – particularly, it seems, against the perennial activities of the Judaisers. 'Beware of the dogs, beware of the evil workers, beware of those who mutilate the flesh!' (Phil. 3.2). The three Greek nouns, *kunas, kakous ergatas, katatomen,* all begin with the same explosive 'k'. It's as though Paul spits the words out. He talks of his previous righteousness in extreme terms. He counts it as rubbish – and the word here is *skubalon,* which means 'excrement, manure, garbage, kitchen scraps'.[45] It's a pile of crap, quite literally. Paul is in tears as he talks of 'enemies of the cross'. The much vaunted Roman citizenship doesn't seem to have got him far: it's the Christian's citizenship in heaven on which he's relying now (Phil. 3.18–20).

Why is the tone so gloomy and down? Clearly things have gone awry. He has been facing opposition from Christians in Rome – Jewish Christians perhaps – who seem to be almost rejoicing in his imprisonment. There are sparks of the old combative Paul, of course, but there's also an unmistakable tone here of tiredness from this old man.

This evidence is supported by Clement, who, in describing the last days of Paul, records, 'By reason of jealousy and strife Paul by his example pointed out the prize of patient endurance.'[46] Clement was in Rome around AD 90, so he seems to be drawing on a strong local tradition. Paul was executed by the Romans, but 'jealousy and strife' seems a strange way of describing their attitude to Christians. It sounds much more as though Clement is talking about disputes between Christians in Rome. It sounds as if people are proclaiming Christ out of envy and rivalry (Phil. 1.15), seeking followers of their own more than of Christ himself, perhaps.

Paul's suffering is quite obvious. The Philippians sent an envoy called Epaphroditus. He also brought money to Paul, to help with his material needs (Phil. 4.18). In the course of this mission, Epaphroditus nearly died through illness. What the illness was, Paul doesn't say. But through the mercy of God he recovered, and Paul says this was a mercy to himself as well, for it spared him from 'one sorrow after another' (Phil. 2:27).

What was this other sorrow? We don't know, but perhaps the ending of Acts affords us a clue. Acts ends in AD 62 and, as we saw, it ends abruptly. The obvious deduction is that Luke wrote Acts before he knew the ending of Paul's story. He was writing in or around AD 62, therefore, when Paul was in prison in Rome. It has been suggested that Theophilus, to whom the book is addressed, was a Roman official who was involved in the case. I'm not sure about that, since both Luke and Acts together would surely provide far too much information for a legal defence.

Whatever the purpose and nature of the book, the question is this: if Luke survived in Rome to know the outcome of Paul's case and to hear about the other events in the world, why didn't he tidy up the ending of Acts to include them? Perhaps because he *didn't* survive. Perhaps Luke died in Rome, a little after AD 62, in the same bout of sickness which nearly killed Epaphroditus. That, certainly, would have been sorrow on sorrow for Paul. And for the Philippians, who knew Luke because it was his home town.

Pure supposition, of course. We have no real evidence. And Paul was not short of sorrows at this time. The storm clouds were massing and the news from elsewhere wasn't good. Timothy himself had been in prison before coming to Rome (Heb. 13.23).

Or maybe he was thinking of problems further afield. Perhaps the behaviour of the Jewish Christians in Rome had thrown into sharper focus what was happening elsewhere. In AD 62, the church in Jerusalem suffered a deep sorrow of its own.

'Jacob, a servant of God and of the Lord Jesus Christ'

In AD 62, the high priest Ananus killed an old man. The procurator Festus had died in Caesarea, and his successor – a man called Albanus – was still on his way. There was a power vacuum. An opportune moment for Ananus to settle an old score. Technically the high priest did not have the right to execute offenders, but this was a chance not to be missed.

Ananus was good at taking chances. He had been appointed by Agrippa, after Festus's death. Agrippa had little political expertise or even ambition, so the likelihood is that Ananus spotted his chance and managed to manipulate himself into, or just plain buy (or both), his high position.[47] He immediately called the Sanhedrin together and called before them Jacob, the leader of the Jerusalem church. According to Josephus, Ananus 'convened a Sanhedrin of judges and brought before them a man named Jacob, the brother of Jesus who was called the Christ, and certain others. He accused them of having acted illegally and delivered them up to be stoned.'

Eusebius records more details, taken from a lost work by Clement of Alexandria:

Now the manner of James' death has already been shown by the words of Clement we have quoted, who has placed it on record that he was cast down from the pinnacle and beaten to death with a club.

Ananus's actions in convening a Sanhedrin of judges and issuing a death sentence were extremely unusual. Josephus does not mention any other high priest doing the same.[48] So why would Ananus take this risk? He's described by Josephus as 'a bold man in his temper, and very insolent; he was also of the sect of the Sadducees, who are very rigid in judging offenders, above all the rest of the Jews, as we have already observed'. But the crucial fact about Ananus is that his full name was Ananus ben Ananus – Ananus son of Ananus. He was from the House of Hanin. His father Ananus, or Annas, had judged Jesus. His brother-in-law had engineered the execution of Jesus. It's a rerun of the old vendetta.

And the punishment? Maybe there's another clue in that. Ancient traditions state that Jacob was beaten by a club or, in one case, 'an altar brand wielded by a priest'. These sources contain a lot of embellishments, but the interesting thing about these details is that they are reminiscent of the ancient Jewish penalty for temple transgressions. According to the Mishnah, a priest who served in a state of impurity was executed by fellow priests outside the temple 'by splitting his brain open with clubs'.[49]

What had Jesus been accused of? What was Stephen's crime? Anti-temple agitation. Jacob was punished for the same thing his brother had been 'guilty' of: crimes against the temple. It was the final malevolent act from the House of Hanin, the aristocrats who had been criticised by Jesus.

It backfired. According to Josephus, Jacob's trial and execution were opposed by 'those of the inhabitants of the city who were considered the most fair-minded and who were strict in observance of the law'. These people informed the incoming procurator Albinus, who wrote a stern letter to Agrippa II. Hurriedly, Ananus was dismissed from power. The last of the high priests from the House of Hanin was Matthias, son of Theophilos. He was deposed in the first days of the revolt. The rebel Jews had had enough of the aristocratic dynasties which had ruled over them for so long.

The House of Hanin had worked with the Romans since old Ananus was appointed high priest in AD 6. But four years after the death of Jacob, Ananus swapped sides. He was appointed the commander-in-chief of the rebels during the Jewish revolt. He died, not at the hands of the Romans, but killed by his own people, by Jewish assassins – the Zealots – in AD 68.[50] For three days they left his body 'naked, meat for dogs and other beasts'.[51]

'I have finished the race'

In that final, heartfelt letter to his old friends in Philippi, Paul talks seriously for the first time about dying. He has faced death many times before, of course, but this time he seems to think that it's really coming. He talks, both in Philippians and in the letter to Timothy, about being poured out like a libation – an offering of wine to the gods (Phil. 2.17; 2 Tim. 4.6). He knows that he's going to be sacrificed by Rome. The race is almost over. And he's prepared for the end.

It has often been suggested that Paul was released from imprisonment in Rome, then went to Spain, came back, was arrested again, and died in Rome sometime around AD 68. The problem with this suggestion is that there's hardly any evidence for it. The only real mention comes from 1 Clement, where he writes that Paul came 'to the extreme limit of the west, and suffered martyrdom under the prefects. Thus was he removed from the world, and went into the holy place, having proved himself a striking example of patience.'[52]

The problem with this is that we don't know what 'the utmost limits of the west' means. It probably means Spain, but Clement offers no other details and the likelihood is that he's simply inferring things from Paul's desire expressed in Romans to go on to Spain after visiting Rome. In fact, there's no evidence at all that Paul ever left Rome. All the theories about Paul being released after the end of Acts are woven from the hopes of visiting Spain he expressed in Romans (15.23, 28), and the attempts to fit some of his letters into a different chronological framework. And all later accounts of Paul's travels – in Eusebius and Clement, for example – seem to draw on Romans, rather than on any actual evidence.

Of course, he may have gone west. He may have been released. But more likely he remained in custody, either forgotten by the courts or, judging perhaps from the tone of 2 Timothy and Philippians, placed into a more severe form of incarceration.

We do know – or at least we can be more confident that we know – that he died in Rome. The tradition is that he was executed by sword. That means it was a judicial execution, not mob violence. He had come to Rome for a trial, but in the end, it seems, the trial must have gone terribly wrong.

Paul was joined in death – at least in the traditional stories – by an old friend and sometime foe. For, sometime around AD 64, some 15 years after his final appearance in Acts, Peter came to Rome.

In 1 Peter he says he's writing 'through Silvanus' and he sends greetings from 'Your sister church in Babylon … and … my son Mark' (1 Pet. 5.13). The import of the letter is hugely contested.[53] This reference to Babylon cannot literally mean Babylon; by this time the original Babylon was a small village on the banks of the

Euphrates. Instead it's used as Revelation used it, as a code word for Rome. Some have seen this as proof that the letter dates from a later time, when the Romans, like the Babylonians before them, had destroyed the temple.[54] But the tone of the letter is less critical. There's no condemnation of Rome in the letter – indeed, the readers are told to obey the emperor and the authorities. So Babylon in this sense might not mean the 'destroyers of Jerusalem', but merely 'a place of exile'. As Babylon was a place of exile for the Jews, so Peter is in 'exile'. His natural home is in Jerusalem, but he's exiled in Rome, the home of the emperor.

Another clue is the presence of Mark, who we know was summoned to Rome by Paul in the AD 60s (2 Tim. 4.11). All of this links Peter with Rome. There's more confirmation outside the Bible. Ignatius, writing around AD 100, shows that there's a tradition of both Peter and Paul teaching in Rome. Writing to the Roman church, he says, 'I do not enjoin you, as Peter and Paul did...'[55] This implies that at some time both Peter and Paul had been in Rome and that the Roman church were so familiar with the fact that they didn't need it explained.

So it ended in Rome, almost certainly. But when? Peter doesn't seem to be there when Paul arrives – surely Paul would have mentioned it in his letters. And there's no mention of him in the last few verses of Acts, which tell of Paul's stay in the city. Nor is there any mention of him in Paul's letter to the Romans, written around AD 57. Had Paul known him to be there it's unlikely he would have been missed from the list of personal greetings.[56] So Peter must have arrived in Rome later, probably around AD 63–64.

It's often claimed that Peter was the first bishop of Rome, but that claim doesn't appear until the third century.[57] All we know of the Roman church indicates that even if smaller networks were in community together, there was certainly no centralised authority over all the churches. However, it's very likely that the tradition reflects a real involvement with the church in Rome. One can imagine the excitement among the churches when this man arrived in the city. Here, after all, was an apostle; a man who could link the church of Rome with the events of Jesus' life; a man who could look back 30 years to when it all started. A man with a lot of memories.

And that's another link with Mark. Mark wasn't just visiting Peter in Rome, he was working alongside him. This comes from a writer called Papias:

> This also the elder used to say. Mark, indeed, having been the interpreter of Peter, wrote accurately, howbeit not in order, all that he recalled of what was either said or done by the Lord. For he neither heard the Lord, nor was he follower of His, but at a later date (as I said), of Peter.[58]

The tradition as recorded by Papias, then, is that Mark was acting as Peter's translator and later wrote down Peter's reminiscences to form the core of the Gospel of Mark.

Clement, recorded in Eusebius, claimed that Mark was responding to 'popular demand':

> When Peter had publicly preached the word at Rome, and by the spirit had proclaimed the gospel, that those present, who were many, exhorted Mark as one who had followed him for a long time and remembered what had been spoken, to make a record of what was said; and that he did this, and distributed the Gospel among those that asked him.[59]

Recent work has shown the importance of eyewitness testimony in the transmission of the Gospel stories and, particularly, the links between Peter and the Gospel of Mark.[60] Mark makes more frequent references to Peter than any of the other Gospels, and there's a strong probability that Peter was the eyewitness source. Mark's Gospel reflects the perspective of 'the twelve', but more than that, it's mediated through Peter's experiences and feelings. Take, for example, Mark 9.5–6, where Peter's babbling is put down to the fact that 'he did not know what to say, for they were terrified'. There are times when Peter seems to be speaking to us, when he becomes clear and distinct as an individual. As Bauckham puts it, 'In the Gospel of Mark, Peter is not only typical of the disciples to some degree, but also the most fully characterized individual in the Gospel, apart from Jesus.'[61]

Mark's Gospel shows Peter at his worst as well as his best. It's a warts-and-all account. If one was creating a spin-doctored, airbrushed portrait of a leader, showing him as a failure at the crucial moment would not be a great idea ... but what if one were writing down the leader's own account?

Anyway, that's the tradition and, if nothing else, it attests to the strong belief that Peter was in Rome.

The implication in the accounts above is that Peter died before Mark got to work. Certainly the traditional view was that Mark's Gospel originated in the teachings of Peter, and there may have been a sense of urgency about the task. By then, there may have been a feeling that these things had to be recorded before it was too late, before everything got lost.

Sadly, Peter arrived in Rome at the worst possible moment. On 19 July AD 64, a fire broke out in the city.

'Drunk with the blood of the saints'

It began in the Circus, between the Palatine and Caelian hills, and spread rapidly. 'There were no walled mansions or temples, or any other obstructions, which could arrest it,' said Tacitus. 'It outstripped every counter-measure. The ancient city's narrow winding streets and irregular blocks encouraged its progress.'[62]

It raced through the dense, crowded streets, destroying homes and buildings and burning for five and a half days. Of the fourteen districts of Rome, only four escaped some kind of destruction. Three were completely destroyed. There was widespread looting and gangs prevented people from fighting the flames. There were conspiracy theories too, ugly rumours of people actually setting light to buildings, spreading the flames, acting 'under orders'.

Nero was at Antium at the time, but hurried back to Rome when he heard how serious the fire was. He seems to have been active in the relief effort, finding places for people to shelter, ordering food to be brought from Ostia and cutting the price of grain. But it was no good. He was deeply unpopular and so the blame fastened on him. The rumours had led people to believe that the fire was started on his orders, to clear the way for a new city to be built, named after himself.

He did his best. He started to plan the rebuilding of the city and he held banquets and nightly vigils to propitiate the gods. But the suspicion still lingered that Nero had ordered this to happen. So the emperor did what leaders always do in such circumstances: he found someone even more unpopular and pinned the blame on them. Nero found the Christians.

The report in Tacitus's history is chilling:

> So, to get rid of this rumour, Nero set up as the culprits and pun-
> ished with the utmost refinement of cruelty a class hated for their
> abominations, who are commonly called Christians ... Accord-
> ingly, arrest was first made of those confessed [to being a Chris-
> tian]; then, on their evidence, an immense multitude was convicted,
> not so much on the charge of arson as because of hatred of the
> human race. Beside being put to death they were made to serve
> as objects of amusement; they were clad in the hides of beasts and
> torn to death by dogs; others were crucified, others set on fire to
> serve to illuminate the night when daylight failed. Nero had thrown
> open his grounds for the display, and was putting on a show in the
> circus, where he mingled with the people in the dress of a chari-
> oteer or drove about in his chariot. All this gave rise to a feeling of
> pity, even towards men whose guilt merited the most exemplary
> punishment; for it was felt that they were being destroyed not for
> the public good but to gratify the cruelty of an individual.[63]

That line, 'not so much on the charge of arson as because of
hatred of the human race', expresses what was to be the common
lot of Christians from then on. It was not the fire: it was *them*.
They were burned and savaged and crucified because they were
different.

Their punishments reflect their 'crimes' and their status. Burning was the punishment for arson and the fact that others were
crucified shows they were not citizens and were viewed as foriegn-
ers or slaves. The effect on the community must have been horrific. Torture was used to extract the names of others. Nero wanted
as big a spectacle as his police could provide.[64]

The persecution by Nero did not start immediately after the
event. Probably it started a few months after the fire, possibly even
as late as spring AD 65.[65] And we don't know how many people
died in the Neronian persecution. Tacitus talks of 'an immense
multitude', but there weren't that many Christians in the city.
Whatever the case, it must have swept up many of the people we
have met in these pages. Priscilla and Aquila, Andronicus and
Junia, Rufus and his mother, Nereus and his sister, Tryphaena
and Tryphosa. Maybe Mark too. Who knows?

We know the name of only one victim of Nero's politically calculated rage: Simon, known as Peter.

One legend has imprinted itself on the Christian conscious-ness: the famous *Quo Vadis* story. In this, Peter is encouraged by 'the brethren' to flee from Rome, but as he is leaving, he sees the figure of Jesus walking into the city. Peter asks Jesus, '*Quo vadis?*' – 'Where are you going?' When Jesus tells Peter that he's going into the city to be crucified again, Peter turns around and follows him to his death.[66]

The source of this legend, *The Acts of Peter*, was written some-time between AD 180 and 225 and can hardly be credited as sober history. However, it does capture something of Peter's charac-ter. And, more to the point, it conforms to the very strong early church tradition that Peter was crucified. A better pointer to this is John's Gospel, written later than the others, where the risen Jesus tells Peter:

> Very truly, I tell you, when you were younger, you used to fasten your own belt and to go wherever you wished. But when you grow old, you will stretch out your hands, and someone else will fasten a belt around you and take you where you do not wish to go. (John 21.18)

John here includes in his Gospel a prophecy which may have circulated independently in the church. That it refers to crucifix-ion seems undeniable: the victim's arms were first stretched out, and then the *patibulum* or cross-beam was bound to them.[67]

The tradition says Peter was crucified upside down. This is not improbable. These deaths, after all, were seen as entertainment. As Hengel has put it, 'Crucifixion was a punishment in which the caprice and sadism of the executioners were given full rein.'[68] Josephus tells how Roman soldiers besieging Jerusalem 'amused' themselves by crucifying their victims in 'various attitudes as a grim joke, till owing to the vast numbers there was no room for the crosses, and no crosses for the bodies'.[69] Seneca reported on a mass crucifixion that he saw: 'I see crosses there, not just of one kind but made in many different ways: some have their victims with their head down to the ground, some impale their private parts, others stretch out their arms.'[70]

Peter, an ageing fisherman from Palestine, probably not much good at Greek, was just one of the multitude to the Romans. Just another pathetic old loser, killed for entertainment at the whim of a paranoid tyrant. They didn't know, they couldn't know, that the man they had just humiliated was Simeon, son of Jonah, Cephas, Petros – the rock, one of the greatest of Jesus' disciples.

'My desire is to depart and be with Christ'

It wasn't just Peter, though. Paul, too, was martyred in Rome.

Clement, writing in the last decade of the first century AD, says that Peter, 'having borne his testimony went to his appointed place of glory', and that later Paul, 'when he had borne his testimony before the rulers, so he departed from the world and went unto the holy place, having been found a notable pattern of patient endurance'.[71] Dionysius, Bishop of Corinth, recorded that Peter and Paul, 'having taught together in Italy, suffered martyrdom at (or about) the same time'.[72] A much later tradition reinterpreted this as meaning that they died on the same day, but that's precisely what the original does not say. By then, the church may have started celebrating these heroes on the same day – 29 June – which may have confused the issue. Jerome (c. 342–420) believed that they died in the same year, but Prudentius (348 – c. 410) and Augustine (354–430) believed that Paul died a year after Peter.[73]

Perhaps there's a clue in that line from 1 Clement, which says that Paul testified 'before the rulers'. Nero remained in Rome through to September AD 66, after which he departed, not returning until March AD 68. He left the city in the charge of Helius and Tigellinus. If we take 1 Clement's mention of 'rulers' as authentic – and there's no reason to think it isn't – this implies that Paul was tried during this period, meaning that he died sometime between late AD 66 and early 68.[74] Sulpicius Severus records a slightly different tradition:

> [After the persecution] laws were enacted and the religion was forbidden. Edicts were publicly published: 'No one must profess Christianity.' Then Paul and Peter were condemned to death. The former was beheaded, Peter was crucified.[75]

The likelihood is that if Peter was crucified – and if he was crucified upside down – then he died in the first wave of punishments. It fits perfectly with the grotesque 'entertaining' punishments organised by Nero. This must have been sometime in AD 65.

But if Paul survived for a bit – and he was a citizen in Roman custody, which might have offered some protection – then it's likely that his punishment was delayed. So we can imagine that he finally did get a judicial hearing, not before the emperor, but before his appointees. But by that time the edict of Nero had been passed. Christianity was banned. Paul never stood a chance of a fair trial.

We can, perhaps, get a glimpse of the process in later accounts. During the reign of Antoninus Pius (86–161) a married woman became a Christian. Her husband sued for divorce and denounced her to the authorities. As she was nobility, she was allowed time to arrange her defence before the emperor. But the man who brought her to Christ – Ptolomaeus – was arrested and imprisoned. When he was finally brought before a magistrate, he was asked one question: 'Are you a Christian?' He replied, 'Yes.' And immediately he was led away to execution. On seeing this, a man called Lucius, who was watching proceedings, shouted out in protest against the injustice of punishing someone just on the strength of the single word 'Christian'. The judge, Urbicus, turned and observed, 'You also seem to me to be such an one.' Lucius replied, 'Most certainly I am,' on which he, too, was led away immediately and executed.[76]

A different emperor, a later time, but the same essential process. By AD 66 it was enough, in Rome, to be called a Christian. If asked, like those two later disciples, 'Are you a Christian?' Paul would never – *could* never – have denied it. Roman death sentences were carried out immediately. He would have been taken out of court and, with the 'mercy' accorded to a citizen, beheaded.

He should, technically, have been offered a choice. The Emperor Tiberius had decreed that citizens sentenced to death could choose permanent deportation to a remote place or a distant island.[77] Their citizenship would be lost, their property forfeit. If he was given such a choice, he didn't take it. He was a citizen of a different world anyway, a different kingdom. Perhaps he felt the time had come to go to his real home.

Both Peter and Paul later had shrines erected to their memory, placed in the areas where it was believed the deaths had happened. Around AD 200, a man called Gaius was opposing the claims of some heretical teachers in Hierapolis that they had the graves of Philip and his daughters. He wrote this:

> But I can show the trophies of the apostles, for if you go to the Vatican Hill or to the highway to Ostia, you will find the trophies of those who have founded this church.[78]

By then the idea had taken root that Peter and Paul were the twin founders of the church in Rome. But the important nugget here is the word *tropaia,* 'trophies'. Does this mean the graves? Or does it mean victory monuments? Eusebius clearly understands it to mean the graves, not least because it's countering claims to the burial place of Philip and his family.

This is the first specific reference to the graves of the apostles, and it comes from 140 years after their deaths. But anyone inventing the locations would not have thought of those places – both at some distance from the centre of Rome. Excavations beneath the main altar of St Peter's Basilica in Rome have revealed a *tropaeum,* a commemorative shrine which is probably that identified by a writer called Gaius around AD 200. Whether the famous bones discovered beneath are those of

The executions of Paul and Peter. This medieval representation records the tradition that Paul was beheaded and Peter crucified upside down. There is nothing historically unlikely in either of these traditions

the apostle is more doubtful, but it certainly marks the site of a very early shrine. So Peter was probably killed in the Circus Nero, which stood just a little way south of Vatican Hill.[79]

The traditional site of the grave of Paul was marked by Constantine, who built a church over the spot. This became the Church of San Paolo fuori le Mura (St Paul Outside the Walls). The name comes from the fact that the original site was beyond the old Roman wall. Recent excavations below the altar of the church have revealed the marble sarcophagus built by Theodosius when he extended the church in AD 386. More recently, on 29 June 2009, Pope Benedict XVI announced that carbon dating of some bone fragments within the sarcophagus confirmed they belonged to someone from the first or second century AD.[80] Although the Vatican announced that this confirmed the 'unanimous and uncontested tradition that they are the mortal remains of the Apostle Paul', there's no way of knowing for sure.

The problem is that the bones of both Peter and Paul were moved. In AD 258, during the persecution under Valerian, their relics were taken from the shrines on the Vatican and the Ostian Way to the catacomb of San Sebastian on the Appian Way.[81] Though they were moved back later, the chances of disruption must be high.

And in any case, for the first-century Christians such things didn't matter. In the first century, the idea of a cult based around relics of the martyrs simply does not exist. The earliest example of that kind of thing comes from the *Martyrdom of Polycarp* around AD 150.[82] The reason is simple: they didn't venerate the relics because they believed that the apostles would very soon be resurrected. At the end of the second century, Polycrates, Bishop of Ephesus, wrote to the Roman Bishop Victor about the places where the 'great stars, who will arise on the last day when Christ returns, have found their resting place'. By that time churches had begun the business of arguing for status on the basis of their association with the apostles, and the whole business of saints, shrines and seniority had swung into action.

But those first Christians in Rome, huddled, hiding, after the terrors of Nero's entertainments – they were not interested in relics.

All they knew was that the stars had gone out.

The Beast: Patmos AD 92

> When he opened the sixth seal, I looked, and there came a great
> earthquake; the sun became black as sackcloth, the full moon be-
> came like blood, and the stars of the sky fell to the earth as the fig
> tree drops its winter fruit when shaken by a gale. (Rev. 6.12–13)

Falling stars. The sun darkened. The winter winds shaking the
fig trees on the Mount of Olives.

Sunday morning, sometime in the first century. A man called
John, a local leader of the churches in Asia, turns round and finds
himself face to face with Jesus. He's on an island called Patmos, a
sea-bound prison. And he's there because he's a Christian.

But that morning, he sees something which makes even the
bright sunlight on the rocks seem dim. It's a vision, of scrolls and
angels and plagues, of bloodthirsty beasts and scarlet whores. He
has an apocalypse.

'Apocalypse' doesn't mean 'end of the world' – at least that's
not what it meant originally. It's Greek for 'revelation'. And what
John sees is the truth of what's going on all around him, the reality behind the reality. It's a vision of the future, certainly, but also
of the present and the past. In the foreground he sees the persecution of the church and the victory of the Roman Empire. But
look through that, beyond that, and you see what's really going
on. You see the fall of Babylon, the utter defeat of the Empire.
And for the Christians, what John sees is victory. He writes all
this down, in a compelling, disturbing word-picture book, a col-
lage of images from the Hebrew Scriptures, mixed with Christian
code words and the sayings of Jesus.

Many years before John saw him, the physical Jesus sat on the Mount of Olives, looked at the temple and likened it to a fig tree that was not producing fruit. With the temple gleaming, gold and white, in the twilight, Jesus told his disciples that it would one day burn with a redder glow, that it would be destroyed, stone by stone. He talked of a time of trial, how his followers would be hated because of his name. Brother would betray brother, fathers their children. And then it would be time to run, to leave everything, head for the hills. 'Just pray,' he said, 'that it won't happen in winter.'

'All will be thrown down'

AD 66. Peter was dead. Paul was dead. In Italy, those Christians who had survived Nero's mad rage had fled from Rome, or buried their faith somewhere deep and secret. In Asia and Greece, Christians looked nervously to the west, hearing bad reports, wondering what was going on.

In Jerusalem, they were collecting their possessions and preparing to leave.

The clouds had been gathering for a long time. The procurators had grown ever more rapacious, greedy and inept. Albinus (AD 60–62) and his successor Gessius Florus (AD 62–66) were accused of taking bribes from Jewish banditry. The flashpoint came in AD 66. In Caesarea, Syrian Gentiles provoked Jewish rage by sacrificing a chicken in the alleyway outside a synagogue. Florus refused to punish the ringleaders, so the Jews of Caesarea decided to leave the city *en masse*. When the citizens of Jerusalem heard about this, they started to complain. Florus punished them by sending people 'to take seventeen talents out of the sacred treasure, and pretended that Caesar wanted them'.[1] This was seen as sacrilege and when Florus next appeared in Jerusalem, a hostile, jeering, mocking crowd was waiting. When the Jewish authorities refused to hand over the ringleaders of these hecklers, Florus let loose his troops in the upper market in the south-west of the city – an area not far from the Christians' Upper Room. Josephus reckoned that over 3,600 people were butchered. Just as shocking were the humiliating punishments: Florus had those of the highest rank scourged and nailed to crosses: 'men of equestrian rank, men, who if Jews by birth were at least invested with that Roman dignity'.[2] The compact between the Jewish aristocracy and the Romans had totally broken down.

From there things escalated rapidly. A young aristocratic priest called Eleazar, son of Ananias, led the action. He was the captain of the temple, usually a post which signified alliance with the forces of law and order, but he led the decision to abandon the daily sacrifice in the temple for the emperor. It was a declaration of war. The city exploded into violence. Ananias son of Nedebaeus, the former high priest who had tried Paul, was murdered and the Roman garrison in Jerusalem was slaughtered. Florus withdrew and sent to the governor of Syria, Cestius Gallus, for help.

In late autumn AD 66, Gallus arrived with a force ready to besiege Jerusalem. He set up camp on Mount Scopus and easily took the outer suburb of Bezetha. The city and its defenders held their breath for the attack.

It didn't come. For some inexplicable reason, Gallus withdrew his forces. Maybe he was worried about the onset of winter (though there were rumours that he had taken a bribe). Whatever the case, the decision was catastrophic. The retreating Romans were ambushed by Jewish forces at a pass near Beth Horon. It was a bloody rout. Five thousand Roman troops were killed and their standard was captured.

Rome struck back. In spring AD 67, Nero sent in 60,000 troops commanded by Vespasian, one of his best generals. They swiftly retook Galilee and Samaria, and moved steadily south. Their task was made easier by the fact that the rebels were not universally supported. Many Jews, especially in Hellenised cities like Tiberias and Sepphoris, knew full well that the Jews could not defeat Rome. King Agrippa tried to persuade the rebels to make a deal: why, he asked, did the Jewish rebels think they could succeed, where the Gauls, the Germans or the Greeks had failed? In Galilee, the local Jewish commander Josephus defected to the Romans. By the winter of AD 67, Vespasian was at Caesarea, planning the recapture of Jerusalem.

Then things stopped. Again. News arrived from Rome: Nero was dead, Vespasian was urgently needed to keep the peace. He went west as soon as possible, leaving his son Titus in charge.

Jerusalem was now in a state of limbo. The Roman forces had isolated the city, but took no further action while the situation in Rome resolved itself. It was the 'year of the four emperors': two claimants to the imperial throne died, a third was proclaimed by legions in Germany, and Vespasian himself was acclaimed by his troops. The rebels, far from using this time of relative peace to prepare their defences, turned inwards, savaging each other in a welter of bloody factionalism.

In Jerusalem, control swung away from any moderates and into the hands of the Zealots, diehard radicals who opposed any talk of compromise. Anyone who talked of peace was a traitor to the cause. Only a small proportion of the city's inhabitants supported the Zealots (and there was massive infighting among the Zealots themselves), but it made no difference. Opposing moderates were removed from their posts of command and excluded from worshipping at the temple. Finally, the Zealots managed to wrest control of the high priesthood from the aristocratic families who had held power for so long, and in the winter of AD 67 they put in place their candidate, Phanias.

This was probably the point at which the Christians left. According to Eusebius, the Christians in Jerusalem fled before the siege, 'because of an oracle given by a revelation', settling in a town called Pella.[3] This story is very open to challenge. Some scholars have argued that the Jewish church did not escape the city and was effectively destroyed. Others say that the story was created by Christians in Pella to 'big up' their town.[4] But Eusebius doesn't say where he got the story from. He lived in Palestine himself, so could certainly have been in touch with a local tradition, and he had access to libraries in both Caesarea and Jerusalem.[5]

It's certainly not hard to imagine the Christians leaving, either as a result of a direct revelation, or as an interpretation of Jesus' statement that the abomination of desolation would stand in Jerusalem. It must have been obvious that the violence would soon engulf everyone. As followers of Jesus, they could not possibly fight. Add to that the belief that the violence and suffering around them must be the 'end times', and you can see why the Jewish Christians – or a significant group of them at any rate – would have decided it was time to go.

It would probably have been before AD 68, because after that the siege set in properly and from then on only the wealthy could buy their way out. Poor refugees were simply cut down. Pella was certainly geographically convenient: the main road to Damascus went straight through it. If the Christians left Jerusalem in AD 67, when the Zealots achieved ascendancy, they would have reached a Pella which had already been 'pacified' by the Romans. And we know from Josephus that the Romans did make terms with some groups of deserters and settled them in cities. Sometimes they were settled in pagan cities as a kind of punitive measure, but one group of high-status Jews who escaped were settled by Titus in Gophna, with the promise that they could return to Jerusalem after the war was finished.[6] Others left, too. Despite the legendary nature of the tales, a significant group of Pharisees certainly also fled Jerusalem to settle in Jamnia.[7]

By AD 70, the situation in Rome had been resolved. Vespasian was emperor and he sent orders to his son Titus to finish the job. Titus surrounded the city with a huge force. The situation inside Jerusalem became truly appalling. People were starving to death, the dead were left unburied, and anyone caught trying to escape was crucified outside the city walls. The final breakthrough came in June, when the Romans breached the city walls and embarked on an orgy of destruction. Temple Mount held out for a little longer, but eventually that, too, fell, leaving the last few, desperate rebels holed up in the temple building itself.

On 29 or 30 July, the Romans gained the outer courts, planning to attack the sanctuary at dawn the next day. But during the night, the fire which had been burning in the outer courts spread to the temple building itself. Soon the temple was ablaze. Its defenders were butchered as they fled, and the temple was ransacked. Jerusalem was systematically destroyed. The most physically robust prisoners were sent to Rome as slaves. The rest found their way to the amphitheatres of the Græco-Roman world, where they were torn apart by beasts. Jerusalem's walls were torn down, the temple dismantled and its treasures taken to Rome. There was never a temple in Jerusalem again.

The destruction of the temple cut the umbilical cord. Despite the sometimes troubled relationship between Gentile Christianity

Detail from the Arch of Titus in the Forum at Rome, showing the sacking of the Jerusalem temple by Roman soldiers, and the removal of the golden candlestick

and the Judean church, there was never any serious question that Jerusalem was the mother church, the fount. But now the temple was gone, the sanctuary destroyed.

There was little sanctuary elsewhere. Things calmed down after Nero's edict, but the church was painfully aware of its prohibited status. And since, to Romans, Christians were mainly indistinguishable from Jews, they also suffered the backlash from the Jewish rebellion.

In Judea the church moved to other places. It established itself in Galilee, in the sites traditionally associated with Jesus. It flourished in Caesarea, which would eventually become a major centre of Christian learning. And some Christians returned to Jerusalem to rebuild their lives and commemorate the holy places.

In Rome, the church was silenced. Crushed. After telling the story of their martyrdoms, Tacitus says nothing more about Christians. Writing at the end of the century, Josephus makes no real reference to them. The earliest post-Neronian Christian documents we have from Rome are 1 Clement (written c. AD 96) and a vision-story called the *Shepherd of Hermas* (written c. AD 140). It all goes quiet, because the Christians simply weren't there. At least not in any number.

Such quiet comprises much of the story for two hundred or so years. The situation of Christianity throughout the Empire was tentative, nervous. The official line was still one of disapproval and disdain, interspersed with occasional violent persecution.

***

17 July AD 180. Carthage, North Africa. Twelve Christians were hauled in for interrogation. Twelve in total: seven male, five female, probably young. They were in possession of a box, which seemed important to them.

The men: Nartzalus, Cittinus, Veturius, Felix, Aquilinus, Laetanius and Speratus.

The women: Donata, Vestia, Secunda, Januaria and Generosa.

Their interrogator, Saturninus the proconsul, offered a pardon if they would only return to good sense, but the Christians' leader, Speratus, replied, 'We have never done evil, we have committed no iniquitious deeds, we have never cursed, but when we were received badly we gave thanks; for we respect our ruler.'

'We *too* are religious,' said Saturninus, 'and our religion is simple: we swear by the genius of our lord the emperor, and we pray for his safety, as you also should.'

Speratus offered to explain their faith, but Saturninus refused to listen. 'I will not lend an ear to you who are about to say evil things about our rites; on the contrary, swear by the genius of our lord the emperor.'

Speratus replied, 'I do not recognise the authority of this age, instead I serve that God whom no man sees or can see with these eyes. I have not committed theft, but if I have bought anything I have paid the tax. For I recognise my Lord, the emperor of kings and of all nations.'

Saturninus offered Speratus and the other Christians 30 days to reconsider, but they refused. When the proconsul asked what was in their precious box, Speratus replied, 'The books and epistles of Paul, a just man.'

The twelve were found guilty of 'living after the Christian fashion'. They were taken out and beheaded.[8]

Not many people died. Just twelve Christians. Killed for being different, for refusing to bow down and worship the emperor, and for having some suspicious, seditious, anti-Imperial writings which they kept in a box.

**

Scholars debate levels of Christian martyrdom as though they were arguing about mere statistics.

I sat once with a TV producer who cheerfully pronounced, 'You know, not many early Christians were martyred,' as though we were talking about figures on a balance sheet. How many is 'not many'? Five thousand? One thousand? One hundred? One? How does anyone say that one unjust death is 'not many'?

We don't know the exact numbers, but we know it was too many. Too many, and not just during the madness of Nero. The reigns of Domitian, Nerva and Trajan also saw Christians imprisoned, punished and killed. Many of the characters we have encountered in this book were executed for their faith. According to Eusebius, Simeon, then leader of the Jewish church, lost his life as a martyr, crucified in the reign of Trajan (AD 97–111).[9] In AD 108, Ignatius was taken to Rome and martyred. On the way he wrote letters, including one to Polycarp, who, some 50 years later, as an old man, was killed in the arena in Smyrna. Two years after Ignatius was killed, Pliny was arresting Christians in Pontus without really knowing anything about them. He had a few casually executed as though he were signing a receipt. In AD 150, Justin complained at the way Christians were being treated – and there was more casual violence against them. Justin himself was, of course, condemned and killed for his defence.

This violence and its illegal status drove the church off the streets. After Nero, the church could no longer speak openly; it could no longer preach on the streets as in the glory days when Paul, Peter and Philip were out on the streets of Antioch, Ephesus and Sebaste. Christians had to keep their meetings covert and quiet. From the mid-first century onwards, the 'general public' were not allowed into Christian worship.

The church was wary of informers and spies in their midst – a situation common to many underground churches today, in places like Iraq and North Korea. One of the roles of the deacon from then on was to act as a security guard at the door.

Even those who had decided to become Christians had to serve a period of training: they were an apprentice, a *catachumen* as it was termed. They had to prove that their life had changed. They were mentored and helped to do this, and the process could take up to two years. It was only after that process that they could be baptised – always on Easter Day – and then admitted to the Eucharist.

But why, in such circumstances, would anyone want to join? Never mind the two-year training/probation period, why would you sign up to a life of looking over your shoulder? And where would you hear about it in the first place?

Clearly in most places Christians got along as best they could. They kept their noses clean and their heads down. Their neighbours would know, but wouldn't make a fuss. 'A good man, this Caius Seius,' they said, 'only that he is a Christian.'[10] They adopted a new term for themselves, to describe their ambivalent relationship with their society and their sense that they were citizens of a different kingdom: they became the *para oikoi,* the 'resident aliens'.

But they could never shed that smell of fear, that sense of otherness, of always being a potential victim. The plain fact is that after Nero, to become a Christian was to sign up willingly to the possibility that you could be ostracised, physically assualted, discriminated against and killed. Celsus describes how Christians were hunted: 'If anyone [Christian] does still wander about in secret, yet he is sought out and condemned to death.' Christians are described as 'a tribe obscure, shunning the light, dumb in public though talkative in corners'.

Yet still people converted. Still people found freedom and acceptance and a new kind of life in this place.

So how did they do it? How did they pass on the good news if they couldn't talk about it?

Beautiful lives

Some of it, indeed, was *because* of the martyrdoms. The crowds watching Christians being killed in the pogrom in Lyons asked themselves, 'What profit has their religion brought them, which is preferred to their own life?' While Tertullian asked, 'At the sight of it [persecution] who is not profoundly troubled to the point of inquiring what may lie behind it all?'[11]

When a group of Christians were put in prison in Carthage in AD 203, their conduct in prison began to affect even their jailers. The junior guard, a man called Pudens, 'began to treat us really well, for he could see that some great power was at work in us'. In the end, he became a believer.[12] And when, just before their deaths, the crowd witnessed the wealthy, high-born Vibia Perpetua give her slave Felicitas the kiss of peace, they saw something of the shocking, startling, wonderful equality of the Christians.

This, I think, brings us closer to why the church had such an effect on the society around it. It was not to do with theology or doctrine; for the most part the people who came to Christ were illiterate. It was not to do with the quality of their worship services, because outsiders were not allowed in. It was to do with their lives. The distinctive practices of the Christians alerted people to the possibility of a different way of life. The way the Christians lived made others think that there was a chance of change. There was no radical wing of the Early Church; the entire organisation was radical to start with.

They lived Jesus-shaped lives. They swam against the tide and tilted at windmills. They did the opposite of what was expected by the society and culture around them. As one of their writers said, 'Beauty of life ... causes strangers to join the ranks ... we do not talk about great things, we live them.'[13]

And it was down to individuals. After Paul, there's no evidence that the church had any kind of organised, official approach to mission. It left everything to the individual. This meant that the only way in which the church could grow was through personal contact. Their lifestyle preached the message that their services could not. Face-to-face communication was 'nearly the only kind of meeting point'.[14]

A good example is the conversion of Justin, who became a Christian around AD 130. His search for truth had taken him to a variety of 'professionals': a Stoic, an Aristotelian, a Pythagorean and a Platonist. But each of these learned, eloquent men failed to convince him. Then he went for a walk on the beach and met a perfectly ordinary old man, a Jewish Christian, who simply began to talk to him. As they talked, Justin's life changed. Justin described it being like gates of light opening up. As he listened, he became more and more awestruck, more and more convinced of the power and truth of what the old man was saying.

> When he had spoken these and many other things, which there is no time for mentioning at present, he went away, bidding me attend to them; and I have not seen him since. But straightway a flame was kindled in my soul; and a love of the prophets, and of those men who are friends of Christ, possessed me; and whilst revolving his words in my mind, I found this philosophy alone to be safe and profitable.[15]

Conversation was just the start. After that, life had to change. As we saw with the catechumens, the would-be disciple was expected to demonstrate proof of conversion. The early church was not interested in some kind of philosophical victory; it could not be belief without changed behaviour. As Christians they kept apart and kept quiet, but as neighbours they were everywhere. The faith was lived out among the people. Stories of healings spread. A neighbour was ill, the Christian offered to pray with them for healing. Another was hungry, a Christian found them food. There were prisoners in jail and the Christians brought them blankets, food and drink.

Perhaps the finest expression of this comes from an anonymous piece of writing called the *Letter to Diognetus*.

> For Christians are not distinguished from the rest of mankind by country or language or speech or customs. They do not live in cities of their own, nor do they speak a different language, nor practice an eccentric way of life. Nor do they possess any teaching discovered through the intellect or study of ingenious men, nor are they leaders in human doctrine like some are. But while they live in both Greek and barbarian cities, as individual circumstances would have it, and follow the native customs in dress and food and the other ways of

life, yet the character of the citizenship which they demonstrate is remarkable, and undeniably unusual. They live in their own countries, but only as nonresidents; they bear their responsibilites as citizens, and they endure all hardships as foreigners. Every foreign country is their fatherland, and every fatherland is foreign. They marry like all other men and they have children; but they do not kill their children. They share their meals, but not their wives. They are in the flesh, but they do not live according to the flesh. They live on earth, but their citizenship is in heaven. They obey the established laws, yet in their own lives they transcend the laws. They love all, and they are persecuted by all. They are ignored, and yet they are condemned. They are put to death, yet they are given life. They are beggars who make many rich. They are in need, and yet they have more than they need. They are dishonoured, and yet they are glorified in their dishonour. They are slandered, and yet they are vindicated. They are hated, and they bless; they are insulted, and they offer respect. When they do good, they are punished as evil-doers; and when they are punished they rejoice, as though brought to life. Jews wage war against them, the Greeks persecute them, and yet those that hate them cannot give a reason of their hostility. In a word, what the soul is in a body, so Christians are in the world.[16]

The church grew strong because it was constantly swimming against the tide. The church stood out because it was visibly different. The kingdom of fools grew, because the kingdom of the world seemed so foolish by comparison.

The first Christians claimed that their ragged, uneducated spokesmen were leaders of a new, powerful kingdom. Their teachers and prophets were tentmakers and travellers, tanners and cobblers. Their heroes were thrown to the animals in the arena or beheaded or crucified. And John the seer – John the overseer – stood on his rocky prison island and dared to claim that what looked like failure was in fact the ultimate victory. These passionate, brave believers were certain that there was victory: even while they were being tortured and killed.

**

No one knows when the final victory that he foresaw will come, or what it will look like when it arrives. As one cleric pondered recently, 'What if we're still the early church?'[17]

In some senses the early church has never gone away. For millions of believers around the world, their experience of life as a Christian resonates strongly with the world of the first followers of Christ. 'A friend of mine is being terribly tortured in prison,' said a Christian leader. 'When he came to faith, he made the decision that one day he would die for Christ.' Those words could have been spoken by a Christian in Carthage, or Smyrna, or Rome. In fact they come from North Korea. 'Every Christian in North Korea has made that choice,' he continues. 'I am convinced he can take the suffering because he constantly reminds himself of the joy that is set before him.'

In the west, we're closer to the world of Peter and Paul than, perhaps, at any time since the fourth century. A walk through the cities of our land will reveal the forums of Rome and Corinth and Athens writ large – swollen, with power and greed. At the heart of our society there are temples, just as there were 2,000 years ago. Only the gods have changed. They had Zeus and Athena and Hermes and Augustus, we have money and sex and power and tribalism. They had gladiators and charioteers, we have footballers. They had emperors, we have celebrities. Worship comes in many forms. And now, as then, there are those who wonder whether these shabby emperors are really the divine beings they claim to be.

But there is further, still, to go. As I write this, it is nearly 1,700 years years since the Edict of Milan made Christianity official; seventeen centuries since Christianity was given a wash and a haircut, dressed up in nice clothes and given a seat at the top table. Christianity got big. It got influential. It was the archetypal victim of its own success and for seventeen centuries the church – in the West, at least – has forgotten that shabby, foolish old kingdom, and happily adopted the wisdom of the world. It moved out of the tentmakers' workshops and the tanners' quarters, and into the cathedrals and the corridors of power; it stopped sharing an actual meal and started handing out wafers and sips of bad wine; it took off the traveller's cloak and started wearing purple.

Oh, I know it's not quite that black and white. In the past centuries there have been many who have refused to play the Emperor's game and sought to return to their roots, to be radical in the true sense of the word. And even before Constantine neutered the church, there were plenty who were eager to bring the kingdom of God down to man's level.

But something changed when the Roman Empire adopted Christianity. Something was lost, shattered.

Now, maybe, things are turning. Perhaps, in the West, it will no longer be acceptable to follow Jesus. Perhaps it will be increasingly seen as anti-social, or stupid, or strange. Maybe, as is the case for so many Christians elsewhere in the world, we will soon have to live in a culture where following Jesus is neither safe nor sensible.

Perhaps western Christianity will, at last, be relieved of the terrible burden of official approval.

If so, then the lessons from the early church will become urgent. At that point, we will be back in their world, we will be true companions, true bread-sharers – with Peter and Paul, with Philip and Priscilla – and then we will need to attend carefully to their example, to the teaching, the training, the *didache* of those first apostles.

Perhaps then, at last, we will really start to grasp the extraordinary wisdom of this kingdom of fools.

Notes

ABBREVIATIONS

Antiquities	Josephus, *Antiquities*
ABD	David Noel Freedman (ed.), *The Anchor Bible Dictionary* (New York: Doubleday, 1999)
ANF	Alexander Roberts, James Donaldson and A. Cleveland Coxe (eds.), *The Ante-Nicene Fathers: Translations of the Writings of the Fathers down to AD 325* (New York: Christian Literature Company, 1885, Accordance electronic edition, 9 vols)
BDAG	William Arndt, Frederick W. Danker and Walter Bauer, *A Greek-English Lexicon of the New Testament and Other Early Christian Literature, 3rd ed.* (Chicago: University of Chicago Press, 2000)
Bock	Darrell L. Bock, *Acts* (Grand Rapids: Baker Academic, 2007)
DSS	Vermès, Géza, *The Complete Dead Sea Scrolls in English* (London: Penguin Books, 2004)
Fitzmyer	Joseph A. Fitzmyer, *The Acts of the Apostles* (New York: Doubleday, 1998)
NIDNTT	Colin Brown (ed.), *New International Dictionary of New Testament Theology* (Exeter: Paternoster, 1986)
War	Josephus, *Jewish War*
Witherington	Ben Witherington, *The Acts of the Apostles: A Socio-Rhetorical Commentary* (Grand Rapids: Eerdmans, 1998)

INTRODUCTION: THE KINGDOM OF FOOLS

1 Minucius Felix, *Octavius*, 8–9, in ANF 4.

2 Tertullian, *Apology*, 16, in ANF 3.

3 Origen, *Contra Celsus*, in Meeks, Wayne A., *The First Urban Christians* (New Haven: Yale University Press, 1983), 51.

4 Origen, *Contra Celsus*, 3.52.

5 Kreider, Alan, *The Change of Conversion and the Origin of Christendom* (Eugene: Wipf & Stock Publishers, 2007), 10; Stark, Rodney, *The Rise of Christianity: How the Obscure, Marginal Jesus Movement Became the Dominant Religious Force in the Western World in a Few Centuries* (San Francisco: HarperSanFrancisco, 1997), 6.

6 Stark, *The Rise of Christianity*, 8–9.

7 Witherington, 52.

8 Witherington, 56.

9 See Robinson, John A. T., *Redating the New Testament* (London: SCM, 1976). For a good overview of Robinson's argument, see McKechnie, Paul, *The First Christian Centuries* (Leicester: Apollos, 2001), 28–30.

10 On Jesus' predictions of the fall of the temple, see Page, Nick, *The Longest Week: The Truth About Jesus' Last Days* (London: Hodder & Stoughton, 2009), 128–130; Wright, N. T., *Jesus and the Victory of God* (London: SPCK, 1996), 348–349.

11 Wedderburn, A. J. M., *A History of the First Christians* (London: T. & T. Clark, 2004), 15.

12 Marshall, I. Howard, *The Acts of the Apostles: An Introduction and Commentary* (Leicester: IVP, 1980), 200.

13 See Neil, William, *Acts: Based on the Revised Standard Version* (Grand Rapids: Eerdmans, 1981), 70–71; Witherington, 65–68.

14 See *Martyrdom of Polycarp* 11, in Holmes, Michael W., *The Apostolic Fathers: Greek Texts and English Translations* (Grand Rapids: Baker Academic, 2007), 317.

15 E.g. Acts 1.2, 15; 2.47; 4.32; 6.1; 9.31, 32.

16 Tertullian, *Against Marcion*, 4.8; Babylonian Talmud, *Ta'anit* 27b, in McKechnie, *The First Christian Centuries*.

17 Quoted in Kreider, *The Change of Conversion and the Origin of Christendom*, xvii.

18 Chrysostom, *Homily on Philemon*.

I. JERUSALEM AD 33

1 Exod. 16.29; Bock, 75.

2 Justin, *Apology*, 1.50; Witherington, 112.

3 Bruce, F. F., *Commentary on the Book of the Acts: The English Text* (London: Marshall, Morgan & Scott, 1954), 39.

4 Epiphanius of Salamis, quoted in Bauckham, Richard, *The Book of Acts in Its Palestinian Setting* (Carlisle: Paternoster Press, 1995), 307.

5 Bauckham, *The Book of Acts in Its Palestinian Setting*, 313–315.

6 Barrett, C. K., *A Critical and Exegetical Commentary on the Acts of the Apostles* (Edinburgh: T. & T. Clark, 1994), 89.

7 On Jesus' family, see Page, Nick, *The Wrong Messiah: The Real Story of Jesus of Nazareth* (London: Hodder & Stoughton, 2011), 45–48.

8 m.Yoma 4.1.

9 Fernando, Ajith, *Acts* (Grand Rapids: Zondervan, 1998), 79.

10 *Hist. Eccl.*, 3.39, in Eusebius, *The Ecclesiastical History and the Martyrs of Palestine*, trans. Hugh Jackson Lawlor and John Ernest Leonard Oulton (London: SPCK, 1927), 1.100, 2.115.

11 Depending, obviously, on whether you think the author of the letters and the Gospel was John, son of Zebedee. I don't, personally.

12 b.Shab. 88b and Philo Decal. 46, in Witherington, 131.

13 For arguments on dating of the crucifixion, see Page, *The Longest Week*, 9–12.

14 Fitzmyer, 234–235. See 11 QT in DSS 196–197.

15 Bruce, F. F., *The Acts of the Apostles: The Greek Text with Introduction and Commentary* (London: Tyndale Press, 1952), 81.

16 See Spencer, F. Scott, *Portrait of Philip in Acts* (Sheffield: JSOT, 1992), 35.

17 Witherington, 135.

18 Bock, 158.

19 Bock, 159.

20 Jeremias, Joachim, *Jerusalem in the Time of Jesus: An Investigation into Economic and Social Conditions during the New Testament Period* (London: SCM, 1974), 161.

21 *Antiquities*, 13.297–298; 18.16–17.

22 Gaechter, P., 'The Hatred of the House of Annas', *Theological Studies* 8. 1947, 7.

23 See Gaechter, 'The Hatred of the House of Annas', 11–12.

24 Notley, R. Steven and Anson F. Rainey, *Carta's New Century Handbook and Atlas of the Bible* (Jerusalem: Carta, 2007), 235.

25 Page, *The Longest Week*, 106ff.

26 Data based on Gaechter, 'The Hatred of the House of Annas', 34.

27 Bock, 195.

28 1QS 6.19–22 in DSS, 106

29 Dunn, James D. G., *Beginning from Jerusalem* (Grand Rapids: Eerdmans, 2008), 182.

30 Bock, 215.

31 Bock, 221.

32 See 1 QS 6, in DSS, 106.

33 See Derrett, quoted in Witherington, 217.

34 For a list of the healings in Acts, see Kelsey, Morton T., *Healing and Christianity: In Ancient Thought and Modern Times* (London: SCM Press, 1973).

35 Hieronymus, *Vita Hilarionis* 8.8f., quoted in MacMullen, Ramsay, *Christianizing the Roman Empire* (New Haven: Yale University Press, 1984), 28.

36 MacMullen, *Christianizing the Roman Empire*, 32.

37 Tertullian, in Kreider, *The Change of Conversion and the Origin of Christendom*, 16.

38 Tertullian, in Kreider, *The Change of Conversion and the Origin of Christendom*, 16; Origen, *Contra Celsus*, 1.6.

39 Justin, *Second Apology*, 6.

40 Tertullian, *To Scapula*, 4.

41 Theophilus of Antioch, *To Autolycus*, 1.13.

42 See Irenaeus, *Against Heresies*, 2.31.2 and 2.32.4.

43 Schwartz, in Bauckham, *The Book of Acts in Its Palestinian Setting*, 409.

44 m.Sota 9.15 and m.Avot 4.11, in Neusner, Jacob, *The Mishnah: A New Translation* (New Haven: Yale University Press, Accordance electronic edition, 1988). See Witherington, 233.

45 See *Antiquities*, 18.23; 20.97.

46 Gaechter, 'The Hatred of the House of Annas', 16.

47 Hengel, Martin, *Between Jesus and Paul: Studies in the Earliest History of Christianity* (London: SCM, 1983), 4–6; Slee, Michelle, *The Church in Antioch in the First Century* CE (London: T. & T. Clark, 1987), 13; Witherington, 240ff.

48 Hengel, *Between Jesus and Paul*, 9.

49 Hengel, *Between Jesus and Paul*, 11.

50 Jeremias, *Jerusalem in the Time of Jesus*, 132.

51 Witherington, 211.

52 See, for example, Luke 7.11–17; 18.1–8; 20.47; 21.1–4.

53 See Spencer, *Portrait of Philip in Acts*, 196. The NRSV, NIV and NET add a 'who', which is not in the Greek text.

54 *Antiquities*, 20.8.8.

55 Gaius, *Institutes*, 1.19 in Knapp, Robert, *Invisible Romans* (London: Profile Books, 2011), 177.

56 Hengel, *Between Jesus and Paul*, 17–18; Page, *The Longest Week*, 102; Barnett, Paul, *The Birth of Christianity: The First Twenty Years* (Grand Rapids: Eerdmans, 2005), 20.

57 Shedd, Ephraim C., 'Stephen's Defense before the Sanhedrin', *The Biblical World* 13(2). 1899, 97.

58 Jackson, F. J. Foakes, 'Stephen's Speech in Acts', *Journal of Biblical Literature* 49(3). 1930, 234.

59 Even if it was his successors, they were still from the House of Hanin: Jonathan son of Ananus and Theophilus son of Ananus. The next one, Simon Cantheras, may also be from the family of Caiaphas. It has been suggested he was Caiaphas's son. Regev, Eyal, 'Temple Concerns and High-Priestly Prosecutions from Peter to James: Between Narrative and History', *New Testament Studies* 56. 2009, 85 n. 73.

60 Hengel, *Between Jesus and Paul*, 11.

61 Sanh. 6.3–4, in Brown, S. Kent, 'Jewish and Gnostic Elements in the Second Apocalypse of James', *Novum Testamentum* 17(3). 1975, 229.

62 Spencer, *Portrait of Philip in Acts*, 192.

2. SAMARIA AD 34

1 Ogg, George, *The Chronology of the Life of Paul* (London: Epworth Press, 1968), 5.

2 Pseudo-Chrysostom, cited in Ogg, *The Chronology of the Life of Paul*, 1.

3 Ogg, *The Chronology of the Life of Paul*, 1; Murphy-O'Connor, J., *Jesus and Paul: Parallel Lives* (Collegeville: Liturgical Press, 2007), 16.

4 *War,* 2.68.

5 Murphy-O'Connor, *Jesus and Paul: Parallel Lives*, 19.

6 *War,* 4.84, in Josephus, Flavius, *The Jewish War* (Harmondsworth: Penguin, 1981).

7 Murphy-O'Connor, *Jesus and Paul: Parallel Lives*, 20.

8 Grant, Michael, *Saint Paul* (London: Phoenix, 2000), 13.

9 Ferguson, Everett, *Backgrounds of Early Christianity* (Grand Rapids: Eerdmans, 2003), 60–61.

10 Philo, *Legatio ad Gaium* 155, quoted in Murphy-O'Connor, *Jesus and Paul: Parallel Lives*, 19.

11 See 'Tarsus', in ABD, 6:334.

12 Witherington, 681.

13 Fitzmyer, 704; Witherington, 668.

14 Orr, William F. and James Arthur Walther, *I Corinthians: A New Translation* (Garden City: Doubleday, 1976), 5.

15 Megillah 21a, in Aberbach, M., 'The Change from a Standing to a Sitting Posture by Students after the Death of Rabban Gamaliel', *The Jewish Quarterly Review*, 52(2). 1961, 168.

16 m.Aboth 1.17, in Murphy-O'Connor, *Jesus and Paul: Parallel Lives*, 51.

17 Certainly later traditions muddled the two. Papias records that Philip the apostle (AD 60–130) lived in Hierapolis with his daughters; Eusebius, *Hist. Eccl.*, 3.39.8–10. It's not unlikely that Philip the apostle ended up in Hierapolis with his family, but the tradition about the daughters emanates from Philip the deacon. Polycrates said that he had two aged virgin daughters and another of his daughters was buried at Ephesus (Eusebius, *Hist. Eccl.*, 3.31.3). Eusebius certainly gets them all muddled up. See 'Philip (Person)', ABD, 5.311–312.

18 Page, *The Wrong Messiah*, 98–99.

19 Gempf, Conrad H. and David W. J. Gill, *The Book of Acts in Its Graeco-Roman Setting* (Grand Rapids: Eerdmans, 1994), 272. Against this, see Bruce, F. F., *The Book of Acts* (Grand Rapids: Eerdmans, 1988), 165; Barrett, *A Critical and Exegetical Commentary on the Acts of the Apostles*, 1.402–403.

20 *Didache*, 3.4.

21 Bock, 331.

22 Bock, 326; Irenaeus, *Against Heretics*, 1.23–27.

23 Hippolytus, *Refutations*, 6.2, 4–15; see McKechnie, *The First Christian Centuries*, 46–47.

24 Rufinus, *Eccl. Hist.*, 2.28–1034.

25 Page, Nick, *The One-Stop Bible Atlas* (Oxford: Lion Hudson, 2010), 103.

26 Herodotus, *The Histories* (London: Penguin Books, 1972), 211.

27 Diodorus Siculus, quoted in Spencer, *Portrait of Philip in Acts*, 150.

28 Esler, Philip Francis, *Community and Gospel in Luke-Acts: The Social and Political Motivations of Lucan Theology* (Cambridge: Cambridge University Press, 1987), 156.

29 Esler, *Community and Gospel in Luke-Acts*, 155.

30 Caner, Daniel F., 'The Practice and Prohibition of Self-Castration in Early Christianity', *Vigiliae Christianae* 51(4). 1997, 398.

31 *Antiquities*, 4.290–291.

32 Philo, *Spec. Leg.*, 1.324–325, in Spencer, *Portrait of Philip in Acts*, 169.

33 Caner, 'The Practice and Prohibition of Self-Castration in Early Christianity', 398–399.

34 Spencer, *Portrait of Philip in Acts*, n. 4, 167.

35 Kuefler, Mathew, *The Manly Eunuch: Masculinity, Gender Ambiguity, and Christian Ideology in Late Antiquity*, (London: University of Chicago Press, 2001), 246–247.

36 Kuefler, *The Manly Eunuch*, 249.

37 Orr and Walther, *I Corinthians: A New Translation*, 5.

38 Fitzmyer, 423.

39 See, for example, 1QS 9.17–18; 10.21, in DSS, 111, 114. For more examples, see Fitzmyer, 424.

40 1QS 8.14–15, in DSS, 109.

41 On this transmission, see McCasland, S. Vernon, 'The Way', *Journal of Biblical Literature* 77(3). 1958.

42 Bishop, Eric. F. F., 'The Great North Road', *Theology Today* 4(3). 1947.

43 For the arguments about the different forms of the verb 'to hear', see Witherington, 312; and Orr and Walther, *I Corinthians: A New Translation*, 57.

44 On all this, see 'ἐκτρομά', BDAG, 311. See 'ἐκτρομα G1765 (*ektrōma*), miscarriage', in 'Birth, Beget, Bear, Become, Miscarriage, Regeneration, Well–born', NIDNTT, 1.182–184.

45 Masterman, E. W. G., 'Damascus, the Oldest City in the World', *The Biblical World* 12(2). 1898, 72–73; Meinardus, Otto F., 'The Site of the Apostle Paul's Conversion at Kaukab', *The Biblical Archaeologist* 44(1). 1981, 57.

3. SYRIA AD 35–37

1 See Hemer, Colin J., 'Observations on Pauline Chronology', in *Pauline Studies: Essays Presented to Professor F. F. Bruce on his 70th Birthday* (Exeter: Paternoster, 1980), 13.

2 See Riesner, Rainer, *Paul's Early Period: Chronology, Mission Strategy, Theology* (Grand Rapids: Eerdmans, 1998), 64–66.

3 Barnett, *The Birth of Christianity*, 26.

4 *Antiquities*, 16.271–284.

5 Tacitus, *Annals*, 6.27, 32.

6 Campbell, Douglas A., 'An Anchor for Pauline Chronology: Paul's Flight from "The Ethnarch of King Aretas" (2 Corinthians 11:32–33)', *Journal of Biblical Literature* 121(2). 2002, 288 n.28.

7 Campbell, 'An Anchor for Pauline Chronology', 288.

8 Riesner, *Paul's Early Period*, 85–87.

9 Marshall, *The Acts of the Apostles*, 178.

10 Tertullian, *To His Wife*, II, iv. in ANF 4.

11 Milavec, Aaron, *The Didache: Text, Translation, Analysis, and Commentary* (Collegeville: Liturgical Press, 2004), 57.

12 Marshall, *The Acts of the Apostles*, 180.

13 See 'Leather in Antiquity', in Forbes, R. J., *Studies in Ancient Technology Vol. 5* (Leiden: Brill, 1966), 38–39.

14 m. B. Bat. 2.9.

15 m. Ketuboth 7.10, in Danby, Herbert, *The Mishnah, Translated from the Hebrew* (London: Oxford University Press, 1933), 255.

16 Appian, *Civil Wars*, 1.100.

17 Marshall, *The Acts of the Apostles*, 183.

18 Ps. 55.17; Dan. 6.10. See Marshall, *The Acts of the Apostles*, 185.

19 Barrett, *A Critical and Exegetical Commentary on the Acts of the Apostles*, 509; Bock, 389.

20 Slee, *The Church in Antioch in the First Century* CE, 17.

21 Jos. Asen. 7.1 and 8.5–7, in Slee, *The Church in Antioch in the First Century* CE, 18.

22 Hopkins, Keith, *A World Full of Gods: Pagans, Jews and Christians in the Roman Empire* (London: Phoenix, 2000), 20–21.

23 Slee, *The Church in Antioch in the First Century* CE, 20.

24 'The Damascus Document', CD 11.14–15, in DSS, 142.

25 Bock, 406. The Greek word is *diekrinontō*.

26 Bainton, Roland H., 'The Early Church and War', *The Harvard Theological Review* 39(3). 1946, 201.

27 Justin, *Trypho*, 110, in Bainton, 'The Early Church and War', 196.

28 Clement, *Protrepticus*, 11, in Bainton, 'The Early Church and War', 196.

29 Tertullian, *De Idolotria*, 19, in Kreider, Alan, 'Military Service in the Church Orders', *The Journal of Religious Ethics* 31(3). 2003, 415.

30 Kreider, 'Military Service in the Church Orders', 419.

31 Bainton, 'The Early Church and War', 193.

32 Sulpicius Severus, *Vita Martini*, 4.

33 The legion was recruited in the province of Melitene in southern Armenia. Later, when a persecuting emperor attempted to enforce idolatry in the region, Armenian Christians took up arms and defeated him. Perhaps the region had a different theology. See Bainton, 'The Early Church and War', 194; Kreider, 'Military Service in the Church Orders', 423.

34 Bainton, 'The Early Church and War', 192. See Tertullian, *Apologeticus*, 37 and *De Corona Militis*, 11.

35 On administrative jobs, see Kreider, 'Military Service in the Church Orders', 425.

36 Bainton, 'The Early Church and War', 198.

37 Athenagoras, *Legatio,* 35, in Kreider, 'Military Service in the Church Orders', 424.

38 Origen, *Contra Celsus,* VIII, 68–69, in Bainton, 'The Early Church and War', 191.

39 Origen, *Contra Celsus,* 8.73, in Bainton, 'The Early Church and War', 193.

40 Bainton, 'The Early Church and War', 205.

41 Tertullian, *Apology,* 38.

42 Kreider, 'Military Service in the Church Orders', 425. *Apostolic Tradition,* 16, Sahidic version quoted in Kreider, 'Military Service in the Church Orders', 419.

43 The first Christian bishop to hold the post of civil magistrate and to employ a bodyguard was Paul of Samosata, in Palmyra in AD 278. Bainton, 'The Early Church and War', 194.

44 Kreider, 'Military Service in the Church Orders', 431.

4. ANTIOCH AD 38–47

1 Slee, *The Church in Antioch in the First Century* CE, 2.

2 Slee, *The Church in Antioch in the First Century* CE, 2.

3 *War,* 7.45.

4 *War,* 3.29.

5 Fitzmyer, 475.

6 Witherington, 366.

7 See Fitzmyer, 476. Also Witherington, 369; Bock, 414.

8 Bock, 413.

9 Green, *Christianity in Rome in the First Three Centuries,* 3.

10 On the cities' population and density, see Stark, Rodney, *Cities of God: The Real Story of How Christianity Became an Urban Movement and Conquered Rome* (New York: HarperOne, 2007), 26ff.

11 Stark, *Cities of God,* 60.

12 Carcopino, Jerome, *Daily Life in Ancient Rome* (London: Penguin, 1962), 57.

13 Carcopino, *Daily Life in Ancient Rome,* 60.

14 Petronius, 79.

15 Johnson, Paul, quoted in Stark, *Cities of God,* 30.

16 Stark, *The Rise of Christianity,* 76.

17 Eusebius, in Stark, *The Rise of Christianity,* 77.

18 Stark, *The Rise of Christianity,* 85–86.

19 Dionysius, *Letter 12 to the Alexandrians.*

20 Tertullian, *Apology,* 39.

21 Quoted in Stark, *The Rise of Christianity,* 84.

22 Stark, *The Rise of Christianity,* 97.

23 Quoted in Stark, *The Rise of Christianity,* 97–98.

24 Quoted in Harris, William V., 'The Theoretical Possibility of Extensive Infanticide in the Graeco-Roman World', *The Classical Quarterly,* 32(1). 1982, 116.

25 Tertullian, *Apology,* 15.

26 Mazower, Mark, *Salonica, City of Ghosts: Christians, Muslims and Jews 1430–1950* (London: Harper Perennial, 2005), 12.

27 Fitzmyer, 475.

28 Cole, Alan, *Mark: An Introduction and Commentary* (Leicester: IVP, 1961), 38.

29 Eph. 11.2; Mag. 4.1; 10.1, 3; Tral. 6.1; Rom. 3.2–3; Phila. 6.1; Poly. 7.3; *Didache*, 12.4. In later writings from the second century, *The Martyrdom of Polycarp* (after c. 167) uses it three times (MPoly. 3.2; 10.1; 12.1–2) and the *Epistle to Diognetus* (c. 150–225) three times. (Diog. 1.1; 2.6, 10; 4.6–5.1; 6.1–9).

30 Witherington, 370.

31 Hengel, Martin, *Paul Between Damascus and Antioch: The Unknown Years* (London: SCM, 1997), 179.

32 Hengel, *Paul Between Damascus and Antioch*, 156; Bruce, *Commentary on the Book of the Acts: The English Text*, 240–241; Barnett, *The Birth of Christianity*, 17–18.

33 Osborne, Robert E., 'St Paul's Silent Years', *Journal of Biblical Literature* 84(1). March 1965, 60–61.

34 Witherington, 370.

35 *Didache*, 10.7.

36 O'Loughlin, Thomas, *The Didache: A Window on the Earliest Christians* (London: SPCK, 2010), 101.

37 Milavec, *The Didache: Text, Translation, Analysis, and Commentary*, 70.

38 It is recorded as reaching 7/8 drachmae per artaba of wheat. Hemer, Colin J., 'Observations on Pauline Chronology', in *Pauline Studies: Essays Presented to Professor F. F. Bruce on his 70th Birthday*, 5.

39 Pliny, *Natural History*, 5.10.58.

40 Hemer, Colin J., 'Observations on Pauline Chronology', 5; Ogg, *The Chronology of the Life of Paul*, 52–53; Gempf and Gill, *The Book of Acts in Its Graeco-Roman Setting*, 63–64.

41 Finegan, Jack, *Handbook of Biblical Chronology: Principles of Time Reckoning in the Ancient World and Problems of Chronology in the Bible* (Peabody: Hendrickson Publishers, 1998), 372.

42 *Antiquities*, 19.6, 2.

43 *Antiquities*, 19.328–330.

44 *Antiquities*, 19.335–337.

45 Gaechter, 'The Hatred of the House of Annas', 29; Ogg, *The Chronology of the Life of Paul*, 42.

46 Ogg, *The Chronology of the Life of Paul*, 42.

47 *Antiquities*, 18.195–200; Finegan, *Handbook of Biblical Chronology*, 373.

48 Ogg, *The Chronology of the Life of Paul*, 40.

49 Orr and Walther, *I Corinthians: A New Translation*, 8.

50 For an overview of such views, see Ogg, *The Chronology of the Life of Paul*, 46ff.

51 Longenecker, Richard N., *Galatians* (Dallas: Word Books, 1990), lxxvii–lxxviii.

52 Orr and Walther, *I Corinthians: A New Translation*, 9.

53 Longenecker, *Galatians*, lxxx–lxxxii.

54 Bruce, F. F., *The Pauline Circle* (Exeter: Paternoster Press, 1985), 59.

55 Longenecker, *Galatians*, 52.

56 Orr and Walther, *I Corinthians: A New Translation*, 11.

5. GALATIA AD 48–49

1 Gempf and Gill, *The Book of Acts in Its Graeco-Roman Setting*, 280.

2 Typically, classical scholars are more prone to identify this senator – at an early stage of his career – with the one mentioned in Acts, while biblical scholars are more cautious. See Gempf and Gill, *The Book of Acts in Its Graeco-Roman Setting*, 285ff.; Witherington, 400.

3 Gempf and Gill, *The Book of Acts in Its Graeco-Roman Setting*, 287.

4 Witherington, 401.

5 *Antiquities*, 20.142.

6 Juvenal, *Satires*, 2.6.

7 Orr and Walther, *I Corinthians: A New Translation*, 11.

8 Witherington, 404.

9 Gempf and Gill, *The Book of Acts in Its Graeco-Roman Setting*, 287.

10 Gempf and Gill, *The Book of Acts in Its Graeco-Roman Setting*, 384.

11 Gempf and Gill, *The Book of Acts in Its Graeco-Roman Setting*, 387.

12 Gempf and Gill, *The Book of Acts in Its Graeco-Roman Setting*, 395.

13 It is found in the *Theologoumena* by Ascplepias of Mendes. In the early second century, Suetonius included the story in a section called 'The Deified Augustus' in his *Lives of the Caesars*, 94.4.

14 Crossan, John Dominic, *God and Empire: Jesus Against Rome, Then and Now* (San Francisco: HarperSanFrancisco, 2007), 108.

15 MacMullen, *Christianizing the Roman Empire*, 15.

16 Benko, Stephen, *Pagan Rome and the Early Christians* (Bloomington: Indiana University Press, 1984), 10.

17 Benko, *Pagan Rome and the Early Christians*, 4.

18 See 'Ἀπόστολος', BDAG, 122.

19 Rom. 1:1; 11:13; 1 Cor. 1:1; 9:1f.; 15:9; 2 Cor. 1:1; Gal. 1:1; Eph. 1:1; Col. 1:1; 1 Tim. 1:1; 2:7; 2 Tim. 1:1; Titus 1:1.

20 *Didache*, 11.4.

21 Iamblichus's *De Mysteriis Aegyptiorum* describes Hermes as 'the god who leads in speaking'.

22 Witherington, 421–22.

23 Gempf and Gill, *The Book of Acts in Its Graeco-Roman Setting*, 393; see 'Lycaonia (Place)', ABD, 5:420.

24 Witherington, 422.

25 Eusebius, *The Ecclesiastical History and the Martyrs of Palestine*, II, 79–80.

26 *Acts of Paul and Thecla*, in ANF 8.

27 See Van Elderen, Bastian, 'Some Archaeological Observations on Paul's First Missionary Journey', in W. Ward Gasque and Ralph P. Martin (eds), *Apostolic History and the Gospel. Biblical and Historical Essays Presented to F. F. Bruce* (Exeter: Paternoster Press, 1970), 158–159.

28 Longenecker, *Galatians*, 182–183.

29 Orr and Walther, *I Corinthians: A New Translation*, 14.

30 Orr and Walther, *I Corinthians: A New Translation*, 13.

31 Slee, *The Church in Antioch in the First Century* CE, 34.

32 See Jewett, Robert, 'The Agitators and the Galatian Congregation', *New Testament Studies* 17. 1971, 206.

33 Holmes, *The Apostolic Fathers: Greek Texts and English Translations*, 357; O'Loughlin, *The Didache: A Window on the Earliest Christians*, 85.

34 Crossan, *God and Empire*, 170.

35 *Didache*, 10.1, in O'Loughlin, *The Didache: A Window on the Earliest Christians*, 92.

36 *Didache*, 14.1.

37 O'Loughlin, *The Didache: A Window on the Earliest Christians*, 99.

38 *Didache*, 10.5; Holmes, *The Apostolic Fathers: Greek Texts and English Translations*, 361.

39 O'Loughlin, *The Didache: A Window on the Earliest Christians*, 97.

40 O'Loughlin, *The Didache: A Window on the Earliest Christians*, 94.

41 *Didache*, 14.1; Holmes, *The Apostolic Fathers: Greek Texts and English Translations*, 365.

42 *Didache*, 14.2.

43 Theodore of Mopsuesta, *Baptismal Homily*, in Kreider, Alan, *Worship and Evangelism in Pre-Christendom* (Cambridge: Grove Books, 1995), 29.

44 Irenaeus of Lyons, in Grant, Robert M., *Second-Century Christianity: A Collection of Fragments* (Louisville; London: Westminster John Knox Press, 2003), 50.

45 See the map in Bauckham, *The Book of Acts in Its Palestinian Setting*, 420.

46 Skarsaune, Oskar and Reidar Hvalvik, *Jewish Believers in Jesus: The Early Centuries* (Peabody: Hendrickson, 2007), 58–59.

47 *Antiquities*, 20.200–201.

48 Bauckham, *The Book of Acts in Its Palestinian Setting*, 436.

49 Bauckham, *The Book of Acts in Its Palestinian Setting*, 440.

50 From Jerome, *De viris illustribus*, in Throckmorton, Burton Hamilton, *Gospel Parallels: A Synopsis of the First Three Gospels with Alternative Readings from the Manuscripts and Noncanonical Parallels* (Nashville: Nelson, 1979). The earliest quotations from the Gospel of Hebrews come from the writings of people who lived in Alexandria, so it probably originated among the Jewish Christians in that region. It's an early gospel – certainly it was known to Papias who died around AD 130. A copy was recorded as being at Caesarea, but it is long lost.

51 Eusebius, *Hist. Eccl.*, 1.2–3, in Eusebius, *The Ecclesiastical History and the Martyrs of Palestine*, 35.

52 Eusebius *Hist. Eccl.*, 2.23.6.

53 See Page, *The Wrong Messiah*, 47–48.

54 Skarsaune and Hvalvik, *Jewish Believers in Jesus: The Early Centuries*, 68; McKechnie, *The First Christian Centuries*, 88–89; Bauckham, Richard, *Jude and the Relatives of Jesus in the Early Church* (Edinburgh: T. & T. Clark, 1990), 116.

55 Fitzmyer, 543; Bock, 486.

56 m.Aboth 3.5, cited in Fitzmyer, 548.

57 There is also a rather convoluted suggestion that the Simeon referred to by Jacob is not Simon Peter, but Simeon called Niger – one of the emissaries sent by the Antioch church. But, as Fitzmyer himself admits, Simeon is 'an apt way for an Aramaic-speaking Jewish Christian like James to refer to Peter'. See Fitzmyer, 552–554.

58 Bock, 505.

59 Bock, 506.

60 Gregory of Nyssa, *Vita Greg. Thaumaturg*, quoted in Witherington, 462.

61 See Gal. 4 3, 9; 1 Cor. 8 8; Col. 2.20–23. See Parker, Pierson. 'Once More, Acts and Galatians', *Journal of Biblical Literature* 86(2). June 1967, 176–177.

62 *Didache*, 6.2–3, in Holmes, *The Apostolic Fathers: Greek Texts and English Translations*, 353–354.

63 Irenaeus, *Against Heretics*, 1.26, in ANF 1.

64 Skarsaune and Hvalvik, *Jewish Believers in Jesus: The Early Centuries*, 90.

6. MACEDONIA AD 49–50

1 Hengel, *Between Jesus and Paul*, 3.

2 m.Kidd 3.12. See Fitzmyer, 575.

3 Bruce, *The Pauline Circle*, 31.

4 Witherington, 478.

5 Riesner, *Paul's Early Period*, 290.

6 Riesner, *Paul's Early Period*, 245.

7 Quoted in Riesner, *Paul's Early Period*, 248.

8 LXX Isa. 66.19, in Pietersma, Albert and Benjamin G. Wright, *A New English Translation of the Septuagint* (New York: Oxford University Press, 2007).

9 *Antiquities*, 1.127.

10 *Antiquities*, 1.144.

11 Y.Meg 71b; b.Yoma 10a.

12 *Antiquities*, 13.421, 18.97.

13 *Antiquities*, 1.127.

14 b.Yoma 10a.

15 All this information is taken from the brilliant, detailed exegesis of this text in Riesner, *Paul's Early Period*, 250–253.

16 Witherington, 480.

17 Bruce, F. F., *The Acts of the Apostles: The Greek Text with Introduction and Commentary* (London: Tyndale Press, 1952), 311.

18 Ramsay, William Mitchell, *St Paul the Traveller and the Roman Citizen* (London: Hodder & Stoughton, 1908), 202.

19 For an overview of this largely debunked theory, see Fitzmyer, 101–102.

20 Witherington, 54.

21 Lewis, Naphtali and Meyer Reinhold, *Roman Civilization: The Empire* (New York: Columbia University Press, 1990), 170.

22 Fitzmyer, Joseph A., *The Gospel According to Luke* (New York; London: Doubleday, 1983), 38–39.

23 Witherington, 485.

24 Landels, John G., *Engineering in the Ancient World* (London: Constable, 2000), 156.

25 Pliny, *Nat. Hist.*, 4.23.

26 Davies, Paul E., 'The Macedonian Scene of Paul's Journeys', *The Biblical Archaeologist* 26(3), 92–93.

27 McRay, John, 'Archaeology and the Book of Acts', *Criswell Theological Review* 5(1). 1990, 75.

28 Ferguson, *Backgrounds of Early Christianity*, 88.

29 Nebreda, Sergio Rosell, *Christ Identity: A Social-Scientific Reading of Philippians 2.5–11* (Göttingen: Vandenhoeck & Ruprecht, 2011), 122.

30 Nebreda, *Christ Identity*, 125.

31 Appian, quoted in Nebreda, *Christ Identity*, 127.

32 Seneca, *Ira III*, 43.5. 'Bowersock, Augustus 69 cites Gellius Noc att 16.13.9 who

refers to the colonies as quasi effigies parvae simulacraque of Rome.' Nebreda, *Christ Identity*, 150 n. 180.

33 Cicero, *Verrine Orations*, 2.5.150, quoted in Nebreda, *Christ Identity*, 154–155.

34 Witherington, 488.

35 Those who see this as an historical inaccuracy of Luke's are clutching at straws, really. He doesn't say it's the capital. See Witherington, 489.

36 Nebreda, *Christ Identity*, 128.

37 Witherington, 490.

38 Demosthenes 59.122 quoted in Ferguson, *Backgrounds of Early Christianity*, 77.

39 Ferguson, *Backgrounds of Early Christianity*, 78.

40 Quoted in Ferguson, *Backgrounds of Early Christianity*, 79.

41 See 'πύθων', BDAG, 896.

42 Plutarch, *De defectu oraculorum*, 9.

43 Bock, 537.

44 Bock, 539.

45 Bainton, 'The Early Church and War', 205.

46 Cyprian, *Letter 1 to Donatus*, 3–4, in Kreider, *The Change of Conversion and the Origin of Christendom*, 9.

47 Kreider, *The Change of Conversion and the Origin of Christendom*, 9.

48 Witherington, 499.

49 Nebreda, *Christ Identity*, 182.

50 Diodorus Siculus, 31.9.2. Tertullian, *To the Martyrs*, 2, quoted in Bock, 539.

51 Witherington, 497.

52 Eusebius, *Martyrs of Palestine*, 4.14, in MacMullen, *Christianizing the Roman Empire*, 26.

53 Fitzmyer, 593.

54 Strabo, *Geography*, 7.7.21; *Palatine Anthology*, 4.228, both in Bock, 549.

55 Witherington, 504.

56 The WT tries to play down the status of the women by reducing them to the wives of prominent men. Priscilla's role in teaching Apollos is also omitted. Witherington, 506.

57 See Aristophanes, *Ranae*, 10.15. Theophrastus, *Char*, 4.2.

58 Fitzmyer, 596.

59 Bock, 551.

60 Benko, *Pagan Rome and the Early Christians*, 11.

61 Benko, *Pagan Rome and the Early Christians*, 13.

62 Minucius Felix, *Octavius*, 8–9, in ANF 4.

63 Harding, *Early Christian Life and Thought in Social Context* (London: Continuum, 2003), 233.

64 Philo, *Det.*, 34, in Winter, Bruce W., *After Paul Left Corinth: The Influence of Secular Ethics and Social Change* (Grand Rapids: Eerdmans, 2001), 188.

65 As outlined in Winter, *After Paul Left Corinth*, 188–189.

66 Ferguson, *Backgrounds of Early Christianity*, 67.

67 Juvenal, *Satires*, 5, in Harding, *Early Christian Life and Thought in Social Context*, 210.

68 Suetonius, *Claudius*, 25.4.

69 Drane, John W., 'Why Did Paul Write Romans?', in *Pauline Studies: Essays Presented to Professor F. F. Bruce on his 70th Birthday*, 216; Green, *Christianity in Rome in the First Three Centuries*, 26. For the alternative view, see Goodman, Martin, *Rome and Jerusalem: The Clash of Ancient Civilizations* (London: Penguin, 2008), 387. But Goodman agrees that it is the same event as detailed in Acts. And he places it in AD 49.

70 Orosius, *Adv. Paganos*, 7.6.15–16. See the detailed account in Lampe, *From Paul to Valentinus* (London: Continuum, 2003), 14ff.

71 Hemer, Colin J., *'Observations on Pauline Chronology'*, 8; Green, *Christianity in Rome in the First Three Centuries*, 26. Another historian, Dio Cassius, put it at the beginning of Claudius's reign, about AD 41; Dio Cassius, *Historia Romana*, 60.6.6. It is probable that Dio Cassius is actually talking about a different event. He says that the Jews were not invited back until the beginning of Nero's reign in AD 54. This is possible if it were AD 49, but not likely for the entire length of Claudius's reign.

72 Dunn, *Beginning from Jerusalem*, 681.

73 Bruce, F. F., *Paul: Apostle of the Free Spirit* (Exeter: Paternoster Press, 1977), 235.

7. ACHAIA AD 51–52

1 Gempf and Gill, *The Book of Acts in Its Graeco-Roman Setting*, 437–438.

2 Horace, *Epist*, 2.2.81, in Fitzmyer, 601. Pliny, *Natural History*, 2.45.117–118 in Lewis, *Roman Civilization: The Empire*, 211.

3 Gempf and Gill, *The Book of Acts in Its Graeco-Roman Setting*, 444–445.

4 Gempf and Gill, *The Book of Acts in Its Graeco-Roman Setting*, 445.

5 Pausanias 1.14; Philostratus, *Vita Ap. Ty.*, 6.3.5.

6 Aeschylus, *Eumenides*, 647–648, quoted in Fitzmyer, 612.

7 Murphy-O'Connor, Jerome, 'The Corinth that Saint Paul Saw', *The Biblical Archaeologist* 47(3). 1984, 147.

8 Murphy-O'Connor, 'The Corinth that Saint Paul Saw', 148.

9 McRay, 'Archaeology and the Book of Acts', 81.

10 McRay, 'Archaeology and the Book of Acts', 81–82.

11 McRay, 'Archaeology and the Book of Acts', 81.

12 Gempf and Gill, *The Book of Acts in Its Graeco-Roman Setting*, 452.

13 Bruce, *The Pauline Circle*, 45.

14 Keller, Marie Noel, *Priscilla and Aquila: Paul's Co-workers in Christ Jesus* (Collegeville: Liturgical Press, 2010, Kindle edition), Loc. 155.

15 See Acts 11.30; 12.25; 13.2–7, then Acts 13.9–12, 43; 14.20; 15.2, 22, 35.

16 Chrysostom, *Homilies on the Second Epistle of Paul to Timothy*, Homily X.

17 Juvenal, 3.61ff., in Lampe, *From Paul to Valentinus*, 191.

18 Murphy-O'Connor, 'The Corinth that Saint Paul Saw', 156–157; Lampe, *From Paul to Valentinus*, 192.

19 Lampe, *From Paul to Valentinus*, 189.

20 Apuleius, Met. 9.24, in Lampe, *From Paul to Valentinus*, 192.

21 Lampe, *From Paul to Valentinus*, 187–188.

22 Keller, *Priscilla and Aquila: Paul's Co-workers in Christ Jesus*, Loc. 456.

23 Still, T. D., 'Did Paul Loathe Manual Labor? Revisiting the Work of Ronald F. Hock on the Apostle's Tentmaking and Social Class', *Journal of Biblical Literature* 124(4). 2006, 781.

24 2 Cor. 10.1; 11.7. See Furnish, Victor Paul, *II Corinthians* (Garden City: Doubleday, 1984), 507.

25 bQidd 30b, in Dunderberg, Ismo, Christopher Tuckett and Kari Syreeni (eds), *Fair Play: Diversity and Conflicts in Early Christianity: Essays in Honour of Heikki Raisanen* (Leiden: Brill, 2001), 355.

26 Hock, Ronald F., *The Social Context of Paul's Ministry: Tentmaking and Apostleship* (Philadelphia: Fortress Press, 1997), 67.

27 Barnett, *The Birth of Christianity*, 36.

28 Bainton, 'The Early Church and War', 203.

29 Tertullian, *De resurr. carn.*, 24.

30 Chrysostom, *Hom. 4 on 2 Thessalonians*, quoted in Bruce, F. F., *1 & 2 Thessalonians* (Waco: Word Books, 1982), 171.

31 Augustine, *City of God,* ch. 20, quoted in Bruce, *1 & 2 Thessalonians*, 175.

32 On Gallio, see Witherington, 551–552; Fitzmyer, 628; 'Gallio', in ABD 3.901.

33 Ogg, *The Chronology of the Life of Paul*, 107; Hemer, Colin J., 'Observations on Pauline Chronology', 6.

34 So Ogg, *The Chronology of the Life of Paul*, 109–110; Murphy-O'Connor, Jerome, 'Paul and Gallio', *Journal of Biblical Literature* 112(2). 1993; against this, or at least arguing that we cannot be that certain, see Slingerland, Dixon, 'Acts 18:1–18, the Gallio Inscription, and Absolute Pauline Chronology', *Journal of Biblical Literature* 110(3). 1991.

35 Seneca, *Letters*, 104.1, in Murphy-O'Connor, 'Paul and Gallio', 315.

36 Dio Cass. 61.20.1.

37 Marshall, *The Acts of the Apostles*, 300.

38 Witherington, 558.

8. EPHESUS AD 53–57

1 Strabo, Geog. 14.1.24, in Gempf and Gill, *The Book of Acts in Its Graeco-Roman Setting*, 306.

2 McRay, 'Archaeology and the Book of Acts', 80–81.

3 Gempf and Gill, *The Book of Acts in Its Graeco-Roman Setting*, 307.

4 Fitzmyer, 657.

5 Ferguson, *The Religions of the Roman Empire*, 21.

6 Fitzmyer, 657; Bruce, *The Acts of the Apostles: The Greek Text with Introduction and Commentary*, 363.

7 Ferguson, *The Religions of the Roman Empire*, 21.

8 Pausanias 4.31.8, in Witherington, 587.

9 Gempf and Gill, *The Book of Acts in Its Graeco-Roman Setting*, 309.

10 Murphy-O'Connor, Jerome, 'John the Baptist and Jesus: History and Hypotheses', *New Testament Studies* 36. 1990, 367.

11 John Chrysostom, *First Homily on the Greeting to Priscilla and Aquila,* in Keller, *Priscilla and Aquila: Paul's Co-workers in Christ Jesus*, Loc. 615.

12 Bruce, *The Acts of the Apostles: The Greek Text with Introduction and Commentary*, 356.

13 On Paul's arrival in summer/autumn AD 53, see Witherington, 84; Ogg argues that Paul *didn't* arrive in Ephesus until AD 54 and left in AD 57. Ogg, *The Chronology of the Life of Paul*, 134, 138. This seems too late and is conditioned by Ogg's desire to fit in a long visit to north Galatia.

14 Gempf and Gill, *The Book of Acts in Its Graeco-Roman Setting*, 316.

15 Walter Harrelson (ed.), *New Interpreter's Study Bible: NRSV with Apocrypha* (Nashville: Abingdon Press, 2003), 2061.

16 For an overview of these arguments, see Blomberg, Craig L., *From Pentecost to Patmos: Acts to Revelation: An Introduction and Survey* (Leicester: IVP, 2006), 205–208. He rightly points out that the question of how two letters got tacked together is difficult. But the argument that 2 Cor. 10 – 13 is a different letter is hardly less convincing than arguing that it is the same letter, only different.

17 Dunn, James, *Romans 9 – 16*, Word Biblical Commentary, New Testament, 38b (Nashville: Thomas Nelson, 1988), 910.

18 Ignatius, Romans 5.1.

19 Welborn, L. L., 'On the Discord in Corinth: 1 Corinthians 1 – 4 and Ancient Politics', *Journal of Biblical Literature* 106(1). 1987, 90–93.

20 Butterworth, Alex and Ray Laurence, *Pompeii: The Living City* (London: Weidenfeld & Nicolson, 2005), 95.

21 Winter, *After Paul Left Corinth*, 46.

22 Thompson, Cynthia L., 'Hairstyles, Head-Coverings, and St Paul: Portraits from Roman Corinth', *The Biblical Archaeologist* 51(2). 1988, 104.

23 Winter, *After Paul Left Corinth*, 122.

24 See 'γυνή, αικος', in BDAG.

25 Winter, *After Paul Left Corinth*, 128.

26 Winter, *After Paul Left Corinth*.

27 Tertullian, *On Veiling of Virgins*, 3.

28 Dio Chrysostom, *The Thirty-third, or First Tarsic, Discourse*, 48.

29 Tertullian, *On Veiling of Virgins*, 17; Thompson, 'Hairstyles, Head-Coverings, and St Paul: Portraits from Roman Corinth', 113.

30 See Orr and Walther, *I Corinthians: A New Translation*, 312–313.

31 Martial, Epigrams 1.20, 3.60, in Crossan, *God and Empire*, 169.

32 Pliny, *Letters*, 2.6.

33 Orr and Walther, *I Corinthians: A New Translation*, 269.

34 Sibylline Oracles, 2.319–324, in Crossan, *God and Empire*, 88.

35 Furnish, *II Corinthians*, 506; *Fair Play: Diversity and Conflicts in Early Christianity: Essays in Honour of Heikki Raisanen*, 365.

36 *Passing of Peregrinus*, 11–13, in Lucian of Samosata, *Lucian* (London: Heinemann, 1936), 5.13–15.

37 *Didache*, 11.4–7, in Holmes, *The Apostolic Fathers: Greek Texts and English Translations*, 363.

38 *Didache*, 12.5.

39 *Didache*, 11.8, 10, in Holmes, *The Apostolic Fathers: Greek Texts and English Translations*, 363.

40 *Didache*, 11.9, in Holmes, *The Apostolic Fathers: Greek Texts and English Translations*, 363.

41 *Didache*, 13.1–4.

42 'Gaius (Person)', ABD, 3:869.

43 'Aristarchus (Person)', ABD, 2:379–380.

44 See Kearsley, 'The Asiarchs', in Gempf and Gill, *The Book of Acts in Its Graeco-Roman Setting*, 368–371; Witherington, 585.

45 Bock, 610; Witherington, 595. For more detail, see Kearsley, 'The Asiarchs', in Gempf and Gill, *The Book of Acts in Its Graeco-Roman Setting*, 364–376.

46 Fitzmyer, 662.

47 There was a third-century tradition that Luke is referred to here. See Bruce, *The Pauline Circle*, 39.

48 Bruce, *The Acts of the Apostles: The Greek Text with Introduction and Commentary*, 369.

49 For an accessible overview of the issues, see Blomberg, *From Pentecost to Patmos: Acts to Revelation*, 343–344. Other letters which are often assumed to be pseudepigraphical are 2 Thessalonians, Colossians and Ephesians.

50 Tertullian, *Baptism*, 7.

51 Page, Nick, *God's Dangerous Book* (Milton Keynes: Authentic Publishing, 2011). On the issue of pseudepigraphy, see Witherington, Ben, *Letters and Homilies for Hellenized Christians* (Downers Grove; Nottingham: IVP Academic Apollos, 2006), 23ff.

52 See 'ἐπίσκοποσ', in BDAG.

53 *Didache*, 15.1–2.

54 *Didascalia Apostolorum*, 2.58, in Kreider, *The Change of Conversion and the Origin of Christendom*, 15.

55 On Paul travelling by ship, see Gempf and Gill, *The Book of Acts in Its Graeco-Roman Setting*, 439.

56 Quoted in Crossan, *God and Empire*, 21.

57 Crossan, *God and Empire*, 23.

58 Crossan, *God and Empire*, 173–174; Dunn, *Romans 9 – 16*, 894–895. Dunn writes, 'The assumption that it must be male is a striking indictment of male presumption regarding the character and structure of earliest Christianity.'

59 The note in the *ESV Study Bible* gives away their reasoning: 'Some have said that this verse proves that Junia was an apostle, and thus women can fill any church office.' Note to Rom. 16.7, *ESV Study Bible* (Wheaton: Crossway Bibles, 2008, Accordance electronic edition).

60 Dunn, *Romans 9 – 16*, 894.

61 See 'ἐπίσεμος' in BDAG.

62 See 'Gaius (Person)', ABD, 3.869.

63 Drane, John W., 'Why Did Paul Write Romans?', in *Pauline Studies: Essays Presented to Professor F. F. Bruce on his 70th Birthday*, 223.

64 Green, *Christianity in Rome in the First Three Centuries*, 29.

9. CAESAREA AD 57–59

1 See Hemer, Colin J., 'Observations on Pauline Chronology', 10–11.

2 Witherington, 609.

3 All these numbers could be used inclusively, making the stay there a little shorter. See Hemer, 'Observations on Pauline Chronology', 9.

4 Hemer, 'Observations on Pauline Chronology', 10.

5 Juvenal, *Satires*, 3, in Lewis, *Roman Civilization: The Empire*, 152–153.

6 The NRSV is the only translation I have found which translates it this way.

7 See Casson, Lionel, *Travel in the Ancient World* (London: Allen & Unwin, 1974), 149–162.

8 Casson, *Travel in the Ancient World*, 154.

9 Hemer, 'Observations on Pauline Chronology', 10.

10 'Mnason (Person)', ABD, 5:881–882.

11 Page, *The Longest Week*, 101–102.

12 Fitzmyer, 698.

13 Page, *The Longest Week*, 68.

14 *War*, 5.5.8 243–245.

15 *War*, 2.254, quoted in Goodman, *Rome and Jerusalem: The Clash of Ancient Civilizations*, 407.

16 Goodman, *Rome and Jerusalem: The Clash of Ancient Civilizations*, 408.

17 Cicero, *Verrine Orations*, 2.5.66.

18 Fitzmyer, 712; Dio Cassius, *Roman History*, 60.17.5–7.

19 *War*, 2.243; Antiquities, 20.131.

20 *War*, 2.426, 429, 441–442.

21 Regev, 'Temple Concerns and High-Priestly Prosecutions from Peter to James: Between Narrative and History', 85 n. 73.

22 Rapske, Brian, *The Book of Acts and Paul in Roman Custody* (Grand Rapids; Carlisle: W. B. Eerdmans; Paternoster Press, 1994), 154.

23 Fitzmyer, 733.

24 Suetonius, *Claudius*, 28.

25 *War*, 2.232–245; *Antiquities*, 15.118–136.

26 *Antiquities*, 20.177–178; *War*, 2.270; cf. *Life*, 13.

27 Suetonius, *Claudius*, 28.

28 Tacitus, *History*, 5.9, in Fitzmyer, 727.

29 Witherington, 78.

30 Rapske, *The Book of Acts and Paul in Roman Custody*, 168.

31 Witherington, 738.

32 Note that Gaius Caligula is tactfully omitted. Warmington, B. H., *Nero: Reality and Legend* (London: Chatto & Windus, 1970), 31.

33 Warmington, *Nero: Reality and Legend*, 36.

34 Tacitus, *Annals*, 14.48; 'Nero (Emperor)', ABD, 4:1,077.

35 Barrett, Anthony A., *Agrippina: Mother of Nero* (London: Routledge, 2002), 225–226.

36 Fitzmyer, 769.

37 Smith, James and Walter Edward Smith, *The Voyage and Shipwreck of St Paul: With Dissertations on the Life and Writings of St Luke, and the Ships and Navigation of the Ancients* (London: Longmans, Green, 1880), 62–63.

38 See Rapske, *The Book of Acts and Paul in Roman Custody*, 378.

39 Pliny, *Epist.*, III.16, quoted in Ramsay, *St Paul the Traveller and the Roman Citizen* 316.

40 Smith and Smith, *The Voyage and Shipwreck of St Paul*, 21ff.

41 Rapske, *The Book of Acts and Paul in Roman Custody*, 269–270.

42 Smith and Smith, *The Voyage and Shipwreck of St Paul*, 67–68; Ramsay, *St Paul the Traveller and the Roman Citizen*, 317.

43 Ramsay, *St Paul the Traveller and the Roman Citizen*, 318.

44 Hirschfeld, Nicolle, 'The Ship of Saint Paul: Historical Background', *The Biblical Archaeologist* 53(1). March 1990, 26.

45 'The Ship: Or, The Wishes', in Lucian of Samosata, *The Works of Lucian of Samosata* (Oxford: Clarendon Press, 1905), v. 4.

46 Casson, *Travel in the Ancient World*, 159. For more on the size of these vessels, see Hirschfeld, 'The Ship of Saint Paul: Historical Background', 27–28; Smith and Smith, *The Voyage and Shipwreck of St Paul*, 187–190; Landels, *Engineering in the Ancient World*, 160ff.

47 Suetonius, *Claudius*, 18.

48 Dio Chrysostom, *Dis.*, 5.9.
49 Green, *Christianity in Rome in the First Three Centuries*, 41.
50 Lampe, *From Paul to Valentinus*, 10.
51 Statius, *Silvae*, 2.2.12.
52 Horace, *Satires*, 1.5.3.

10. ROME AD 60–70

1 Lewis, *Roman Civilization: The Empire*, 136.
2 Carcopino, *Daily Life in Ancient Rome*, 30.
3 Seneca, *Moral Epistles*, 56.1–2, in Lewis, *Roman Civilization: The Empire*, 142.
4 From Juvenal, *Satires,* 3, in Lewis, *Roman Civilization: The Empire*, 153.
5 From Juvenal, *Satires,* 3, in Lewis, *Roman Civilization: The Empire*, 152.
6 From Juvenal, *Satires,* 3, in Lewis, *Roman Civilization: The Empire*, 151.
7 Lampe, *From Paul to Valentinus*, 10.
8 *War*, 2.80; *Antiquities,* 17.300–303.
9 Green, *Christianity in Rome in the First Three Centuries*, 3.
10 Tacitus, *Histories*, 5.5, in Green, *Christianity in Rome in the First Three Centuries*, 4.
11 Green, *Christianity in Rome in the First Three Centuries*, 12.
12 Green, *Christianity in Rome in the First Three Centuries*, 22-23.
13 Green, *Christianity in Rome in the First Three Centuries*, 33.
14 Green, *Christianity in Rome in the First Three Centuries*, 34.
15 Eusebius, *Hist. Eccl.*, 5.24.14–17; Grant, *Second-Century Christianity: A Collection of Fragments*, 52.
16 Lampe, *From Paul to Valentinus*, 22–23.
17 Lampe, *From Paul to Valentinus*, 42.
18 Lampe, *From Paul to Valentinus*, 47.
19 Lampe, *From Paul to Valentinus*, 55.
20 Fitzmyer, 788.
21 Drane, 'Why Did Paul Write Romans?', 215.
22 On all these names, see Dunn, *Romans 9 – 16*, 897–898; Lampe, *From Paul to Valentinus*, 164ff. Names in this list found frequently among slaves are: Ampliatus, Urbanus, Stachys, Herodion, Narcissus, Tryphaena, Tryphosa, Persis, Rufus, Asyncritus, Phlegon, Hermes, Patrobas, Hermas, Philologus, Julia, Nereus, Olympas.
23 Lampe, *From Paul to Valentinus*, 166.
24 Dunn, *Romans 9 – 16*, 897.
25 Augustine, *Epistle to Firmus*, 2.4.17, quoted in Kreider, *Worship and Evangelism in Pre-Christendom*, 17.
26 1 Clement 59.4.
27 WT, Acts 28.16, in Fitzmyer, 788.
28 Rapske, *The Book of Acts and Paul in Roman Custody*, 177.
29 Rapske, *The Book of Acts and Paul in Roman Custody*, 238.
30 Green, *Christianity in Rome in the First Three Centuries*, 43.
31 *Epistle of Ignatius to the Ephesians*, 1, in ANF 1.
32 Tertullian, *De Fuga in Persecutione*, in ANF 4.

33 *Apostolic Constitutions*, 7, *The Ecclesiastical Canons of the Same Holy Apostles,* no. 82, in ANF 7.

34 *Apostolic Constitutions*, 46, in ANF 7.

35 Chrysostom, *De Lazaro*, 6.7–8, in Mitchell, Margaret M., 'John Chrysostom on Philemon: A Second Look', *The Harvard Theological Review* 88(1). 1995, 141.

36 Chrysostom, *An Exhortation to Theodore After His Fall*, Letter I. 18. See John Chrysostom, *Homily XLIII. Matthew 12.38 and Matthew 12.39; Homilies on the Acts of the Apostles, XX*; also twice in his *Homilies on Romans*. The clearest statement is, unsurprisingly, in Chrysostom's *Homily on Philemon*.

37 See Callahan, Allen Dwight, 'Paul's Epistle to Philemon: Toward an Alternative Argumentum', *The Harvard Theological Review* 86(4). 1993. Also Mitchell, 'John Chrysostom on Philemon: A Second Look', 135; and in rebuttal, Callahan, Allen Dwight, 'John Chrysostom on Philemon: A Response to Margaret M. Mitchell', *The Harvard Theological Review* 88(1). 1995.

38 Callahan, 'Paul's Epistle to Philemon: Toward an Alternative Argumentum', 359.

39 Knox, *Philemon*, 20, quoted in Callahan, 'Paul's Epistle to Philemon: Toward an Alternative Argumentum', 360.

40 See Frilingos, Chris, '"For My Child, Onesimus": Paul and Domestic Power in Philemon', *Journal of Biblical Literature* 119(1). Spring, 2000.

41 Seneca, *On Clemency*, 1.29.1, in Lewis, *Roman Civilization: The Empire*, 176.

42 Page, *The Longest Week*, 224.

43 1 Clement 55.2.

44 Murphy-O'Connor, 'John the Baptist and Jesus: History and Hypotheses', 102.

45 'σκύβαλον', BDAG, 932.

46 Clement of Rome, *Letter to the Corinthians*, 5, in Lightfoot, *The Apostolic Fathers*, 59.

47 Gaechter, 'The Hatred of the House of Annas', 30.

48 Regev, 'Temple Concerns and High-Priestly Prosecutions from Peter to James: Between Narrative and History', 77.

49 m.Sanh. 9.6, in Regev, 'Temple Concerns and High-Priestly Prosecutions', 81.

50 Goodman, *Rome and Jerusalem: The Clash of Ancient Civilizations*, 525.

51 *War*, 4.6.2.

52 1 Clement 5, in ANF 1.

53 For a good overview of the issues, see Blomberg, *From Pentecost to Patmos: Acts to Revelation*, 441–443.

54 Blomberg, *From Pentecost to Patmos: Acts to Revelation*, 443.

55 Ignatius, *Letter to Romans*, 4, in Lightfoot, *The Apostolic Fathers*, 151.

56 Cullmann, Oscar, *Peter: Disciple, Apostle, Martyr* (London: SCM, 1953), 79.

57 Brown, Raymond Edward and John P. Meier, *Antioch and Rome: New Testament Cradles of Catholic Christianity* (London: Geoffrey Chapman, 1983), 98.

58 Eusebius, *The Ecclesiastical History and the Martyrs of Palestine*, I, 101.

59 Eusebius, *Hist. Eccl.*, 2.15.2.

60 See especially Bauckham, Richard, *Jesus and the Eyewitnesses: The Gospels as Eyewitness Testimony* (Grand Rapids: William B. Eerdmans, 2006), 155ff.

61 Bauckham, *Jesus and the Eyewitnesses*, 175.

62 Tacitus, *Annals*, 15.39–45.

63 Tacitus, *Annals*, 15.44; Bettenson, Henry Scowcroft, *Documents of the Christian Church*, 2nd ed. (Oxford: Oxford University Press, 1986), 1–2.

64 Green, *Christianity in Rome in the First Three Centuries*, 52.

65 Robinson, *Redating the New Testament*, 145–146.

66 Acts of Peter 35, in James, M. R, *The Apocryphal New Testament: Being the Apocryphal Gospels, Acts, Epistles and Apocalypses: With Other Narratives and Fragments* (Oxford: Clarendon, 1924), 333.

67 Cullmann, *Peter: Disciple, Apostle, Martyr*, 87 n. 82.

68 Hengel, Martin, *Crucifixion in the Ancient World and the Folly of the Message of the Cross* (London: SCM, 1977), 25.

69 *War*, 5.449–451.

70 Quoted in Page, *The Longest Week*, 223.

71 Clement of Rome, *Letter to the Corinthians*, 5, in Lightfoot, *The Apostolic Fathers*, 59. For a full treatment of this evidence, see Cullmann, *Peter: Disciple, Apostle, Martyr*, 89ff.

72 Quoted in Eusebius, *Hist. Eccl.*, 2.25.8.

73 Robinson, *Redating the New Testament*, 143.

74 Finegan, *Handbook of Biblical Chronology*, 387–388.

75 Sulpicius Severus, *Chronicle*, 2.29.3, in Robinson, *Redating the New Testament*, 147.

76 Justin Martyr, *Second Apology*, 2, in ANF 1.

77 Murphy-O'Connor, *Jesus and Paul: Parallel Lives*, 104.

78 Eusebius, *The Ecclesiastical History and the Martyrs of Palestine*, I, 60; Cullmann, *Peter: Disciple, Apostle, Martyr*, 117–118.

79 Brown and Meier, *Antioch and Rome: New Testament Cradles of Catholic Christianity*, 97.

80 'Pope: Scientific analysis done on St Paul's bones', in *Guardian*, Monday 29 June 2009, http://www.guardian.co.uk/world/feedarticle/8581822.

81 Cullmann, *Peter: Disciple, Apostle, Martyr*, 126–127.

82 Cullmann, *Peter: Disciple, Apostle, Martyr*, 119.

THE BEAST: PATMOS AD 92

1 *War*, 2.293.

2 *War*, 2.301–308.

3 *Hist. Eccl.*, 3.5.3, in Eusebius, *The Ecclesiastical History and the Martyrs of Palestine*, 68.

4 See Brandon, S. G. F., *The Fall of Jerusalem and the Christian Church: A Study of the Effects of the Jewish Overthrow of AD 70 on Christianity* (London: SPCK, 1951); On Aristo of Pella, see Bauckham, *The Book of Acts in Its Palestinian Setting*, 317; see also Sowers, S., 'The Circumstances and Recollection of the Pella Flight', *Theologische Zeitschrift*, 26. 1970; and Bourgel, Jonathan, 'The Jewish Christians Move from Jerusalem as a Pragmatic Choice', in Dan Jaffe (ed.), *Studies in Rabbinic Judaism and Early Christianity: Text and Context of Ancient Judaism and Early Christianity* (Leiden: Brill, 2010), 248.

5 Bourgel, 'The Jewish Christians Move from Jerusalem as a Pragmatic Choice', 111.

6 See *War*, 6.115–116. It is subject to Josephus's pro-Roman spin, but it probably records a real tradition.

7 Bourgel, 'The Jewish Christians Move from Jerusalem as a Pragmatic Choice', 131.

8 Grant, *Second-Century Christianity: A Collection of Fragments*, 48. From H. Musurillo, *The Acts of the Christian Martyrs* (Oxford: Oxford University Press, 1972), xii–xxiii, 86–89.

9 Hegesippus says that he was 120. The age is legendary, but it's not unreasonable to assume that this man, Jesus' cousin, met his death at an old age in the wave of persecution at the end of the first century. *Hist. Eccl.*, 3.32.3, Eusebius, *The Ecclesiastical History and the Martyrs of Palestine*, 1.92–93, 2.104.

10 Tertullian, *Apology*, 3.1, in Kreider, *Worship and Evangelism in Pre-Christendom*, 13.

11 Tertullian, *Apology*, 50.15.

12 'Martyrdom of Perpetua and Felicitas', in White, Carolinne, *Lives of Roman Christian Women* (London: Penguin, 2010), 10, 14.

13 Minutius Felix, *Octavius*, 31.7; 38.5, in Kreider, *Worship and Evangelism in Pre-Christendom*, 19.

14 MacMullen, *Christianizing the Roman Empire*, 21.

15 Justin, *Dialogue with Trypho*, 8, in ANF 1.

16 *Epistle to Diognetus*, 5.1–6.1.

17 A friend of mine attributed this profound question to Archbishop Rowan Williams.

Bibliography

Aberbach, M., 'The Change from a Standing to a Sitting Posture by Students after the Death of Rabban Gamaliel', *The Jewish Quarterly Review*, 52(2). 1961

Bainton, Roland H., 'The Early Church and War', *The Harvard Theological Review* 39(3). 1946

Barnett, Paul, *The Birth of Christianity: The First Twenty Years* (Grand Rapids: Eerdmans, 2005)

Barrett, Anthony A., *Agrippina: Mother of Nero* (London: Routledge, 2002)

Barrett, C. K., *A Critical and Exegetical Commentary on the Acts of the Apostles* (Edinburgh: T. & T. Clark, 1994)

Bauckham, Richard, *Jesus and the Eyewitnesses: The Gospels as Eyewitness Testimony* (Grand Rapids: Eerdmans, 2006)

Bauckham, Richard, *The Book of Acts in Its Palestinian Setting* (Carlisle: Paternoster Press, 1995)

Bauckham, Richard, *Jude and the Relatives of Jesus in the Early Church* (Edinburgh: T. & T. Clark, 1990)

Benko, Stephen, *Pagan Rome and the Early Christians* (Bloomington: Indiana University Press, 1984)

Bettenson, Henry Scowcroft, *Documents of the Christian Church* (Oxford: Oxford University Press, 1986)

Bishop, Eric. F. F., 'The Great North Road', *Theology Today* 4(3). 1947

Blomberg, Craig L., *From Pentecost to Patmos: Acts to Revelation: An Introduction and Survey* (IVP, 2006)

Bock, Darrell L., *Acts* (Grand Rapids: Baker Academic, 2007)

Bourgel, Jonathan, 'The Jewish Christians Move from Jerusalem as a Pragmatic Choice', in Dan Jaffe (ed.), *Studies in Rabbinic Judaism and Early Christianity: Text and Context of Ancient Judaism and Early Christianity* (Leiden: Brill, 2010)

Bradstock, Andrew and Christopher Rowland (eds), *Radical Christian Writings: A Reader* (Oxford: Wiley-Blackwell, 2002)

Brandon, S. G. F., *The Fall of Jerusalem and the Christian Church: A Study of the Effects of the Jewish Overthrow of* AD 70 *on Christianity* (London: SPCK, 1951)

Brown, Raymond Edward and John P. Meier, *Antioch and Rome: New Testament Cradles of Catholic Christianity* (London: Geoffrey Chapman, 1983)

Brown, S. Kent., 'Jewish and Gnostic Elements in the Second Apocalypse of James', *Novum Testamentum* 17(3). 1975

Bruce, F. F., *1 & 2 Thessalonians* (Waco: Word Books, 1982)

Bruce, F. F., *The Book of Acts* (Grand Rapids: Eerdmans, 1988)

Bruce, F. F., *Commentary on the Book of the Acts: The English Text* (London: Marshall, Morgan & Scott, 1954)

Bruce, F. F., *Paul: Apostle of the Free Spirit* (Exeter: Paternoster Press, 1977)

Bruce, F. F., *The Acts of the Apostles: The Greek Text with Introduction and Commentary* (London: Tyndale Press, 1952)

Bruce, F. F., *The Pauline Circle* (Exeter: Paternoster Press, 1985)

Butterworth, Alex and Ray Laurence, *Pompeii: The Living City* (London: Weidenfeld & Nicolson, 2005)

Callahan, Allen Dwight, 'John Chrysostom on Philemon: A Response to Margaret M. Mitchell', *The Harvard Theological Review* 88(1). 1995

Callahan, Allen Dwight, 'Paul's Epistle to Philemon: Toward an Alternative Argumentum', *The Harvard Theological Review* 86(4). 1993

Campbell, Douglas A., 'An Anchor for Pauline Chronology: Paul's Flight from "The Ethnarch of King Aretas" (2 Corinthians 11:32–33)', *Journal of Biblical Literature* 121(2). 2002

Caner, Daniel F., 'The Practice and Prohibition of Self-Castration in Early Christianity', *Vigiliae Christianae* 51(4). 1997

Carcopino, Jerome, *Daily Life in Ancient Rome* (London: Penguin, 1962)

Casson, Lionel, *Travel in the Ancient World* (London: Allen & Unwin, 1974)

Cole, Alan, *Mark: An Introduction and Commentary* (Leicester: IVP, 1961)

Crossan, John Dominic, *God and Empire: Jesus Against Rome, Then and Now* (San Francisco: HarperSanFrancisco, 2007)

Cullmann, Oscar, *Peter: Disciple, Apostle, Martyr* (London: SCM, 1953)

Davies, Paul E., 'The Macedonian Scene of Paul's Journeys', *The Biblical Archaeologist* 26(3). 1963

Drane, John W., 'Why Did Paul Write Romans?', in *Pauline Studies: Essays Presented to Professor F. F. Bruce on his 70th Birthday* (Exeter: Paternoster, 1980)

Dunderberg, Ismo, Christopher Tuckett and Kari Syreeni (eds), *Fair Play: Diversity and Conflicts in Early Christianity: Essays in Honour of Heikki Raisanen* (Leiden: Brill, 2001)

Dunn, James, *Beginning From Jerusalem* (Grand Rapids: Eerdmans, 2008)

Dunn, James, *Romans 9 – 16* (Nashville: Thomas Nelson, 1988)

Esler, Philip Francis, *Community and Gospel in Luke-Acts: The Social and Political Motivations of Lucan Theology* (Cambridge: Cambridge University Press, 1987)

Eusebius, *The Ecclesiastical History and the Martyrs of Palestine*, trans. Hugh Jackson Lawlor and John Ernest Leonard Oulton (London: SPCK, 1927)

Ferguson, Everett, *Backgrounds of Early Christianity* (Grand Rapids: Eerdmans, 2003)

Ferguson, John, *The Religions of the Roman Empire* (London: Thames and Hudson, 1970)

Fernando, Ajith, *Acts* (Grand Rapids: Zondervan, 1998)

Finegan, Jack, *Handbook of Biblical Chronology: Principles of Time Reckoning in the Ancient World and Problems of Chronology in the Bible* (Peabody: Hendrickson Publishers, 1998)

Fitzmyer, Joseph A., *The Acts of the Apostles* (New York: Doubleday, 1998)

Fitzmyer, Joseph A., *The Gospel According to Luke* (New York: Doubleday, 1983)

Forbes, R. J., *Studies in Ancient Technology Vol. V* (Leiden: Brill, 1964)

Freedman, David Noel (ed.), *The Anchor Bible Dictionary* (New York: Doubleday, 1999)

Frilingos, Chris. '"For My Child, Onesimus": Paul and Domestic Power in Philemon', *Journal of Biblical Literature* 119(1). 2000

Furnish, Victor Paul, *II Corinthians* (Garden City: Doubleday, 1984)

Gaechter, P., 'The Hatred of the House of Annas', *Theological Studies* 8. 1947

Gempf, Conrad H. and David W. J. Gill, *The Book of Acts in Its Graeco-Roman Setting* (Grand Rapids: Eerdmans, 1994)

Goodman, Martin, *Rome and Jerusalem: The Clash of Ancient Civilizations* (London: Penguin, 2008)

Goodman, Martin, *The Ruling Class of Judaea: The Origins of the Jewish Revolt Against Rome, AD 66–70* (Cambridge: Cambridge University Press, 1987)

Grant, Michael, *Saint Paul* (London: Phoenix, 2000)

Grant, Robert M., *Second-Century Christianity: A Collection of Fragments* (Louisville: Westminster John Knox Press, 2003)

Green, Bernard, *Christianity in Rome in the First Three Centuries* (Edinburgh: T. & T. Clark, 2010)

Harding, *Early Christian Life and Thought in Social Context* (London: Continuum, 2003)

Harris, William V., 'The Theoretical Possibility of Extensive Infanticide in the Graeco-Roman World', *The Classical Quarterly*, 32(1). 1982

Hemer, Colin J., 'Observations on Pauline Chronology', in *Pauline Studies: Essays Presented to Professor F. F. Bruce on his 70th Birthday* (Exeter: Paternoster, 1980)

Hengel, Martin, *Between Jesus and Paul: Studies in the Earliest History of Christianity* (London: SCM, 1983)

Hengel, Martin, *Crucifixion in the Ancient World and the Folly of the Message of the Cross* (London: SCM, 1977)

Hengel, Martin, *Paul Between Damascus and Antioch: The Unknown Years* (London: SCM, 1997)

Herodotus, *The Histories* (London: Penguin Books, 1972)

Hirschfeld, Nicolle, 'The Ship of Saint Paul: Historical Background', *The Biblical Archaeologist* 53(1). 1990

Hock, Ronald F., *The Social Context of Paul's Ministry: Tentmaking and Apostleship* (Philadelphia: Fortress Press, 1997)

Holmes, Michael W., *The Apostolic Fathers: Greek Texts and English Translations* (Grand Rapids: Baker Academic, 2007)

Hopkins, Keith, *A World Full of Gods: Pagans, Jews and Christians in the Roman Empire* (London: Phoenix, 2000)

Jackson, F. J. Foakes, 'Stephen's Speech in Acts', *Journal of Biblical Literature* 49(3). 1930

James, M. R., *The Apocryphal New Testament* (Oxford: Clarendon, 1924)

Jeremias, Joachim, *Jerusalem in the Time of Jesus: An Investigation into Economic and Social Conditions during the New Testament Period* (London: SCM, 1974)

Jewett, Robert, 'The Agitators and the Galatian Congregation', *New Testament Studies* 17. 1971

Josephus, Flavius, *The Works of Josephus : Complete and Unabridged*, (Peabody: Hendrickson Publishers, 1987 Accordance electronic edition)

Josephus, Flavius, *The Jewish War* (Harmondsworth: Penguin, 1981)

Keller, Marie Noel, *Priscilla and Aquila: Paul's Coworkers in Christ Jesus* (Collegeville: Liturgical Press, 2010, Kindle edition)

Kelsey, Morton T., *Healing and Christianity: In Ancient Thought and Modern Times* (London: SCM Press, 1973)

Knapp, Robert, *Invisible Romans* (London: Profile Books, 2011)

Kreider, Alan, 'Military Service in the Church Orders', *The Journal of Religious Ethics* 31(3). 2003

Kreider, Alan, *The Change of Conversion and the Origin of Christendom* (Eugene: Wipf & Stock Publishers, 2007)

Kreider, Alan, *Worship and Evangelism in Pre-Christendom* (Cambridge: Grove Books, 1995)

Kuefler, Mathew, *The Manly Eunuch: Masculinity, Gender Ambiguity, and Christian Ideology in Late Antiquity* (London: University of Chicago Press, 2001)

Lampe, Peter, *From Paul to Valentinus: Christians at Rome in the First Two Centuries* (London: Continuum, 2003)

Landels, John G., *Engineering in the Ancient World* (London: Constable, 2000)

Lewis, Naphtali and Meyer Reinhold, *Roman Civilization: The Empire* (New York: Columbia University Press, 1990)

Lightfoot, Joseph Barber, *The Apostolic Fathers* (London: Macmillan and Co., 1893)

Longenecker, Richard N., *Galatians* (Dallas: Word Books, 1990)

Lucian of Samosata, *Lucian* (London: Heinemann, 1936)

Lucian of Samosata, *The Works of Lucian of Samosata* (Oxford: Clarendon Press, 1905)

Macmullen, Ramsay, *Christianizing the Roman Empire:* AD *100–400* (New Haven: Yale University Press, 1984)

Macmullen, Ramsay, *Paganism in the Roman Empire* (New Haven: Yale University Press, 1981)

Macmullen, Ramsay, *Romanization in the Time of Augustus* (New Haven; London: Yale University Press, 2008)

Marshall, I. Howard, *The Acts of the Apostles: An Introduction and Commentary* (Leicester: IVP, 1980)

Masterman, E. W. G., 'Damascus, the Oldest City in the World', *The Biblical World* 12(2). 1898

Mazower, Mark, *Salonica, City of Ghosts: Christians, Muslims and Jews 1430–1950* (London: Harper Perennial, 2005)

McCasland, S. Vernon, 'The Way', *Journal of Biblical Literature* 77(3). 1958

McEvedy, Colin, *Cities of the Classical World: An Atlas and Gazetteer of 120 Centres of Ancient Civilization* (London: Allen Lane, 2011)

McKechnie, Paul, *The First Christian Centuries: Perspectives on the Early Church* (Leicester: Apollos, 2001)

McRay, John, 'Archaeology and the Book of Acts', *Criswell Theological Review* 5(1). 1990

Meeks, Wayne A., *The First Urban Christians* (New Haven: Yale University Press, 1983)

Meinardus, Otto F., 'The Site of the Apostle Paul's Conversion at Kaukab', *The Biblical Archaeologist* 44(1). 1981

Milavec, Aaron, *The Didache: Text, Translation, Analysis, and Commentary* (Collegeville: Liturgical Press, 2004)

Mitchell, Margaret M., 'John Chrysostom on Philemon: A Second Look', *The Harvard Theological Review* 88(1). 1995

Murphy-O'Connor, J., *Jesus and Paul: Parallel Lives* (Collegeville: Liturgical Press, 2007)

Murphy-O'Connor, J., 'John the Baptist and Jesus: History and Hypotheses', *New Testament Studies* 36. 1990

Murphy-O'Connor, J., 'Paul and Gallio', *Journal of Biblical Literature* 112(2). 1993

Murphy-O'Connor, J., 'The Corinth that Saint Paul Saw', *The Biblical Archaeologist* 47(3). 1984

Nebreda, Sergio Rosell, *Christ Identity: A Social-Scientific Reading of Philippians 2.5–11* (Göttingen: Vandenhoeck & Ruprecht, 2011)

Neil, William, *Acts: Based on the Revised Standard Version* (Grand Rapids: Eerdmans, 1981)

Neusner, Jacob, *The Mishnah: A New Translation* (New Haven: Yale University Press, 1988, Accordance electronic edition)

Notley, R. Steven and Anson F. Rainey, *Carta's New Century Handbook and Atlas of the Bible* (Jerusalem: Carta, 2007)

O'Loughlin, Thomas, *The Didache: A Window on the Earliest Christians* (London: SPCK, 2010)

Ogg, George, *The Chronology of the Life of Paul* (London: Epworth Press, 1968)

Orr, William F. and James Arthur Walther, *I Corinthians: A New Translation* (Garden City: Doubleday, 1976)

Osborne, Robert E., 'St Paul's Silent Years', *Journal of Biblical Literature* 84(1). 1965

Page, Nick, *God's Dangerous Book* (Milton Keynes: Authentic Publishing, 2011)

Page, Nick, *The Longest Week: The Truth About Jesus' Last Days* (London: Hodder & Stoughton, 2009)

Page, Nick, *The Wrong Messiah: The Real Story of Jesus of Nazareth* (London: Hodder & Stoughton, 2011)

Page, Nick, *The One-Stop Bible Atlas* (Oxford: Lion Hudson, 2010)

Page, Nick, *What Happened to the Ark of the Covenant and other Bible Mysteries* (Milton Keynes: Authentic, 2007)

Parker, Pierson, 'Once More, Acts and Galatians', *Journal of Biblical Literature* 86(2). 1967

Pietersma, Albert and Benjamin G. Wright, *A New English Translation of the Septuagint* (New York: Oxford University Press, 2007)

Ramsay, William Mitchell, *St Paul the Traveller and the Roman Citizen* (London: Hodder & Stoughton, 1908)

Rapske, Brian, *The Book of Acts and Paul in Roman Custody* (Grand Rapids: Eerdmans, 1994)

Regev, Eyal, 'Temple Concerns and High-Priestly Prosecutions from Peter to James: Between Narrative and History', *New Testament Studies* 56. 2009

Riesner, Rainer, *Paul's Early Period: Chronology, Mission Strategy, Theology* (Grand Rapids: Eerdmans, 1998)

Roberts, Alexander, James Donaldson and A. Cleveland Coxe (eds), *The Ante-Nicene Fathers: Translations of the Writings of the Fathers down to AD 325* (New York: Christian Literature Company, 1885, Accordance electronic edition, 9 vols)

Robinson, John A. T., *Redating the New Testament* (London: SCM, 1976)

Shedd, Ephraim C., 'Stephen's Defense before the Sanhedrin', *The Biblical World* 13(2). 1899

Skarsaune, Oskar and Reidar Hvalvik, *Jewish Believers in Jesus: The Early Centuries* (Peabody: Hendrickson, 2007)

Slee, Michelle, *The Church in Antioch in the First Century CE* (London: T. & T. Clark, 1987)

Slingerland, Dixon, 'Acts 18:1–18, the Gallio Inscription, and Absolute Pauline Chronology', *Journal of Biblical Literature* 110(3). 1991

Smith, James and Walter Edward Smith, *The Voyage and Shipwreck of St Paul: With Dissertations on the Life and Writings of St Luke, and the Ships and Navigation of the Ancients* (London: Longmans, Green, 1880)

Sowers, S., 'The Circumstances and Recollection of the Pella Flight', *Theologische Zeitschrift* 26. 1970

Spencer, F. Scott, *Portrait of Philip in Acts: A Study of Roles and Relations* (Sheffield: JSOT, 1992)

Stark, Rodney, *Cities of God: The Real Story of How Christianity Became an Urban Movement and Conquered Rome* (New York: HarperOne, 2007)

Stark, Rodney, *The Rise of Christianity: How the Obscure, Marginal Jesus Movement Became the Dominant Religious Force in the Western World in a Few Centuries* (San Francisco: HarperSanFrancisco, 1997)

Still, T. D., 'Did Paul Loathe Manual Labor? Revisiting the Work of Ronald F. Hock on the Apostle's Tentmaking and Social Class', *Journal of Biblical Literature* 124(4). 2006

Swain, Joseph Ward, 'Gamaliel's Speech and Caligula's Statue', *The Harvard Theological Review* 37(4). 1944

Thompson, Cynthia L., 'Hairstyles, Head-Coverings, and St Paul: Portraits from Roman Corinth', *The Biblical Archaeologist* 51(2). 1988

Throckmorton, Burton Hamilton, *Gospel Parallels: A Synopsis of the First Three Gospels with Alternative Readings from the Manuscripts and Noncanonical Parallels* (Nashville: Nelson, 1979)

Van Elderen, Bastian, 'Some Archaeological Observations on Paul's First Missionary Journey', in W. Ward Gasque and Ralph P. Martin (eds), *Apostolic History and the Gospel. Biblical and Historical Essays Presented to F. F. Bruce* (Exeter: Paternoster Press, 1970)

Vermès, Géza, *The Complete Dead Sea Scrolls in English* (London: Penguin Books, 2004)

Walker, Peter, *In the Steps of Saint Paul: An Illustrated Guide to Paul's Journeys* (Oxford: Lion Hudson, 2008)

Warmington, B. H., *Nero: Reality and Legend* (London: Chatto & Windus, 1970)

Wedderburn, A. J. M., *A History of the First Christians* (London: T. & T. Clark International, 2004)

Welborn, L. L., 'On the Discord in Corinth: 1 Corinthians 1 – 4 and Ancient Politics', *Journal of Biblical Literature* 106(1). 1987

White, Carolinne, *Lives of Roman Christian Women* (London: Penguin, 2010)

Winter, Bruce W., *After Paul Left Corinth: The Influence of Secular Ethics and Social Change* (Grand Rapids: Eerdmans, 2001)

Witherington, Ben, *Letters and Homilies for Hellenized Christians* (Downers Grove; Nottingham: IVP Academic Apollos, 2006)

Witherington, Ben, *The Acts of the Apostles: A Socio-Rhetorical Commentary* (Grand Rapids: Eerdmans, 1998)

Wright, N. T, *Jesus and the Victory of God* (London: SPCK, 1996)

INDEX

Do you wish this wasn't the end?
Are you hungry for more great teaching, inspiring
testimonies, ideas to challenge your faith?

Join us at www.hodderfaith.com, follow us on Twitter
or find us on Facebook to make sure you get the latest from
your favourite authors.

Including interviews, videos, articles, competitions
and opportunities to tell us just what you thought about
our latest releases.